THE CIVILIZATION OF THE AMERICAN INDIAN SERIES

ATLAS OF GREAT LAKES INDIAN HISTORY

The preparation and the publication of the *Atlas of Great Lakes Indian History* were supported in part by a grant from the Program for Research Tools and Reference Works of the National Endowment for the Humanities, an independent Federal agency that supports the study of such fields as history, philosophy, literature, and language.

ATLAS OF GREAT LAKES INDIAN HISTORY

EDITED BY HELEN HORNBECK TANNER

Adele Hast, Associate Editor

Jacqueline Peterson

Robert J. Surtees

CARTOGRAPHY BY MIKLOS PINTHER

Published for The Newberry Library by the
UNIVERSITY OF OKLAHOMA PRESS : NORMAN

Books by Helen Hornbeck Tanner

Zéspedes in East Florida, 1748-1790 (Coral Gables, 1963)
The Territory of the Caddo Tribe of Oklahoma (New York, 1974)
The Ojibwa, A Critical Bibliography (Bloomington, Indiana, 1976)
(editor) *Atlas of Great Lakes Indian History* (Norman, 1986)

Library of Congress Cataloging-in-Publication Data

Atlas of Great Lakes Indian history.

    (The Civilization of the American Indian series: v. 174)
    Bibliography: p. 187
    Includes index.
    1. Indians of North America—Great Lakes Region—History.   2. Great Lakes Region—History.   I. Tanner,
Helen Hornbeck.   II. Hast, Adele.   III. Series: Civilization of the American Indian series: v. 174.
E78.G7A87   1986   977   86-4353
ISBN: 0–8061–1515–7 (cloth)
ISBN: 0–8061–2056–8 (pbk.)

The paper in this book meets the guidelines for permanence and durability of the Committee on Production Guidelines for Book Longevity of
the Council on Library Resources, Inc. ♾

5 6 7 8 9 10 11 12 13 14 15 16 17 18 19 20 21 22 23 24 25 26 27

To
Erminie Wheeler-Voegelin
in recognition of her indispensable contribution
to Indian history
as creator of the Ohio Valley-Great Lakes Ethnohistorical Archive

CONTENTS

ILLUSTRATIONS

PREFACE AND ACKNOWLEDGMENTS

The chain of events leading to the creation of an atlas of Indian history began in 1963, when I agreed rather casually to find out what Indians lived around my home base, Ann Arbor, Michigan, at the time of the American Revolution. The inquiry was posed by lawyers representing Indian tribes in litigation before the Indian Claims Commission in Washington, D.C., an arena of legal and scholarly jousting about which I was as yet totally ignorant. Nevertheless, fortified by a recently acquired doctoral degree in history involving some study of the Creeks and Seminoles, I viewed the request as eminently reasonable, and looked forward to completing the research in short order. It was a naive expectation.

Unwittingly, I had been drawn into the most singularly unexplored area of Indian history in the eastern United States —the Ohio country. It turned out, Ann Arbor and southeastern Michigan were only on the periphery of the total area to be investigated for that particular land claims case. Allied litigation involved all of northern Ohio and eastern Indiana, and everything that happened in northern Ohio was linked to developments in southern Ohio. While the geographical area for study enlarged, the time frame expanded to encompass Great Lakes Indian history from about 1640 to 1820. I finally understood that the ultimate goal for this research was to determine what tribes had claims to which land in eastern Michigan and Ohio country. The historical data would be presented to the Indian Claims Commission, a body created in 1946 to hear claims against the federal government arising out of the provisions of Indian treaties. (A typical claim in behalf of a tribe asserted that two cents an acre was inadequate payment to Indians for land being sold for $1.25 an acre to settlers and speculators.)

For initial orientation in my own research assignment, I turned to maps prepared by The Smithsonian Institution and The National Geographic Society, and was dismayed by what I found. These standard maps of Indian tribes in the United States exhibited bright colored patterns and specific tribal names for most of the country, but only pale grey for much of Ohio, along with cryptic comments, "little known area," or "insufficient information."

Apparently the Ohio country held little interest for anthropologists because Indian society was too "inter-tribal" and too early contaminated by "white contact" to be of major professional concern. The Ohio country was also an unsatisfactory research field for colonial historians because so few reports emerged before the 1750s, and then suddenly the historical chronicle became extraordinarily complicated by the presence of many Indian tribal groups, with shifting factions, coalitions, and European alliances.* For Indian residents, the Ohio country swiftly changed in the eighteenth century from hunting ground and homeland to battle zone.

A clear grasp of the mid-eighteenth-century scene seemed vital to comprehension of the Revolutionary War era and the better-known events leading up to Anthony Wayne's military victory over the Indian confederacy in northwest Ohio in 1794. To get the proper background, I decided to start research at the beginning of French contacts in the Great Lakes Region in the early seventeenth century and expected historical maps to provide helpful guidance. I soon collected half a dozen maps with conflicting representations of early tribal distribution in Ohio and the Great Lakes Region, and yet no single map suggested there might be a lack of unanimity on the subject.

Historical accounts raised puzzling questions as well. For example, all historians used eloquent prose to describe the destruction wrought by Iroquois warriors during major expeditions into southern Ontario during the mid-seventeenth century. Yet fifty years later, when the Iroquois war era was over, the "conquered" region was occupied by Missisaugas and Ojibwas. How did this happen? In 1963 there was no ready answer. Further investigation revealed the discrepancies between the documentary and cartographic records of history. Map makers of the eighteenth century continued to place Iroquois villages on the north shore of Lake Ontario for fifty years after sites had been deserted by the Iroquois. Furthermore, these and similar errors were faithfully copied for twentieth-century publications.

Ploughing through more source material on Great Lakes history, I continued to find maps that were discouragingly inaccurate, or misleading because of absent information. Maps of frontier areas conventionally showed newly established white towns and omitted long-existent Indian communities. Maps of military expeditions recorded the location of forts, but not the Indian towns that were targets for attack. The successive sites of Indian communities seemed particularly elusive and difficult to trace. Published maps usually included scattered townsites that were never occupied concurrently. In those early days of rather solitary historical exploration, I was sustained largely by the encouraging direction of Donald E. Worcester, first at the University of Florida and later at Texas Christian University, and by frequent consultation with two exceptionally helpful staff members at the University of Michigan Museum, Richard H. Ford and the late Volney Jones.

My initial sortie into Great Lakes and Ohio Valley Indian history brought further revelations. The assignment was not

*At that time, the Ohio Valley–Great Lakes Ethnohistory Project was under way at Indiana University, supported by the Department of Justice, but results of this collective research were not open to perusal until 1978.

purely academic investigation into eighteenth-century history, but concerned present-day Indian people who were living not on reservations "out west," but in the Great Lakes states. Up to that time, like most residents of the Midwest, I was scarcely aware of the reservations still surviving in the region from New York to Minnesota. The usual supposition seemed to be that Indian people had ceded their land and left, or were removed west of the Mississippi. When I was made a commissioner of Indian affairs in Michigan in 1966, I came to know the pockets of Indian population scattered throughout the state, but found no written history to explain their presence at those specific places.

After about a dozen more legal cases, and inquiries into the history of Indian people as far west as the Sioux country of the Dakotas and as far south as Texas and Louisiana, I became convinced that new maps were desperately needed to clarify Indian history in North America. Although I had drafted maps for my own publications, the first opportunity for formal cartographic representation came in 1974 through contact with the *Atlas of Early American History* project at the Newberry Library, under the direction of Lester Cappon with Barbara Petchenik as Cartographic Editor. Adele Hast, a staff member, thought that the volume should include maps of Indian locations and asked me to prepare manuscript compilations. When that work was completed, she suggested that we undertake a separate atlas concentrating on Indian history, an idea that developed into a formal proposal through the Newberry Library to the National Endowment for the Humanities. The proposal was approved, with a starting date on September 1, 1976.

The decision to concentrate on the Great Lakes Region was based on the obvious need for correlating the chronologies of Euro-American population advance west of the Appalachian Mountains, military campaigns, and repeated displacement of Indians of many tribal affiliations. The coverage had to include parts of Canada, for the tide of Indian history flowed back and forth across the artificial American-Canadian boundary. In the final analysis, it was also important to demonstrate the continuing presence of Indian people in the northern districts of the Great Lakes Region and at the same time provide a pre-reservation history for Great Lakes Indian people who had removed to Iowa, Kansas, and Oklahoma, or had fled to Canada or some isolated hideout. Maps provide a perspective different from the "history" constructed by scholars and different from the views of the past still recounted by Indian people.

Preparation of historical maps for the *Atlas* has been a cooperative team effort with a geographic division of research responsibility; Hast for the eastern section including New York and Pennsylvania; Tanner for the central section including Ohio, Michigan, and parts of Indiana; Peterson for the western section including Minnesota, Wisconsin, Illinois, and part of Indiana; and Surtees for the Canadian sections of all maps. Partially as a consequence of this division, individual staff members have had primary roles in the development of particular topics: Hast, the Iroquois Wars as well as epidemics and reservations; Tanner, the transitional frontier of the eighteenth century; Surtees, the War of 1812 and Canadian land surrenders; Peterson, the 1830s era and especially the Black Hawk War. To map the environmental setting and the very early history of the region, we brought in two specialists, ethnobotanist Nancy Nowak Cleveland and Charles E. Cleland, who has devoted much of his professional career to Great Lakes archaeology and ethnohistory. Miklos Pinther designed and made the final ink compilations of maps drafted by the research staff. As project director, Tanner was responsible for final review of all maps, and synthesis of written material for the text.

Administrative assistants in charge of data files were Catherine Dieckman, Kathleen Mallon, and Ira Jacknis, who also organized the collection of illustrations. Nancy Morbeck Haak corrected the 1:25 M base maps to make them conform as nearly as possible to the eighteenth-century drainage pattern.

The number of people contributing to this atlas goes far beyond the basic team of staff members and consultants. Following announcement of the project, representatives of tribal groups throughout the Great Lakes Region of the United States and Canada telephoned, came to the Newberry to talk, and carried on correspondence concerning their familiar territories. County historical societies supplied descriptive information and sketch maps. As manuscript maps were drafted, these were taken to professional meetings for comment by historians, anthropologists, and geographers.

The Newberry Library provided a stimulating environment for research and map compilation. John Aubrey of the Special Collections Department, himself an internationally appreciated bibliographic resource, aided the staff—as he has many other researchers—in extracting pertinent materials from the manuscript and printed collections. Robert Karrow, Curator of Maps, located scarce and indispensable cartographic items. The staff often turned to John H. Long, director of a separate project plotting changes in mid-western county boundaries. David Woodward, then Director of the Hermon Dunlap Smith Center for the History of Cartography, was also a frequent adviser. F. Peter Weil photographed many of the illustrations.

The Library serves as an intellectual clearing house, visited by a constant stream of scholars, many with interests related to topics mapped in this atlas. Each year of the active research period, a new contingent of Fellows arrived at the Center for the History of the American Indian, and along with the director, Francis Jennings, were drawn into discussions of individual maps. We benefitted particularly from the contributions of Indian Center fellows investigating similar or overlapping fields of history: Gary Clayton Anderson, Mary A. Druke, Michael D. Green, Richard Haan, and Paul Stevens. We were also fortunate to have on hand Henry F. Dobyns, whose broad knowledge and massive files supplemented data collected on the subject of epidemics. With the inauguration of the Iroquois documentary project, Mary A. Druke as associate director continued to provide assistance along with David Reed Miller.

A number of routine tasks for the *Atlas* were handled by students at the Newberry enrolled in the joint program of the Associated Colleges of the Midwest and the Great Lakes College Association. Kelly Sharp undertook a major responsibility as coordinator of the bibliography. Volunteers from the membership of the Newberry Library Associates also aided the project. The longest and most demanding term of service was contributed by Chalkley J. Hambleton, a trustee of the Newberry Library.

Among the many individuals whose aid we gratefully acknowledge are friends and colleagues dispersed over a broad geographic area. From the beginning to the end of the Atlas project, Nancy O. Lurie of the Milwaukee Public Museum supplied advice, support, and general guidance. Others who shared with us their personal accounts, research notes, unpublished writings, and special expertise were: David Beaulieu, University of Minnesota; Donald Berthrong, Purdue University; Jennifer S. H. Brown, University of Winnepeg; Jack Campisi, State University of New York-New Paltz; Harvey Carter, Colorado College; James A. Clifton, University of Wisconsin-Green Bay; Raymond J. DeMallie, Indiana University; R. David Edmunds, Texas Christian University; William N. Fenton, State University of New York-Albany; Raymond D. Fogelson, University of Chicago; Elizabeth Glenn, Ball State University; Robert Hall, University of Illinois-Chicago; Theodore Karamanski, Loyola University; Thomas Krasnean, Vincennes University; G. Malcolm Lewis, Sheffield University, England; Russell Magnaghi, Northern Michigan University; Dwight Mikkelson, Taylor University; John Moore, University of Oklahoma; Keewaydinoquay Peschel, University of Wisconsin, Milwaukee; Joseph Peyser, University of Indiana-South Bend; Janet Spector, University of Minnesota; Robert K. Thomas, University of Arizona; Gerald Vizenor, University of California-Berkeley; Nancy and Alan Woolworth, White Bear, Minnesota; and W. William Wykoff, Ithaca, New York.

For interpreting and spelling place names in Indian languages, we had the advice of Marianne Mathun, State University of New York, Albany; Kenneth Miner, University of Kansas; John Steckley, Thornhill, Ontario; Roy Wright, Trent University, Peterborough, Ontario; Lorraine Winneshiek, Wisconsin Rapids, Wisconsin; and John Nichols, University of Manitoba.

A necessary and valuable adjunct to the production of the Atlas has been the cooperation of other institutions and organizations in the United States and Canada. We want to express our thanks to Joan Freeman and Edward Oerichbauer, State Historical Society of Wisconsin, Rhoda Gilman and Douglas Birk, Minnesota Historical Society; Leroy Barnett and David Olson, Map Archives, History Division, Michigan Department of State; John Dann, Clements Library, Ann Arbor, Michigan; Joseph Marconi, Bayliss Library, Sault Ste. Marie, Michigan; Archie Motley, Chicago Historical Society; Gordon L. Olson, Grand Rapids (Michigan) Public Library and Museum; Mary Jo Pugh, Bentley Library, Ann Arbor, Michigan; Carol Morris Waddell, Tippecanoe County (Indiana) Historical Society; James Kellar, Glenn A. Black Laboratory, Indiana University; Edward Lace, Cook County (Illinois) Forest Preserve; Robert Haltiner, Jesse Besser Museum, Alpena, Michigan; Harold O. Bernhardt, Iron County (Michigan) Historical and Museum Society; J. Dee Ellis, Lapeer County (Michigan) Historical Society; Herbert Nagel, Oqueoc River, Michigan; Jean McGroarty, Battle Ground, Indiana; Betty Jo Gioffre, Huron (Ohio) Public Library, Larry Sommers, St. Louis County (Minnesota) Historical Society, and Harrison Palmer, Danbury, Wisconsin. We also appreciate assistance from staffs of the Minnesota Archeological Survey, Architectural Resources Inc. of Duluth, Minnesota; Indiana State Library and Indiana Historical Society, Indianapolis; Cass County (Indiana) Historical Society; Illinois State Library, Springfield; Brown County (Wisconsin) Historical Society; Wisconsin Archaeological Survey, Fulton County (Indiana) Historical Society; Michigan Archaeological Survey; Vassar College Library, Poughkeepsie, New York; New York Public Library and Museum of the American Indian, New York City; State Library of New York, Albany.

In Ottawa, research inquiries received the kind attention of Gordon Day, National Museum of Man, as well as Edward Dahl and David Hume at the Public Archives of Canada. For promptly sending us new publications, we thank John Leslie, Treaties and Research Branch, Department of Indian Affairs.

Significant data came to the Atlas staff from people who had accumulated personal knowledge through Indian heritage or from intensive study of a particular locality. We want to acknowledge contributions of the late George Cook, Houghton Lake, Michigan; Richard Criss (Little Hawk), Imlay City, Michigan; Robert Gough, Daniel and Judith Poler, Mole Lake, Wisconsin; John Hall, Kampsville, Illinois; Dean Jacobs, Walpole Island, Ontario, the late Norbert Hill, Oneida, Wisconsin; Willard La Mere, Chicago; William Gribb and James McClurken, Michigan State University; Jerry W. Lewis (Niswemakek), Midlothian, Illinois; Jerry Pope (Tukemas), Xenia, Ohio; Howard LaHourreau (Big Owl), Fort Wayne, Indiana; and Jerry Wagner, Oscoda, Michigan.

Dr. Robert O'Neill, Narragansett, Rhode Island, generously presented to The Newberry Library the original watercolor portraits of Black Hawk and The Winnebago Prophet for publication in this atlas. We also wish to express our gratitiude for the enthusiasm and kindly interest of the late Cable Gordon Ball and Mrs. Ball, Lafayette, Indiana, who granted permission to reproduce drawings and paintings from the George Winter collection.

In the lengthy process of creating the Atlas, we realize that there were several people who made a critical difference in carrying out the entire project. We especially appreciate the faith expressed by George H. Farr and the staff of the Research and Tools Division of the National Endowment for the Humanities, in initially supporting this project. We also thank Richard H. Brown, Academic Vice President of the Newberry Library, for his assistance in formulating the original and supplementary proposals. The technical quality of the maps can be attributed to the painstaking efforts of Jon Leverenz, Pat Healy, and Jill Metz of the Cartographic Services Division of Rand, McNally, Inc. Lawrence W. Towner, President and Librarian of the Newberry Library assured realization of our goal by his earnest fund-raising endeavors. In addition to outright grant and matching funds from the National Endowment, financial support for the Atlas came from the generous gifts of a number of private foundations and individuals: the late Ray A. Billington, The Bush Foundation, Mr. and Mrs. Leo J. Carlin, C. J. Hambleton in memory of D'Arcy McNickle, Robert R. McCormick Charitable Trust, Andrew W. Mellon Foundation, and Mr. and Mrs. Samuel R. Rosenthal.

In summary, the entire Atlas staff is grateful to a host of named and unnamed people, organizations, and institutions who have helped in many ways.

HELEN HORNBECK TANNER

Chicago, Illinois

ATLAS OF GREAT LAKES INDIAN HISTORY

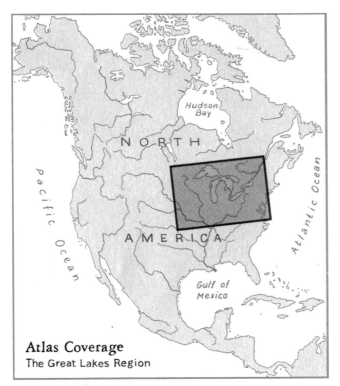

Atlas Coverage
The Great Lakes Region

MAP
1

removal, and land allotments. The sequence of maps in this atlas traces the changing pattern of Indian village locations as a result of all these factors. The time span begins with the period of Iroquois warfare (1641-1701) and ends with the last phase of the transfer from Indian to white dominance, occurring in the northern Great Lakes Region in the 1870s.

The Indian People

The Indians involved in the history of the Great Lakes Region can be divided into three classes: (1) the resident people, (2) refugees principally from the Atlantic seaboard, and (3) temporary allies or opponents coming from areas south or west of the Great Lakes.

Indian people with homelands in the Great Lakes Region were: members of the League of the Iroquois, the Five Nations, originally formed in northern New York by the Mohawk, Oneida, Onondaga, Cayuga and Seneca; Huron settled southeast of Georgian Bay in Canada and other western Iroquois, whose survivors in eighteenth century Ohio and Michigan were called Wyandot; Ottawa located in the straits region of northern Lake Huron and Lake Michigan; Ojibwa communities prominent in territory surrounding Lake Superior; Menominee living west of Green Bay; Dakota of eastern Minnesota; Mesquakie (commonly called Fox) as well as Sauk and Winnebago of Wisconsin; Potawatomi based in southwestern Michigan; Kickapoo of central and eastern Illinois who often had Mascouten living with them; Miami and their allies along the Wabash River of Indiana; and the Shawnee of southern Ohio.

Successive waves of refugee people originating along the eastern seaboard or the southern Appalachian piedmont reached the Great Lakes Region by the eighteenth century. Mahican from New England were living with Potawatomi and Miami near southern Lake Michigan before 1700. The Tuscarora of North Carolina became the sixth nation in the Iroquois League about 1717. Surviving remnants of neighboring southern tribes, the Saponi and Tutelo of Virginia and North Carolina, formed minority populations among the Iroquois towns along with Nanticoke and Piscataway from the Chesapeake Bay area of the middle Atlantic seaboard.

Most transient of all Indian people on the Great Lakes scene were the Delaware. Munsee and Delaware from New Jersey and eastern Pennsylvania brought refugees with them when they reached the Ohio country by 1725. Some Nanticoke and Piscataway (or Conoy) migrated directly to Ohio from the Chesapeake Bay region at the end of the American Revolution and usually joined Delaware communities where others of their people were already living. Although

Within the area of the Great Lakes and upper Ohio River valley, the disruption of Indian life has been so extensive and so frequent that the history can be clarified only with the visual aid of maps. For this reason, an atlas appears to be the best method of conveying information about places where Indian people have lived in the vicinity of the Great Lakes during the historic era. The *Atlas of Great Lakes Indian History* focuses on the Great Lakes as a distinct geographic unit with an equally distinct historical development embracing parts of both Canada and the United States. Roughly outlined, the geographic unit is an almost triangular area beginning at Montreal, Quebec, extending westward to the Lake of the Woods on the Ontario-Manitoba-Minnesota boundary, with the Mississippi and Ohio rivers forming the western and southeastern boundaries. This outline surrounds the five Great Lakes and three large peninsulas: Lakes Ontario, Erie, Huron, Michigan and Superior; and the peninsulas of Upper and Lower Michigan and southwestern Ontario.

Influential factors in the complex picture of this part of North America have been: territorial conquest by inter-tribal warfare, refugee movements, epidemics, French-English trade rivalry and wars, international treaties, Indian-white hostilities, inter-tribal alliances, encroachment by settlers, Indian treaties ceding land to state and national governments, and imperfectly administered arrangements for reservations,

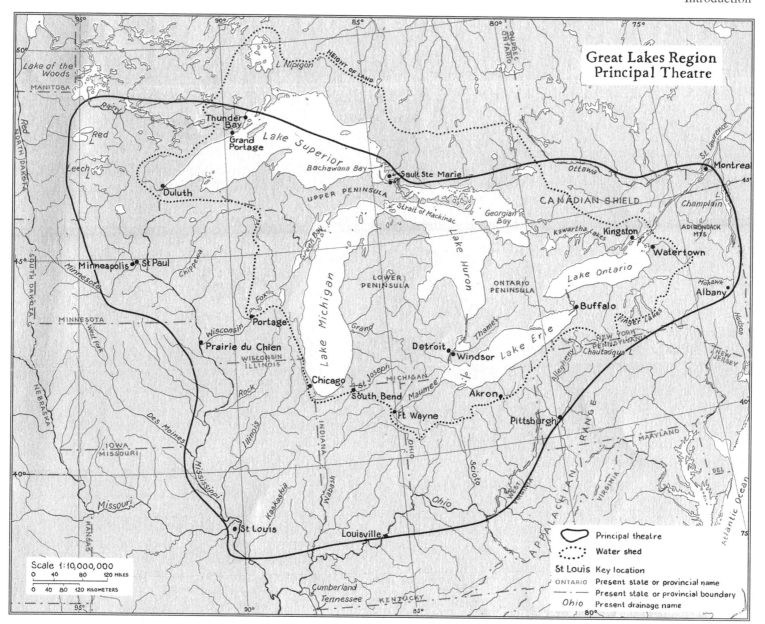

MAP
2

a few of these easterners eventually became permanent residents of southern Ontario, others born within 50 miles of Philadelphia, Pennsylvania, were removed from Indiana in 1819 to reservations across the Mississippi River.

Less involved with the continuity of Great Lakes history were representatives of southern and western Indian people. Osage from Missouri were reported near Detroit during warfare in 1712 and claimed presence at Braddock's defeat in Pennsylvania 40 years later. Chickasaw from present Mississippi invaded southern Indiana in the 1730s; a later generation of Chickasaw supplied scouts for General Wayne's Legion of American troops in Ohio in 1794. During the post-Revolutionary warfare on the Ohio frontier, southern allies came chiefly as warriors, but in some cases they brought families and resided for a period of years. A contingent of Chicamauga Cherokee from the Tennessee mountains lived with Shawnee in Ohio in the 1790s. Creek towns in Alabama also sent warriors to the Ohio front. At the outset of the War of 1812, a British Indian agent recruit-

ed Dakota from as far west as the Minnesota-South Dakota border to fight near Detroit and western Lake Erie.

The broad area covered by the double-page maps in the *Atlas of Great Lakes Indian History* further includes Indian people who have only an incidental connection with activities in the central Great Lakes theatre. Algonquin along the Ottawa River, Cree northwest of Lake Superior, and Iowa close to the Mississippi River lived on the fringe of the Great Lakes action.

Indians of the Great Lakes operated in a dynamic intertribal environment. The resident people spoke several languages and dialects that can be grouped in three major linguistic divisions: Algonquian, Iroquoian, and Siouan. Most of the Indian languages of the northeastern United States and adjacent Canadian territory were Algonquian. Indeed, knowledge of Ojibwa could carry a traveler across more than a thousand miles of land from east to west in the Great Lakes, although not all the Algonquian languages were mutually intelligible. Iroquoian speakers, composing the membership of

3

Canadian Forest Campsite.
By W. H. Bartlett. From
Willis, *Canadian Scenery,* vol. 1.
The Newberry Library.

the League of Iroquois, allied Huron, and later Wyandot, constituted a linguistic island surrounded by speakers of the various Algonquian languages. On the western side of the Great Lakes Region, the Winnebago and Dakota spoke Siouan languages. Many Indian people were conversant in several languages, and leaders acquired considerable facility in French but were less acquainted with English. Any major Indian council in the Great Lakes Region included representatives of about a dozen tribes, thus interpreters served an important function.

In the *Atlas of Great Lakes Indian History*, commonly used names have been employed in identifying most of the Indian tribes. Generally, Indian names for their own groups can be translated as "the people," or "the real people" or "the allies." On the other hand, they often become known by names given by outsiders or by geographic identification. "Ojibwa" is a word referring to the practice of recording information by drawing glyphs and signs on birch bark. The Atlas uses this spelling rather than the corrupted form "Chippewa" or the Canadian "Ojibway," or any recent linguistic innovations. The Mesquakie people prefer their own name to "Fox," the term that became current in French documents.

Similarly, many Dakota people avoid the term "Sioux" derived from the French spelling for an Ojibwa word meaning "little snake" or enemy, "nadowasieux." Without the diminutive suffix, "nadowa" referred to the principal early enemies of the Ojibwa, members of the Iroquois league. Although the Delaware have acquired the name of the river valley homeland of their several tribal divisions, their traditional name is Lenape. In the Atlas separate identification is given to the Christian Indian settlements supervised by Moravian missionaries. Residents of

the Moravian towns were principally Delaware and Mahican, but included remnants of other New England and Middle Atlantic tribes.

Although every Indian town carried an identifying tribal name, the resident population included people connected with other tribes. They may have come to live in the village because of marriage alliances made during a trading visit or a journey to a neighboring tribe. Some were captives acquired during inter-tribal wars, or Indian slaves known as "panis," French version of "Pawnee," the term for almost any Indian captured west of the Mississippi and traded as a slave to eastern towns. Refugees were not always moving from east to west. Part of the Mesquakie of Wisconsin went to live with the Iroquois in New York and Pennsylvania during the "Fox Wars" of the early eighteenth century. The Atlas indicates significant minorities in villages of other tribes, the mixed villages notable along the border between neighboring tribes, and multitribal communities that developed during wartime dislocations.

Among the residents of Indian towns involved in eighteenth-century border warfare, there were frequently people of European and African heritage captured as children or adults. Occasionally the blacks were escaped slaves; others were traders, or servants and employees of traders. European traders, usually French, Scottish or Irish, lived in the major Indian towns with their Indian families, and occasionally a highly useful blacksmith was one of the important townspeople. Except in the most isolated localities, an Indian village regularly provided hospitality for native couriers, visiting tribal delegations, European missionaries and travelers. Indian parties frequently made lengthy sojourns distant from their home villages.

Indian Villages

The maps in the *Atlas* emphasize the location of Indian villages at significant dates in the history of the Great Lakes Region. Indian villages were the recognized home bases for their inhabitants, yet, unlike white settlements, were seldom fully occupied during the entire year. In the northern Great Lakes Region, where people have been heavily dependent upon fish for nutrition, the major fishing sites were the places regularly occupied during the spring to fall period of tolerable weather. To the south, where Indians were more dependent upon agriculture, villages had their maximum population during the summer planting and harvesting seasons. The *Atlas* maps identify summer agricultural villages and fishing communities that have been the fixed geographical bases for specific groups of people, as well as sites occupied all year.

An extended period of residence in the home base, which might be called a "town" or a "village," was part of the annual round followed by most Great Lakes Indian people. After the harvest or fishing season in the fall, the village customarily split into smaller groups to depart for winter hunting camps, then moved to maple groves for sugar making in the early spring and often took in a short-term spring fish run before returning to plant corn and other vegetables and visit a major trading center. In mid-winter, an Indian village site might be entirely vacant or house only elderly people left behind with dried food supplies to serve as general caretakers during the four-month winter hunting season. Although sites of many winter camps, sugar groves, and fishing runs have been identified, they are too numerous to be plotted on maps at the scales used in this atlas.

Indian villages varied in size and changed considerably in appearance during the course of the two-century time span of this atlas. Seventeenth-century Huron and Iroquois villages were surrounded by protective palisades, but away from battle zones, villages were not laid out with exterior walls and fortifications. Kaskaskia, the Grand Village of the Illinois, had between 7,000 and 8,000 residents in 1680. Among the largest villages in the Great Lakes Region in the mid-eighteenth century was the Seneca headquarters in northern New York with an estimated population of 1,200. In 1830, the Sauk village at present Rock Island, Illinois, a large community for that date, sheltered close to six hundred people living in peak-roofed homes along neatly squared streets. By contrast, the small Mississauga and Ojibwa hamlets of the northland might have a population of only fifty people.

Although the style of architecture in the Great Lakes was not uniform, Indian-designed buildings universally were constructed of pole frames covered over by large sheets of elm or birch bark, or rush mats. Multiple family dwellings were used by seventeenth-century Illinois as well as by New York Iroquois and Ontario Huron. The longhouses, the largest accommodating ten families, had high arched roofs with separate smoke holes for each pair of resident households. Large council houses 100 feet in length were conspicuous buildings in the Wyandot and Shawnee towns of Ohio, and elongated ceremonial lodges were constructed in other Great Lakes Indian communities.

The wigwam, a round or oval domed structure, was

Interior of a Long House, typical dwelling of Huron and Iroquois people. The American Museum of Natural History.

the most common house type for individual families in the northern lakes region. In the summer, the heavy sheets of bark could be replaced with woven reed mats. A circle of poles with the slender ends criss--crossed at the top created the conical outline of a "tipi," in the woodlands covered with bark or mats, but out on the prairies covered with skins. Quickly erected, a shelter of this design was utilized also for temporary housing and traveling. A simple A-frame building was created by placing two forked poles in the ground and connecting them with a ridge pole resting in the forks. The frame was then covered with the sheets of flattened bark. The addition of sidewalls, rafters, and other braces tied together with hickory bark thongs made a larger and more substantial house of rectangular shape.

During the late eighteenth century, prominent Great Lakes Indian leaders frequently changed to the use of frontier-type log cabins, some with glazed windows and stone fireplaces. By the 1830s, log houses and fenced yards made Indian communities and nearby white settlements appear much alike to the casual observer. But in regions of the Great Lakes remote from white population, many Indian people lived in traditional housing throughout the nineteenth century.

Indian villages were located on banks of streams, along sheltered bays, or near springs where a supply of fresh water was available. Extensive cornfields often lay across a stream from the village site, or beyond the concentration of houses. Using seeds procured from French residents, Indians planted apple and peach orchards in settlements situated where the climate was suitable for raising fruit. After horses became common in the southern section of the Great Lakes Region about 1770, ponies with bells around their necks were a common sight around Indian villages, along with stocks of cattle and hogs. In fishing communities, the outdoor fire with racks for smoking fish, seines and nets spread out to dry, and overturned canoes in view on the sandy beach were distinguishing elements of the village scene. A large dog population was another characteristic feature of an Indian village.

White Towns, Forts, and Trading Posts

During the period of time covered by the *Atlas*, white towns were usually larger than Indian villages, although this differential did not exist in frontier areas. The same dot on the map can represent a population of a few hundred or several thousand. Along the St. Lawrence River, dots indicate the location of parish churches, central points in the district of French farms, each with narrow frontage on the river bank.

In creating maps keyed to specific dates, problems have arisen concerning the time a town came into existence. When county histories, recollections of settlers, and census data did not agree, conflicting data were weighed for decisions concerning the inclusion of the place on a map for a particular date. Diaries and accounts of travelers proved helpful in evaluating other sources of information.

The working definition of a white town is a recognizable population center with a name. Evidence of five or six houses with the addition of a church, store, or mill has been considered in some cases sufficient to map a frontier settlement. The American census records for 1830 list hamlets of only about fifty people as subdivisions of townships. In a region of scattered farms, the actual time a town center developed may be difficult to establish. Local histories are apt to hail the building of the first house as a founding date. Towns were sometimes plotted on paper for real estate sales long before a single building was erected. The lonely roadside tavern, , ferry, or postal stop could be a place of considerable local importance without meeting the criteria for mapping a "town."

The fort symbol has been used only to identify regular garrisons or places where troops were officially stationed. Both Indian and white communities, as well as isolated frontier establishments, were constructed with attention to defense. In Kentucky, immigrants of the Revolutionary War era used the term "stations" to identify their semi-military bases in the wilderness. These are mapped as white towns. A special symbol has been employed for the combined fort and white town, a military and governmental center such as Detroit or Montreal. Two symbols are used for the rare occasions where a fort existed at an Indian town. An example is Fort Miami at present Fort Wayne, Indiana, where there were also traders among the permanent population.

The trading post symbol indicates that the chief enterprise at the location is Indian trade. Subsidiary trading posts or stopping points for itinerant traders in the back country are usually omitted from the maps. Throughout the area of present Canada, major trading posts called "forts" were the property of large mercantile establishments with headquarters in Montreal or London. The company employees might number fifty people, but such locations are distinguished by the symbol for a trading post and are not mapped as either forts or white towns. Some of these places, such as Fort William, present Thunder Bay on the northwest shore of Lake Superior, eventually became cities. Although British fur trading posts actually served a military function in providing supplies for troops during the War of 1812, in *Atlas* maps the post personnel are not considered the equivalent of a garrison. Trading posts were often unnecessary in frontier regions where Indian and white communities existed in close proximity. In these areas neighborhood bartering was a common practice and Indians were among the customers at the general stores.

The Geographic Region

The geometric outline of the Great Lakes Region already presented points out a roughly triangular area with three easily located corners: Montreal, at the juncture of the Ottawa and St. Lawrence rivers, on the east; Lake of the Woods, on the American-Canadian boundary beyond Lake Superior, on the west; and St. Louis, near the juncture of the Ohio and Mississippi rivers, on the south. This brief definition requires supplementary information in order to provide a more accurate understanding of the dynamics of Great Lakes history.

A rigid geographic definition of the Great Lakes Region would be limited to the land where streams flow into the Great Lakes. The watershed closely circumscribes the outer shorelines of the five Great Lakes, with no major tributary streams except in the large interior peninsulas, Upper and Lower Michigan, and southwestern Ontario (see map 2). This entire system is drained by the St. Lawrence River. Any account of activities around the Great Lakes, however, takes in adjacent parts of the Ohio and Mississippi river valleys. Historical developments within the total space identify a principal Great Lakes theatre as well as border regions and peripheral areas.

A complete geographic description of the Great Lakes Region's principal theatre, the space where the main developments occurred during the historical period covered by the *Atlas*, draws attention first to the Straits of Mackinac connecting Lake Huron and Lake Michigan, and to the St. Marys River flowing from Lake Superior to Lake Huron. This vital crossroads was the center of a trade and communications network permeating the Great Lakes Region and by extensions reaching the Great Plains of the Canadian and American West, Hudson Bay, the Atlantic Ocean and the Gulf of Mexico.

Although the Great Lakes Region had a pattern of land trails approximating the modern highway system, waterways were the main thoroughfares. These water routes are the key to understanding Great Lakes history. Portage points and river junctures along the waterways were important locations, the sites of trading posts, towns, and forts. The low watershed south of the Great Lakes often flooded during spring and fall rains, facilitating canoe travel in all directions over an estimated fifty available portages. The major portages connecting watercourses are shown by red lines on map 9, "The French Era 1720-c. 1761."

From the Straits of Mackinac* the main route south bor-

*The vicinity of the Straits of Mackinac was known by its longer original name, "Michilimackinac," until well into the nineteenth century. As a more specific geographic reference, the term "Michilimackinac" applied first to the St. Ignace locale on the north side of the straits in the late seventeenth century; then in the early eighteenth century to the tip of Michigan's Lower Peninsula south of the straits, and finally to present Mackinac Island at the entry to Lake Huron, where a British fort was relocated in 1781.

dered the north shore of Lake Michigan to Green Bay, then followed the Fox-Wisconsin waterway to the Mississippi River at present Prairie du Chien, Wisconsin. From this point a northward jog of 150 miles led to the Minnesota River and access to the prairies and western plains, while the southward course of the Mississippi River carried travelers to the Gulf of Mexico. An alternate southern route from Mackinac lay along the west shore of Lake Michigan to the Chicago River and the short portage to the Des Plaines, headwaters of the Illinois River, entering the Mississippi north of St. Louis. Along the eastern shore of Lake Michigan, the main canoe route continued southward by way of the St. Joseph River to present South Bend, portage point to the Kankakee River, flowing across northern Indiana and Illinois.

The region west of the tip of Lake Superior was reached by circuiting through the St. Marys River, crossing the Keweenaw Peninsula, and ascending the St. Louis River near present Duluth. This route to the Savanna portage continued to Sandy Lake and Leech Lake population centers and the headwaters of the Mississippi River.

Southeast from the Straits of Mackinac, two main routes led to the lower lakes. The first route followed the western shore of Lake Huron through the St. Clair River, Lake St. Clair, and the Detroit River to Lake Erie. In good weather, canoes used an island-hopping course across Lake Erie to Sandusky Bay, then a river and trail system to many points in the Ohio county and southern United States. At the western end of Lake Erie, the Maumee River was a main route to the, Wabash River by way of a short portage at modern Fort Wayne, Indiana. A second route southeastward from the Mackinac area crossed Lake Huron to the base of Georgian Bay, and through the Severn River reached Lake Simcoe in the neck of the Ontario Peninsula. Here the main route split, one branch going directly south to present Toronto and another continuing eastward through the chain of lakes and streams of the Kawartha Lake district to the Trent River entering Lake Ontario at present Belleville. Fifty miles farther east, at modern Kingston, the St. Lawrence River opened passage directly to the Atlantic Ocean. When travelers were crossing from Toronto to the south side of Lake Ontario, the Oswego River was a frequently used entry point for reaching Oneida Lake and the Wood Creek portage to the Mohawk River, the principal thoroughfare to the Albany region on the Hudson River in eastern New York.

Overarching the entire communications network of the Great Lakes principal theatre was the main thoroughfare from Montreal to the Lake of the Woods, particularly important for the fur trade. This many-portaged route from Montreal followed the Ottawa River to the forks at the Mattawa River, then branched west to Lake Nipissing, the French River, and Georgian Bay. Brigades of traders heading for Mackinac then crossed Lake Huron to the straits region. Others passed through the sheltered channel north of Manitoulin Island, ascended the St. Marys River and either boldly crossed Lake Superior from Keweenaw Point to Isle Royale, or skirted the northern shore. Ultimate streams for reaching the Rainy River route to far northwest country were the Pigeon River, entered north of Grand Portage, Minnesota, or the Kaministiquia River that flows into Lake Superior at present Thunder Bay, Ontario.

These communication lines radiating from the Straits of Mackinac provided both unity and continuity for the course of Great Lakes Indian history. Significant events concerned a total space extending to border regions and peripheral areas tapped by these channels. An explanation of the outer limits of the principal theatre will begin with the eastern section and progress south, west, and north.

East of Lake Ontario, the principal theatre extends to Albany, New York, and Montreal, primarily to include the Mohawk, the eastern division of the Iroquois living in the valleys of the Mohawk and St. Lawrence rivers. Furthermore, Albany and Montreal were rivals for trade and political influence among the Great Lakes Indians from the first quarter of the seventeenth century until the rise of the Pennsylvania traders about 1730. Albany, situated on the north-south course of the Hudson River, is only ten miles below the mouth of the Mohawk River, the east-west travel route splitting the mountain barrier of eastern New York. Montreal, two hundred miles to the north at the juncture of the Ottawa and St. Lawrence rivers, marked the eastern terminus of water transportation routes from the entire Great Lakes area. The corridor from Montreal to Lake Champlain and the upper Hudson River valley is the eastern border region separating the linguistically diverse Great Lakes district from New England's uniformly Algonquian-speaking people.

A southeastern and southern line surrounding the principal theatre follows the Mohawk valley westward to intersect the Great Lakes watershed south of the Finger Lakes district of western New York state, then follows the Allegeny and Ohio river valleys to the "Falls of the Ohio" at present Louisville. The Ohio River is a reasonable southern territorial boundary, since the river course is also the southern limit of Indian villages in this region of North America. There were no Indian villages south of the Ohio River banks in present Kentucky and West Virginia during the period covered by the *Atlas* except for the brief occupation by Shawnee in the mid-eighteenth century.

From the "Falls of the Ohio," a line defining the outer geographic limit of the Great Lakes principal theatre strikes across southern Indiana and Illinois to the Mississippi River at the mouth of the Kaskaskia, fifty miles south of St. Louis. Below the confluence of the Wabash and Ohio rivers and along the Mississippi south of St. Louis, the country's history is increasingly in the orbit of Gulf Coast and southeastern influences. On the lower Ohio River, the principal tributaries are the Cumberland and Tennessee rivers, main arteries from the southern country of the Cherokee, Creek, and Chickasaw. A general orientation toward the south rather than the Great Lakes has always been evident from pre-historic times in the lower Wabash section of present Illinois and Indiana (see map 5).

The course of the Mississippi River is a natural western boundary for the Great Lakes Region and, like the Hudson River valley on the east, forms a border region. Indian settlements along the Mississippi and on the lower Kaskaskia and Illinois rivers had connections for both peaceful trade and warfare with Indians living in territory beyond the western banks. St. Louis, Missouri, identifies an important transitional zone, serving as the southwest terminus for the Great Lakes Region and origin point for travel up the Missouri

Menominee Village in Wisconsin, 1838. From Castlenau, *Vues et Souvenirs du L 'Amerique du Nord,* pI. 22. The Newberry Library.

and down the Mississippi, with eastern routes by way of the Ohio River.

The headwaters of the Mississippi River near Leech Lake indicate the western spread of the Great Lakes principal theatre in Minnesota. Western Minnesota, beyond the elbow of the Minnesota River 80 miles southwest of Minneapolis St.. Paul, is a borderland facing the Dakota plains. On the extreme western edge of the Great Lakes Region, Red Lake, to the northwest of Leech Lake, drains westward to the Red River of the North, emptying into Lake Winnipeg in Manitoba. Directly north of Red Lake, the Lake of the Woods on the Ontario-Manitoba-Minnesota boundaries marks a transitional zone more in the hinterland of Lake Winnipeg than Lake Superior, particularly after the establishment of Canadian Fort Garry in 1821. Lake Winnipeg is outside the mapped area of the *Atlas.*

North of Lake Superior and Lake Huron, beyond the geographic barrier known as the "Height of Land," the focus of life for Indians was toward the Hudson Bay region; these Indians do not figure in the chronology of Great Lakes Indian history. The scattered population living along the northern rim of Lake Superior northwest of Michipicoten was remote from the warfare and population changes of the lower lake region, but was connected with the fur trade economic complex based at Sault Ste. Marie and Mackinac. Northwest of Lake Superior the country was not opened up until the mining era of the 1870s, a development stimulated by completion of the Sault Ste. Marie ship canal on the American side of the river in 1855

and subsequent Indian land cessions and surrenders.

The foregoing description of the principal theatre of action for the Great Lakes Region encompasses close to 200,000 square miles of land in the present United States and Canada, and almost 100,000 square miles of the surface waters of the five Great Lakes. The eighteenth-century homelands of the Great Lakes Indians, their major intertribal councils, and their joint military actions were confined to this arena. Within the principal theatre, the central staging area for the historical drama shifted from one section to another, generally moving in a northwesterly direction during the time period covered by the *Atlas.* The frontier in the east had stabilized by the 1790s but did not approach stability in the northwestern Great Lakes until a century later.

The Mapping Process

Sources of information for mapping Great Lakes Indian history are accounts of traders, missionaries, Indian agents, surveyors, military personnel, travelers, and early settlers. These people frequently have recorded Indian tradition about population distribution and village sites, as well as their own direct observations. A limited number of archaeological reports and the few publications by authors of Indian heritage have also been used in locating historic Indian villages. Printed maps are unreliable for establishing Indian locations unless they are based on actual surveys. Old maps of the

Dakota Village of the 1840s. Watercolor by Seth Eastman. Jerome Hill Reference Library.

seventeenth and eighteenth centuries generally reveal the limited state of knowledge and erroneous impressions of the Great Lakes Region prevalent at that period. A printed map of the eighteenth century may reflect a ten-year delay in adding new places and a fifty-year delay in removing obsolete information. Manuscript maps, with careful interpretation, have been very helpful. A crude sketch by a novice familiar with a remote area can be more valuable in mapping Indian villages than a printed map compiled far from the scene.

All sources of information are apt to reveal geographic errors and obscurities, for there are many pitfalls. A few streams mentioned in Great Lakes Indian treaties still defy attempts at identification, but name repetition poses greater problems. The great watercourse of the Ottawa River in Canada was often called the "Grand." There are also Grand rivers entering both the Ontario and Ohio sides of Lake Erie, as well as an important Grand River in western Michigan known to the Indians as "Washtenong." Two Huron rivers flow into eastern Lake Erie; two other Huron rivers in southeastern Michigan were later renamed Cass and Clinton. The present Cuyahoga River in Ohio was originally one of many called "White," and there have been Delaware villages on this White River as well as White rivers in Indiana and Missouri. The names St. Joseph and St. Mary have been given to missions, forts, rivers, trading posts, and villages dispersed over a broad geographic area. The above examples are a small selection of the name duplications that can lead to misinterpretation of geographic references.

In the course of research for the Atlas, data have been collected on more than 1,500 Indian village sites in the Great Lakes Region. All information has been organized by state or province and subdivided according to tribe and geographic location. The resulting permanent data file, continually corrected and redefined, was used for compiling all the Atlas maps. The locations of some Indian villages are accurately established from surveyor archaeological reports. Other locations may be only approximations fixed with reference to travel time or estimated distance upstream from a known point, or forks in a stream, or a lake or bay.

Assigning names to Indian villages on maps in the Atlas has required making choices among a number of alternatives. Although many villages are designated only by a tribal name, others are identified by the name of the principal leader or by some geographical association. The Shawnee towns carried the name of their individual tribal division with them when they moved, so there is a succession of places called "Piqua" or "Chillicothe," and the single name may refer to a cluster of villages. In contrast, Delaware towns frequently changed names with the advent of each new leader in addition to having a geographic or descriptive name. The Delaware town near present Lancaster, Ohio, was known successively as French Margaret's, Hockhocking, Beaver's New Town, Assinink or Standing Stone, and Captain Johnny's Town. A number of Indian villages in different states were identified with salt licks or salt springs.

In printed and manuscript sources, several spellings may

be found for any well-known Indian village name. The differences usually depend on the native language of the reporter, translator, and scribe, each team of two or three combining the talents of persons of Indian, Dutch, French, English, or German heritage. Present specialists in Iroquoian and Siouan languages have reached some degree of general understanding about spelling, but this recent agreement did not affect the individuality of writers in the eighteenth and nineteenth centuries. No standard spelling of the numerous Algonquian languages has been set by linguistic experts, and village names in the *Atlas* include several spellings for syllables with the same pronunciation.

For the *Atlas*, the spelling found first or most frequently in historical records has generally been adopted; when there is a choice, the shortest form is preferred. Sometimes the selection process has favored a brief English name rather than a long Indian name, simply because of restricted space on the map-for example, in the Winnebago area of Wisconsin. No alternative spelling has been possible for the longest village name in the *Atlas*, Shingabawassinekegobawat, an Ojibwa community in Michigan, fortunately located where the name can extend across Lake Huron. Present spelling is used where the town exists today. Thus "Sheboygan" appears for the community on the Lake Michigan shore of Wisconsin, and "Cheboygan" for Michigan's Lower Peninsula towns. Several spellings for tribal designations are also found in source material for the *Atlas*, but they are generally enough alike to avoid confusion. Yet, "Odawa" might not be recognized as "Ottawa." In a recent major change on the Mohawk reservation south of Montreal, "Kahnawake" has officially replaced the long-used name "Caughnawaga."

In preparing for cartographic presentation of Great Lakes Indian history, the first task was to secure a suitable base map covering both American and Canadian territory. National maps conventionally do not extend beyond the political boundaries. This historical atlas has utilized drainage and shaded relief from *The National Atlas* (Washington, 1970) with supplementary information to complete the Canadian section of the map bases. Maps are on Albers equal area projection. Manuscript maps were drawn at scale. All the double page maps are compiled on the 1: 5 million base for which a one-inch measurement approximates 5,000,000 inches or about 80 miles distance (5,068,800 inches, to be exact) across the earth. Two groups of single page maps, the "Frontier in Transition" and "Indian Villages 1830" series are double in scale, 1 :2.5 million or an inch equalling approximately 40 miles.

The second cartographic step involved redrawing river courses and removing artificial lakes from the contemporary map base, so that the final result would conform as nearly as possible to the drainage pattern before the era of dam construction, canal building, and extensive harbor engineering. Consequently, the Atlas does not show the Welland, Erie, or Sault Ste. Marie canals, or other canals built in the 1830 to 1850 period during the heyday of internal improvements.

Since all map bases are generalizations of the complete system of lakes and streams in a given area, map makers exercise choices in selecting the water courses to be drawn on a base. For the Atlas, some inconspicuous drainage features have been added to the standard base because they were associated with Indian occupation. These include the Gananoque River at the head of the St. Lawrence, Little Detroit Island near the entry to Green Bay of Lake Michigan, and Tinker's Creek, now obscured in present metropolitan Cleveland, Ohio. Some swampy regions noted on the Atlas maps have been drained by ditches that appear as watercourses on present maps.

In order to improve legibility, special rules of style have been adopted for the Atlas maps. No punctuation is used for abbreviations or possessive forms except for apostrophes in the present spelling of the same name. The word "river" is omitted. To reduce the density of type, the word "town" or "village" frequently is deleted from the end of the name of an Indian community.

Summary of Contents

In the sequence of thirty-six maps prepared for the Atlas, the first two, appearing in the introduction, provide a general geographic orientation to the Great Lakes Region. The next three full-size maps of natural vegetation, subsistence patterns of Indian people, and proto-historic cultural groups cover essential background information. These maps concentrate on the environmental setting, natural resources, and lifestyles of Indian communities. The story of life throughout the Great Lakes Region before the Europeans arrived is known in general detail. American and Canadian archaeologists, through the investigation of thousands of prehistoric sites have worked out the sequence of cultural development in the Great Lakes Region after A.D. 800. Because of European diseases and intertribal warfare that disrupted much of the region before the first French observers arrived early in the seventeenth century to report on the country and its people, it is very difficult to compare and contrast the archeological and archival records.

Historians agree, however, that the first major phenomenon of the historical era in the Great Lakes Region was the warfare originating with the Five Nations of Iroquois in northern New York State following the introduction of firearms about 1640. Standard treatment of the Iroquois Wars, ending in 1701, has stressed the offensive directed against the Huron towns around Lake Simcoe, Ontario, in 1649 and the rapid depopulation of the area. The Atlas map of this period illustrates as well the subsequent counteroffensive launched by the Missisauga and their allies that routed the Iroquois from townsites north of Lake Ontario in the 1680s and carried the attacks into the Iroquois homeland in New York.

The map of the French Era (1720-61) focuses attention on the fur trade and population movements in response to trade expansion and the rivalry of Indian middlemen and French and British firms. For this period, colonial history usually highlights the French and Indian War (1754-60) along the St. Lawrence, the Hudson River corridor, and the Pennsylvania frontier, as part of a European conflict, the Seven Years' War (1756-63). The Atlas mapping shows the results of the earlier mercantile offensive led by Pennsylvania traders in the 1740s and French-sponsored military retaliation in the early 1750s before the officially-recognized French and Indian War. Pontiac's Indian uprising in 1763 was the final Indian episode aimed at retaining French trade contacts and opposing continued Anglo-American acquisition of Indian land.

The quartet of maps showing "Changes in Sovereignty" is placed on a single page to facilitate comparing the terms of a sequence of international treaties, 1763, 1783, 1794, and 1795, all drawn up in Europe but affecting the Indian country. The concept of "sovereignty," a fundamental reality in the minds of European heads of state, was untranslatable and incomprehensible to eighteenth-century Indian leaders.

The 1768 map featuring both Indian villages and surrounding tribal estates can be considered the basic map for the beginning of the modern era in Great Lakes Indian history. The time emphasizes a brief interval of relative equilibrium when no European wars exerted pressure on Indians in the Great Lakes Region, although the Ojibwa-Dakota warfare was still in progress southwest of Lake Superior. The year 1768 also marks the establishment of the "permanent" Ohio River boundary between areas of Indian and white settlements by the Treaty of Fort Stanwix, an agreement that Indian people expected would exclude European settlers from the Great Lakes Region. The mid-eighteenth century is the earliest time for which sufficient data are available to present tribal distribution for the Great-Lakes. This map is the first to show the location of Missisauga and Ojibwa villages that dominated southeastern Ontario at the conclusion of the Iroquois wars.

Population shifts during the years from 1770 through 1794 are traced in the series of five maps grouped under the heading, "Frontier in Transition." Attacks on the integrity of the Fort Stanwix line were the basic causes for frontier warfare until the allied Indians were defeated in northwest Ohio in 1794. An interval of this war over the Indian boundary coincided with the American Revolution, 1776-1783. This map sequence is the first cartographic analysis of a complex chapter in Indian and frontier history.

The three dates selected for mapping Indian and white townsites during the nineteenth century, 1810, 1830, and 1870, indicate thresholds of three historic eras in Great Lakes Indian history. For each map, the objective is to present the number and distribution of Indian villages as accurately as possible for the particular date. The same attention to the overall pattern of settlement has been followed in portraying the increasing density and geographical extent of white towns, hence the advancing frontier phenomenon is apparent on the sequence of maps.

The 1810 map portrays population distribution just before the widespread Indian opposition to American encroachment signaled by the Battle of Tippecanoe in 1811. The Indian war in the Old Northwest continued throughout the British-American War of 1812. The 150 events and incidents mapped for the Atlas version of the War of 1812 illustrate the dual nature of the hostilities spread over a broad area in the Great Lakes theatre. Exclusively Indian-American conflicts, the majority mapped for the first time, predominated in the area southwest of Detroit extending to eastern Missouri, while the British-American warfare was confined to the area east of Detroit.

The year 1830 heralded the inauguration of new Indian programs in both Canadian and American territory. It was the year of the passage of the Indian Removal Act by the American Congress. Indian agents in Canada were about to institute a new reserve policy. It marked the beginning of accelerated westward migration of settlers using the new Erie Canal route and increased passenger transportation facilities on the Great Lakes. The 1830 era is the subject of the second series of large-scale maps providing a closer view of Indian villages and white settlements. These six maps portray the Indian tribal distribution on the eve of the Black Hawk War, 1832, the last great Indian war in the Great Lakes Region. The complete mapping of all elements in this episode has led to the conclusion that British involvement was of greater consequence than generally credited by historians.

Three topical maps covering the entire period of the Atlas are included to indicate factors affecting Indian village locations and population numbers over long periods of time. The concurrent completion of Indian land cessions and surrenders on the American and Canadian sides of the international border is evident in the land cessions map. From a review of the treaties, it is clear that many Indian groups straddling the international border have dealt with two governmental structures. Although the subject of land cessions has been mapped in other publications, the Atlas is presenting an accompanying map of all land reserved for Indian people by these same treaties, as well as reserves created by American state governments. Epidemic disease throughout the Great Lakes Region has never been studied, and consequently presents another new topic for mapping. Some of the Indian population dislocation and decline can be attributed to specific epidemics, particularly outbreaks of smallpox.

The 1870 date for the final map of Indian village locations approximates the commencement of the last stage of the frontier in the upper Great Lakes Region. This late frontier was delayed until after the Civil War in the United States (1861-65) and after Canadian Confederation in 1867. The year 1870 is selected as a representative date for a combination of developments. It indicates the advent of intensive mining and lumber operations, coordinated with the arrival of the first railroad lines in the northern Great Lakes Region. It is near the conclusion of Indian treaty making in the United States, ended by law in 1871, and at the same time it signifies the beginning of greater attention in Canada to the Canadian West in the wake of the Louis Riel uprising at Red River in 1869. Major land surrenders by Indians living in Canadian territory northwest of Lake Superior were made in 1871 and 1873. The final pattern of Indian population distribution in the Great Lakes Region was established by this time.

The foregoing summary of the content of Atlas maps stresses main developments in the principal theatre of the Great Lakes Region. Since the total area framed by the double-page maps in the Atlas is greater than the irregular shape of the Great Lakes principal theatre, these large maps cover outlying territory surrounding the Great Lakes Region.

The peripheral sections of the maps have been treated in different ways. The small section of New England east of the Hudson River is considered a "non-subject area" and has no data on any of the Atlas maps. On the other hand, Quebec, Ottawa, Philadelphia, and Washington have seemed to be useful geographic reference points for some of the map topics.

Trading posts have been mapped in marginal regions of Canada to infer the presence of Indian people in the vicinity. The stations occupied by pioneer Americans in Kentucky are mapped to indicate the source of the expeditions against the Indians during the era of the rapidly transitional frontier. The map of population distribution in 1870 includes a part of the Great Lakes Indian population that had been removed to Kansas.

The four corners of the map pages are too confining to indicate the full geographic range of Great Lakes Indian people. Winnebago from Wisconsin traveled to Santa Fe, New Mexico, in the eighteenth century to get horses; Delaware from Ohio went to Pensacola, Florida, in 1790 on a diplomatic mission to Spanish authorities. A delegation of Ojibwa Indians from north of Lake Huron was received by royalty in the courts of France, England, and Belgium in 1845. These few examples of a multitude of individual long-distance journeys illustrate the diversity of contacts made by Great Lakes Indians in the larger world outside the principal theatre of action more immediately affecting their lives.

Taken as a whole, the series of maps of Indian village locations shows the changing pattern of population distribution in the Great Lakes over more than two hundred eventful years. Indian people maintained control of their lands as long as they were numerically dominant. As white settlers flooded a section or determined to develop resources of an area, Indian people were forced northward and westward by population pressure exerted through the medium of land cession treaties. Once Indians became a minority, they could no longer retain tribal lands except for reservations conceded by British, American, and Canadian governments.

The *Atlas* maps graphically demonstrate the persistent Indian element in Great Lakes history. From the first map of Indian villages in the seventeenth century during the Iroquois Wars to the final map for 1870, there are Iroquois in New York and along the St. Lawrence River, Ojibwa on the Ontario peninsula and around Lake Superior, Ottawa on the Straits of Mackinac, Potawatomi in southwestern Michigan and other parts of the Great Lakes, Miami on the Wabash River in northern Indiana, and Winnebago and Menominee in Wisconsin. Although Indian people were almost completely swept from the main line of westward white emigration through Ohio, Indiana, and Illinois, they have never abandoned the less populated northern country of the Great Lakes Region. The states of New York, Michigan, Wisconsin and Minnesota numbered about 150,000 Indians in 1980, and an estimated 90,000 lived in adjacent sections of Ontario. A substantial portion of the population of the area included Indian people among their forbears. Within the entire Great Lakes Region, the growing Indian population by 1985 was close to 300,000.

The distribution of major vegetation communities as they existed in the Great Lakes Region during late prehistoric times is depicted in map 3. The degree to which Indian land use practices had an effect on natural communities is a matter of scholarly debate. Certainly, over time, all plant communities were disturbed by either natural or cultural causes, so that on the microenvironmental level, plant communities are dynamic. On the macroenvironmental level, like those shown in map 3, stability should be emphasized over change. This is probably true even on the prairie-woodland margin, where Indian burning was a major factor in ecological succession. Although small tracts of land have been continually disturbed by the burning and land clearing activities of native peoples, major disturbance in the Great Lakes environment awaited the arrival of Europeans. The ecology of the region was altered as early as the seventeenth century by the selective trapping of furbearers, yet it was not until settlers and entrepreneurs established themselves in the region during the nineteenth century that the environment, was greatly altered. The clearing of land for lumber and agriculture, drainage of swamps and bogs, and the widespread introduction of exotic plant and animal species altered forever the plant communities of the Great Lakes Region.

At the time of European contact, there were five major plant communities in the region: coniferous forests, deciduous-coniferous forests, deciduous forests, grassland-

Aboriginal Forest. By W. H. Bartlett. From Willis, *Canadian Scenery,* vol. 1. The Newberry Library.

Felling a tree by burning and scraping until it falls to the ground. The American Museum of Natural History.

deciduous forests, and grasslands. Deciduous forests covered most of the region extending throughout the south central and eastern portions of the Great Lakes where temperatures are moderate and humidity high. These broadleaf forests graded into grasslands to the west and the north. Intermediate areas supported either prairie grasses intermixed with deciduous forest components or forests composed of both deciduous and coniferous elements.

One of the difficulties in preparing vegetation maps arises from the lack of uniformity or standardization in the basic reference material originally prepared for a variety of political entities-states, provinces, and countries. Large regional maps must of necessity encompass many smaller political entities. Their construction, therefore, poses problems that result from discrepancies in scale and the degree of

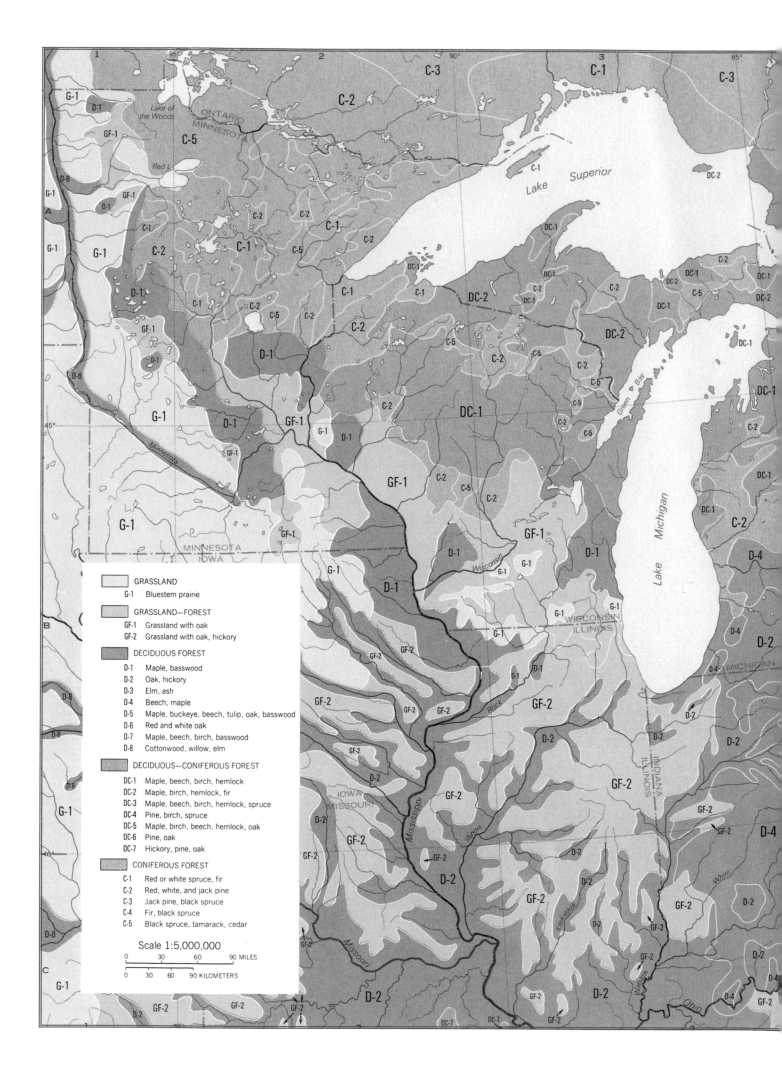

GRASSLAND
G-1   Bluestem prairie

GRASSLAND—FOREST
GF-1   Grassland with oak
GF-2   Grassland with oak, hickory

DECIDUOUS FOREST
D-1   Maple, basswood
D-2   Oak, hickory
D-3   Elm, ash
D-4   Beech, maple
D-5   Maple, buckeye, beech, tulip, oak, basswood
D-6   Red and white oak
D-7   Maple, beech, birch, basswood
D-8   Cottonwood, willow, elm

DECIDUOUS—CONIFEROUS FOREST
DC-1   Maple, beech, birch, hemlock
DC-2   Maple, birch, hemlock, fir
DC-3   Maple, beech, birch, hemlock, spruce
DC-4   Pine, birch, spruce
DC-5   Maple, birch, beech, hemlock, oak
DC-6   Pine, oak
DC-7   Hickory, pine, oak

CONIFEROUS FOREST
C-1   Red or white spruce, fir
C-2   Red, white, and jack pine
C-3   Jack pine, black spruce
C-4   Fir, black spruce
C-5   Black spruce, tamarack, cedar

Scale 1:5,000,000

0   30   60   90 MILES

0   30   60   90 KILOMETERS

Natural Vegetation c. 1600

MAP
3

Manuscript map by Nancy Nowak Cleland

Indian Sugar Camp, showing sap collection from maple trees and open-fire boiling to produce sugar. By Seth Eastman. From Schoolcraft, *History of the Indian Tribes of the United States*, pt. 2, p. 59.

A herd of buffalo on the prairie. By Seth Eastman. From Schoolcraft, *History of the Indian Tribes of the United States*, pt. 4, p. 97. The Newberry Library.

detail provided for various plant communities. Professional judgment must often be exercised in reconciling differences found in the many sources consulted in the course of research.

General cultural associations in the use of plant complexes are superficially apparent. For example, those Indian groups occupying regions predominantly forested by the various combinations of deciduous species built dugout canoes, frequently used elm bark to cover houses, and relied heavily upon nuts for subsistence supplement. Tribes of the mixed conifer-deciduous and conifer regions used birch bark for house covering and for building canoes, and depended more on berries than nuts as a dietary supplement.

It is no doubt possible to go far beyond these general kinds of conclusions concerning the relationship between Indians and specific vegetative associations. Without elaborating or attempting to arrive at causal relationships, the following possible associations may be noted: (1) the westward limit of the expansion of early Ojibwa villages on the north shore of Lake Superior to Michipicoten Bay and the westward limit of mixed deciduous-conifer forests north of Lake Superior; (2) the strong relationship of the maple-birch-hemlock and the maple-beech-birch association with Ojibwa settlements on the south shore of Lake Superior; (3) the close relationship between the northern limits of Potawatomi expansion and the northern limits of the deciduous forest formation; (4) the relationship of Miami with the eastern extent of the grassland-forest association. These are but a few of the many relationships which will bear close investigation in the future.

Principal Sources: Kuchler 1964; Rowe 1972.

The subsistence regimes of Indian people living in the Great Lakes Region reveal the close relationship between the distribution of natural and cultural communities. By the time of contact with Euro-Americans, Great Lakes Indians had developed means of gaining a living by methods that were the cumulation of thousands of years of trial and error in which countless choices for the investment of human effort were balanced against possible yield of food resources. Although making a living depended to some degree on the caprice of nature, the evidence suggests that a stable balance was reached in which population, group size, seasonal movements, and the division of labor combined to produce a successful accommodation to specific sets of environmental resources. This map illustrates the approximate boundaries of the major subsistence patterns as they existed from about A.D. 1000 to A.D. 1900.

In the Great Lakes Region, four basic subsistence patterns can be identified, based primarily upon domesticated plants, fishing, hunting, and wild rice. The first subsistence pattern appears in the oak-hickory and to some extent in the beech-maple forests of what is now lower Ontario, southern Michigan and Wisconsin, and southeastern Minnesota, where Indian people depended for their livelihood on the cultivation of domesticated plants-particularly corn, beans, and squashes. These species, domesticated in the tropical and semitropical climates of Middle America, were gradually adapted to more northern climates of the forested regions of northeastern North America. Although each species arrived at a different time, all of the major crops of the Eastern Agricultural Complex had arrived by A.D. 1000. Yarnall's report of a survey of plant remains recovered archaeologically from the Great Lakes area has shown that agri-

Ojibwa women harvesting wild rice, Wisconsin, c. 1850. By Seth Eastman. The American Museum of Natural History.

Spearing Fish in Winter. By Seth Eastman. From Schoolcraft, *History of the Indian Tribes of the United States*, pt. 2, p. 53. The Newberry Library.

culture was practiced in areas that received at least 120 frost-free growing days, and that 140 growing days were generally necessary for reliable corn production. Although the northern extent of this agricultural complex has undoubtedly shifted with climatic fluctuation and the development of more rapidly maturing corn strains, the modern 140 frost-free day line provides a conservative indicator of the northern extent of the practice of agriculture since A.D. 1000 (see inset, map 3).

It would be a mistake to think of these agricultural Indians-of which the Iroquoian tribes, Potawatomi, Miami, Illinois, and various Siouan groups are examples-as entirely dependent upon agriculture. They also hunted, fished, and collected wild plant foods. Deer, bison, elk, bears, turkeys and a large variety of other species were important sources of protein. The storage of corn, however, differentiated these part-time hunters from peoples to the north and the west.

The second major economic adaptation was based upon hunting and occurred in the boreal and mixed deciduous-conifer transition forests north and northeast of the Great Lakes. Here, northern Ojibwa, Cree, and Assiniboine Indians were dependent on moose, woodland caribou, and bears for most of their subsistence needs. Smaller game such as beaver, hare, partridge, and geese, as well as fish, were very important and, collectively, were probably vital for survival.

The third and fourth subsistence patterns arose in the transitory forests of the central Upper Great Lakes where two very distinctive subsistence patterns emerged, each centered on a unique constellation of resources. West of Lake Michigan and south and west of Lake Superior in the maple-beech and conifer-dominated mixed forests where shallow limey lakes are a major feature of the landscape, Indians such as the Menominee, southwestern Ojibwa, and some Winnebago and Dakota developed an economy based upon wild rice, described by Jenks. Although hunting of moose, caribou, elk, and even local cultivation of corn were important subsistence enterprises, wild rice provided the economic mainstay. Farther east, the southeastern Ojibwa, Ottawa, and some Huron groups occupying the transition forests at the heads of Lakes Michigan and Huron and the eastern end of Lake Superior developed an economy centered on water rather than land resources. Again, hunting, collecting, occasional gardening, and, especially, maple sugar production were important subsistence activities; but these people were, above all, fishermen. This fishery was first studied by Rostlund, who called it the Inland Shore Fishery. A great variety of fishing techniques were devised, including such novel methods as those used in the rapids of the St. Marys River, where fish were scooped from the water by a man standing in the prow of a bark canoe. The use of gill nets set on off-shore shoals for the capture of whitefish and lake trout constituted the heart of this fishery.

The Indians of the Great Lakes thus developed four very different subsistence patterns, which were based upon agriculture, large game hunting, rice, and fishing. The extent to which one or another of these resources were favored was

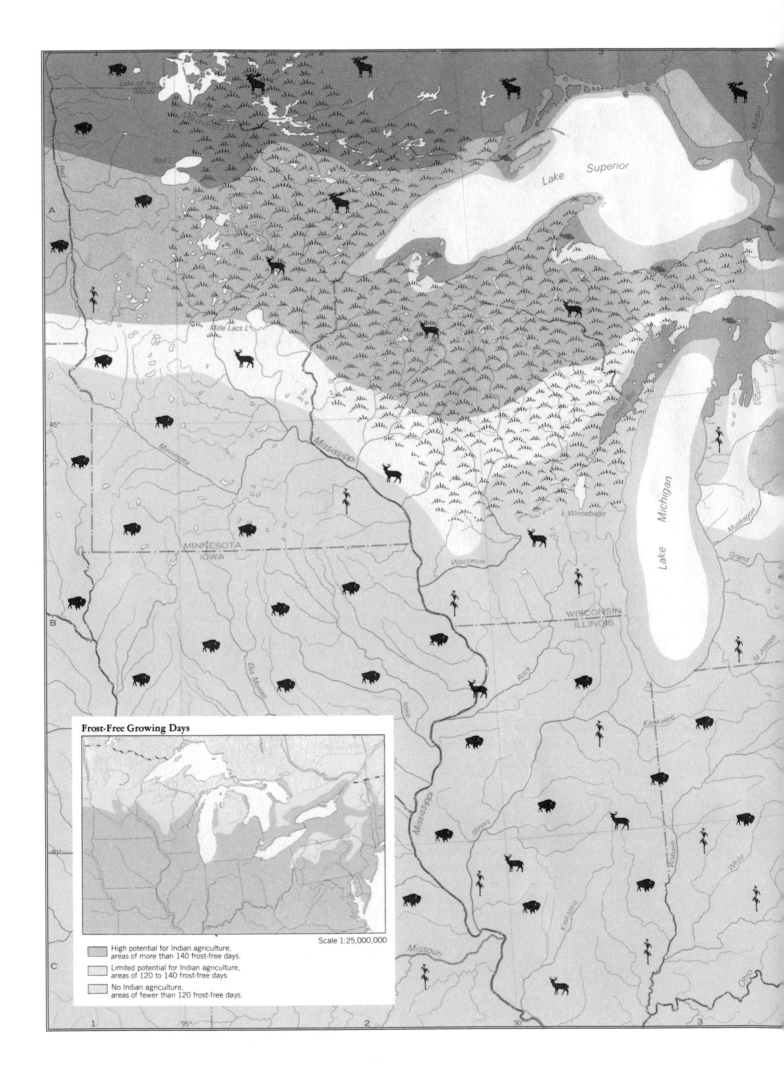

Frost-Free Growing Days

High potential for Indian agriculture,
areas of more than 140 frost-free days.

Limited potential for Indian agriculture,
areas of 120 to 140 frost-free days.

No Indian agriculture,
areas of fewer than 120 frost-free days.

Scale 1:25,000,000

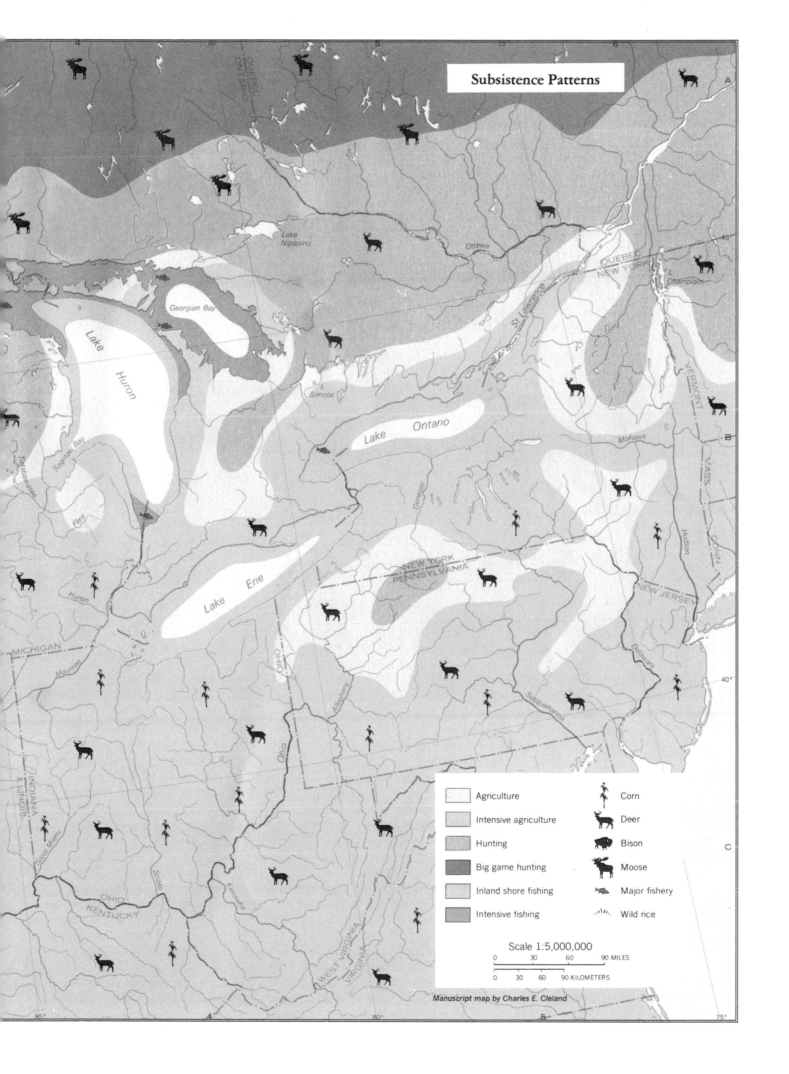

Subsistence Patterns

MAP
4

Agriculture

Intensive agriculture

Hunting

Big game hunting

Inland shore fishing

Intensive fishing

Corn

Deer

Bison

Moose

Major fishery

Wild rice

Scale 1:5,000,000

| 0 | 30 | 60 | 90 MILES |

| 0 | 30 | 60 | 90 KILOMETERS |

Manuscript map by Charles E. Cleland

Guarding the corn crop. By Seth Eastman. From *Schoolcraft, History of the Indian Tribes of the United States*, pt. 3, p. 63. The Newberry Library.

not necessarily a matter of opportunity. Indeed, some Indian people may well have systematically exploited all of the resources in the course of a yearly subsistence round. Yet, the identifiable patterns arising before European contact and persisting into the historic era were based on specialized technologies, knowledge, and the adaptation of social institutions in order to "capitalize" on a few of the total array of resources available.

Which resource or resources became central to the economy depended not only on availability but also on the efficiency with which they could be exploited. Thus, corn could be and was grown in many areas where the growing season was so short that little or no reliance could be placed on the possibility of producing a large corn crop. In other areas, people actively fished for short periods but conditions for the preservation of the catch mitigated against a long-term economic benefit from this activity. For these reasons it was a combination of unique environmental and cultural conditions that eXplained the local form of the subsistence pattern. The guiding principle that seems to transcend both cultural change and fluctuations in the ecology of the landscape is development of a storable food surplus to be used in periods of food scarcity.

Following this principle, when Indians could depend on a corn crop (in areas with 140 frost-free days), they practiced agriculture to the exclusion of all other major subsistence enterprises. Corn and beans are high-energy foods that could be produced in abundance and easily stored. For these reasons, and because surplus production could be stimulated by added labor, agriculture was a superior subsistence pat-

tern constantly pushed to the northern limits of successful production.

The least secure of the four major Great Lakes subsistence patterns and the one least under human control was the hunting pattern in the conifer-dominated forests of the north. Low population in this region is a direct reflection of the absence of a reliable food source. Moose and woodland caribou, the large "meat packages" of the region, could be preserved by freezing but were relatively low in density and most difficult to capture when other foods were in short supply in late winter and early spring.

The wild rice and Inland Shore Fishery patterns are, in effect, agricultural surrogates in areas north of the effective climatic limits of the tropical domesticates upon which the agricultural complex is based. The parallel between rice and corn production is easy to comprehend. The link between the fishery and agriculture is harder to see, but understood by at least one modern Ojibwa who noted that "having a hundred feet of good gill net is like having 40 acres. . ." Gill nets have been used primarily to capture whitefish and lake trout when they spawn in the late fall and early winter on offshore shoals. These fish can be preserved by freezing or smoking and, like wild rice, stored for winter use. Like the harvesting of wild rice, production can usually be increased by increased labor. Fishing, however, seemed to have provided a more reliable food source than rice production.

The written descriptions of the lifeways of Great Lakes Indians beginning in the seventeenth century provided a quantitative leap in the understanding of many aspects of the cultures of these people. Unfortunately, when it comes to

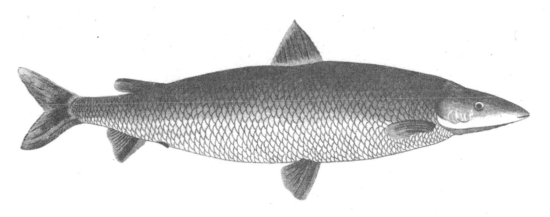

Whitefish, for Indians the most delectable staple of the Upper Great Lakes. Drawn by J. C. Tidball. From *Schoolcraft, History of the Indian Tribes of the United States*, pt. 5, p. 117. The Newberry Library.

consideration of the relationship between Indians and the natural environment, the historic literature up to the 1830s is so dominated by the drama of the fur trade that Indian people appear to have been exclusively concerned with furbearing animals. Closer attention to the less exciting aspects of the historic literature reveals that Indians continued to procure food in traditional ways, and that the pressures of Euro-American contact had the effect of intensifying the four basic subsistence strategies already present in the region. Even with the introduction of items of European technology (including firearms, traps, and metal fishing gear), depopulation caused by European diseases, and major population movements, Indians maintained their vital links with the environment.

In fact, it was not until the destruction of the environmental resources base in the twentieth century that these traditional subsistence patterns were substantially modified. Lumbering, draining of lakes and bogs, and over-hunting and fishing by an expanding non-Indian population brought an end to the subsistence patterns that had proved equal to the cycles of nature and the immense social changes of the fur trade era. Despite the magnitude of the overall social and economic changes, corn agriculture, wild rice production, and the Inland Shore Fishery have continued to be viable economic pursuits for modern Great Lakes Indian communities.

Principal Sources: Cleland 1966, 1982; Jenks 1900; Rostlund 1952; Yarnall 1964.

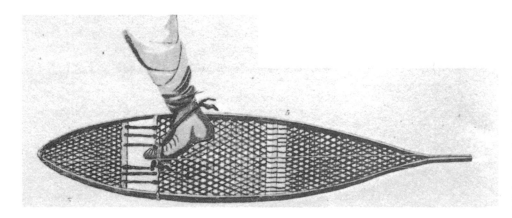

Snowshoe. Tied to moccasins, they were used to cross deep snow in winter. Drawn from the original by Seth Eastman. From *Schoolcraft, History of the Indian Tribes of the United States*, pt. 3, p. 68. The Newberry Library.

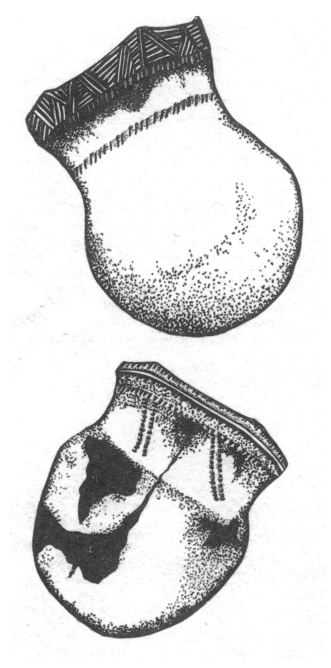

Late Woodland Pottery.
The Museum, Michigan State University.

The use of archaeological data for cartographic purposes poses specific difficulties. The archaeological record, like the written documents, permits only occasional glimpses into the cultural past. Evidence from the soil often speaks softly and indistinctly, leaving uncertainty concerning facts of ethnic and cultural relationships. In the case of archaeology, determining the degree of these relationships usually requires making a judgment about the degree of similarity or difference between two assemblages of excavated artifacts. Such judgments are based on the assumption that the more similar the artifacts from two sites, the more direct is the cultural continuity between them. Since this assumption applies to space as well as time, it is possible to map areas of prehistoric cultural homogeneity.

Archaeologists in the eastern United States have a long tradition of thinking about cultural boundaries in terms of differences and similarities of pottery types. Most maps of the distribution of prehistoric cultures are, in reality, maps of the distribution of broadly defined ceramic wares and styles. The map presented here follows the same pattern. While it is widely recognized that there is no necessary correlation between the mode of decoration applied to a ceramic vessel and the specific ethnic or linguistic identity of the pottery maker, most archaeologists believe that at least broad relationships exist between the material and the social and ideological aspects of society. This map of prehistoric cultures of the Great Lakes is presented in that spirit.

One of the difficulties with mapping "archaeological cultures" is that the traditions described cartographically are not strictly contemporaneous in time. An attempt has been made here to show the latest prehistoric cultures where possible. As a general rule, most of the divisions shown represent cultures extant between A.D. 1300 and A.D. 1600, but some extend somewhat earlier and later.

A few words also are in order concerning boundaries, another feature of maps of prehistoric cultures that probably have far more meaning for modern students than prehistoric Indians. Generally, prehistoric cultures conform in their distributions to features of the natural as well as the cultural landscape. To this extent, prehistoric cultural boundaries often correspond to boundaries of watersheds, climate zones, or biotic communities. In some cases where the boundaries of prehistoric cultures are not known, natural features of the environment were used to estimate their approximate location for the purpose of this map.

Finally, it is perhaps self-evident that the more distinctive the archaeological material and the greater the number of sites located in a region, the more accurately the boundaries can be drawn. For an example of this contrast, attention can be drawn to the Fort Ancient manifestation in southern Ohio as opposed to the Juntunen culture of northern

Michigan. The boundaries of Fort Ancient are quite accurate, while the limits of Juntunen, circumscribing Michipicotin Bay, the eastern half of the Upper Peninsula, and the northern part of the Lower Peninsula of Michigan, are strictly an estimate.

In the Great Lakes, it is possible to identify three broad cultural (ceramic) traditions. Each is distinguishable by at least A.D. 1000 and may be traced clearly in time until the era of European contact. These traditions are the Woodland, of the Atlantic seaboard and the northern Midwest; the Upper Mississippian, of the upper Ohio and upper Mississippi river valleys; and the Mississippian of southern parts of Indiana and Illinois.

The Woodland is by far the dominant tradition in the Great Lakes area. Virtually all of the village farmers and northern hunters who inhabited the shores of the five Great Lakes proper are of this tradition. The pottery that characterizes the Woodland is most often tempered with coarse grit; the surface has a cord-roughened finish produced by malleting the pot with a cordwrapped paddle. The upper portion of the globular vessels often have pronounced shoulders and collars. Decoration is accomplished with repeated application of twisted cords, punctates, or incised lines placed in geometric patterns on the upper rim and lips.

Within the Woodland tradition, it is possible to identify at least two subtraditions. These have been associated with the Iroquoian and Algonquian language groups, associations that are justified on the basis of ethnohistoric data. MacNeish and Wright have illustrated the in situ development of both New York and Ontario Iroquois cultures from an earlier Woodland base. These works lay to rest the idea of recent Iroquoian migration into the Great Lakes Region from the south. Tuck, in fact, provides a detailed developmental sequence for a single Iroquoian tribe, the Onondaga, and thus the hope that archaeologists will eventually be able to trace the ascendancy of other specific tribal groups in the region.

Although the development of the Algonquian aspects of the Woodland tradition is not as well-documented, McPherron has provided a long developmental sequence for the ceramics of the Straits of Mackinac region that documents ceramic development from A.D. 800 until A.D. 1350. Work in Manitoba, Ontario, and states on the southern shores of the Great Lakes indicates a relatively unbroken continuity of Woodland styles from at least A.D. 1000 until European contact.

The areas mapped for Upper Mississippian tradition illustrate the complexity of relating prehistoric culture to cultures known during the protohistoric and historic periods. In both the upper Mississippi and upper Ohio valleys, archaeologists have found sites of village agriculturalists with a material culture very similar to the Woodland tradition; the exception is a well-made ceramic tempered with grit or ground clam shell. Globular pots have smoothed surfaces and loop or strap handles. Rims are frequently sharply out-turned at the neck and the shoulder below decorated with broadly incised trailed designs of a geometric type, usually triangles.

The Fort Ancient culture of the upper Ohio Valley was carefully studied by Griffin and, despite the lack of direct archaeological evidence, Fort Ancient culture has been widely identified with historic Shawnee, who are Algonquian speak-

Upper Mississippian Pottery.
The Museum, Michigan State University.

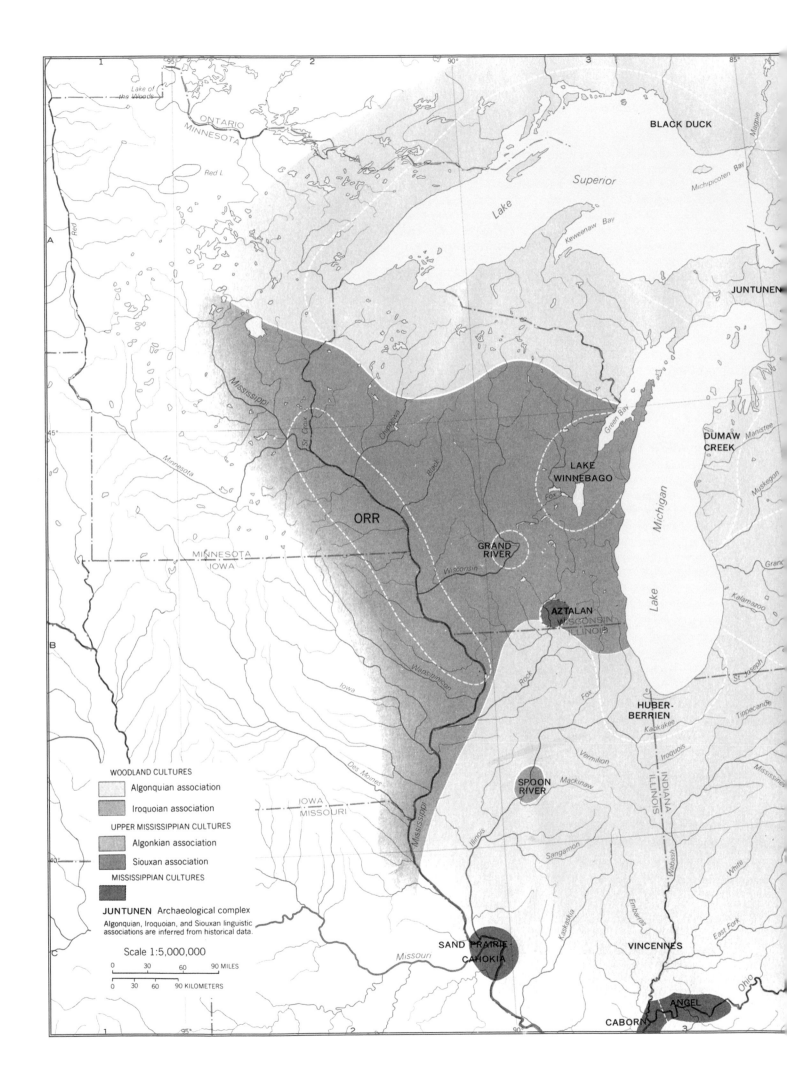

BLACK DUCK

JUNTUNEN

DUMAW
CREEK

Superior

Keweenaw Bay

Michipicoten Bay

Lake

Red L

Lake of
the Woods

ONTARIO
MINNESOTA

Red

Mississippi

Minnesota

St. Croix

Chippewa

Black

Fox

Green Bay

LAKE
WINNEBAGO

ORR

GRAND
RIVER

Wisconsin

Lake

Michigan

MINNESOTA
IOWA

AZTALAN
WISCONSIN
ILLINOIS

HUBER-
BERRIEN

Kalamazoo

Grand

Manistee

Muskegon

St. Joseph

Iowa

Wapsipinicon

Des Moines

Rock

Fox

Kankakee

Vermilion

Mackinaw

SPOON
RIVER

Tippecanoe

Iroquois

INDIANA
ILLINOIS

Mississinewa

IOWA
MISSOURI

Mississippi

Illinois

Sangamon

WOODLAND CULTURES

Algonquian association

Iroquoian association

UPPER MISSISSIPPIAN CULTURES

Algonkian association

Siouxan association

MISSISSIPPIAN CULTURES

JUNTUNEN Archaeological complex

Algonquian, Iroquoian, and Siouxan linguistic
associations are inferred from historical data.

Scale 1:5,000,000

0   30   60   90 MILES

0   30   60   90 KILOMETERS

Kaskaskia

Embarras

White

Wabash

East Fork

VINCENNES

SAND PRAIRIE
CAHOKIA

Missouri

ANGEL

CABORN

Ohio

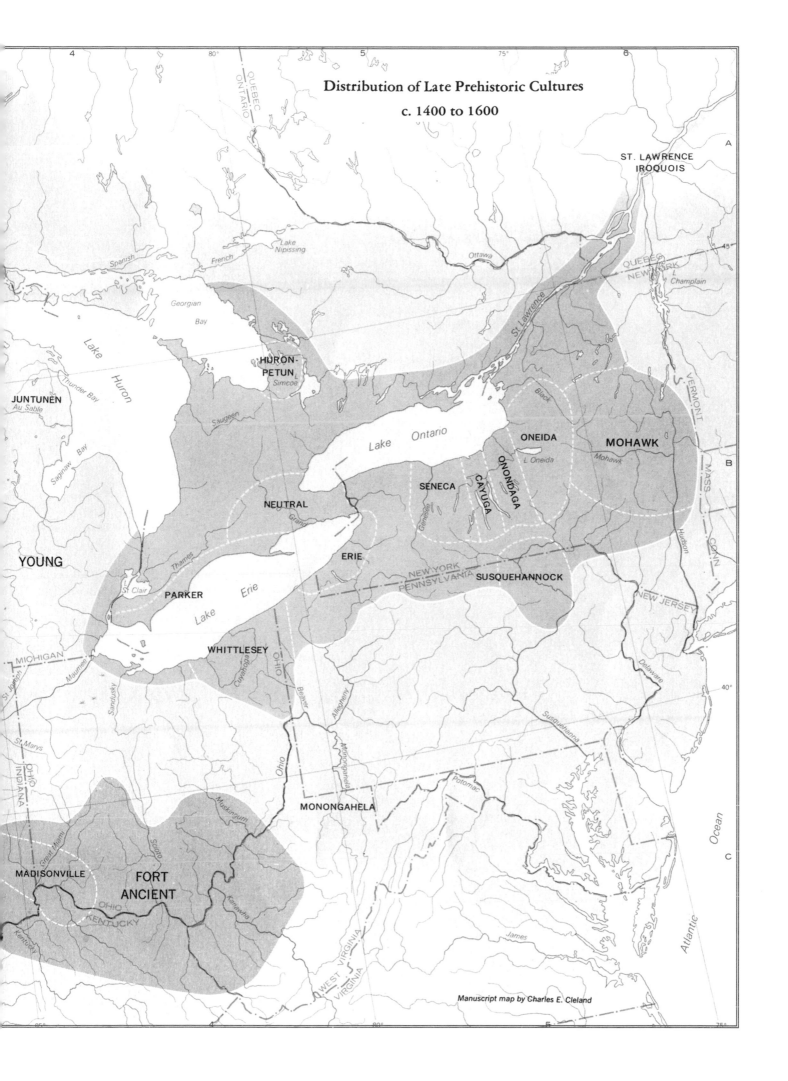

Distribution of Late Prehistoric Cultures
c. 1400 to 1600

ST. LAWRENCE
IROQUOIS

HURON-
PETUN
Simcoe

JUNTUNEN
Au Sable

YOUNG

Lake Ontario

ONEIDA

MOHAWK

SENECA

CAYUGA

ONONDAGA

NEUTRAL

ERIE

PARKER

Lake Erie

NEW YORK
PENNSYLVANIA

SUSQUEHANNOCK

WHITTLESEY

MICHIGAN

MONONGAHELA

MADISONVILLE

FORT
ANCIENT

Manuscript map by Charles E. Cleland

MAP
5

Mississippian Pottery. The Museum, Michigan State University.

ers. On the other hand, the broadly similar Upper Mississippian cultures of the upper Mississippi River valley and central Wisconsin have long been associated with Siouan-speaking groups such as the Winnebago. Although Mason has recently called attention to the near absence of archaeological evidence for such assumptions in the case of the Winnebago, the Siouan-Upper Mississippian association is well-fixed in the minds of prehistorians in this region. Thus, an Upper Mississippian-Siouan connection has been noted in one region and an Upper Mississippian-Algonquian connection in another—both on the basis of very tenuous archaeological evidence.

The Mississippian tradition is predominate on the Gulf Coast and in the lower Mississippi Valley and is therefore both geographically and culturally marginal to a consideration of Great Lakes prehistory. Nevertheless, several very large and influential Mississippian centers existed on the southern margin of the Midwest. These included Cahokia near St. Louis, with satellites in the Illinois River valley extending as far north as the site of Aztalan in southern Wisconsin, and another center focusing on the Angel site in southern Indiana. These were large ceremonial sites with impressive earthen mounds that served as platforms for temples. The Cahokia site is the largest prehistoric site north of Central Mexico, which Fowler estimates may have been occupied at one point by as many as ten thousand people. Mississippian material culture is very distinct from the Woodland and Upper Mississippian, which bear a much closer resemblance to each other than either does to Mississippian. The Mississippian ceramic tradition is extremely rich, showing a large variety of vessel forms. Ceramics are well-fired, tempered with crushed shell, and show a smoothed surface. The vessels were decorated by incising broad designs, many curvilinear, or often by painting. Ethnic and linguistic associations for Mississippian are poorly understood in the Great Lakes Region, but the most productive correlations would probably be found with tribes of the southeastern United States.

Principal Sources: Fowler 1969; Griffin 1943, 1960; MacNeish 1976; Mason 1976; McPherron 1967; Tuck 1971; Wright 1966.

The long series of confrontations in the second half of the seventeenth century that are known as the Iroquois Wars resulted from a combination of old hostilities and new factors related to the fur trade. With few exceptions, intertribal relationships did not change, but actions against traditional enemies heightened from occasional raids and taking of prisoners to long-range excursions by large numbers of warriors and repeated attacks on fur brigades. The result was vanquishment, dislocation, and disappearance of some Indian groups as cultural entities, notably the Erie and Wenro, through absorption by other tribes.

Sources of Conflict

Great Lakes Indians were involved in fur trade with Europeans. The Five Nations of the Iroquois Confederacy, the Seneca, Cayuga, Onondaga, Oneida, and Mohawk living in northern New York, brought pelts as exchange for trade goods to the Dutch at Fort Orange (present Albany). These Indian's continued trading at the same place with the English after the English conquest of New Netherlands in 1664, when the name of the colony changed to New York. Indians living west of Lake Huron and Huron living near the base of Georgian Bay traded principally with the French at Montreal, Trois Rivieres, or Quebec. The Huron acted as middlemen dealing directly with the French for furs brought to them by Indians from the west and north, and providing European trade goods to Indian suppliers.

By the 1640s the beaver supply in Iroquois territory was exhausted, or insufficient for their needs. They went to war to obtain furs from the Huron and other nations trading with the French, and to harvest furs in the hunting grounds of neighboring tribes. At the time the wars began, the Five Nations of Iroquois and the Huron Confederacy were of equal strength numerically, with about 12,000 in each group. Since 1600, they had lost a third to a half of their populations through epidemics of European diseases (see map 32). More adequate firearms secured from traders at present Albany, New York, gave the Iroquois initial military superiority.

Aspects of the War Era

In order to appreciate the diverse military activity of the Iroquois War era, a few general statements should be made. First of all, despite the periodic intensity of warfare between 1641 and 1701, fighting was sporadic, with several intervals of peace by treaty. Furthermore, warfare was not exclusively directed toward the Great Lakes Region. At various times, the range of expeditions extended east into New England, south to Chesapeake Bay and the southern Appalachian highlands, and north beyond the headwaters of the Ottawa river. Warfare outside the Great Lakes Region has not been mapped.

The course of the warfare was affected by disunity among the Iroquois; the Five Nations often acted independently of one another. In 1645 the Mohawk observed a peace agreement with the Huron and other Indians of the western Great Lakes that lasted until 1646. At the same time, the Seneca, Oneida, and Onondaga were raiding western fur brigades along the St. Lawrence River. The Mohawk alone fought the Mahican, neighbors to the east in the Hudson River valley. This longstanding hostility subsided following the Mohawk victory in 1669 at Hoffman's Ferry (now Hoffman's), New York, nine miles up the Mohawk River from Schenectady.

Some of the other Indian tribes engaged in the Iroquois wars were also involved in conflicts of a more limited scope. The Ojibwa and Nipissing were fighting with the Dakota and Mesquakie west and south of Lake Superior at the same time they were resisting the Iroquois. Refugees from King Philip's War in New England came to the Miami village on the St. Joseph River at present Niles, Michigan, in the 1680s, and joined the fight against the Iroquois. The Mahican group shown on the map at that location included New England Indian refugees as well. Among the Miami living there were related Wea and Piankashaw groups. As a consequence of such factors, the entire population of the Great Lakes Region became involved in numerous military conflicts during the long course of the Iroquois Wars. Individual incidents ranged from quick raids by small war parties to large-scale battles involving 2,000 warriors.

Although inter-tribal warfare is the focus of this map, it is important to be aware that the first French explorers, traders and missionaries reached Indian communities in the upper Great Lakes and the Illinois and Mississippi valleys during this same time period. Before combat occurred on the St. Marys River, missionaries preached to Ojibwa at Bawating in 1641, and venturesome traders penetrated Lake Superior and the northwestern shores of Lake Michigan to Green Bay. In 1673, the trader Louis Joliet set forth from Michilimackinac on an expedition to the lower Mississippi River, during which his companion Pere Jacques Marquette established a mission among the Illinois tribes. Rene Robert Cavelier, Sieur de la Salle, and Henri Tonti explored the Great Lakes and also descended the Mississippi during two journeys, 1678-83 and 1684-87. The establishment of Fort St. Louis on the Illinois River in 1682, with a trading post and mission, was a factor in assembling a temporary local population estimated at 18,000 Illinois, Miami, and Shawnee. Indians in Illinois became objectives of attack during later stages of Iroquois warfare.

View of the Indian village of Lorette, mission community established near Quebec for Huron refugees from Iroquois warfare. Clements Library.

Summary Narrative

At the outset of warfare in 1641, the Iroquois, with newly-acquired guns, increased the frequency and duration of their raids against the Huron in southern Ontario. Attacks on trade canoes along the Ottawa and St. Lawrence rivers occurred year-round. The Wenro had already fled from the Niagara River area to the Neutral in 1638 to escape the Iroquois. In 1648, the Iroquois carried warfare into the heart of Huronia, destroying two villages and dispersing the inhabitants of St. Ignace I (Taenhatentaron) near the southern end of Georgian Bay. The next year a force of 1,000 Seneca and Mohawk wiped out St. Ignace II and St. Louis in the same region. The destruction of the towns brought about the end of Huronia.

Believing their villages indefensible, the Huron, with the Jesuit missionaries among them, burned and abandoned the remaining villages and missions and became refugees. Some took shelter among the neighboring Tionontati, Neutral, and Erie living south of Lake Erie; others fled to St. Joseph Island (now Christian Island in Georgian Bay). From the latter group, a few hundred Huron moved to safer quarters with the French at Quebec, forming the community later called Lorette. Captive Huron set up a separate village, Gandougarae, in Seneca territory in present New York.

The collapse of the Huron had disastrous consequences for neighboring tribes. Small groups like the Allumette along the Ottawa River left the area for their own safety. The Nipissing moved north of Lake Superior to Lake Nipigon, though they later returned and many located at Oka on the Lake of Two Mountains near Montreal. A few months after the Huron dispersal, the Tionontati fled their lands. The majority, including the Huron refugees, moved to Ottawa villages on Manitoulin Island; others joined the Huron at St. Joseph Island. By 1653 the Neutral were scattered after an earlier defeat in 1647 at the hands of the Iroquois. The Iroquois also defeated the Erie, who left their lands by 1656.

With Huronia temporarily depopulated, the focus of the fur trade with the French shifted west. The group generally labeled Huron, but actually including more Tionontati than Huron, became the new middleman group, joined by the Ottawa. Refugees from the southern Great Lakes gathered on Green Bay, forming an intertribal community estimated to exceed 10,000 at peak population concentration. Green Bay became a major center of French trade.

Since the area around Lake Erie, on the Ontario peninsula and south of the lakes, was now depopulated, the Iroquois sent war parties 600 to 800 miles across the Great Lakes Region to strike at their enemies. The Iroquois raided west in two thrusts, first to northern Lake Michigan and eastern Lake Superior, and later south of the Great Lakes into Ohio and Illinois country (see map 7). The first large-scale Iroquois invasion west of Lake Michigan failed in 1655 when the Iroquois were unable to find sufficient food and were forced to retreat from Mechingan Village on Green Bay. The Illinois pursued those who went south, while the Ojibwa attacked and destroyed another group at Sault Ste. Marie. In 1657, Huron and Ottawa on Rock Island, at the entrance to Green Bay, prevented attack by a party of 1,200 Iroquois through the vigilance of scouting parties. Even this far west of the Iroquois country, the refugee Ottawa, Huron, and Tionontati felt uneasy about the Iroquois threat, and began another migration in 1657 to the Mississippi River, returning to Wisconsin in 1660 near the Black River and Chequamegon Bay of Lake Superior.

When war parties failed to stop the western Indian fur trade, the Iroquois attempted, with some success, to blockade the Ottawa River and prevent fur brigades from reaching the French. Iroquois warriors suffered a major defeat in 1662 at Iroquois Point in Michigan by the Ojibwa, Ottawa, and Nipissing Indians. The final flight of the Ottawa and Huron, this time to escape the Dakota, occurred in 1671 when the majority returned to Michilimackinac, establishing a major population center at present St. Ignace on the north side of the Straits of Mackinac.

During the same period, the Iroquois were fighting the Susquehannocks, New England Indians, and Shawnee, and decreased their attacks along the Ottawa River. By the time this phase of warfare ended in the late 1670s in an area further ravaged by epidemic diseases, the Ottawas and their allies had strengthened their position sufficiently so that the Iroquois could not dominate the western trade.

The year 1680 marked the last important military success of the Iroquois in the west before the beginning of a serious counterthrust into Five Nations country by the western Indians and the French. Shawnee in the Ohio Valley probably departed because of Iroquois attacks, leaving the area free for westward traveling war parties. In 1680 the Iroquois attacked in the Illinois River valley, beginning at Kaskaskia and pursuing the retreating Illinois Indians along the river. All of the Illinois except the Tamaroa fled across the Mississippi River. The Tamaroa were defeated, with more than 700 captured or killed. The Illinois returned in 1682 when LaSalle established Fort St. Louis at Starved Rock on the Illinois River near present Utica, Illinois. This was one of a number of forts set up by the French in the 1680s and 1690s to protect their western allies and prevent Iroquois incursion. The last Iroquois expeditions into Illinois were an unsuccessful attempt to besiege Fort St. Louis in 1684, and an attack south of Chicago in 1687.

The French and allied western Indians now carried the war into Iroquois lands with a victorious expedition against the Seneca villages in 1687. For this later stage of warfare, traditional histories of the tribes opposing the Iroquois mention defeat of the Seneca in a canoe battle on Lake Erie, inter-tribal mobilization near Lake St. Clair, and success in overrunning all of southern Ontario. A dramatic series of western Indian victories took place along the water routes through old Huronia and the chain of lakes leading to the Trent River outlet into eastern Lake Ontario. A division of this joint campaign against the Iroquois veered southward at Lake Simcoe toward present Toronto, aiming attacks at the western end of Lake Ontario.

As a consequence of the counteroffensive, raids led by Ottawa, Huron, Missisauga, and Ojibwa forced the Iroquois away from the north shore of Lake Ontario. The Iroquois had established several villages along the lake during the 1660s, but abandoned these sites for their New York homeland by 1687. In the final decade of the wars, the Missisauga and their allies defeated the Iroquois in several battles on

Huron Indians of Lorette c. 1838. From Castlenau, *Vues et Souvenirs du L 'Amerique du Nord*, pl. 30. The Newberry Library.

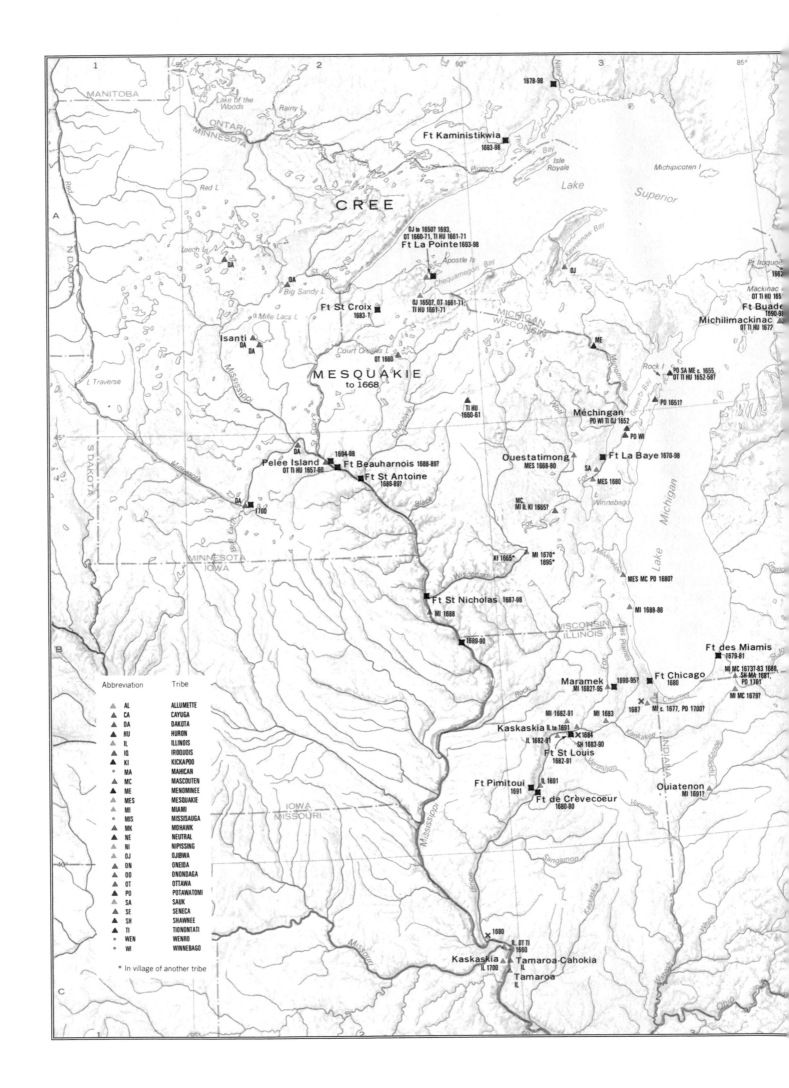

MANITOBA

ONTARIO
MINNESOTA

Lake of the Woods

Rainy L

Red L

1678-98

Ft Kaministikwia
1683-98

CREE

Thunder Bay

Isle Royale

Pigeon

Michipicoten I

Lake Superior

Pt Iroquois
1662

OJ to 16507 1693,
OT 1660-71, TI HU 1661-71
Ft La Pointe 1693-98

Apostle Is
Chequamegon Bay

Keweenaw Bay

OJ

Mackinac
OT TI HU 165

Ft Buade
1690-98
Michilimackinac
OT TI HU 1677

Leech Is

DA

DA

Big Sandy L

Ft St Croix
1683-?

OJ 16507, OT 1661-71;
TI HU 1661-71

MICHIGAN
WISCONSIN

Isanti
DA
DA

Mille Lacs L

Court Oreilles L
OJ 1660

ME

Rock I

PO SA ME c. 1655,
OT TI HU 1652-587

MESQUAKIE
to 1668

TI HU
1660-61

Méchingan
PO WI TI OJ 1652

PO 1651?

Menominee

Green Bay

PO WI

N DAKOTA

St Louis

Chippewa

Wolf

Ouestatimong
MES 1668-80

Ft La Baye 1670-98

SA

L Traverse

Mississippi

45

DA

1694-98

Pelee Island
OT TI HU 1657-60

Ft Beauharnois 1688-89?

Ft St Antoine
1686-89?

MES 1680

L Winnebago

Fox

S DAKOTA

Minnesota

DA
1700

Black

MC
MI IL KI 1665?

MINNESOTA
IOWA

Blue Earth

KI 1665*

MI 1670*
1695*

Wisconsin

Ft St Nicholas 1687-98

MI 1688

MES MC PO 1680?

MI 1688-88

WISCONSIN
ILLINOIS

B

1689-90

Rock

Des Plaines

Ft des Miamis
1679-81

Maramek
MI 1682?-95

1690-95?

Ft Chicago
1680

MI MC 16737-83 1688,
SH-MA 1681,
PO 1701

MI MC 1679?

×
1687

Calumet

MI c. 1677, PO 1700?

Abbreviation   Tribe

▲ AL   ALLUMETTE
▲ CA   CAYUGA
▲ DA   DAKOTA
▲ HU   HURON
▲ IL   ILLINOIS
▲ IO   IROQUOIS
▲ KI   KICKAPOO
∘ MA   MAHICAN
▲ MC   MASCOUTEN
▲ ME   MENOMINEE
▲ MES   MESQUAKIE
▲ MI   MIAMI
∘ MIS   MISSISAUGA
▲ MK   MOHAWK
▲ NE   NEUTRAL
▲ NI   NIPISSING
▲ OJ   OJIBWA
▲ ON   ONEIDA
▲ OO   ONONDAGA
▲ OT   OTTAWA
▲ PO   POTAWATOMI
▲ SA   SAUK
▲ SE   SENECA
▲ SH   SHAWNEE
▲ TI   TIONONTATI
∘ WEN   WENRO
∘ WI   WINNEBAGO

* In village of another tribe

MI 1682-91

MI 1683

Kaskaskia IL to 1691
IL 1682-91

×1684

SH 1683-90

Ft St Louis
1682-91

Kankakee

INDIANA

Ouiatenon
MI 1691?

IOWA
MISSOURI

Ft Pimitoui
1691

IL 1691

Ft de Crèvecoeur
1680-80

Vermilion

Mississippi

Sangamon

Illinois

Kaskaskia

× 1680

IL, OT TI
1660

Tamaroa-Cahokia
IL

Kaskaskia
IL 1700

Tamaroa
IL

Missouri

Ohio

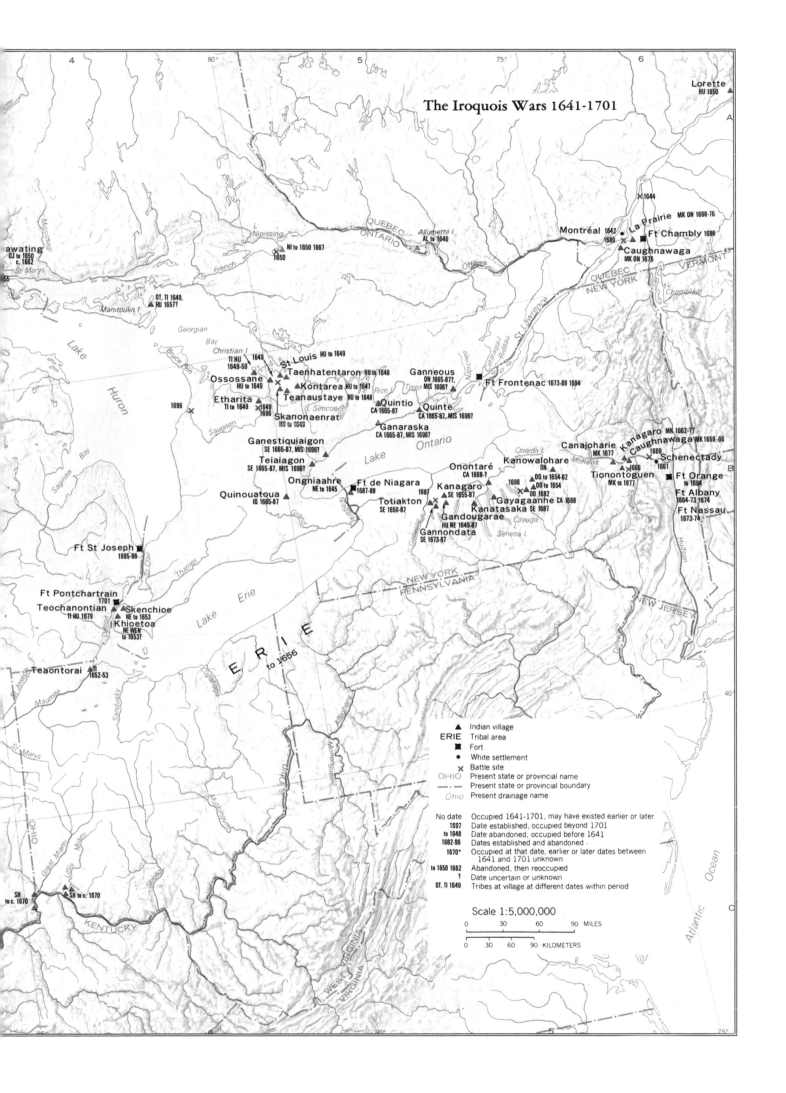

The Iroquois Wars 1641-1701

Lorette
HU 1650

×1644

Montréal 1642 • La Prairie MK ON 1668-76
1689 × ■ Ft Chambly 1686
Caughnawaga
MK ON 1676

QUEBEC
ONTARIO
Allumette I
AL to 1646

L
Nipissing

French R

QUEBEC
NEW YORK
VERMONT

L
Champlain

NI to 1650 1667
1650

awating
OJ to 1650
c. 1662
St Marys

OT, TI 1649,
HU 1657?

Manitoulin I

Lake
Huron

Georgian

Bay

Christian I
TI HU
1649-50

St Louis HU to 1649
Taenhatentaron HU to 1648
Ossossane
HU to 1649
Kontarea HU to 1647
Teanaustaye HU to 1648

1649

Ganneous
ON 1665-877,
MIS 1696?

Ft Frontenac 1673-89 1694

Napanee

St Lawrence

Cataraqui

Rideau

Bruce Pen

1696

Etharita
TI to 1649

1649
1696

Skanonaenrat
HU to 1649

L Simcoe

Rice L
Trent

Quintio
CA 1665-87

Quinte
CA 1665-87, MIS 1696?

Saugeen

Ganaraska
CA 1665-87, MIS 1696?

Lake

Ontario

Ganestiquiaigon
SE 1665-87, MIS 1696?

Teiaiagon
SE 1665-87, MIS 1696?

Ongniaahre
NE to 1645

Ft de Niagara
1687-88

Onontaré
CA 1668-?

Canajoharie
MK 1677

Kanowalohare
ON

Kanagaro MK 1662-77
Caughnawaga MK 1659-66
1669
Schenectady
1661
1666

Oneida L

Mohawk

Schoharie

Tionontoguen
MK to 1677

Ft Orange
to 1664

Ft Albany
1664-73 1674

Ft Nassau
1673-74

Quinouatoua
IQ 1665-87

Kanagaro
SE 1655-87

1687

Totiakton
SE 1650-87

×

Gandougarae
HU NE 1649-87

Gannondata
SE 1673-87

Gayagaanhe CA 1668

Kanatasaka SE 1687

1696
OO to 1654-82
OO to 1654
OO 1682

Genesee

Cayuga

Seneca L

Ft St Joseph ■
1685-86

St Clair

Thames

Grand R

Niagara R

Hudson

NEW YORK
PENNSYLVANIA

NEW JERSEY

MAP
6

Ft Pontchartrain
1701
Teochanontian
TI HU 1679
Skenchioe
NE to 1653
Khioetoa
NE WEN
to 1653?

Detroit R

Lake

Erie

Cuyahoga

E   R   I   E

to 1656

Susquehanna

Delaware

Teaontorai
TI
1652-53

Maumee

St Joseph R

Sandusky

Allegheny

Ohio

NEW YORK
PENNSYLVANIA

Atlantic

Ocean

St Marys

OHIO

Great Miami

Little Miami

Scioto

Muskingum

Monongahela

W VIRGINIA

VIRGINIA

SH
to c. 1670

SH to c. 1670

KENTUCKY

WEST VIRGINIA

80°

5

75°

40

Legend

▲ Indian village
ERIE Tribal area
■ Fort
● White settlement
× Battle site
OHIO Present state or provincial name
--- Present state or provincial boundary
Ohio Present drainage name

No date — Occupied 1641-1701, may have existed earlier or later
1697 — Date established, occupied beyond 1701
to 1648 — Date abandoned, occupied before 1641
1682-96 — Dates established and abandoned
1670* — Occupied at that date, earlier or later dates between 1641 and 1701 unknown
to 1650 1662 — Abandoned, then reoccupied
? — Date uncertain or unknown
OT, TI 1649 — Tribes at village at different dates within period

Scale 1:5,000,000

0   30   60   90   MILES

0   30   60   90   KILOMETERS

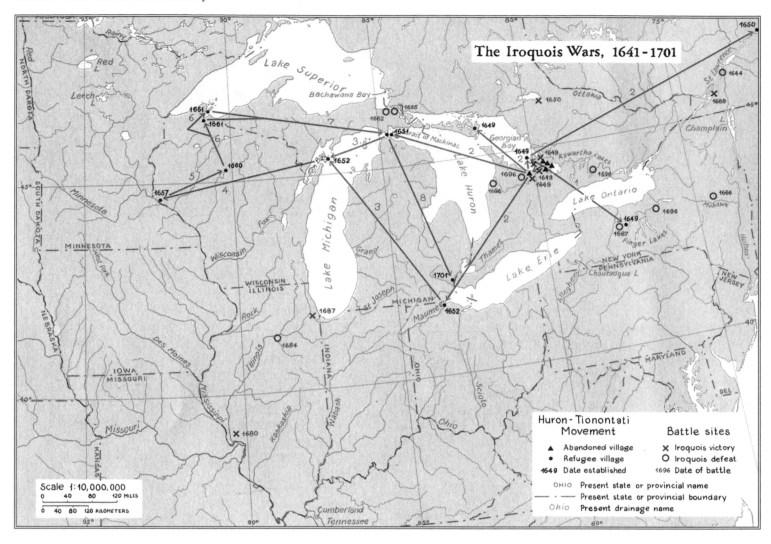

MAP
7

the Ontario peninsula, at or near the sites of early encounters in 1649. The wars had come full circle to their place of origin. By 1696 the northern lakeshore village sites of the Iroquois were occupied by Missisauga, establishing a new element in the population pattern of the Great Lakes Region. When peace was assured, villages of Miami and Potawatomi gradually returned to more traditional locations south and east of Lake Michigan.

Steps Toward Peace

Forced to defend their own villages instead of carrying the war to the west, the Iroquois sued for peace. In bringing an end to the prolonged warfare, councils took place in 1701 at three political centers: Onondaga, diplomatic headquarters of the Five Nations of the Iroquois Confederacy; Albany, with British authorities presiding over negotiations between the Five Nations and the "Waghanes," a term interpreted as Ottawa; and Montreal, where a comprehensive peace agreement under French auspices included more than twenty western, eastern, and northern Indian groups. An additional Indian council possibly was held in the fall in the Detroit area.

Preliminary peace arrangements had been made in Montreal in 1700 by representatives of the Huron, Ottawa, Seneca, and Onondaga. The final council at Montreal in August, 1701, to proclaim general peace and return prisoners of war, was attended by leading men of the Ottawa, Huron, Missisauga, Nipissing, Algonquin, Temiscaming, Ojibwa, Potawatomi (who also represented the Sauk), Menominee, Winnebago, Mesquakie, Mascoutin, Miami, Illinois, Kickapoo, Indians of the French missions at Sault St. Louis and Lake of the Two Mountains near Montreal, Abenaki, Onondaga, Seneca, Oneida, and Cayuga. The Mohawk of the Mohawk River valley did not participate but later added their approval. The geographic range of the Indians gathering at Montreal in 1701 reached the fringe of the Great Lakes Region. On the outer edges were the Abenaki of the St. Lawrence River valley to the east, Temiscaming at the head of the Ottawa River on the north, Cree living west of Lake Superior, and Kaskaskia of southwestern Illinois near the Mississippi River. As a result of the agreements in 1701, the Iroquois could hunt in Canada; at the same time the Ottawa could travel peacefully through Iroquois lands to trade at Albany, and the Five Nations adopted a policy of neutrality between the French and the British.

At the conclusion of the major military events during the period of the Iroquois Wars, the French regime reversed its seventeenth-century policy of exploration and expansion into the Great Lakes Region. In 1696 a depleted war chest, a glut on the European fur market, and Jesuit complaints persuaded the King to revoke fur-trading privileges and close down the western forts. Trade was not reopened until forts were reestablished in the Upper Great Lakes region between 1715 and 1720 (see map 9). In the interim, the only French post in the Upper Great Lakes was Fort Ponchartrain, established at present Detroit, Michigan, in 1701 by Antoine de la Mothe Cadillac, who had been the last commander of Fort Buade at Michilmackinac. The safe occupation of a site only eighteen miles from the western end of Lake Erie was made possible by the 1701 peace treaty signed in Montreal.

Mapping the War Era

Map 6 shows the dislocations of Indian groups throughout the Great Lakes area during the long period of intermittent Iroquois warfare. Some village locations are more precise than others, based on archaeological findings or continuous use into the eighteenth and nineteenth centuries when data are more extensive than for the seventeenth century. Where approximate locations are known, the villages have been mapped to present an accurate general pattern of settlement and movement. Village sites also were often locations of fortified trading posts and French missions (see map 8).

When the Iroquois Wars were over, only two widely separated groups of Indians retained the name "Huron," one near Quebec and one at Detroit. The movement of the Huron and Tionontati who went to Detroit in 1701 is shown on map 7. Called Huron by the French, this refugee community became known to the British as the Wyandot, an adaptation of their name for their ancient alliance, usually spelled "Wendat."

The following encounters are indicated on the map as important battle sites of the Iroquois Wars in the Great Lakes Region :

Date	Present Site	Event
1644	near mouth of Richlieu River, Que.	Huron and Algonquin attack Iroquois
1649	near Lake Simcoe, Ont.	Iroquois disperse Huron
1649	Collingwood area, Ont.	Iroquois disperse Tionontati
1650	near Lake Nipissing, Ont.	Iroquois massacre Nipissing
1655	near Sault St. Marie, Mich.	Ojibwa attack Iroquois
1662	Point Iroquois, Mich.	Ojibwa, Ottawa, Nipissing defeat Iroquois
1666	near Canajoharie, N.Y.	French destroy Tionontoguen
1669	near Schenectady, N.Y.	Mohawk defeat Mahican
1680	mouth of the Illinois River	Iroquois defeat Tamaroa
1684	at Starved Rock, near Utica, Ill.	Iroquois siege at Fort St. Louis fails
1687	near Chicago, Ill.	Iroquois massacre Miami
1687	between Seneca Lake and Genessee River, N.Y.	Western Indian allies and French destroy four Seneca villages
1689	Lachine, Que.	Iroquois attack Lachine
1696	near Manlius, N.Y.	French burn Onondaga village
1696	mouth of Saugeen River, Blue Mountains, and Rice Lake, Ont.	Missisauga, Ottawa, Ojibwa defeat Iroquois

Principal Sources: Blair 1911; Blasingham 1956; Clifton 1977; Coyne 1895; Eid 1979; Fenton 1940; Franquelin 1684, 1685, 1688; Hast MS 1978; Heidenreich 1971; Hunt 1940; Konrad MS 1977, 1981; Minet 1685; Norton 1974; Schmalz 1977; Tooker 1964; Trigger 1960, 1976; Voegelin 1974d; White 1961; Wright 1963.

Map 8 presents a panoramic view of the Great Lakes Region looking southward from Sault Ste. Marie, Michigan, midpoint in the main thoroughfare from Montreal to the western end of Lake Superior. Here, in 1671, the French representative formally announced the royal claim to interior North America as part of New France, with the specific objective of searching for a copper mine. Accompanied by music and medieval pageantry, he addressed delegates of fourteen groups of Indian people living south, west, and north of Lake Superior. The ceremony took place at the Jesuit mission established at Bawating, Ojibwa village situated at the rapids of the river outlet from Lake Superior (see map 6). Jesuits had already explored the entire shoreline of Lake Superior, and that very year, 1671, completed a map little known to contemporaries but not rivaled in accuracy until the nineteenth century.

The French perception of the frontier south of the Great Lakes is evident from the map. The present Upper Peninsula of Michigan was considered the mainland. In the center foreground is the prominent Michigan peninsula dividing the main routes southward, to the east by way of Lake Huron and Georgian Bay, and to the west by way of Green Bay and Lake Michigan. On the distant southern horizon is the Ohio Valley, an area that became the focus of contention between France and Great Britain in the early eighteenth century (see map 9).

Missions shown on the map were part of a worldwide foreign missionary program begun by French Jesuits in the seventeenth century. Earliest written accounts of the Great Lakes country and Indian people are from annual reports of about seventy priests who served in New France before 1700.

Scant information came from the area south of the Great Lakes, where no missions were established between western New York and the Illinois River, as the map shows. Jesuits concentrated their efforts on missions among the Huron living in the district between Georgian Bay and Lake Simcoe (nos. 2, 8, 12, 14, 17, 22). Indian village sites in Huronia as well as locations of other Indian villages and French forts are shown on map 6 of the Iroquois Wars. After the destruction of Huronia, the Jesuits followed Huron refugees westward and established missions among tribes in present Wisconsin, Illinois, and Michigan.

In 1671, the Huron and Ottawa at St. Esprit mission on Chequamegon Bay, Wisconsin (no. 3) fled from Dakota invaders and settled at present St. Ignace, Michigan, where the Jesuits established the St. Ignatius mission (no. 9). During the next two decades, several thousand Indians representing many tribes gathered every summer at this location, called Michilimackinac, for inter-tribal ceremonies and trade.

The most prominent missions were founded near forts where the local French community included traders and military personnel. In addition to Michilimackinac, major centers of religious activity were on the St. Joseph River of Michigan (no. 16), Green Bay (nos. 5, 29), and among the Illinois Indians (nos. 1, 30). Principal missions often had subsidiary mission stations not shown on the map. For example, a mission station for the Ottawa on Manitoulin Island was established, and one for Mesquakie on the Wolf River of Wisconsin. Some mission ventures were of short duration or were itinerant, as in the case of the Nipissing.

Jesuits were not alone in their evangelizing work among

MAP
8

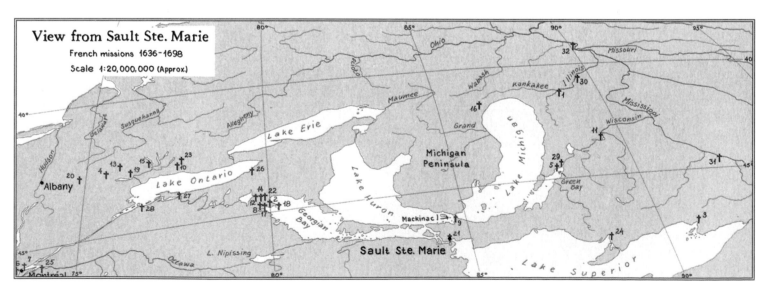

Great Lakes Indians. In 1670, Recollect missionaries, who to compete for western missions. Discouraged by the Jesuits had not been in New France since 1632, returned to Canada at Sault Ste. Marie, they later returned to their monastery with royal support. That same year the Sulpicians attempted at Montreal.

French Missions in the Great Lakes 1636-1 698

Name	Location	Date Founded	Seventeenth-century Village Site and/or Tribe
1. Immaculate Conception	Near Utica, Ill.	1675	Kaskaskia, Illinois
2. La Conception	Ontario	1636	Ossossane, Huron
3. St. Esprit	Chequamegon Bay, Wisc.	1665	La Pointe, Huron and Ottawa
4. St. Francois Xavier	Near Oneida Lake, N.Y.	1667	Oneida
5. St. Francois Xavier	Green Bay, Wisc.	1669	Sauk, Mesquakie, Potawatomi, Winnebago
6. St. Francois Xavier des Pres	La Prairie, Que.	1670	Kentake, Iroquois
7. St. Francois Xavier du Sault	Caughnawaga, Que.	1676	Caughnawaga, Iroquois
8. St. Ignace	Ontario	1645	Taenhatentaron, Huron
9. St. Ignatius & St. Francis de Borgia	St. Ignace, Mich.	1671 1672	Ottawa Huron
10. St. Jacques	New York	1656	Seneca
11. St. Jacques	near Berlin, Wisc.	1669	Mascouten and Miami
12. St. Jean Baptiste	Ontario	1639	Contarea, Huron
13. St. Jean Baptiste	near Manlius, N.Y.	1654	Onondaga
14. St. Joseph	Ontario	1638	Teanaustaye, Huron
15. St. Joseph	Cayuga Lake, N.Y.	1656	Gayagaanhe, Cayuga
16. St. Joseph	Niles, Mich.	1688	Potawatomi and Miami
17. Ste. Marie I	Wye Lake, Ont.	1639	Huron
18. Ste. Marie II	Christian Island, Ont.	1649	Huron refugees
19. Ste. Marie	Lake Onondaga, N.Y.	1656	Ganentaa, Onondaga
20. Ste. Marie	New York	1667	Tionontoguen, Mohawk
21. Ste. Marie	Sault Ste. Marie, Mich.	1668	Bawating, Ojibwa
22. St. Michel	Ontario	1638	Scanonaenrat, Huron
23. St. Michel	New York	1656	Gandougarae, captive Huron
24. L'Anse	Keweenaw Bay, Mich.	1660	Ojibwa
25. Lac des Deux Montagnes	Oka, Que.	1663	Algonquin and Iroquois
26. ———	North Shore, Lake Ontario	1668	Teiaiagon, Seneca
27. Quinte	North Shore, Lake Ontario	1668	Quinte, Cayuga
28. Cataraqui	Kingston, Ont.	c. 1670	Fort Frontenac, Oneida
29. St. Xavier	De Pere, Wisc.	1671	Mesquakie
30. La Conception	Peoria, Ill.	1680	Fort Pimitoui, Illinois
31. St. Michel	Lake Pepin, Mississippi River	1683	Fort Beauharnois, Dakota
32. Cahokia	20 mi. below mouth of Illinois River	1698	Tamaroa-Cahokia, Illinois

Principal Sources: Heidenreich 1971; Konrad MS 1977; Mealing 1967; Shea 1882.

The St. Marys River c. 1838, looking west. Fort Brady on the south shore in the foreground, and rapids upstream in the distance. From Castlenau, *Vues et Souvenirs du L'Amerique du Nord* pl. 28. The Newberry Library.

Lake of the Two Mountains, early mission site on the Ottawa River above Montreal, as it appeared about 1840. By W. H. Bartlett. From Willis, *Canadian Scenery*, vol. 1. The Newberry Library.

Rivalry between France and Great Britain over the Indian trade in the Great Lakes Region is the theme of map 9. Called the French Era because of French dominance in trade, the period ended with the British occupation of former French posts in 1761, following military victory over the French at Montreal in 1760.

This map includes trading posts and forts as well as Indian villages that were trading centers or otherwise important in Indian life. French and British trade with the Indians differed in method. The British issued licenses to traders who went to villages and there set up trading posts. The official French traders ran combined forts and trading posts to which the Indians brought furs. Extensive illegal trade was also carried on by *coureurs de bois* who circulated through winter hunting camps.

In addition, the map calls attention to the water transportation system in the Great Lakes Region. Waterways provided the communication channels for trade, warfare, diplomacy, and casual exchange of hospitality. The main portage locations are marked by red lines to aid in tracing the principal routes across dividing ridges between water courses.

Discussion of the history of the French Era is divided into four topics, each emphasizing a different geographic zone. These topics, all involving Indian trading alliances and changes in village locations, are: (1) Mesquakie wars carried on west and south of Lake Michigan, (2) Ojibwa expansion west of Lake Superior encroaching on Dakota lands, (3) repopulation of the Ohio country by Huron with British trade connections, and (4) inter-colonial warfare between France and Great Britain in Pennsylvania, New York, and Canada.

Background

At the opening of the eighteenth century, French contacts with Indians in the interior of North America were concentrated at two widely separated locales, the new mission villages of Illinois Indians on the Mississippi River near the mouth of the Kaskaskia River, and at present Detroit, Michigan. Antoine de la Mothe Cadillac,last commandant at Fort de Buade (1690-98) on the north side of the Straits of Mackinac, built Fort Ponchartrain at Detroit in 1701 with the view of spearheading French fur trade in the direction of the Ohio River. As part of his plan for the development of the new post, Cadillac invited tribes from the Upper Great Lakes to settle in the vicinity of the fort and associate with French traders. Within a few years he had drawn villages of Huron and Ottawa from the Straits of Mackinac, Potawatomi and Miami from the St. Joseph River of southwestern Michigan, and Sauk, Mesquakie, and Mascouten from the Green Bay area of Wisconsin.

Missisauga and Ojibwa from northern Lake Huron were settled on the north side of Lake St. Clair.

The attempt to concentrate 6,000 Indians in the vicinity of Detroit strained resources and tempers. Inter-tribal animosities flared first in 1706, when the French commandant protected the Ottawa chief after an Ottawa attack on the Miami. By 1708, the Miami had removed to the head of the Maumee River, location of the principal Miami community. Fear and resentment of the large Mesquakie delegation that arrived at Detroit in 1711 led to concerted local action. Aided by the French garrison and tribal allies, the Huron and Ottawa at Detroit besieged and slaughtered several hundred Mesquakie, launching the first of a series of so-called "Fox Wars" in the western Great Lakes. Surviving Mesquakie re-turned to their kinsmen in Wisconsin. As a result, after 1712 only the Huron and Potawatomi remained close by the French fort on the north bank of the Detroit river, with the Ottawa on the opposite shore in present Ontario.

The reestablishment of French forts in the Great Lakes, delayed until after the European Peace of Utrecht in 1713, commenced with the reoccupation of the Straits of Mackinac. The new French fort was built on the south side of the straits, present Mackinaw City, Michigan, rather than the former site, present St. Ignace on the north side. By the beginning date for this map, 1720, the licensed fur trade was again in full swing at these additional strategic location: Fort LaBaye, Green Bay, Wisconsin; Fort Lapointe on Madeleine Island of Chequamegon Bay, Lake Superior; Fort Ouiatenon on the Wabash River near present West Lafayette, Indiana; Fort Miami, present Fort Wayne, Indiana; Fort St. Joseph, Niles, Michigan; Fort Pimitoui on the Illinois River at Peoria, Illinois; and Fort Chartres on the Mississippi River above the mouth of the Kaskaskia River. An impetus promoting the fort building and allied fur trading was the sudden rise in demand for beaver. Paris merchants discovered in 1714 that three-quarters of their beaver pelts were unusable after long years in storage.

The twenty-year ban on the French trade caused by the oversupply of furs had worked a great hardship on the Great Lakes Indians. Although some of them loyally carried their furs to Montreal, others sought out the Albany traders in New York, who were much closer to many Indian hunters. Beyond Lake Superior, Indians traveled northward to British posts of the Hudson's Bay Company.

South of Lake Ontario, increasing rivalry between French and British interests is indicated by the founding dates of new posts along the lake shore. In 1721, the French built Fort Niagara at the mouth of the Niagara River, while the British constructed a short-lived trading post, Irondequoit, seventy-five miles distant at the mouth of the Genesee River. A firm

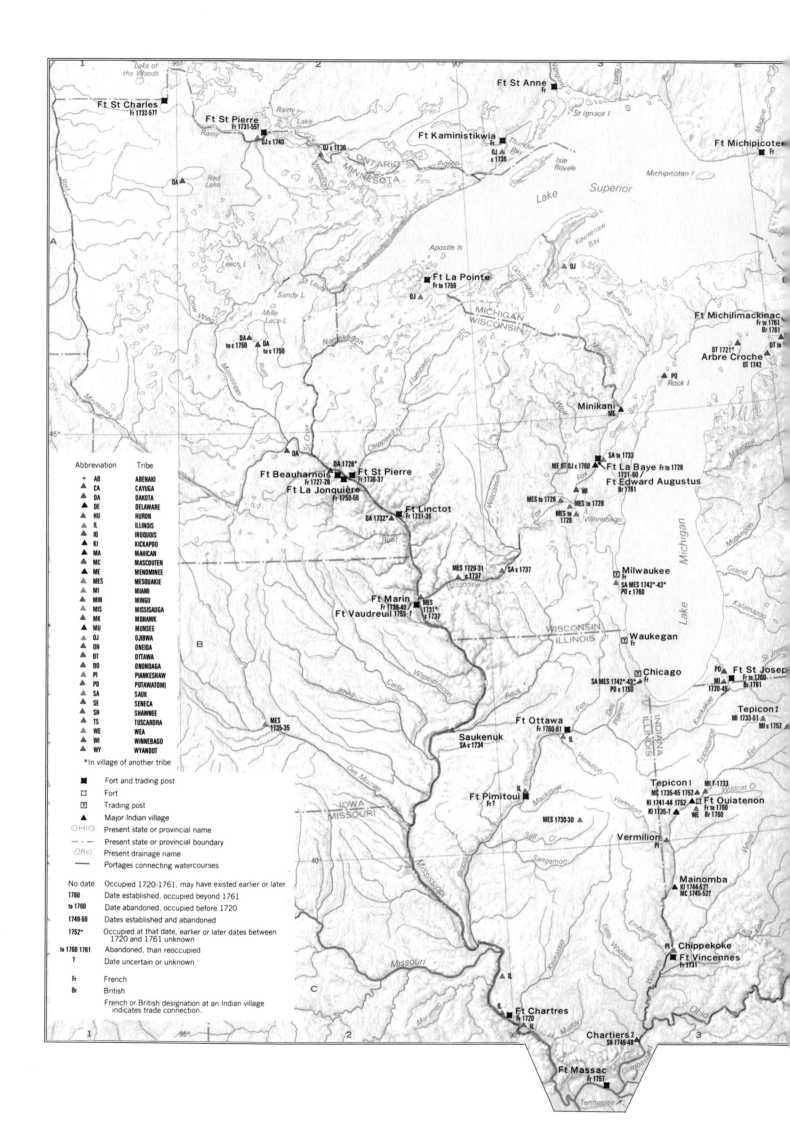

Ft St Charles
Fr 1732-57?

Lake of
the Woods

Ft St Pierre
Fr 1731-55?

OJ c 1740

OJ c 1736

Rainy
Lake

Rainy

Red

Red
Lake

DA

ONTARIO
MINNESOTA

Ft St Anne
Fr

St Ignace I

Ft Kaministikwia
Fr

OJ
c 1736

OJ
c 1736

Thunder
Bay

Isle
Royale

Ft Michipicoten
Fr

Michipicoten I

Lake   Superior

Leech L

St Louis

Sandy L

Apostle Is

Keweenaw
Bay

Ft La Pointe
Fr to 1759

OJ

OJ

Mille
Lacs L

Namekagon

MICHIGAN
WISCONSIN

Ft Michilimackinac
Fr to 1761
Br 1761

Escanaba

Rum

Crow Wing

DA
to c 1750

DA
to c 1750

OT 1721*

Arbre Croche
OT 1742

OT to

Mississippi

Flambeau

Menominee

PO
Rock I

Minikani
ME

Green Bay

Manistee

Chippewa

DA

DA 1728*

St Croix

Fox

SA to 1733

ME OT OJ c 1760

Ft La Baye Fr to 1728
1731-60

Ft Edward Augustus
Br 1761

Muskegon

Lake Michigan

Kalamazoo

Ft Beauharnois
Fr 1727-28
Ft La Jonquière
Fr 1750-56

Ft St Pierre
Fr 1736-37

Black

Wisconsin

WI

MES to 1728

MES to 1728

MES to
1728

Winnebago

DA 1732*

Ft Linctot
Fr 1731-36

Root

MES 1729-31
c 1737

SA c 1737

Wisconsin

Milwaukee
Fr

SA MES 1742*-43*
PO c 1760

Ft Marin
Fr 1738-40
Ft Vaudreuil 1753-?

MES
1731*
c 1737

WISCONSIN
ILLINOIS

Waukegan

Grand

St Joseph

Abbreviation	Tribe
• AB	ABENAKI
▲ CA	CAYUGA
▲ DA	DAKOTA
▲ DE	DELAWARE
▲ HU	HURON
▲ IL	ILLINOIS
▲ IO	IROQUOIS
▲ KI	KICKAPOO
▲ MA	MAHICAN
▲ MC	MASCOUTEN
▲ ME	MENOMINEE
▲ MES	MESQUAKIE
▲ MI	MIAMI
▲ MIN	MINGO
▲ MIS	MISSISAUGA
▲ MK	MOHAWK
▲ MU	MUNSEE
▲ OJ	OJIBWA
▲ ON	ONEIDA
▲ OT	OTTAWA
▲ OO	ONONDAGA
▲ PI	PIANKESHAW
▲ PO	POTAWATOMI
▲ SA	SAUK
▲ SE	SENECA
▲ SH	SHAWNEE
▲ TS	TUSCARORA
▲ WE	WEA
▲ WI	WINNEBAGO
▲ WY	WYANDOT

*In village of another tribe

Chicago
Fr

SA MES 1742*-43*
PO c 1750

PO
MI
1720-49

Ft St Joseph
Fr to 1760
Br 1761

Wapsipinicon

Iowa

Cedar

Rock

Des Plaines

Fox

INDIANA
ILLINOIS

Tepicon 2
MI 1733-51

MI c 1752

Kankakee

Tippecanoe

Fel

■ | Fort and trading post
□ | Fort
T | Trading post
▲ | Major Indian village
OHIO | Present state or provincial name
—·—· | Present state or provincial boundary
Ohio | Present drainage name
—— | Portages connecting watercourses

Ft Ottawa
Fr 1760-61

Saukenuk
SA c 1734

IL

Tepicon 1
MC 1735-45 1752
KI 1741-44 1752
KI 1735-?

MI ?-1733

Wildcat Cr

Ft Ouiatenon
Fr to 1760
WE Br 1760

MES
1735-35

Des Moines

IOWA
MISSOURI

Ft Pimitoui
Fr ?

IL

Mackinaw

MES 1730-30

Vermilion

Vermilion
PI

Sangamon

Salt Cr

White

No date | Occupied 1720-1761, may have existed earlier or later
1760 | Date established, occupied beyond 1761
to 1760 | Date abandoned, occupied before 1720
1749-59 | Dates established and abandoned
1752* | Occupied at that date, earlier or later dates between 1720 and 1761 unknown
to 1760 1761 | Abandoned, than reoccupied
? | Date uncertain or unknown
Fr | French
Br | British

French or British designation at an Indian village
indicates trade connection.

Mainomba
KI 1744-52?
MC 1745-52?

Embarras

Little Wabash

Missouri

Chippekoke
Ft Vincennes
Fr 1731

Wabash

PI

Kaskaskia

IL

Ft Chartres
Fr 1720

IL

Maramec

Muddy

Chartiers 2
SH 1745-48

Ohio

Ft Massac
Fr 1757

Cumberland

Tennessee

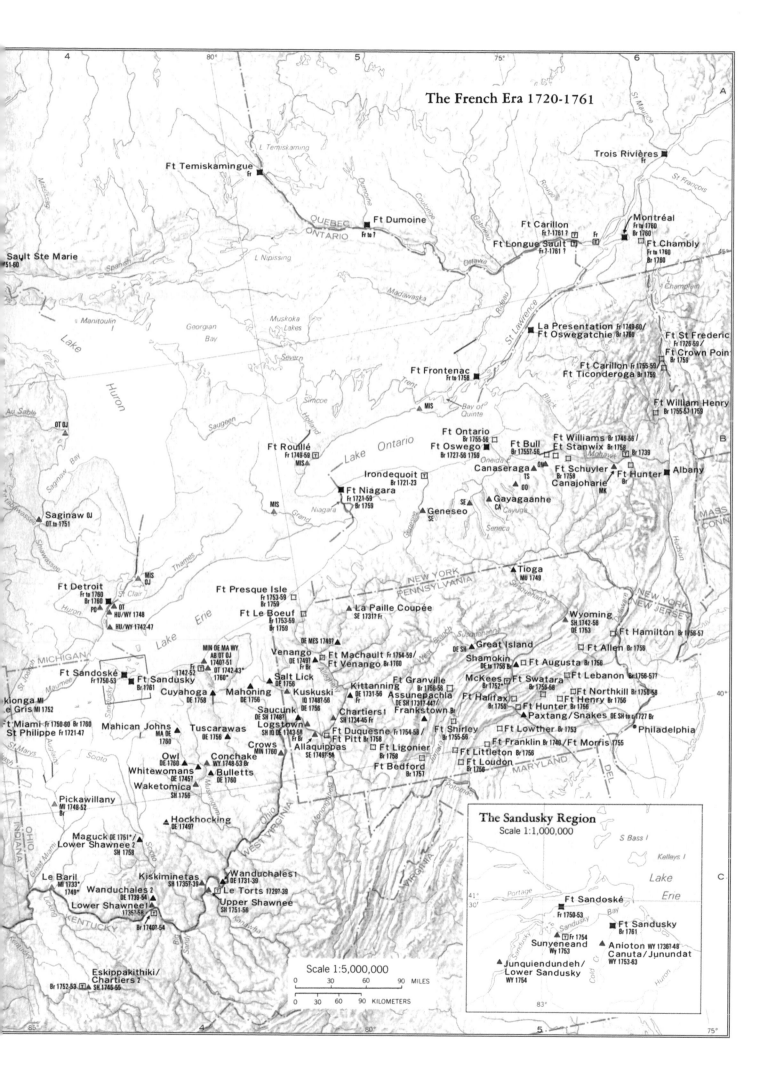

The French Era 1720-1761

MAP
9

Ft Temiskamingue Fr ⊠

Ft Dumoine Fr to ? ■

L Temiskaming

QUEBEC
ONTARIO

Trois Rivières Fr ■

Montréal Fr to 1760 / Br 1760 ■

Ft Carillon Fr ?-1761 ? ⊡
Ft Longue Sault Fr ?-1761 ? ⊡ Fr ⊡

Ft Chambly Fr to 1760 / Br 1760

Sault Ste Marie ■ 51-60

L Nipissing

Manitoulin

Georgian Bay

Lake Huron

Muskoka Lakes

La Presentation Fr 1749-60 / Ft Oswegatchie Br 1760

Ft St Frederic Fr 1726-59 / Ft Crown Point Br 1759

Ft Frontenac Fr to 1758 ■

Ft Carillon Fr 1755-59 / Ft Ticonderoga Br 1759

Ft William Henry ⊡ Br 1755-57 / 1759

OT OJ ▲

Saginaw OJ ▲ OT to 1751

Ft Roullé Fr 1749-59 ⊡
MIS ▲

Lake Ontario

MIS ⊠

Ft Ontario Br 1755-56 ⊡
Ft Oswego Br 1727-56 / 1759 ■

Ft Bull Br 1755?-56 ⊡

Ft Williams Br 1746-56 /
Ft Stanwix Br 1758 ⊡ ⊡ Br 1739 ⊡

Irondequoit ⊡ Br 1721-23

Ft Niagara Fr 1721-59 / Br 1759 ■

MIS ▲

Canaseraga TS ▲ OM
OO ▲

Ft Schuyler Br 1759 ▲
Canajoharie MK

Ft Hunter Br ▲ Albany ●

Geneseo SE ▲

SE ▲ Gayagaanhe CA ▲

MASS CONN

Ft Detroit Fr to 1760 / Br 1760 ■
PO OT HU/WY 1748 ▲

MIS OJ ▲

Tioga MU 1749 ▲

Ft Presque Isle Fr 1753-59 / Br 1759 ⊡

Wyoming SH 1742-58 / DE 1753 ▲

Ft Hamilton Br 1756-57 ⊡

HU/WY 1742-47 ▲

Ft Le Boeuf Fr 1753-59 / Br 1759 ⊡

La Paille Coupée SE 1731? Fr ▲

Ft Sandoské Fr 1750-53 ■
Ft Sandusky Br 1761 ■

DE MES 1749? ▲

Venango DE 1749? ▲
1742-52 ⊡
Fr ⊡
MIN DE MA WY AB OT OJ 17407-51 OT 1742-43? 1760? ▲

Ft Machault Fr 1754-59 /
Ft Venango Br 1760

DE SH ▲ Great Island

Ft Allen Br 1756 ⊡

Shamokin DE to 1756 Br ▲

Ft Augusta Br 1756 ⊡

Ft Lebanon Br 1756-57? ⊡

Cuyahoga DE 1758 ▲

Mahoning DE 1756 ▲

Salt Lick DE 1756 ▲

Kuskuski IO 1748?-56 ▲

Kittanning DE 1731-56 Fr ▲

Ft Granville Br 1756-56 ⊡

McKees Br 1752? ▲
Ft Swatara Br 1755-58 ⊡

Ft Northkill Br 1756-58 ⊡

Ft Sandoské Fr 1750-53 ■
Ft Sandusky Br 1761 ■

Chartiers DE SH 1748? ▲

Ft Halifax Br 1756 ⊡

Assunepachla DE SH 1731?-44?/ ▲

Ft Hunter Br 1756 ⊡
Ft Henry Br 1756 ⊡

ukionga MI Le Gris MI 1752 ▲

Mahican Johns MA DE 1760 ▲

Tuscarawas DE 1756 ▲

Logstown SH IO DE 1743-58 Fr Br ▲

Frankstown Br ▲

Paxtang/Snakes DE SH to c.1727 Br ▲

Ft Miami Fr 1750-60 Br 1760 ▲
St Philippe Fr 1721-47

Crows MIN 1760? ▲

Ft Duquesne Fr 1754-58 /
Ft Pitt Br 1758 ⊡

Ft Shirley Br 1755-56 ⊡

Ft Lowther Br 1753 ⊡

Philadelphia ●

Owl DE 1760 ▲

Conchake WY 1748-53 Br ▲

Allaquippas SE 1749?-54 ▲

Ft Ligonier Br 1758 ⊡

Ft Franklin Br 1749 / Ft Morris 1755

Whitewomans DE 1745? ▲
Bulletts DE 1760 ▲

Ft Littleton Br 1756 ⊡

Ft Bedford Br 1757 ⊡

Ft Loudon Br 1756 ⊡

Waketomica SH 1756 ▲

MARYLAND

Pickawillany MI 1748-52 Br ▲

Hockhocking DE 1749? ▲

The Sandusky Region
Scale 1:1,000,000

S Bass I

Maguck DE 1751? ▲
Lower Shawnee 2 SH 1758

Kelleys I

Lake Erie

Le Baril MI 1733? 1749? ▲

Kiskiminetas SH 1735?-39 ▲

Wanduchales 1 DE 1731-39 ▲

Wanduchales 2 DE 1739-54 ▲
Lower Shawnee 1 1735?-58 ⊡ Br 1740?-54

Le Torts 1729?-39 ▲
Upper Shawnee SH 1751-56

41° 30'

Portage

Ft Sandoské Fr 1750-53 ■

Ft Sandusky Br 1761 ■

KENTUCKY

Sunyeneand Wy 1753 ▲ Fr 1754

Anioton WY 1736?-48 ▲
Canuta/Junundat WY 1753-63

Junquiendundeh / Lower Sandusky WY 1754 ▲

Eskippakithiki / Chartiers 2 Br 1752-53 ⊡ SH 1745-55 ▲

Scale 1:5,000,000

0 30 60 90 MILES

0 30 60 90 KILOMETERS

83°

75°

base for the British Indian trade was established in 1727 at Fort Oswego, located at the river entry to the central Iroquois country.

French trade on the western frontier of Canada expanded with the addition of Fort Beauharnois among the Dakota on the upper Mississippi River in 1727, followed by Fort St. Pierre on the Rainy River west of Lake Superior in 1731, and Fort St. Charles on Lake of the Woods in 1732. To the south, on the lower Wabash River, Fort Vincennes among the Piankeshaw was built in 1731, Vincennes was the north-eastern outpost of French Louisiana, a province invigorated since the founding of New Orleans above the Mississippi River delta in 1718. The dividing point between the two French colonies, Canada and Louisiana, was marked on the Wabash River at "the Highlands," present Terre Haute, In-diana, about midway between Fort Ouiatenon and Fort Vincennes, or Post Vincennes as it was often called.

Mesquakie Wars

Following the attack on the Mesquakie by the allied Indians of Detroit in 1712, the Wisconsin-based Mesquakie made the Great Lakes waterways unsafe for the French and their Indian enemies for about four years. The belligerent Mesquakie and their allies the Sauk, Mascouten, Kickapoo, and Dakota persisted in warfare with the strongly French-partisan Illinois again between 1719 and 1726, when a formal peace was finally effected by the French. A major objective of the French was to break the Mesquakie blockade of the Fox-Wisconsin waterway that had prevented French traders from direct access via Green Bay to the Dakota hunting territory on the upper Mississippi River. After the peace, the building of Fort Beauharnois in 1727 was an effort to detach the Dakota from the Mesquakie. Nevertheless, by 1727 the Mesquakie resumed war against the Illinois and threatened to carry their trade to the English.

This renewal of warfare persuaded the French to attempt to exterminate the Mesquakie. In a combined French and Indian assault, the Mesquakie were driven from their villages around Lake Winnebago in 1728. Two years later, the Mesquakie were besieged by a force of 1,400 men in their prairie fortification near Leroy, Maclean County, Illinois. Losses were heavy as they attempted to escape in darkness. The following year, 1731, a war party of Christian Iroquois, Huron, and Ottawa raided the Mesquakie camps on the lower Wisconsin River, killing and capturing more than 300. By 1733, the 50 to 100 remaining Mesquakie were living among the Sauk at Green Bay and asking for mercy. French demands led to further hostilities, however, and both the Sauk and Mesquakie fled to the west bank of the Mississippi,where the latter remnant wandered in exile until clemency was granted in 1737. Shortly thereafter the Mesquakie and Sauk reestablished villages on the east bank of the Mississippi, locating at Saukenuk on the Rock River, at the mouth of the Wisconsin River (present Prairie du Chien), and at several sites upriver. Trade with these tribes resumed with the erection of Fort Marin in 1738 on the Mississippi River below and opposite the mouth of the Wisconsin River.

By the end of the Mesquakie threat about 1740, the tribal landscape west and south of Lake Michigan had considerably altered. Both the Sauk and Mesquakie had left the Green Bay region. About 1749, one group of Mesquakie joined a Delaware village on the Allegheny River in northwestern Pennsylvania. A small portion of the Potawatomi remained at the entrance to Green Bay on Rock Island and the Winnebago continued to live on Lake Winnebago. The ancestral village of the Menominee at the mouth of the Menominee River split about 1760, some of its people moving to the bottom of Green Bay.

The French trading post at Fort Ouiatenon on the upper Wabash River drew hunters southeastward from Wisconsin. By 1735, Mascouten and Kickapoo bands had accepted the invitation to settle upon Miami lands. Mascouten and Kickapoo villages were first established on the west bank of the Wabash opposite the Wea towns, and, a decade later, farther south at present Terre Haute in Piankeshaw territory. Prairie rather than river dwellers, the Kickapoo and Mascouten no doubt had other villages during the French Era in north central Illinois, near the Rock, Fox, Vermilion and Mackinaw rivers, but the locations of such villages are unknown.

The tragedy of the French Era in the western Great Lakes was the population loss of the Illinois. In this period of migration and trade expansion, western tribes—including the Mesquakie after the end of hostilities—increased in population. But the Illinois, the people most closely attached to the French through intermarriage, Christianization, and commerce, declined dramatically. Between 1700 and 1763, the number of Illinois dropped from about 6,000 to 2,000 persons. Although disease, alcohol, and factionalization all contributed to this decrease, the most important factor was the constant raiding and warfare upon the Illinois by their anti-French tribal enemies, particularly the Iroquois in the seventeenth century, followed by Mesquakie, Sauk, and Dakota from the north and the Chickasaw from the south in the first half of the eighteenth century.

Ojibwa-Dakota Conflict

After 1731 and until the renewal of French-English warfare in 1744, French fort-building activity and exploration focused on the search for a route to the "Western Sea." By 1734, under the leadership of Pierre Gaultier de Varennes, Sieur de la Vkrendrye, the French had penetrated the rich fur-bearing lands west of Lake Superior, then occupied by Cree, Assiniboine, and Monsoni (Ojibwa) hunting bands. La Vkrendrye erected the trading posts at Rainy Lake and Lake of the Woods.

The opening of the Rainy River route and the French-Cree trade further disrupted the intertribal equilibrium of the Wisconsin and Minnesota area already involved in Mesquakie warfare. Before 1731, the Minnesota Dakota in temporary alliance with the Ojibwa of Lake Superior had fought against the Cree and Assiniboine on their northern border. As part of this alliance, the Ojibwa had been allowed to hunt on Dakota lands west of the St. Croix River and, as middlemen, to funnel Dakota furs through Fort La Pointe. They had not established permanent villages beyond the shores of Lake Superior by this time, however.

British base at Oswego, New York, looking north into Lake Ontario, 1760. The port at Oswego channeled part of the fur trade of French Canada to British traders in Albany. From *London Magazine*, 1760, original engraving entitled "A South View of Oswego, on Lake Ontario, in North America." Clements Library.

Irritated by the French-Cree compact, the Dakota killed La Virendrye's son and nineteen other Frenchmen near Fort St. Charles in 1736. In retaliation, the Ojibwa broke with their former allies and joined the Cree. By 1736, Ojibwa villages were noted at Thunder Bay of Lake Superior, at the mouth of the Vermilion River on Rainy River, and by 1740 the Ojibwa were lodged at Rainy Lake. From these locations, as well as from their villages on the southern shore of Lake Superior, the Ojibwa attacked the Dakota via the Vermilion, St. Louis, and St. Croix river warroads.

The Ojibwa-Dakota conflict, which raged well into the nineteenth century (see maps 13,20, and 28),barred exploration, mission establishment, and long-term survival of forts and trading posts along the upper reaches of the Mississippi River throughout the French era. An uninhabited "war zone" stretched from the headwaters of the Mississippi south to the vicinity of Mille Lacs Lake. This region had formerly been occupied by the Dakota, whose pre-1736 villages probably skirted the shores of Sandy Lake, Leech Lake, Red Lake and smaller lakes around the Mississippi headwaters. However, the precise location of these early Dakota villages and the dates of their abandonment and subsequent reoccupation by the Ojibwa remains uncertain.

Nineteenth-century Ojibwa oral tradition implied that the Dakota were driven from their villages at Mille Lacs Lake south to the Minnesota River in 1745. The Ojibwa also claimed that their villages replaced Dakota villages at the mouth of the St. Louis River and at Sandy Lake during the 1740s. In the absence of corroborative documentary evidence, however, only the probable location of the northern-most Dakota village at Red Lake is shown on the map.

Similarly, a Dakota village symbol has been placed at the juncture of the Minnesota and Mississippi rivers in order to indicate traditional Dakota occupation of this region. The documented presence of Dakota villages adjacent to Fort Beauharnois in 1728 and Fort Linctot in 1732 affirm that Dakota use of the Mississippi River near the St. Croix predated and was unrelated to Dakota-Ojibwa animosities. The Ojibwa apparently did not secure a firm toehold in Minnesota until the 1760s.

Repopulation of the Ohio Country

While the French and the Indian tribes of the western Great Lakes were embroiled in Mesquakie warfare and Ojibwa-Dakota hostilities, Delaware and Shawnee in Pennsylvania were being forced westward across the Appalachian mountains by population pressure and attendant land sales managed by Iroquois sachems. At new hunting bases in the upper Ohio valley, including the Allegheny River headwaters, they were supplied with British manufactured goods brought by Pennsylvania and Virginia traders. The vanguard of this movement is marked on the map by LeTort's trading post established about 1729 on the Ohio above the Kanawha River.

Farther downstream on the Ohio River, the Shawnee established a new headquarters, Lower Shawneetown, at the mouth of the Scioto River. In the late seventeenth century, Shawnee had been living at LaSalle's Fort St. Louis on the Illinois River, with the Creek in Alabama, and in eastern Tennessee, where they traded with the Spanish at St. Augustine, Florida. In the opening years of the eighteenth century they were on the Potomac River in Maryland and in eastern Pennsylvania. Beginning in the 1730s, they drew together on the Scioto River segments of the Shawnee divisions that had been scattered since the period of the Iroquois Wars. The early appearance of LeBaril's Miami community on the Ohio River near the mouth of the Miami about 1733 probably indicates flight from the smallpox epidemic that struck the Wabash towns in 1732.

The first prominent Delaware leader to enter the Ohio country was Wandochale, whose successive locations and those of his son make it possible to trace this Delaware group through the entire course of their short residence in the Great Lakes Region. Wandochale was reported: (1) near LeTort's trading post on the Ohio River in 1739, (2) on the Scioto north of Lower Shawneetown in 1751, (3) on the Walhonding between Killbuck and Mohican creeks in 1775, probably after returning for several years to western Pennsylvania, (4) with his son Buckongahelas on the upper Mad River in 1779 (map 16). Buckongahelas subsequently lived on the Auglaize River in northwestern Ohio in 1790, and at Telipokshy on the White River of Indiana in the early nineteenth century (map 20), a region from which the Delaware were removed west of the Mississippi River in 1819.

One clan of Detroit Huron (Wyandot) under Orontony and Anioten made a permanent move from the Detroit River to Sandusky Bay about 1736, establishing towns near the tribal hunting grounds on the headwaters of the Scioto rivers. Away from French supervision, they were in contact with British traders and also made peace with their British-supported southern Indian enemies. Since this action was carried out without consulting the Ottawa, they created a temporary rift with their traditional allies.

In northeastern Ohio, the French endeavored to maintain control over the Cuyahogaregion where a French trading post was in operation periodically at a location on the Cuyahoga River opposite the mouth of Tinker's Creek in present Cleveland.The multi-tribal population clustered in that vicinity in 1742 included: Seneca, Cayuga, Oneida, Onondaga, Mohawk, Mahican, Ottawa, Abenaki of St. Francis, and Ojibwa from the lower end of Lake Ontario. On the map, the abbreviation for "Mingo" covers the first five tribes on the list. In the eighteenth century, this term referred to splinter groups of Iroquois who moved to Ohio and were considered outside the control of the Six Nations confederacy. Since specific information is lacking, this tribal mixture is represented by a single symbol placed near the mouth of the Cuyahoga River. The total population, estimated at 2,000, was probably scattered at several sites along the banks of the river as far upstream as the river bend, present Akron, where the Cuyahoga Town of the Delawares located in 1758.

The Cuyahoga valley was a major transportation corridor. From the river bend a portage led directly south to the Tuscarawas, Muskingum and Ohio rivers. Both ends of the portage were locations for Indian towns, trading posts and forts. Farther up the Cuyahoga beyond the falls another portage formed part of a route southeast to Mahoning Creek and the upper Ohio Valley.

Better prices and more adequate supplies of trade goods attracted the Indian hunters of the Lower Great Lakes to the British traders. The British financial advantage in the Indian trade improved when the French in 1742 adopted a new system of auctioning trading posts, a policy

that increased costs. Furthermore, the European conflict known as King George's War (1744-48) particularly handicapped French trade after the British captured French ships carrying Indian goods to Canada in 1745.

The outcome of these developments was the uprising against the French in 1747 organized by Orontony, the Huron (Wyandot) leader at Sandusky, whose French name was Nicholas. The critical incident in this so-called "Conspiracy of Nicholas" was the killing of five French traders at Sandusky on their way back to Detroit from winter quarters on the Cuyahoga River, but there were other attacks on French traders in the Great Lakes area. The commandant at Detroit took precautionary defense measures after a secret plot against the French town was revealed through information conveyed to the Jesuit priest. On the other hand, the pro-British Miami made a successful attack on Fort St. Phillipe (present Ft. Wayne), pillaging the French traders.

Following the abortive 1747 uprising, two notable population transfers took place involving the Huron (Wyandot) and the Miami. The Huron at Sandusky precipitously burned their village early in 1748 and went first to the Cuyahoga River (also called the White River), then to Beaver Creek in Pennsylvania, finally establishing a new town called Conchake on the Muskingum River across from modern Coshocton. In that year they attended the first of a series of British councils at Logstown, founded in 1743, an important intertribal center for the Iroquois, Delaware, and Shawnee, who became the major population group. Alliance with the Six Nations was a prominent feature of the council, attended also by Delaware, Shawnee, Mahican, and Missisauga.

At the same time the Shawnee persuaded a group of Miami to establish a new town, Pickawillany, near present Piqua, Ohio, on the upper waters of the Great Miami River. Here Pennsylvania merchants penetrated farthest into the French trading territory, even carrying trade goods north to a winter hunting base at the juncture of the Maumee and Auglaize rivers in northwest Ohio in the very hinterland of Detroit.

Concurrent but of lesser importance was the move of the Huron (Wyandot),who were loyal to the French, from the mouth of the Detroit River to a location closer to, but still opposite, the French fort. This was their third townsite in the Detroit area; their original location was adjacent to the French fort.

French efforts to prevent the inroads of British traders initially were unsuccessful,but positive measures were undertaken at the conclusion of King George's War in 1748. Additional troops were sent to Detroit and Michilimackinac. The Indian population was aggravated but not threatened by a French official trip down the Ohio River in 1749, asserting French authority by placing lead markers at river mouths. More effective was the arrest of British traders on the Auglaize and Cuyahoga rivers in 1750. Since French authorities could not secure the support of Detroit Indians, their first attempt against Pickawillany in 1751 was unsuccessful. Vigorous action between 1752 and 1754, however, expelled British traders from the Ohio Valley.

On the western trading frontier, French troops and Ottawa warriors from northern Lower Michigan captured the British traders at Pickawillany in 1752 and "made a broth"

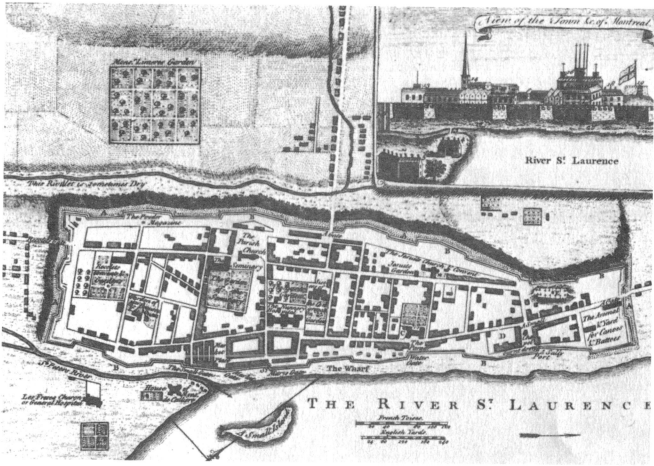

Town and fortifications at Montreal, government and trade headquarters of french Canada, conquered by the British in 1760. From *London Magazine,* 1760, engraving entitled "Plan of the Town and Fortifications of Montreal, or Ville Marie in Canada." Clements Library.

out of the local Miami leader known as "La Demoiselle" or "Old Britain." With the destruction of Pickawillany, the Miami returned to their former residences on the Wabash River and to French alliance.

During the same year, 1752, French and Indian forces struck far south of the Ohio River to the British trading post at Eskippakithikion Lulbegrud Creek in Kentucky. This location was occupied beginning in 1745 by part of Peter Chartier's band of Shawnee. The band had lived on the Allegheny River above Pittsburgh, but moved down the Ohio River, splitting to form two short-term villages, one at present Shawneetown, Illinois and the other in Kentucky.

The French successfully staked their claim along the eastern front of the Ohio country beginning in 1753 with the construction of a road and a new chain of four posts from Fort Presque Ile (Erie, Pa.) to present Pittsburgh, where they seized a post being constructed by a Virginia trader in February, 1754 and made it Fort Duquesne. This activity and a devastating smallpox epidemic in 1752 were factors in the return of the Huron to Sandusky Bay in 1753 (see inset map). British traders were eliminated from Lower Shawnee town at the mouth of the Scioto River and from the Muskingum River in 1754. The French regained the upper hand in Indian trade and diplomacy, and demonstrated their control of the Ohio Valley two years before the outbreak of the Seven Years War in Europe (1756-1763).

Intercolonial Warfare

Competition between France and Great Britain over trading territory in the Ohio Valley expanded into full-scale warfare following French seizure of the uncompleted British post that became Fort Duquesne in 1754. Despite protests of Indian leaders against European powers fighting their battles on Indian land, international encounters took place for the next five years in the eastern section of the Great Lakes Region, resulting in the end of the French empire in North America. Indians fought on both sides of this struggle, but principally on the side of the French. Action occurred in two war zones, western Pennsylvania and the Canada-New York corridor from Montreal south past Lake Champlain.

The French and Indian War (1754-60) began with the resounding defeat of General Edward Braddock's British expedition attempting to take Fort Duquesne in November, 1755. The garrison of about 300 French soldiers and Canadian militia drew major support from a multi-tribal army of almost a thousand Indians. British losses included close to 900 casualties, two-thirds of the force, as well as horses, provisions, and supplies. Indian tradition records that the Huron and Potawatomi of Michigan acquired their first horses at Braddock's defeat.

Indian military assistance for the French came from almost every section of the Great Lakes Region during the

Working a canoe up a rapid. The route of seventeenth-century voyageurs up the Ottawa River continued in use for passengers and freight until the mid-nineteenth century, when this drawing was made. From Willis, *Canadian Scenery,* vol. 2, p. 44. The Newberry Library.

course of the war. The French administration consolidated seven mission establishments along the St. Lawrence River as the "Seven Nations of Canada." Members included four groups living near Montreal: Iroquois, Algonquin and Nipissing from the Lac des Deux Montagnes community called Oka; and Caughnawaga, a mixed Iroquoian settlement at Sault St. Louis that later became Mohawk in language. At various times, membership in the Seven Nations of Canada included the Abenaki of St. Francis and Bkcancour, Huron of Lorette near Quebec City, and the Cayuga and Onondaga at Oswegatchie, some of whom later joined the Mohawk of Akwesasne at the mouth of the St. Regis River.

A second coalition called the "Lakes Indians" included the four tribes around Detroit, the Huron, Ottawa, Chippewa, and Potawatomi. Although more inclined to neutrality, some Delaware, Shawnee, and Iroquois on the Allegheny River joined in the defense of Fort Duquesne in 1755.

The beginning of the Seven Years' War in Europe (1756-63) led to intensified warfare on the colonial frontier of North America. The Great Lakes Indians, perceiving the war as a contest between French fur-trading interests and British settlers' land-owning aspirations, attacked frontier settlements of Pennsylvania. Lives were lost and several hundred people held captive until the end of the war. To defend settlers against French and Indian raids, the British built forts in the thinly populated Appalachian mountain district, most of which were dismantled during or after the war. Fifteen are shown on the map.

In the major expeditions of the inter-colonial war, French and Indian troops secured initial victories on the New York frontier, capturing Fort Oswego on Lake Ontario in 1756, then advancing from Montreal down Lake Champlain to take Fort William Henry in 1757. Both of these forts were retaken by the British in 1759. The Indian force with the

French army operating south of Lake Champlain in 1757 numbered 855. They included 160 Ojibwa, called Sauteurs by the French, from as far west as Chequamegon Bay of Lake Superior; 337 Ottawa from the Michilimackinac vicinity, Saginaw Bay, and Detroit; 88 Potawatomi from Detroit and the St. Joseph River; 129 Menominee from Green Bay; as well as 144 other Indian warriors of the Winnebago, Mesquakie, Iowa, Sauk, and Miami. Lake Superior Ojibwa were also present at the fall of Quebec in 1759.

Charles Michel de Mouet Langlade, a trader of French and Ottawa heritage from Michilimackinac, exercised decisive leadership in the French military victory at Fort William Henry in 1757, as he had at Fort Duquesne in 1755 and Pickawillany in 1752. Unfortunately, Indians entering the smallpox ward at the fort brought back the fatal disease to their villages, causing heavy loss of life among the Menominee and the Potawatomi of the St. Joseph River (see map 32).

The tide of battle began to favor the British in the fall of 1758. Again called to defend Fort Duquesne, the "Lakes" Indians defeated the advance detachment of the British attacking force in September, but then returned to their villages. Lacking the necessary Indian support when the main body of the British army arrived in November, the French garrison burned the fort and fled up the Allegheny River. The British army took over the site on November 24, 1758, renaming the place Pittsburgh and the military post Fort Pitt.

The focus of warfare between France and England in the Pittsburgh area brought about a shift in the regional Indian population. Eager to leave the war zone, Delaware made arrangements with the Huron (Wyandot) to settle in eastern Ohio. During 1755 and 1756 they began to move up the Beaver River to Kuskuski (Newcastle, Pa.), Salt Lick near Niles, Ohio, and Mahoning near present Newton Falls,

Old French graveyard at Traverse des Sioux on the Minnesota River, sketched July 16, 1851,along with encampment of American officials engaged in treaty negotiations with the eastern Dakota. Frank B. Mayer, Drawing No. 3. The Newberry Library.

Ohio. By 1758, Delaware were living at Cuyahoga Town (Akron), the frequently occupied site at the bend of the Ayahoga River. Turkey Division people settled at Tuscarawastown, also called Beaver's town, at present Bolivar, Ohio. Two years later, Mingo and Delaware were living at Mahican John's town, two miles below present Jeromesville, a way station on the main land trail between Detroit and Pittsburgh. Delaware occupied the site at intervals until the War of 1812.

Another wave of western migration took place when the British occupied Pittsburgh in 1758. The largely Shawnee population left Logstown, trading center on the Ohio River eighteen miles below Pittsburgh. Shawnee also left Wyoming, on the Susquehanna River of eastern Pennsylvania, at this time. As the Shawnee population in Ohio increased, village locations changed as well. The Upper Shawnee at the mouth of the Kanawha River established a new community, Wakatomica, in 1756 on the fringe of the newly formed Delaware population on the headwaters of the Muskingum River. In 1758, Lower Shawneetown, at the mouth of the Scioto River, moved upriver fifty miles to the plains near Circleville, Ohio.

When the British military supremacy on the New York and Pennsylvania frontier was established in 1759, Indian leaders promptly made contact with George Croghan, Irish trader in the British Indian service, to insure adequate future supplies of trade goods. At this juncture, Ottawa in Detroit split on the issue of continued adherence to the French, and a pro-British faction moved across Lake Erie to the Cuyahoga River. In August, 1760, Croghan held a council at Pittsburgh to win the friendship of tribes that had supported the French. He entertained over a thousand Indians: Mingo, Huron (henceforth called Wyandot by the British), Delaware, Shawnee, Ottawa, Ojibwa, Potawatomi, Miami and Kickapoo. Old French graveyard at Traverse des Sioux on the Minnesota River, sketched July 16, 1851, along with encampment of American officials

engaged in treaty negotiations with the eastern Dakota. Frank B. Mayer, Drawing No. 3. The Newberry Library.

The final battle of the French and Indian War in North America, the French defeat at Montreal on September 8, 1760, included in the terms of capitulation the surrender of all military posts in French Canada. In November, British Rangers peacefully assumed command of the fort and palisaded town of 80 houses at Detroit. Croghan accompanied the advance occupation force to council with Indian leaders and arrange the exchange of prisoners. British detachments went immediately to replace the French at Fort Miami on the Maumee River (Fort Wayne) and Fort Ouiatenon on the Wabash, southwesternmost post in French Canada.

Ice in the upper lakes prevented the reoccupation of Fort Michilimackinac, the most important post in the Upper Great Lakes until the following year. In the fall of 1761, the British landed troops at Michilimackinac and continued on a circuit of Lake Michigan. They took over Fort LaBaye at Green Bay, renaming it Fort Edward Augustus, reestablished Fort St. Joseph at present Niles, Michigan, abandoned by the French in 1760; and constructed a new defense post, Fort Sandusky, on the south side of Sandusky Bay.

Principal Sources: Anson 1970; Berthrong 1974; Blasingham 1956; Bond 1927; Carte du Fort 1731; Clifton 1977; Corbett 1977; Darlington 1892; Dobbs 1744; Donehoo 1928; Edmunds 1979; Gibson 1963; Gist 1893; Hanna 1911; Hickerson 1974a, b; Hutchins 1942; Kellogg 1925; Illinois 1960-1961; Kinietz 1942; Krauskopf 1955; Lajeunesse 1960; Marin 1975; Montgomery 1916; Norton 1974; Pease and Jenison 1940; Peckham 1961; Peyser 1980; Robinson 1965; Rawlyck 1975; Smith 1870; Smith 1977; Stevens and Kent 1940; Temple 1958; Thwaites 1902-1908; Tucker 1942; Warren 1885; Voegelin 1962; Voegelin, Blasingham, and Libby 1974; Volwiler 1926; Vrooman 1943; Zoltvany 1974.

Pontiac, an Ottawa leader living on the Detroit River, was the dominant figure in a season of Indian warfare, May through October of 1763. His objective, shared by many tribal groups, was to eliminate the British from the Great Lakes Region. Pontiac and other Indian leaders had three objections to British behavior. First of all, British officers discontinued the generous French practice of giving out powder and ammunition needed for hunting. Second, the British exhibited every intention of taking over the whole country rather than being content with widely separated military and trading posts. A third factor was the arrogance and the dislike of Indians so obvious in the personal attitudes of most British officials.

The idea of an uprising was not independently generated in Detroit, for Pontiac had three outside influences: (1) an earlier appeal for war against the British circulated by the Seneca as early as 1761, (2) the teachings of Neolin, the newly acclaimed Delaware Prophet, at Tuscarawas Town in Ohio, and (3) the encouragement of local French residents of, Detroit as well as the French in the Illinois country. The settlements in present Illinois on the east bank of the Mississippi River near Fort Chartres were part of French Louisiana, a province unconquered and not yet transferred to the British when Pontiac's War broke out.

The violent Indian protest erupted during the short time between the British occupation of posts in former French Canada, 1760-61, and news of the formal ending of hostilities by terms of the Treaty of Paris in February, 1763, which reached Detroit by way of New Orleans on October 30 (see maps 12A and 12B).The Delaware Prophet's message spread among Great Lakes Indians during that same time interval. Ideological seed for his revelation may have come from western Indians who visited the Delaware a few years earlier and explained that they were not dependent on white people, and used no guns or other articles made by Europeans. In his oratory, the Prophet graphically demonstrated the menace of white people with a diagram painted on a deerskin portraying white people in a large rectangle blocking the pathway of Indians from earth to happiness, with associated lines representing the sins Indian people had acquired from contact with Euro-Americans. The image was copied and distributed among Great Lakes Indians.

Two small maps are a guide to the sequence of military events of Pontiac's War and the results of the warfare. Sharing Pontiac's immediate objective were Seneca, Delaware, Shawnee, Miami, Ottawa, Ojibwa, and Missisauga. Of the "British Forts Affected," nine of eleven in the Great Lakes Region were lost to the British between May 16 and June 20, 1763, and the two more strongly fortified positions at Detroit and Pittsburgh were under siege.

Indian warfare did not seriously threaten Ligonier and Bedford, east of Fort Pitt on the Pennsylvania frontier (see map 10). The area bounded by Detroit, Pittsburgh, and Fort Niagara formed the "Principal Theatre" for aggressive Indian action in 1763 and for two retaliatory peace-enforcing British expeditions in 1764, led by General John Bradstreet and Colonel Henry Bouquet (see map 11).Within this war theatre, Potawatomi, Ottawa, Wyandot and Delaware villages changed their locations or abandoned sites during the two years 1763 and 1764.

British Forts Affected

Indian plans to remove the British from the Great Lakes and upper Ohio Valley were under way for almost a year before Pontiac's first overt action in May, 1763. At the Ottawa village opposite Detroit, a secret council took place in the summer of 1762, involving local Indian leaders and others from as far north as Lake Superior. War belts were en route that year from the French in Illinois to the Wabash River villages. Indian people also became aware that Spain had joined France in European warfare and anticipated a joint expedition that would reconquer Quebec. In the Seneca country, Kyashuta and Tahaidoris, who may have been the son of a French official, actively promoted war against the British. They had come to Detroit to propose immediate war in 1761, but their initial appeal was not accepted. In February, 1763, a Seneca belt reached the Miami living at the head of the Maurnee River in Indiana. The message called for a strike against the British as soon as the belt reached Ouiatenon on the Wabash.

In April, 1763, Pontiac began coordinating strategy for the three Indian villages at Detroit. These were the Potawatomi two miles south of Detroit and Ottawa and Wyandot living across the river from the fortified town. Pontiac's speech inciting warriors to action outlined the vision-inspired message of the Delaware Prophet urging Indians to drive out the British and return to a traditional life-style. He proposed taking his Ottawa warriors into the British fort ostensibly for a council, then at a signal seizing control by using weapons concealed under blankets. Opening the gates to armed Wyandot and Potawatomi surrounding the fort would assure a quick victory, since the British garrison numbered only about 120 and the combined local warrior strength totaled about 400. The British commandant learned about the plan, however, and it could not be pursued. Pontiac's followers struck the first blows outside the fort on May 9 and began a siege lasting six months.

At the beginning of the war, Pontiac sent out messengers to Wyandot, Potawatomi, and Wea living near other

Pontiac's War 1763
British Forts Affected

- Forts destroyed or abandoned, Indian victory
- Forts attacked or besieged by Indians, held by British

5.25 May 25
5.9-11.30 May 9 to November 30, siege

1:25,000,000

0 ——— 300 MILES

0 ——— 300 KILOMETERS

Ottawa, Ojibwa, and Pontiac's War Wyandot contingents sent from Detroit. Warriors of the four tribes conducted successful siege operations leading to the surrender of the fort on June 20.

Delaware brought news of the fall of the three northwest Pennsylvania forts to Fort Pitt on June 24, advising the captain to surrender rather than face a large Indian army. Recently reinforced to a strength of 338 men, Fort Pitt seemed strong enough to withstand attack, although small-pox had broken out. The captain presented the Delaware delegation with blankets from the smallpox hospital, starting an epidemic that raged through the Delaware, Mingo, and Shawnee towns of Ohio until the following spring.

The siege of Fort Pitt, commenced on May 29, was relieved on August 10 by the expedition of Colonel Henry Bouquet, organized at Carlisle, Pennsylvania. On August 6 the expedition was attacked twenty-six miles east of Pittsburgh by Shawnee, Delaware, and Sandusky Wyandot. Bouquet's superior strategy forced the Indian assailants to retreat into the forest, but only at the cost of 110 British casualties. He then marched on to Pittsburgh, and the fort was never again seriously threatened by Indian attack.

Therefore, as a consequence of a series of Indian actions beginning in May, Pittsburgh and Detroit were the only British-held forts in the Great Lakes Indian country by late summer of 1763. Bouquet regretted that he did not have time to import British hunting dogs to track down elusive Indian fighters.

Principal Theatre

MAP
10

The war commenced by Pontiac produced hostile incidents over a broad area, but the most persistent fighting occurred in the vicinity of Detroit and along the British supply line extending from Fort Niagara on Lake Ontario, along the Niagara River, and across Lake Erie to the Detroit. As early as June 2, the day of the historic lacrosse game at Michilimackinac, Missisauga captured three Detroit-bound barges of goods and eleven traders at the mouth of the Grand River on the northeast shore of Lake Erie.

Although losses were frequent on the supply route from Niagara, an armed vessel safely made its way up the Detroit River past Indian breastworks in June, 1763. In late July, fourteen batteaux brought additional troops to Fort Detroit under cover of a night fog. The head of this relief expedition attempted a middle of the night attack on Pontiac's camp five miles north of Detroit, with disastrous results. His men were ambushed beside a bridge over a small stream in the early dawn of July 31, and 19 were killed and 42 wounded before the soldiers retreated back to the fort.

Another major confrontation took place on September 14 at the Niagara portage. Seneca led a force of about 300 against a British convoy of horse and ox-drawn supply wagons that broke away and fell over the cliffs. Of the convoy escort and subsequent relief expedition from Fort Niagara, 72 men were slain in the heaviest fighting of the entire war period.

At peak military strength, Pontiac at Detroit had an army estimated at 870 men: 150 Potawatomi under Ninevois; 50 Huron under Take after withdrawal of the Christian

British forts. Using various ruses, local warriors killed or captured all personnel at Fort Sandusky on May 16, Fort St. Joseph on May 25, Fort Miami on May 27, and Fort Ouiatenon on June 1. The surprise attack at Michilimackinac on June 2, probably the most widely known incident of Pontiac's War, was devised by the nearby Ojibwa. During a game of lacrosse with visiting Sauk, they hooked a ball over the stockade wall and then all rushed in to recover it. Once inside the fort, the Ojibwa began to kill and take prisoners.

Offended at being left out of the plot, Ottawa from L'Arbre Croche came to Michilimackinac, seized the British prisoners from the Ojibwa, and demanded part of the loot. These Ottawa also crossed Lake Michigan by canoe and brought back men ordered to evacuate Fort Edward Augustus on Green Bay. This garrison and survivors of Michilimackinac eventually made their way from L'Arbre Croche to Montreal.

On June 2, the day of the Michilimackinac attack, Pontiac dispatched 200 Ottawa, Ojibwa, and Wyandot from Detroit to Presque Isle on the southeast side of Lake Erie. In mid-June, Seneca of the Genesee valley in New York entered active warfare. They first attacked Fort Venango (Franklin, Pa.), probably on June 16, leaving no survivors. At Fort Le Boeuf (Waterford, Pa.) two days later, the defending detachment was able to escape after dark, but the fort was destroyed. Moving north to Fort Presque Isle (Erie, Pa.), the Seneca joined forces with the

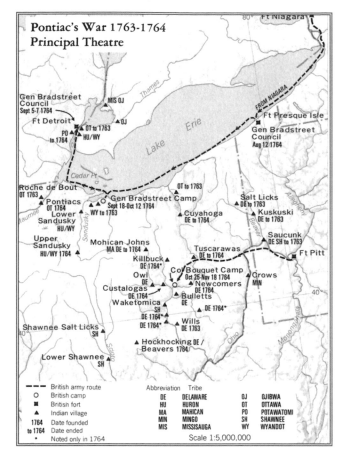

MAP
11

and individual Indian leaders came to make peace with the commandant at Fort Detroit. The warning of winter came with a giant snow squall on October 14 and a hard freeze and heavy snow on October 29. The next day, a messenger from the French commandant at Fort Chartres arrived with the advice that France and England were at peace and all the Indians should cease fighting. This message was a response to Pontiac's appeal for French aid sent to Fort Chartres in early September. Indians had already begun to disperse to winter hunting grounds.

The season of warfare in 1763 had caused violence and atrocities far beyond the scenes of military engagements. Attacks on isolated white settlements had inflamed the frontier from New York to Maryland with reprisals against Indians who were not involved in Pontiac's war. Virginia had mobilized a militia of 1,000 men, and Pennsylvania raised 700 to try to protect the frontier population. Cornstalk, the Shawnee leader, took a war party up the Kanawha River, striking deep into present West Virginia. British military losses were more than 400, and the intertribal Indian forces lost 90 of their best warriors. Including the losses along the frontier, the total casualty list for the British population was estimated at 2,000.

Reaction and Continuation

Within the area of the warfare during 1763, there was still evidence of hostility in 1764, despite the efforts of British authorities to bring tribal leaders into peace councils and gain permission to reoccupy lost forts. In August, 1764, General James Bradstreet and 1,200 men set out from Fort Niagara for Detroit, where he called together Indian leaders in an attempt to make an effective peace. Pontiac, at that time living on the Maumee River, did not attend. Bradstreet was able to send a new garrison up to Fort Michilimackinac, since Upper Great Lakes Indians were eager for restoration of trade.

Stopping at Presque Isle (Erie, Pa.) en route to Detroit, Bradstreet encountered Delaware and Shawnee who duped him into thinking they were peaceable. These Indians then hurried to the Maumee River in advance of Bradstreet's representative and made sure that he received an unfriendly reception. Although the British officer received permission from Pontiac to proceed upriver and was accompanied by an Iroquois delegation including the distinguished Oneida leader Thomas Kin, he was nevertheless seized at the Miami villages and forced to turn back.

The second British expedition sent out in 1764 was more effective. In October, Colonel Henry Bouquet left Fort Pitt with a force of 1,500 to subdue the Delaware and Shawnee in Ohio and bring back prisoners of war. The threatening size of Bouquet's army brought the Ohio Indians to terms at a council held across the river from present Coshocton, on the site of the former Wyandot town, Conchake. Bouquet returned with 200 white captives and the promise of 100 more.

During the two year period 1763-64, Indian people moved their homesites because of the disruptions of warfare. At Detroit, Pontiac and his Ottawa following moved to the Maumee River, establishing two towns, one at Roche de Bout, a rocky landmark above the rapids, and another on an

Huron; 250 Ottawa under Pontiac; 250 Ojibwa from Saginaw Bay under Wasson; and 170 Missisauga-Ojibwa from the Thames River under Sekahos. He also secured some local French assistance, a few Menominee from Green Bay, and short-term support of Wabbibomigot's Missisauga from Toronto. They could have stormed the fort at Detroit, but since that action definitely would have meant sacrifice of many Indian lives, the project was never seriously considered.

The early weeks of the war under Pontiac's leadership were marked by a series of victories, yet deterrents to long-range success were also noticeable from the beginning. Acts of torture and cannibalism during drunken celebrations at the Ottawa camp near Detroit drew criticism from other tribal leaders. Kinochameg, son of the respected Ojibwa leader Minevavana or "Le Grand Saulteur," came from northern Michigan to deliver a speech censuring treatment of prisoners. Spokesmen for the visiting Delaware and Shawnee pointed out at a council that the Delaware Prophet had said not to harm their French brothers, and the war was bringing hardship to the French inhabitants. Pontiac had requisitioned supplies from all the farmers along the Detroit River, and taken over fields for raising corn. Potawatomi at St. Joseph became convinced that the rumor of international peace was true. Christian Huron were dissuaded from warfare by their priest.

With the approach of fall, fighting was suspended

Ruins of Old Fort Michilimackinac, 1763, looking across the Straits toward St. Ignace. Mackinac Island at the right. From Schoolcraft, *History of the Indian Tribes of the United States*, pt. 4, p. 242. The Newberry Library.

island, both near present Waterville, Ohio. The Potawatomi, living two miles south of the fort at Detroit, were among the first to withdraw from active warfare. They left the Detroit River and probably moved to the Huron River west of Detroit. Another small Potawatomi community had moved away about 1761.

Wyandot on the south shore of Sandusky Bay, alarmed at the approach of the British relief expedition headed for Detroit in July of 1763, fled from their villages. The abandoned towns were Junundat, original townsite of the Sandusky Wyandot at present Castalia, and Sunyeneand on Pickerel Creek at the west end of Sandusky Bay (see inset map "The Sandusky Region" on map 9).By 1764, the two Wyandot villages in Ohio were Lower Sandusky (Fremont) and Upper Sandusky, located about three miles southwest of the present townsite.

Closer to Pittsburgh, Delaware vacated sites in the potential line of march of Bouquet's troops in October, 1764. In addition, Newcomer left Cuyahoga Town (Akron, Ohio) to establish a headquarters for the consolidating Delaware divisions at present Newcomerstown; Beaver moved from Tuscarawas Town to the head of the Hocking River (present Lancaster, Ohio). A number of "New Towns" noted in 1764 never appeared in later records. Their disappearance is probably attributable to the small-pox epidemic.

The Bradstreet and Bouquet expeditions in 1764 were the delayed British military reaction to Pontiac's war. They curbed but did not quell Indian power in the Great Lakes Region. By the spring of 1764, the center of resistance to British occupation of the Great Lakes Region had transferred to the Illinois country, where Indian leaders were still seeking French assistance. News of Pontiac's War had been carried through the southern tribes with the result that war parties on the lower Mississippi River turned back the British detachment from Mobile, Alabama, endeavoring to occupy Fort Chartres in March, 1764. Pontiac sent belts to the Quapaw at the mouth of the Arkansas River and also to the Osage in Missouri, to prevent any later British attempt to ascend the Mississippi.

The French commandant at Fort de Chartres, Captain Louis St. Ange de Bellerive, recently transferred from Fort Vincennes, curtailed warfare that spring by distributing only limited quantities of powder and ammunition. In addition to the local Illinois and Pontiac's Ottawa following, Captain St. Ange dealt with delegations of militantly anti-British Ojibwa, Potawatomi, and Shawnee during the summer of 1764. Leaders of the Shawnee and Illinois independently went to New Orleans to seek assistance from the French governor.

During the winter 1764-65, Pontiac held a secret meeting in the Illinois country with the powerful Ojibwa Le Grand Saulteur and French inhabitants eager to prevent British rule in their homeland. Not until April, 1765, did Pontiac become convinced that his former allies in Detroit and the Ohio country had made peace with the British. He was also persuaded that the Treaty of Paris in 1763 applied to the Illinois country, part of the Province of Louisiana, as well

Sleeping Bear Sand Dunes on northeastern shore of Lake Michigan during a storm. The dune was a prominent land-mark along the water-course from Michilimackinac to the post on the St. Joseph River in southwestern Michigan. From Castlenau, *Vues et Souvenirs du L 'Ameriquedu Nord* pl. 29. The Newberry Library.

as to Canada. The agent effectively transmitting this information to Pontiac was a French-speaking lieutenant from Fort Pitt who had set out for Fort Chartres in advance of George Croghan, deputy Indian agent for the Northern Department. At an assembly of 500 Indians, Pontiac announced his decision to make peace, though the local Illinois, who had never dealt with the British, would have continued warfare eagerly at his behest.

At the same time that Pontiac began promoting peace, Indian couriers brought news that the British were planning to organize the southern Indians against the northern tribes. Also, a French trading boat arrived from New Orleans with large supplies of powder and ammunition and the false report that the French were about to declare war against the British. These developments may explain why George Croghan and his Shawnee and Delaware escort, mistakenly thought to be Cherokee, were attacked just below the mouth of the Wabash River in June, 1765. Two whites and three Indians were killed, and Croghan and the wounded were taken as prisoners to Ouiatenon. Fear of retaliation by the Ohio Indians was a factor in his success

in securing the Wabash tribes' consent to the reestablishment of British forts.

Croghan also conferred at Ouiatenon with Pontiac, who came from Kaskaskia for that purpose with representatives of the four Illinois tribes, and Seneca, Delaware, and Shawnee deputies. A follow-up general council took place in Detroit in August, 1765. Deciding that peace must be made with the British, Pontiac sent a peace pipe to Sir William Johnson, superintendent of Indian affairs for the Northern Department, whose headquarters were at present Johnstown, N.Y. With the pipe he sent a message stating the conditions of peace. He declared that the British could occupy the former French forts but had no permission for settlements. He also made it clear that the French were tenants and not owners of land and could not transfer territory to the British. Indian hunting grounds must be undisturbed.

Croghan's hazardous but successful mission was the fourth British attempt in 1765 to gain Indian consent to the occupation of Fort Chartres. In addition to the lieutenant from Fort Pitt, two delegations had been sent overland from the British command at Mobile. With their lives in danger, all three parties returned to their respective bases by way of New Orleans. When Fort Chartres finally changed hands in October, 1765, Captain St. Ange and the French garrison moved across the Mississippi River to St. Louis, a town established by French settlers of the Illinois country in 1764. St. Ange continued in charge of Indian affairs and local government in St. Louis until a permanent Spanish commandant for Upper Louisiana arrived from New Orleans in 1769.

In 1766, Pontiac's oratory dominated the formal peace council with Sir William Johnson at Fort Ontario (Oswego, N.Y.). The western Indians refused to go inland to the Indian superintendent's residence, Johnson Hall, ninety miles distant. After this appearance, Pontiac's prestige among Indian people diminished rapidly; he became a virtual exile attended only by a small group of relatives. In April, 1769, he was murdered by an Illinois Indian while on a trading trip to Kaskaskia, possibly in retaliation for an attack made the previous year at Detroit. At the time of his death, sporadic attacks against British traders were still occurring in the Great Lakes area, along the Ohio River, and in Kentucky.

Principal Sources: Hutchins 1778; Johnson 1921-1951; Knapp 1872; Musick 1941; Peckham 1961; Slocum 1905; Smith 1868; Stagg 1981.

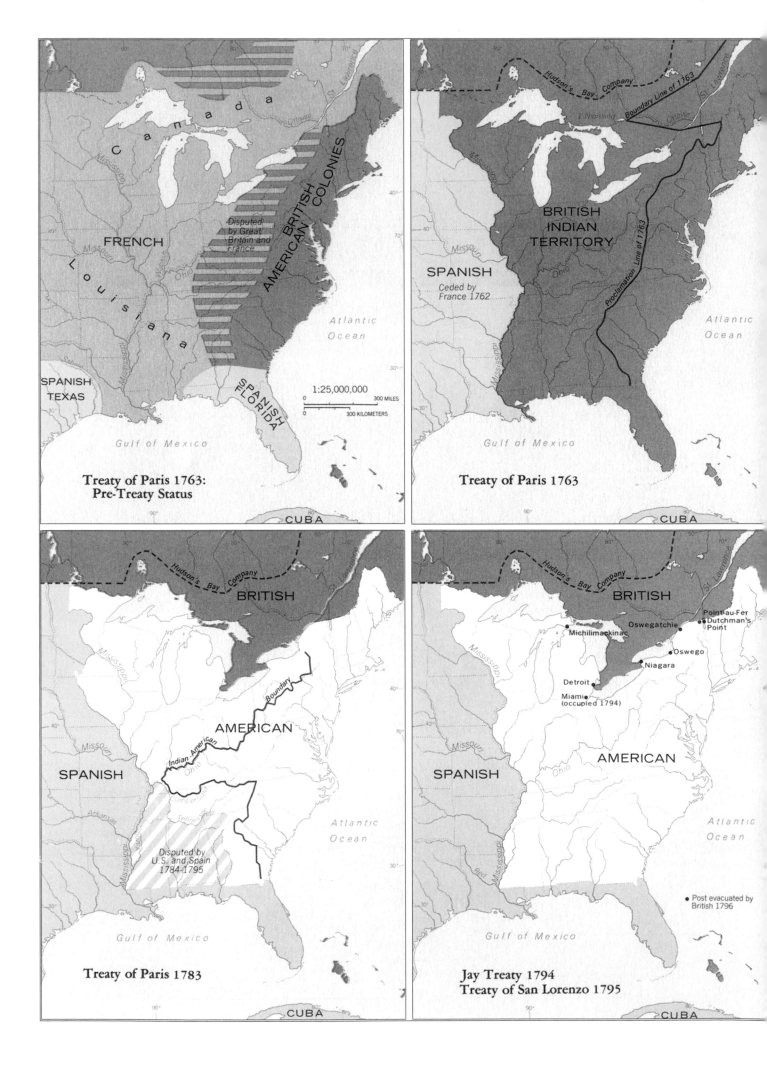

MAP
12

Treaty of Paris 1763: Pre-Treaty Status

FRENCH

Louisiana

Canada

BRITISH AMERICAN COLONIES

Disputed by Great Britain and France

SPANISH TEXAS

SPANISH FLORIDA

Gulf of Mexico

Atlantic Ocean

1:25,000,000

0   300 MILES
0   300 KILOMETERS

CUBA

Treaty of Paris 1763

SPANISH
Ceded by France 1762

BRITISH INDIAN TERRITORY

Hudson's Bay Company   Boundary Line of 1763

Proclamation Line of 1763

Atlantic Ocean

Gulf of Mexico

CUBA

Treaty of Paris 1783

Hudson's Bay Company

BRITISH

SPANISH

Boundary

Indian-American

AMERICAN

Disputed by U.S. and Spain 1784–1795

Atlantic Ocean

Gulf of Mexico

CUBA

**Jay Treaty 1794
Treaty of San Lorenzo 1795**

Hudson's Bay Company

BRITISH

Point-au-Fer
Dutchman's Point
Oswegatchie
Michilimackinac
Oswego
Niagara
Detroit
Miami (occupied 1794)

SPANISH

AMERICAN

Atlantic Ocean

• Post evacuated by British 1796

Gulf of Mexico

CUBA

Changes in sovereignty are shown on four maps that portray geographic changes in French, British, and Spanish colonial possessions in North America as well as territory of the new independent American republic according to terms of European treaties. By European perception, the major portion of the Great Lakes Region was transferred from French to British to American jurisdiction in the course of thirty-two years. Concepts of international law prevailing in Europe allowed no territorial rights to non-Christian or technologically underdeveloped people. The eighteenth-century treaties were drawn up without accurate information about the geography of the Great Lakes Region. Although Jesuit missionaries had a detailed knowledge of Lake Superior by 1671, the first reasonable maps of the Ohio valley appeared only in 1755, and the source of the Mississippi River, one of the geographic reference points, was not known until 1820.

A. Pre-Treaty Status, 1763

British colonies in North America with indefinite western limits were founded along the Atlantic seaboard starting in 1607. French settlement in Canada began in 1608 on the lower St. Lawrence River, and exploration advanced westward toward the upper Great Lakes. The development of Louisiana commenced with a base on the Gulf of Mexico in 1699. The dispute between the French and the British for control of the region west of the Appalachian mountains developed early in the eighteenth century. Consequently, Indian people were subject to the pressures of both British and French colonial administrators on this eastern margin of the Great Lakes Region (see map 9). North of French Canada, the southern boundary for the sparsely populated territory of the British Hudson's Bay Company established in 1670 was never precisely delineated but was understood to lie somewhere within the drainage of Hudson Bay.

In the southeastern section of the present United States, Indian nations were subject to a three-way struggle between the British, French, and Spanish. Spanish outposts in Florida, principally for the protection of Cuba, existed from 1565 on the Atlantic Coast and from 1698 on the Gulf Coast.

B. Treaty of Paris 1763

The treaty signed in Paris in February, 1763, concluded the Seven Years' War, the first European war fought on a global scale, with engagements in Europe, Africa, Asia, and South America as well as in the North American colonies. The North American phase, the French and Indian War, ended in September, 1760, when the French surrendered Montreal to British forces (see map 9). Spain was drawn into the war on the side of France in 1761. The British claimed conquest of Cuba after successfully laying siege to Havana in 1762.

The secret treaty conveying the area of Louisiana lying west of the Mississippi from France to Spain in 1762 became part of the final treaty settlement. The 1763 treaty redistributed the Indian country from the Great Lakes Region south to the Gulf of Mexico. French Canada and the portion of Louisiana lying east of the Mississippi were ceded to Great Britain, ending the French colonial empire on the North American mainland. The British also acquired East and West Florida but, returned Cuba to Spain.

Following the first treaty of Paris, the British reorganized administration of the North American colonies. The "Boundary Line of 1763" shown on this map defines the western borders of the Province of Quebec converging at Lake Nipissing. Settlement was officially restricted to the Province of Quebec; actually the population concentrated along the lower St. Lawrence River east of Montreal. Within the present United States, the "Proclamation Line" announced in October, 1763, officially confined white settlement to the area east of the crest of the Appalachian Mountain range but was ineffective in practice (map 11).

Implementing the territorial transfers of French posts in the upper Mississippi River valley required an additional seven years after the 1763 treaty was signed. Indian opposition held off British occupation of Fort Chartres in Illinois until October, 1765. The first Spanish governor for Upper Louisiana did not take control from the French commandant at St. Louis until 1770.

C. Treaty of Paris, 1783

At the conclusion of another European war, this time involving the independence of thirteen British colonies on the Atlantic seaboard, North American territory east of the Mississippi River again was distributed by European diplomats gathered in Paris. The American colonies, after declaring their independence in 1776, gained French support in 1778. Spain joined France in 1779 to oppose the British without supporting the concept of independence potentially dangerous for her own colonial possessions. Warfare ended in America in 1781.

By terms of the 1783 treaty the Canadian-American border extended from the Atlantic Ocean through the Great Lakes to the Lake of the Woods. In the same treaty, Spain regained the provinces of East and West Florida and retained

Louisiana, beyond which Spanish claims extended westward to the Pacific coast and northward past Vancouver Island. A boundary between American territory and Spanish Florida was left for later bilateral settlement.

The "Indian Boundary Line" shown on the same map indicates the territorial limits of the new American nation according to British-Indian treaties up to 1770, extended by land company purchase of western Kentucky in 1775 (see map 13).

D. Jay Treaty, 1794, and Treaty of San Lorenzo, 1795

The continued existence of British garrisons on American territory after 1783 was ended by the Jay Treaty of November, 1794, between the United States and Great Britain, providing for the removal of troops from posts on American soil by June 1, 1796. British traders and settlers could remain, and Indian people were permitted to move freely back and forth across the international border. Despite the removal of military posts, British influence remained supreme north and west of Lake Michigan for another quarter century. Spanish control scarcely extended north of present Missouri.

The Treaty of San Lorenzo in 1795, between the United States and Spain, restricted the territory of West Florida to the boundary prescribed originally by the British in 1763. Indians of the Great Lakes Region were involved in the diplomacy of Great Britain, the United States, and Spain continuously until Louisiana was receded to France in 1802 and purchased by the United States in 1803.

Principal Sources: Billington 1944; Cappon 1976; Downes 1940 ; Johnson Papers (6) 1928 and (12) 1957; Marshall 1967; O'Callaghan (8) 1857; Sosin 1971.

The year 1768 is significant in Great Lakes Indian history as the date of the Treaty of Fort Stanwix, establishing the Ohio River as the intended permanent borderline between the northwestern Indian country and white settlements on the colonial frontier of New York, Pennsylvania, and Virginia. The time of the 1768 treaty is appropriate for surveying the tribal distribution of Indian people in the Great Lakes Region, since it was an interval of relative stability in eastern North America. For a brief period there were no European-directed military campaigns, no conspicuous Indian-white hostilities, and no active intertribal conflicts except the persistent Ojibwa-Dakota warfare in present Wisconsin and Minnesota, the northwest corner of the Great Lakes Region.

The Indian-white boundary settlement at Fort Stanwix took place midway between the end of the French and Indian War in North America in 1760 and the outbreak of the American Revolution in 1775. During this period, Indian tribes were released from the opposing trade and territorial rivalries of the French and British in the Ohio Valley and were not yet embroiled in the War for Independence of Great Britain's American colonies. Temporarily, Indian people in the Great Lakes Region contended only with a single foreign nation, Great Britain, acknowledged by other European powers (but not universally accepted by Indians) as "sovereign" over the entire area east of the Mississippi River.

The year 1768 also marks the threshold of Spain's active participation in Great Lakes Indian diplomacy. Although France had formally ceded the Louisiana territory west of the Mississippi River to Spain in 1763, the first gesture of Spanish occupation of Upper Louisiana did not take place until 1767, when an advance military contingent began construction of Fort Don .Carlos at the mouth of the Missouri. In 1768, two years after the arrival in New Orleans of the first Spanish governor, French citizens staged an uprising forcefully suppressed by Spanish troops. Piedro Piernas, new commandant for Fort Don Carlos, did not arrive until 1769 to begin dealing with Great Lakes Indian tribes. Appointed lieutenant governor of the Illinois District in 1770, he immediately assumed authority at St. Louis, replacing the interim French official who had served since the town's founding in 1764.

Treaty of Fort Stanwix, 1768

The need for an Indian boundary had been apparent since the time of Pontiac's War in 1763. American colonists were settling on tribal lands without authorization of the British ministry, colonial governments, or native occupants. Colonial administrators reasoned that a new boundary would at least provide compensation to the Indians for land that had been lost to them. The agreement made at Fort Stanwix in 1768 marked the end of four years of discussion at a series of Indian councils. In May, 1765, Sir William Johnson, British Indian Superintendent for the Northern District, and representatives of the Six Nations arrived at a tentative boundary with the northernmost point located at Owego village near the present New York-Pennsylvania boundary. At conferences with deputy Indian agent George Croghan at Fort Pitt in May, 1766, and June, 1767, Shawnee, Delaware, Mingo and Wyandot representatives complained further of squatters pouring into their lands unhindered by Pennsylvania proclamations to stop such settlement. A third council at Fort Pitt in April, 1768, included Iroquois and Mahican representatives as well as those present at the earlier meetings.

Delegates began gathering in September for the formal council at Fort Stanwix, situated at the head of the Mohawk River near present Rome, New York. Close to the fort was the residence of Sir William Johnson, who organized the deliberations. The opening session for the largest Indian treaty council held by the British in North America took place on October 24, and the treaty was signed on November 5. About 3,400 Indians attended, including the Six Nations and their refugee minorities of Nanticoke, Conoy, Tutelo and Saponi; the Seven Nations of Canada constituting the mission communities around Montreal, and Shawnee, Delaware and Mingo of the Ohio country. Fewer women and children were present than expected, because they had remained at their villages to finish harvesting the corn crop. In advance of the final sessions, Nanticokes met privately with Johnson. The Stockbridge (Mahican) reached agreement on an intertribal boundary with the Mohawk, enabling them to leave by September 30.

Colonist representation included government officials and military personnel, as well as Indian traders, land speculators, and missionaries, who all tended to promote their special interests. The governor of Pennsylvania attended preliminary sessions and left two council members to sign the treaty, but the governor of New Jersey and his chief justice signed in person. Samuel Wharton and William Trent, present in behalf of the "suffering traders" of Pennsylvania, requested and secured land in present West Virginia as compensation for traders' losses during Pontiac's uprising. Commissioners from Virginia sought land from the Iroquois south of the Ohio River on the western frontier of their colony. Two missionaries, linking spreading the gospel with preservation of Indian lands, attempted to prevent the Oneida from ceding land. Oneida leaders Canaghquieson and the head of the warriors, Tagawaron, strongly opposed Johnson's ultimately successful effort to move the eastern end of the line north-

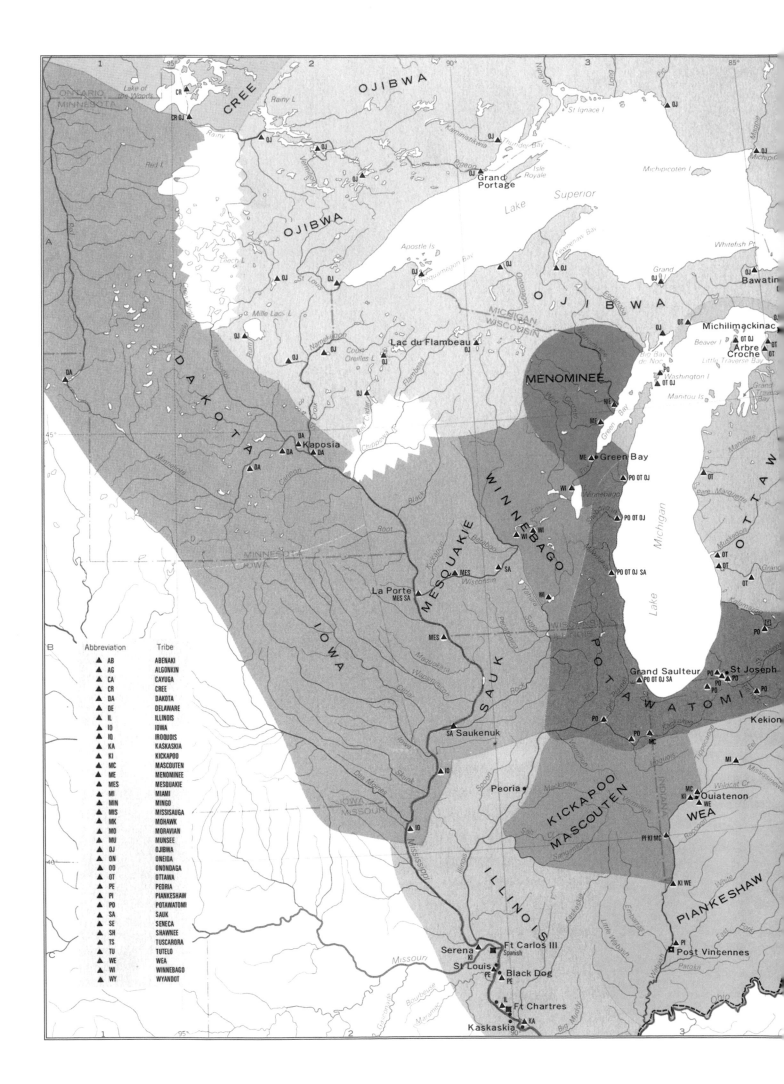

CREE

OJIBWA

OJIBWA

OJIBWA

DAKOTA

Kaposia

Grand Portage

Lake Superior

Apostle Is

Lac du Flambeau

MICHIGAN
WISCONSIN

O J I B W A

Bawatin

Michilimackinac

Arbre Croche

MENOMINEE

Green Bay

WINNEBAGO

MESQUAKIE

La Porte

SAUK

IOWA

Peoria

Saukenuk

POTAWATOMI

Grand Saulteur

St Joseph

Kekion

KICKAPOO
MASCOUTEN

WEA

Ouiatenon

PIANKESHAW

ILLINOIS

Serena

St Louis

Black Dog

Ft Carlos III
Spanish

Ft Chartres

Kaskaskia

Post Vincennes

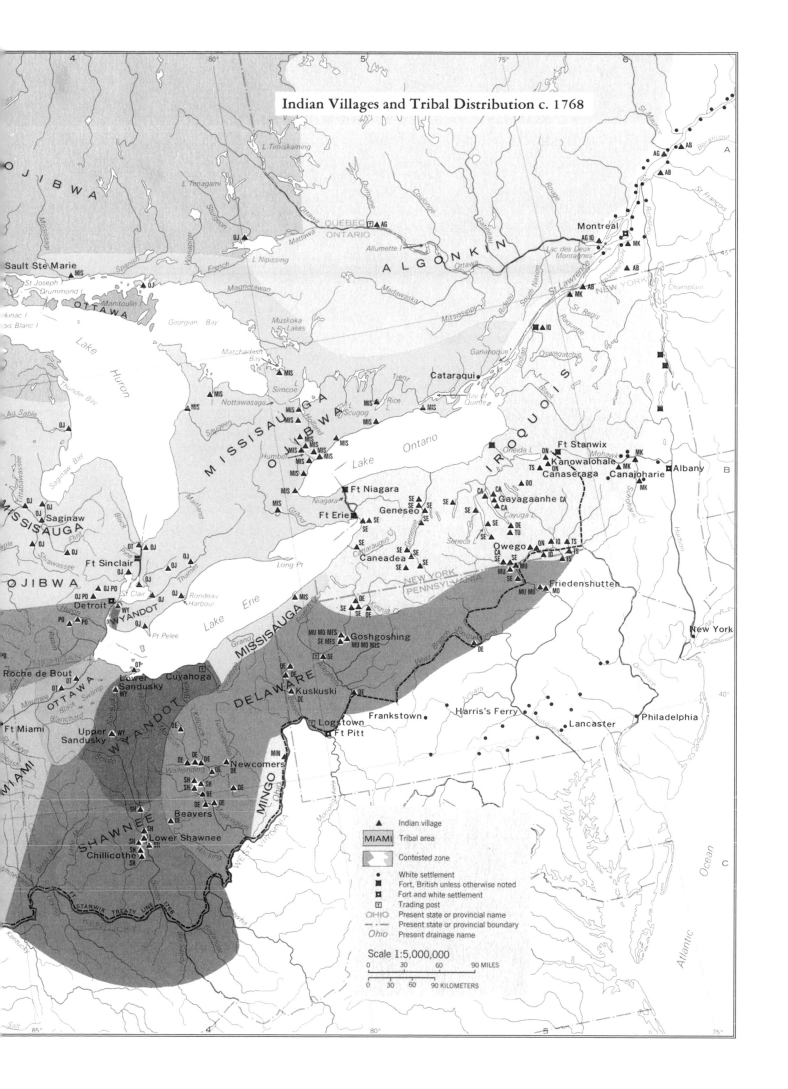

Indian Villages and Tribal Distribution c. 1768

OJIBWA

ALGONKIN

Sault Ste Marie
St Joseph I
Drummond I

OTTAWA
Manitoulin I
Mackinac I
Bois Blanc I

Lake Huron

Georgian Bay

L Timiskaming

L Timagami

QUEBEC
ONTARIO

L Nipissing

Allumette I

MONTREAL

Lac des Deux
Montagnes

NEW YORK

L Champlain

IROQUOIS

MISSISAUGA OJIBWA

Thunder Bay
Au Sable

Saginaw Bay

MISSISSAUGA

Saginaw

Ft Sinclair

OJIBWA

Detroit

Roche de Bout

OTTAWA

Ft Miami

MIAMI

L Simcoe
Nottawasaga

Matchedash Bay

Lake Ontario

Cataraqui

Bay of Quinte

Rice

Ft Niagara

Ft Erie

Geneseo

Caneadea

Cattaraugus

Lake Erie

Long Pt

Rondeau Harbour

Pt Pelee

WYANDOT

St Clair

MISSISAUGA

DELAWARE

Cuyahoga

Lower Sandusky

Kuskuski

Upper Sandusky

WYANDOT

Newcomers

SHAWNEE

Beavers

Chillicothe

Lower Shawnee

MINGO

Fort Stanwix

Kanowalohale
Canaseraga

Gayagaanhe

Owego

Friedenshutten

Goshgoshing

Logstown
Ft Pitt

Frankstown

Harris's Ferry

Albany

Canajoharie

NEW YORK
PENNSYLVANIA

New York

Lancaster

Philadelphia

Atlantic Ocean

STANWIX TREATY LINE

KENTUCKY

WEST VIRGINIA

MAP
13

Indian village

MIAMI   Tribal area

Contested zone

White settlement

Fort, British unless otherwise noted

Fort and white settlement

Trading post

OHIO   Present state or provincial name

Present state or provincial boundary

Ohio   Present drainage name

Scale 1:5,000,000

0   30   60   90 MILES

0   30   60   90 KILOMETERS

ward from Owego to Wood Creek, a stream entering Oneida Lake west of Fort Stanwix. The change from the boundary accepted in 1765 meant that the important and financially profitable portage from Oneida Lake to the Mohawk River passed out of Oneida control and into the area of white occupancy .

In the final negotiations, sachems of the Six Nations Iroquois acted as proprietors of all the territory involved and were the only Indian signatories. The line defined in the Fort Stanwix Treaty ran from a point a few miles west of Fort Stanwix southward to the Delaware River, then along the West Branch Susquehanna and the Allegheny, finally following the course of the Ohio from Pittsburgh to the mouth of the Tennessee River (see map 12). In extending the line down the Ohio River past the mouth of the Kanawha, Johnson made another change from the boundary prescribed by the Board of Trade in Great Britain in 1765. Johnson insisted on the right of the Six Nations to cede land they had "conquered" but never used south of the Ohio River in Kentake, the Iroquois word for prairie land that converted into English as Kentucky. The Six Nations land cession at Fort Stanwix covered land utilized chiefly by Seneca, Delaware, and associated Indians in western Pennsylvania, and Shawnee hunting grounds in Kentucky as well. as part of the Cherokee country in Tennessee. In the treaty, the Six Nations declared that the Tennessee River had always been their boundary with the southern Indians.

Sir William Johnson's boundary extension to the Tennessee River confused the results of a concurrent southern , Indian congress being held in South Carolina. By the Treaty of Hard Labor signed on October 14, 1768, the Cherokees ceded land south of the Ohio River with a western boundary line drawn directly from the head to the mouth of the Kanawha River, leaving Kentucky land west of the Kanawha still part of the Indian territory. The Indian boundary line achieved by the Treaty of Hard Labor was intended to connect at the mouth of the Kanawha River with the boundary being approved at Fort Stanwix.

There were obvious elements of dissatisfaction with the particular terms of the Fort Stanwix treaty. Shawnee and Delaware were displeased not only with the land cession but also with the decision that the Iroquois would receive all the monetary reward of the treaty, amounting to over ten thousand pounds sterling. A number of Indian nations remote from the frontier disapproved of any land concessions by the Six Nations. Nevertheless, Indians affected by the treaty came to recognize the Fort Stanwix boundary line between areas of Indian and white occupancy as a guarantee of protection to their remaining tribal lands. Indian people considered the agreement made in 1768 as definitive. Immediately after the treaty however, General Thomas Gage advised Sir William Johnson that British troops were insufficient to force settlers to adhere to the Fort Stanwix line.

Tribal Distribution

The Fort Stanwix line serves as a guide for the southeastern boundary of the Great Lakes Indian country in 1768. Northwest of the line defined by the Fort Stanwix treaty, mapping tribal distribution in 1768 has been determined by combining diverse kinds of information and relying on four premises:

(1) Each Indian group had a main geographic focal point, either a summer agricultural community, fishing station, or traditional ceremonial center, mapped as a village site.

(2) Indian people knew the extent of their home country and the general dimensions of the lands of neighboring and even distant tribes.

(3) In the case of territorial conflict, the area of contention could be defined.

(4) Divisions in the Indian country were most often identified by distinctive geographic features, usually a stream or lake, or a ridge between two river systems.

In preparing the 1768 map, the first stage was the location of principal villages of each tribe. This procedure established a spatial pattern indicating the relative position of a tribe with respect to adjacent tribes. Supplementary information about hunting grounds helped to clarify the extent of the territory of a single tribe or closely allied people. For the 1760s, contemporary data came from the accounts of a small number of traders and travelers and from official correspondence. Information that came to light later than the 1760s has also been utilized when it appears to reveal long-established custom or traditional tribal boundaries.

Some tribal boundary markers are stated precisely, while other lines are described in general terms, and information may be lacking for areas little used or remote from well-traveled routes. In the absence of better data for completing the map, topographic features serve as guides for estimating the probable land distribution of adjoining tribes.

The picture of distinct tribal countries does not imply that each area was occupied solely by one tribal group. Diverse population in any tribal country can be attributed to (1) intertribal arrangements to accommodate refugees, (2) concessions permitting seasonal hunting by other tribes, and (3) hospitality accorded to allies, travelers and delegations of visitors who might remain several years.

Although a number of approximations have been made in constructing the map, the range of possible variation is limited because each of the seventeen separate tribal areas is bordered by three to five adjoining areas, forming a system of interdependent line segments. Experimentation with possible adjustments has led to the conclusion that no single intertribal line could be altered significantly without diminishing the overall accuracy of the map. Viewed as a whole, the map can be considered a reliable representation of the distribution of tribes in the Great Lakes Region in 1768.

Northern Section

In the northeast, the Algonquin area included the St. Maurice River drainage and stopped at the string of French settlements along the north bank of the St. Lawrence River in Quebec. Algonquin also occupied the Ottawa River valley, their territory probably extending across the little used highland of the Laurentian shield southwest of the Ottawa River. Directly west of the Algonquin, the area is divided between two closely related Ojibwa-speaking groups identified as Missisauga-Ojibwa and Ojibwa. Lake Nipissing appears to have

Maiden Rock, landmark on the Wisconsin shore of Lake Pepin, the broadening of the Mississippi River above the mouth of the Chippewa River. From Keating, *Narrative of an Expedition to the Source of the St. Peter's River.* The Newberry Library.

been the locality where three regions converged, with the Algonquin on the south and east, the Ojibwa on the north and the Missisauga-Ojibwa on the west. The Lake Nipissing village at this time was Ojibwa, most of the Nipissing having moved to the Lake of Two Mountains near Montreal.

The large Ojibwa tribe has been considered, on one hand, an unorganized collection of perhaps fifty local bands, or, at the other extreme, a single people with widely scattered sub-groups. For this map, the broad expanse on the north shore of all the Great Lakes is divided into districts of the Missisauga-Ojibwa and the Ojibwa, essentially eastern and western divisions.

The Missisauga identified the extreme eastern end of their territory as the Gananoque River, a short tributary of the upper St. Lawrence. During land surrender discussions with a British representative in 1783, the Missisauga explained that on arriving at the Gananoque they would be crossing into the lands of the Iroquois. The map shows this boundary. The northwestern limit of Missisauga villages was the mouth of the Missisauga River on the north shore of Lake Huron. The term "Missisauga" never occurs west of this point, but farther east in Canada often appears in conjunction with or interchangeable with various spellings of "Ojibwa." The principal Missisauga concentration is found on the northwest side of Lake Ontario near the Humber River in the vicinity of modern Toronto. The Missisauga-Ojibwa bands were located on the Ontario peninsula, along the east coast of Georgian Bay, and around the southern end of Lake Huron into southeastern Michigan. By 1768, Missisauga-Ojibwa were the predominant population in the Saginaw Valley. Most of the earlier Ottawa occupants joined other tribal members at L'Arbre Croche by 1750.

French reports from Detroit in the first quarter of the eighteenth century refer to the communities on Lake St. Clair as mixed Missisauga and "Saulteur," the latter term used by the French to identify Ojibwa from Sault Ste. Marie, the falls or rapids of the St. Marys River. After occupying Detroit in 1760, the British commonly used the term "Chippewa," a corruption of "Ojibwa," in referring to the Indian communities on both sides of the St. Clair River and their relations in the Saginaw Valley. This variation became popular in the nineteenth century in Ontario and the northern United States. The northernmost village of the Saginaw Valley group of Missisauga-Ojibwa, a village still retaining an Ottawa minority, was located at the mouth of the Au Sable River near the entrance to Saginaw Bay. These people maintained close ties with their kindred on the St. Clair and Thames rivers.

When the Saginaw Indians ceded land in 1819, the western and southern cession lines conformed reasonably to the watershed of Saginaw Bay (see map 30). It was probably the best geometric representation that could be stated for an unknown interior region. This watershed has been used for the western border in Lower Michigan for the Missisauga-Ojibwa district. Although the 1819 land cession began at the mouth of the Thunder Bay River, that bay area in 1768 was a hunting ground for Ojibwa from the Upper Peninsula of Michigan who have always differentiated themselves from the Ojibwa of the Saginaw Valley in the Lower Peninsula.

The name Ojibwa originally applied to a single village on the north shore of Lake Superior, but usage has given the word a broader linguistic and tribal meaning. On this map, the vast area designated Ojibwa surrounding Lake Superior includes people who had common language bonds but were locally differentiated by descriptive or geographic names. Northeast of Lake Superior were the Têtes de Boule or Roundheads, who might be considered Algonquin; farther west were other migratory groups called Gens de Terre and Monsoni, the latter probably indicating moose clan affiliation. Bawating, the village at the falls of the St. Marys River, means in Ojibwa the place at the falls or rapids. Saulteurs, the French translation for the "people at the falls" applied as well to other Ojibwa, including a population north of the confines of the map. The Bay de Noc, on the northwest side of Lake Michigan, is probably associated with an early community of Ojibwa called Noquets by the French.

Southeastern Section

The Iroquois were confined to an area east of the Niagara River. In 1764, Sir William Johnson, British Indian superintendent, concluded a treaty with the Seneca ceding a tract of land four miles wide on each side of the Niagara River, partly as a punishment to the Seneca, who had opposed the British during and following the French and Indian War. This cession placed a western limit on the Iroquois territory. The Iroquois country extended east of the 1768 Fort Stanwix Treaty line in a region not occupied by white settlers until several years after the treaty. Mohawk villages continued in existence near white settlements in the Mohawk Valley. The Iroquois also had a narrow band of territory north of the St. Lawrence River recognized by the Missisauga. The majority of the Iroquois were loosely united in the Six Nations confederacy. As stated earlier, the original, Five Nations, located from east to west in present New York, were the Mohawk, Oneida, Onondaga, Cayuga, and Seneca. The league was enlarged to Six Nations about 1717 with the admission of the Tuscarora, Iroquois-speaking people who continued migrating from North Carolina at intervals during the eighteenth century. The Iroquois living in mission villages along the St. Lawrence River formed the nucleus of a separate group known as the Seven Nations of Canada (see p. 46).

In Pennsylvania, the 1768 treaty line reflects the approximate northern limit of Delaware and Munsee settlement at this time. The Seneca and Munsee-Delaware villages along the present New York-Pennsylvania boundary indicate the border between the regions of Iroquois and Delaware occupancy. The small section along the Ohio River marked "Mingo" identifies independent splinter groups from the Iroquois towns who rejected the authority of the Onondaga Longhouse and moved to the Ohio country. Mingo also lived with the Shawnee, Delaware, and Wyandot.

The Missisauga, allies of the Iroquois since the 1701 treaty at Montreal, were their neighbors on the west side of the Niagara River. With Six Nations approval, they crossed Lake Erie to use land along the southern shoreline. This narrow strip is shown on the map as ending at the Cuyahoga River, the indicated western limit of Six Nations land jurisdiction. Actually, the Cuyahoga Valley was an intertribal zone. The river served as a transportation corridor from Lake Erie to several points on the Ohio River. The lower Cuyahoga below the falls at the river bend was occupied at intervals in the eighteenth century by several different tribes, never for more than a few years and always peaceably (maps 9, 11, 16).

In the Ohio country, the Wyandot exercised administrative supervision over land, and their leadership was recognized and respected by the other tribes. Through arrangements with the Wyandot, the Delaware moved into the Muskingum valley shortly after the Wyandot abandoned Conchake in 1753. On Beaver Creek in Pennsylvania, they had dealt with the Iroquois. The actual territory assigned to the Delaware in Ohio is described differently in contemporary reports, but always covers parts of eastern and central Ohio. The map shows that the Delaware in 1768 were living on all the branches of the Muskingum River and on the Hocking. Part of the Shawnee lived among the Delaware from 1756 until 1774 (maps 9 and 16). The Shawnee in south central Ohio were clustered in the Scioto River valley between the modern towns of Chillicothe and Circleville. The tribe hunted south of the Ohio River in the Kentucky country and along the Great and Little Miami rivers west of their towns.

The Wyandot, whose influence was much greater than their small population would indicate, were settled at two points on the Sandusky River of north central Ohio and a third location on the south side of the Detroit River. A small section on the tip of the Ontario peninsula identifies the presence of the Detroit Wyandot. Here they had a Jesuit mission and extensive croplands. Hunting grounds for the Detroit and the Sandusky Wyandot were the headwaters of the Sandusky River and adjacent streams flowing into Lake Erie, and the upper branches of the Scioto River. In northwest Ohio the Black Swamp, virtually impassable except during arid or freezing weather, bordered the land principally used by the Wyandot. The Wyandot gave the Ottawa and Ojibwa permission to hunt along the south shoreline of Lake Erie, easily reached for Ontario Ojibwa who island-hopped south from Point Pelee.

Ottawa are shown at three places in the central section of the map: Manitoulin Island of Lake Huron, the west end of Lake Erie, and surrounding northern Lake Michigan. Manitoulin is the traditional Ottawa homeland often called the Ottawa Island. At the west end of Lake Erie, the Ottawa contingent represented two factions that moved from the Detroit River at the end of Pontiac's war. The followers of Pontiac established one village on the north bank of the Maumee River in late 1764, and by 1764 there were four communities between the head and the foot of the rapids. By 1766, however, the faction opposing Pontiac, led by Manitou, was settled on the Marblehead peninsula north of Sandusky Bay. In 1768, Pontiac and his personal attendants were living at Ouiatenon on the middle Wabash River. This Ottawa area included the Maumee drainage east of the Auglaize and its tributary Blanchard River. Ottawas established villages on these streams during the American Revolution (see map 16).

Headquarters for the Ottawa in 1768 was L'Arbre Croche in northwest Lower Michigan, where Ottawa had moved from Michilimackinac in 1742. The fort marked a division between the Ottawa on the west and Ojibwa country to the east. Ottawa continued exploiting the fisheries on the shoals of the islands and shores of northern Lake Michigan, including the Door Peninsula of Wisconsin between Green Bay and Lake Michigan. In winter, they hunted along the streams of western Lower Michigan, where permanent village sites were of recent origin in 1768. Both Ottawa from northern Lake Michigan and Ojibwa from the Bay de Noc region filtered southward along the Wisconsin shore of Lake Michigan.

The Potawatomi, spreading westward from the St. Joseph River region in southern Michigan, were by 1768 firmly lodged at the mouth of the Chicago River, near the forks of the Iroquois and Kankakee rivers (present Kankakee), the mouth of the Des Plaines (present Joliet), and at river mouths of western Lake Michigan at present Milwaukee, Sheboygan, and Two Rivers. Although predominantly Potawatomi, these lakeside villages contained large numbers of Ottawa and Ojibwa, and frequently smaller numbers of Sauk and Mesquakie. Occasionally, when the leader of a given village in this region was Ottawa or Ojibwa, as at Milwaukee, the village appears in the historical record with the tribal identification of the leader. At Milwaukee, the Potawatomi joined kinsmen who had resided on the western shore of Lake Michigan since dislocations caused by the Iroquois Wars (see map 6). At the tip of the Door Peninsula the Potawatomi were located on Rock Island and the Ottawa-Ojibwa on Little Detroit Island, both noted fishing bases on the north and south sides of larger Washington Island.

The Kalamazoo River was the traditional boundary between Ottawa and Potawatomi country in southwestern Michigan. On the eastern side of the state, the Potawatomi and Ojibwa countries met on the west side of Lake St. Clair, where mixed villages are located near modern Birmingham. Missisauga-Ojibwa permission was needed to settle on the Clinton River, the unnamed stream showing flowing into the west side of Lake St. Clair.

The Miami country has been mapped as the drainage of the Wabash River and the headwaters of the Maumee River. All village sites for the Miami, Wea, and Piankeshaw, are on the Wabash River, and hunting grounds were not far from their villages (see also map 9).

Ojibwa Woman and Child. Published by E. C. Biddle, Philadelphia, 1837. The collection of C. J. Hambleton.

Western Section

Intertribal warfare and land encroachment in the decades surrounding 1768 contributed to an unstable pattern of tribal distribution in the western Great Lakes Region, making tribal territories fluid and difficult to define for this specific date. Illinois, western Wisconsin, and Minnesota were the scenes of protracted struggles.

The once-dominant Illinois tribes, whose ancestral domain stretched as far north as Chicago, had been reduced from more than six thousand in 1700 to about twenty-two hundred persons in 1768. Their territory was being compressed in a triangular squeeze by Sauk, Potawatomi, and Kickapoo advancing from the north and east. The boundaries drawn for this map reflect the last possible date at which the Illinois remnant occupied hunting grounds in the central portion of the state. In 1761, the Peoria were still hunting along the upper Illinois River, and in 1769 a small number were reported living on Starved Rock directly below the juncture of the Fox and Illinois rivers and east of the Illinois-Potawatomi line shown on this map.

Illinois domination of central Illinois was nonetheless tenuous by 1768. Many Kaskaskia and Peoria had migrated to the west bank of the Mississippi after the terms of the Treaty of Paris in 1763 became known (see map 12). The few Peoria who remained at the town bearing their name soon followed or merged with invading Potawatomi and Kickapoo bands. As early as 1763, the Potawatomi were reported hunting 200 miles down the Illinois River, at least to the Fox River junction near present Ottawa, and possibly within 20 miles of Peoria. Before 1780, however, the Illinois tribes had been pushed south of the mouth of the Illinois River, retaining only the headwaters of the Kaskaskia and Big Muddy rivers for hunting purposes (see map 19).

In 1768, the majority of Kickapoo and Mascouten hunted north of the mouth of the Sangamon River in Illinois. Village sites on the Wabash River were at Ouiatenon, the mouth of

Old Ford Across the Eel River, near juncture with the Wabash River in Indiana. Watercolor by George Winter. From "Judge Horace Biddle's Journal," MS in Cass County Historical Society, Logansport, Indiana. Cass County Historical Society.

the Vermilion River of Indiana where they lived with the Piankeshaw, and at Terre Haute near the present Indiana-Illinois state boundary. Serena's Kickapoo band had already settled on the Missouri about thirty miles from the mouth, where Fort Don Carlos III was established by the Spanish in 1767. Serena's band, who had supported Pontiac's opposition to the British, moved west of the Mississippi after the British finally secured Indian assent to the occupation of Fort Chartres in 1765. Although the Kickapoo were to occupy the interior prairies of Illinois by the 1790s, the dates and direction of the eighteenth-century Kickapoo-Mascouten migration into the Sangamon River valley and towards the headwaters of the two Vermilion rivers are still somewhat questionable.

In northern Illinois, a region little known in 1768, the Sauk and Potawatomi probably shared a common boundary at the Rock River, a key geographical feature. Sauk hunters may have ranged as far east as the Upper Fox River; a few Sauk lived in the predominantly Potawatomi towns at Chicago and Milwaukee. The Iowa, adjoining the Sauk on the west, by 1768 had established two villages on the east bank of the Mississippi on the margin of traditional Iowa lands. The locations were mapped by Hutchins.

Problems of territorial definition are compounded in Wisconsin and Minnesota, where warfare between the eastern Dakota and Ojibwa persisted for more than a century. Information is particularly scarce for the little-used area of north central and northwestern Wisconsin, where hunting territories of the Sauk, Mesquakie, Ojibwa, Winnebago, and Menominee converged. Boundaries suggested for this region are more dependent upon estimates than those shown elsewhere on the map.

In the century since their decimation by smallpox, the Winnebago by 1768 had grown sufficiently to expand beyond their ancestral village at the entrance to Lake Winnebago on Doty Island. New villages were located at Lake Puckaway, Buffalo Lake, and on the upper Rock River at Lake Koshkonong.

The Menominee, whose principal villages traditionally stood at the mouths of rivers flowing into the west shore of Green Bay, had established a new village at the base of Green Bay by mid-century (map 9). A small number of Menominee utilized the resources of the islands at the tip of the Door Peninsula, although the principal inhabitants of these islands were the Ottawa living there in conjunction with Potawatomi and Ojibwa.

In upper Wisconsin, the Mesquakie were located south of the Chippewa River and west of the Wisconsin, with their principal villages on the lower Wisconsin. In the mid-seventeenth century, these Mesquakie, in alliance with the Dakota, had occupied the northwest corner of the present state, so their 1768 position represented a southern migration. Their affiliates, the Sauk, still controlled the critical Fox-Wisconsin River portage, according to Carver's observations. However, both the Sauk and Mesquakie were steadily being drawn south and west toward the banks of the Mississippi, and it is doubtful that these two tribes made more than minimal use of the northern reaches of their estimated territory. By the last quarter of the eighteenth century, the Winnebago and Menominee were beginning to fill the vacuum created by the southward-migrating Sauk and Mesquakie, hunting in central and western Wisconsin.

Eighteenth-century Ojibwa-Dakota warfare, originating in 1736 at the Lake of the Woods, by 1768 had resulted in considerable redistribution of tribal territory south and west of Lake Superior (see also map 9). From bases at Chequamegon Bay and at Fond du Lac on the lower St. Louis River near modern Duluth, the Ojibwa made serious inroads into former Dakota territory in eastern Minnesota and western Wisconsin. Permanent villages had been or were about to be established at Lac du Flambeau and Lac Court Oreilles, and incipient communities were hunting as far west as Mille Lacs Lake and at Sandy Lake on the portage from the St. Louis River to the headwaters of the Mississippi River. West of Grand Portage, the Ojibwa and Cree had pushed the Dakota from the headwaters of the Mississippi and by 1768 occupied fishing sites at Vermilion River, Rainy Lake, and the mouth of the Rainy River at the entrance of Lake of the Woods. While the Cree and Assiniboine continued to trade at Grand Portage at this time, their principal hunting activities utilized lands north and west of the Lake of the Woods and they soon moved outside the Great Lakes Region.

Many former Dakota village and camp sites around Leech Lake and Red Lake were still unsafe for the Ojibwa occupancy iJ,11768. Instead, a broad swath of space on the headwaters of the Mississippi River was described as a "war road," a contested zone little used or occupied except by traversing war parties of Dakota, Ojibwa and Cree. Similarly, land between the Red Cedar and Chippewa rivers in western Wisconsin was an uninhabited route of warfare between the Ojibwa at the headwaters of those rivers and the Dakota villages clustered on the upper Mississippi and lower Minnesota rivers.

The Dakota people were first described in terms of two geographic divisions, the "Sioux of the East and the Sioux of the West," according to their location with reference to the Mississippi River. Alternate terminology was "Sioux of the Woods or Rivers and Sioux of the Prairies or Meadows." The line between the more densely wooded eastern area of the Mississippi valley and the beginning of the western prairies corresponds closely to the line bounding the principal theatre of Great Lakes Region (see map 2). The grassland commencing at the angular bend in the Minnesota River and extending across northern Iowa is shown on map 3.

Of the Dakota, only the river bands, including the more or less fixed villages largely occupied by the Mdewakanton, were active in the Great Lakes theatre. Kaposia, an important Mdewakanton village, was located on the Mississippi on the southern side of modern St. Paul. The Tincton (Teton) of the western division had a base at Lake Traverse on the watershed between the Minnesota River and the Red River of the North. Here they were adjacent to the buffalo hunting grounds on the plains of present North and South Dakota. At this date, no additional geographic bases can be identified for the majority of the Dakota population separated into bands of fluctuating numbers of lodges, shifting from camp sites in the Red River and upper Minnesota River valleys westward to the Missouri River. Some bands frequented the headwaters of the Des Moines River in northern Iowa. The map actually covers less than half of the total territorial range of the Dakota. A number of prairie bands were intermittently within the Dakota area included in the map, while others might appear in this eastern range occasionally or perhaps only once in several years. Cheyenne, who in the seventeenth century were associated with the Dakota in Minnesota, by the late eighteenth century were along the Sheyenne River and other undesignated locations west of the Red River.

Population

At the time of the Treaty of Fort Stanwix in 1768, tribes in the Great Lakes Region probably numbered about 60,000 persons. The estimated total population of 80,000 for the tribal areas of the map includes close to 20,000 who were peripheral to the action taking place in the Great Lakes theatre. Clearly outside the scope of most Great Lakes Indian concerns were part of the Algonquin, about 3,000 Ojibwa north and east of Lake Superior, Cree at the Lake of the Woods, and about 15,000 Dakota of the prairie divisions. Although the Iowa were among the western Indians going to Michilimackinac to receive presents from the British commandant, they actually belong to the plains-oriented Indian population west of the Mississippi River.

In the vicinity of Montreal, the Lake of the Two Mountains population has been listed separately because of its intertribal composition. The three communities, Algonquin, Nipissing and Iroquois, together called Oka, composed one of the mission settlements collectively called the Seven Nations of Canada (see p. 46). The Abenaki on the St. Lawrence River directly below Montreal, numbering over 1,000, and the few hundred Huron at the Lorette mission on the outskirts of Quebec were not included in the total count for the Great Lakes Region.

Most eighteenth-century population data in original sources are given in terms of warriors, with the ratio of warrior count to total population figured as 1: 5, although ratios of 1:4 and 1:6 were also mentioned. In modern studies, the recommended ratio varies from 1 :3.5 to 1 :6. For the computations in the 1768 population table, the ratio of 1:4 was used chiefly for the Iroquois, and 1: 5 for most of the balance of the tribes. Dakota population is usually stated in terms of lodges, each lodge counting from ten to fifteen persons, but part of the eastern division was village based and estimated in terms of warriors.

Although population estimates varied for all tribes, the greatest spread occurred in the figures for the two largest groups, the Dakota and the Ojibwa combined with the Missisauga-Ojibwa. For the 1763-78 period, warrior count and lodge numbers reported for the Dakota indicate populations of 21,500, as well as 30,000 and 40,000. Similarly for the composite Ojibwa, reported populations varied from 20,000, with a separate estimate of 10,000 for the Missisauga, to 25,000 and 40,000. In the population table for 1768 the lowest estimate for the Dakota was used, along with other

Indian Population Estimates for 1768

Tribe	Subtotal	Total
Algonquin		1,500
Cree, Lake of the Woods district		1,000
Dakota		22,000
River bands, including 3,500 with villages	6,000	
Prairie bands, including 4,000 Teton	16,000	
Delaware and Munsee		3,500
Illinois		2,200
Iowa		1,000
Iroquois		9,800
Six Nations	7,500	
Refugees in Six Nations country (Nanticoke, Conoy, Tutelo, Saponi)	800	
St. Lawrence Iroquois	1,500	
Kickapoo and Mascouten		2,000
Lake of the Two Mountains (Iroquois, Algonquin, Nipissing)		500
Mahican (principally with the Wyandot)		300
Menominee		800
Mesquakie		1,500
Miami, Wea, Piankeshaw		4,000
Mingo		600
Missisaga-Ojibwa		7,000
Saginaw Bay district	2,200	
Lake St. Clair, Thames River, Lake Erie	2,100	
Lake Ontario to Lake Huron	2,700	
Ojibwa		8,000
South of Lake Superior, and Grand Portage to Rainy River	5,000	
North and east of Lake Superior, Thunder Bay to Ottawa River	3,000	
Ottawa		5,000
Lake Michigan	4,000	
Northwest Ohio	1,000	
Potawatomi		3,000
Sauk		2,000
Shawnee		1,800
Winnebago		1,500
Wyandot		1,000
Total		80,000
Total within Great Lakes Principal Theatre		60,000

reports for individual villages and for the river bands living in the eastern section of the Dakota country. Populations for the Ojibwa and Missisauga-Ojibwa were based on a collection of local and sub-regional reports and estimates. This process may have left uncounted a few thousand Ojibwa within the area mapped, and no additional estimate of Ojibwa outside the map has been calculated.

Summary

The Indian scene in eastern North America never was completely static: always there was a geographical locus of population pressure, tension, and change. In summarizing the 1768 situation in the Great Lakes Region, two broad generalizations may be made. First of all, the tribal distribution in the northern two-thirds of the map had achieved, or was in the process of achieving, long-term stability. Second, the tribal distribution across the southern part of the map was on the verge of rapid and violent alterations.

This map serves as a basis for describing and measuring later changes in tribal distribution and the decreasing tribal estates of Indian people. For comparison, see coverage of the same area in 1810 (map 20), tribal distribution in 1830 (map 22), and Indian reserved land (map 31).

Principal Sources: Ainsse 1888; Alvord 1908, 1922; Alvord and Carter 1916, 1921; Berthrong 1974; Braider 1972;

War Dance of the Menominee at Green Bay, Wisconsin. From Castlenau, Vues et Souvenirs du L'Amerique du Nord, pI. 17. The Newberry Library.

Bushnell 1919; Canada 1876; Carver 1781; Clifton 1977; Coates 1888; Croghan 1939; DeVorsey 1961; Dobie 1888; Edmunds 1978; Epping 1911; Feiler 1962; Gibson 1963; Gist 1893; Gorell 1903; Green and Harrington 1932; Gussow 1974; Haldimand 1765? 1782; Hanna 1911; Hickerson 1974b, c, d; Howard 1976; Hutchins 1778, 1942; Jenks 1900; G. Johnson 1781; Johnson Papers (4) 1925, (6) 1928, (12) 1957; Lees 1911; List 1892; Long 1791,1904; McCarty 1779; Melscheimer 1891; Morris 1943; O'Callaghan 1855; Ojibwa 1973; Parker 1976; Quaife 1921; Raisz 1957; W. Smith 1868; Sosin 1971; W. Stone 1965; Stout 1974b; Summary 1908; Tanner 1974a, c; Thwaites 1904; Trent 1871; Trigger 1978; Voegelin 1962, 1974b, c, d; Warren 1885; Wedel 1974.

INTRODUCTION TO THE FRONTIER IN TRANSITION

The quarter century from 1770 through 1794 was the time of frequent transition in the homesites of Indian people living in the area of present western New York, Pennsylvania, and southern and eastern Ohio. Consequently, this southeastern frontier of the Great Lakes Region is the primary focus in the series of five maps headed "Frontier in Transition." Migration from 1770 to 1772 represented adjustments to the Indian boundary agreement made by the Iroquois at Fort Stanwix in 1768 (see also maps 12c and 13). Later Indian population movements northward and westward, extending to British Canada and Spanish Louisiana, were directly related to the state of potential or actual warfare prevailing between 1774 and 1794.

The summary guide to "Expeditions into the Northwest Indian Country 1774-1794" (map 14) indicates the broad geographic area covered by these two decades of military campaigns into the Indian country and the general location of tribal groups affected by these campaigns. Indian villages that were military targets or in the line of march are shown at a larger scale on maps 15 to 19. These Indian village maps divide the total area covered by the expeditions map into three sections: (1) New York, Pennsylvania, and Canada, (2) Ohio Country and Canada, and (3) Illinois Country. The more detailed maps give terminal dates for specific Indian villages affected by the campaigns, and where possible the new locations for the same communities. Three of the five large-scale series, maps 16, 17, 18, are devoted to the complex sequence of changes in the central section of the southeastern frontier including most of Ohio and eastern Indiana.

Summarizing a series of military campaigns into the Great Lakes frontier, the guide map exhibits the approximate routes of thirty-four expeditions and sites of significant hostile action, all differentiated by color pattern to identify the year of the event. The accompanying chart lists these expeditions in chronological order. The two decades of hostilities can be divided into three discrete periods separated by intervals of diminished warfare within the Indian country: 1774, 1777-82, and 1786-94. Map and chart do not include the almost continual Indian forays against white settlements, some in conjunction with British troops, or the frequent clashes along the Ohio River.

During the single year 1774, events are associated with the initial onset of violence known as Dunmore's War because the only official expedition was led by John Murray, Earl of Dunmore and royal governor of Virginia. Lord Dunmore's expedition was a move to forestall anticipated aggression by Shawnee who were angered over continued advance of settlers into their traditional hunting grounds in present West Virginia and Kentucky. In the treaty at Camp Charlotte in October, 1774, the Shawnee leaders agreed to recognize the Ohio River boundary between Indian and white settlement, accepting the line set by the Iroquois at the Treaty of Fort Stanwix in 1768. Many Indian and white participants in Dunmore's War fought in later expeditions climaxing in Wayne's campaign of 1794.

The outbreak of the American Revolution in 1775 did not bring immediate reaction in the Indian country, because Indian leaders viewed the conflict as a "father and son" quarrel in which they had no part. Furthermore, both British and American authorities at first urged the Indians to remain neutral. By 1777, however, officers on both sides were exhorting the Indians to become active partisans.

The period 1778-82, concurrent with the American Revolution, accounts for twenty-three expeditions from different points of origin variously organized by divisions of the Continental army, governments of Virginia, Pennsylvania and Kentucky militias, British army, Spanish administration of Louisiana, and French inhabitants of St. Louis, Kaskaskia, and Cahokia.

Throughout years of interaction between these diverse European population elements and Indian people, the motivation and ultimate objectives of each group remained virtually constant. On a personal level, French and Indian people continued friendships and family ties developed over many generations. Indians and British traders shared an interest in preserving the land for a hunting economy that further provided the vital trade goods for the Indians. American colonists wanted to acquire land for farming and speculation, objectives more easily achieved without the constraints imposed by British policy. The emotional patriotic zeal for independence was scarcely noticeable in the western country along the Great Lakes frontier.

The small pockets of French inhabitants and Spanish authorities at St. Louis and New Orleans shared a long European tradition of antipathy to the British, reinforced during the American Revolution by the Franco-American treaty of alliance against Great Britain signed in 1778, with Spain joining France in 1779. Spanish Louisiana, already a refuge for many old French families of the Illinois country, became a third alternative residential base for Indian people disillusioned by dealing with British and American authorities.

By 1784, when the British-American phase of the hostilities was over, the eastern Great Lakes frontier had stabilized with the establishment of reservations for the Six Nations Indians remaining in New York and Pennsylvania, and the transfer of British partisans among the Six Nations to Canada (see map 31). On the other hand, the peace treaty at the end of the American Revolution became the basis for

Tavern Scene near Montreal, 1775. Group includes Indian dancers, drummer, and spectators, as well as soldiers in uniform and women dancing, trapper, small child, and landlady holding candle in the background. Music provided by piano, not visible. Reproduced from a pencil sketch by John Andre, in his correspondence for 1775. Clements Library.

a final period of warfare, 1786-94, concentrated in the central section of a broad band of frontier borderland a thousand miles long. Members of the Indian confederacy formed during the Revolution were incensed by the new American government's declaration that Indian lands had been acquired from the British by terms of the Treaty of Paris in 1783. American demands for Ohio land cessions in three unacceptable "treaties" signed by inadequate Indian representation at Fort Stanwix in 1784, Fort McIntosh in 1785, and Fort Finney in 1786 led to plainly-stated objections on the part of the Indian confederacy. Although revised federal policy later acknowledged Indian land ownership, Indian leaders militantly denied the validity of two more land cession "treaties" signed separately by the Six Nations and by the Western Confederacy at sparsely attended councils at Fort Harmar in 1789.

The frequency of expeditions into the northwest Indian country peaked during the thirteen months beginning in October, 1790, when four expeditions set out against the "hostile tribes on the Wabash." In the final engagement of this intensive period, the combined Indian army triumphantly routed General Arthur St. Clair's army near the present Ohio-Indiana border in November, 1791. However, in 1794, the warriors of the Indian confederacy gave up their struggle when they were unable to achieve any similar success at the battle of Fallen Timbers against General Anthony Wayne's better-trained soldiers (see map 19).

Throughout the struggles of the 1774-94 period, Indian leaders agreed on the importance of maintaining their hunting grounds and trading channels, yet they faced perplexing choices of strategy. Under many pressures, often with a need for rapid action and without the time to discuss a decision at length to achieve unity, Indians were never of one opinion. Among the alternatives were securing American protection or British aid, uniting in tight village formations or scattering to hunting grounds, making a sacrificial peace or continuing warfare. The most militant warriors generally lived remote from the fighting front and closer to British supply posts. Indian communities nearer to American forts were apt to be inclined toward peace. On the crucial issues of war, peace, and treaty-making, splits developed among the Six Nations Iroquois, Delaware, and Shawnee people. Divergent locations of villages of the same tribe reflect these different choices.

The great issue in this era was the permanency of the Ohio River boundary for separating the Indian country from white settlements. After Wayne's victory in 1794, Indian people faced the reality that they would be compelled to give up the southern Ohio land so forcefully demanded by the American government. The territory definitively ceded the next year at Greenville, Ohio, included a large area that in 1770 had been a homeland only for the Delaware, and Shawnee, and allied Mingo, and a hunting ground for the Wyandot; but all Great Lakes Indians realized they had a stake in the outcome of this contest.

The Treaty of Greenville in 1795 marked the end of the Indian war to maintain the Fort Stanwix treaty line of 1768 (see "Land Cessions" map 30), Tribes represented at Greenville were the: Wyandot (or Huron), Delaware, Shawnee,

Pittsburgh in 1790. Watercolor by Seth Eastman, from original by Lewis Frantz. View from the south side of the Monongahela River. From Schoolcraft, *History of the Indian Tribes of the United States,* pt. 3, p. 336. The Newberry Library.

Ottawa, Ojibwa, Potawatomi, Wea, Miami, Kickapoo, Piankeshaw and Kaskaskia. A century earlier they had all been united in opposing Iroquois expansion and were present together at the peace conference convened by the French at Montreal in 1701 (see p. 34).

By 1795, peace could be imposed all along the southeastern frontier of the Great Lakes Region on the basis of obvious numerical strength of the growing white population. In 1775, the population of present Kentucky had been only 300; by 1790, Kentucky had 73,000 inhabitants and became a state in 1792. Population figures in 1790 for other regions adjoining the northwestern Indian country were: 121,000 in northern New York, 92,000 in western Pennsylvania, 36,000 in western Virginia. At that time, Indian population in the area mapped for the "Frontier in Transition" probably was not much over 30,000.

FRONTIER IN TRANSITION 1774-1794:
EXPEDITIONS INTO THE NORTHWEST INDIAN COUNTRY, Map 14

Date	Event
Apr., 1774	Massacre of family of Mingo chief Logan on Ohio River opposite mouth of Yellow Creek.
Aug., 1774	Maj. Angus McDonald and 400 Virginia militia burned 5 Wakatomica towns of the Shawnee west of the Muskingham River.
Oct., 1774	Lord Dunmore's force proceeded from base at mouth of Hocking River in Ohio to Camp Charlotte, 6 miles from Cornstalk's town east of the Scioto. Sent side expedition to burn the Mingo town at the Salt Licks.
Oct.,1774	Battle of Point Pleasant. About 900 Shawnee and Indian allies withdrew after attack on 1,200 Virginia militiamen fortified at mouth of the Kanawha River.
Feb., 1778	"Squaw Campaign" when Gen. Edward Hand and 500 Westmoreland (Pa.) militia attacked Delaware women making salt in northeast Ohio; intended to strike British trading post at mouth of the Cuyahoga River.
July, 1778	Gen. George Rogers Clark, starting from Redstone (Brownsville, Pa.), arrived at Kaskaskia, Illinois, with 175 volunteers to establish fort under authority of Virginia. Capt. Joseph Bow man continued to Cahokia.
Aug., 1778	Lt. Leonard Helm advanced from Kaskaskia to Vincennes. French inhabitants already pro-American.
Sept., 1778	Col. Thomas Hartley from Fort Munsee struck 2 Munsee towns on Susquehanna River in northern Pennsylvania.
Oct., 1778	Col. William Butler from fort on Schoharie Creek destroyed 3 Iroquois and Tuscarora towns on Susquehanna River in New York.
Dec., 1778	Gen. Henry Hamilton, British commander at Detroit, and a principally Indian force of 500 men gained control of Vincennes on Wabash River, Indiana.
Feb., 1779	Clark marched from Kaskaskia to recapture Vincennes.

Mar., 1779 Clark attacked Delaware camps on lower White River, Indiana.

Apr., 1779 Col. Goose Van Schaick with 500 men marched from Fort Stanwix and struck the Onondaga settlements.

May, 1779 Col. John Bowman and about 300 Kentuckians attacked Chillicothe, Shawnee town near Little Miami River, Ohio.

Aug.,1779 Col. Daniel Brodhead's expedition from Pittsburgh with 600 men destroyed 12 Seneca and Delaware villages on upper Allegheny River, Pennsylvania.

Aug.,1779 Gen. John Sullivan and Gen. James Clinton directed combined expedition of about 5,000 men, destroying 40 villages of Six Nations in New York.

May, 1780 British-Indian force originating at Mackinac, Michigan, assembled estimated 750 to 1,000 men at Prairie du Chien, Wisconsin. Attack on St. Louis and Cahokia under leadership of Calve, Hesse, and Ducharme rebuffed by Spanish and French defenders.

June,1780 Spanish and American force of 300 to 500 led by Gen. John Montgomery pursued British and burned Sauk-Mesquakie village at Rock Island, Illinois.

July, 1780 Mohawk leader Joseph Brant led expedition from British-controlled Niagara; burned pro-American Oneida and Tuscarora towns near Oneida Lake.

Aug., 1780 Clark's expedition of about 1,000 Kentucky militia and Virginia regulars destroyed Chillicothe and Piqua, Shawnee towns near Little Miami and Mad Rivers, Ohio.

Nov.,1780 Col. Augustin Mottin de la Balme with combined French, American, and Indian force of 100 from St. Louis and Cahokia destined for Detroit, took Fort Miami but were attacked during retreat by Little Turtle and Miami Indians.

Expeditions into the Northwest Indian Country 1774-1794

MAP
14

Dec., 1780 J. B. Hamelin and 16 men from Cahokia sacked British Fort St. Joseph while Potawatomi were on winter hunt. Only three escaped counterattack by Potawatomi and British under Dagneau de Quindre at Petit Fort on Lake Michigan.

Feb., 1781 Don Eugenio Perré and Louis Chevalier with 65 Spanish militiamen and estimated 100 Indians captured British post at Fort St. Joseph in collusion with local Potawatomi; after 24 hours returned to St. Louis.

Apr., 1781 Col. Daniel Brodhead with 300 Continentals and militia destroyed principal Delaware town, Coshocton, as well as Lichtenau. Booty sold at Wheeling for 80,000 pounds.

Oct., 1781 Col. David Williamson and Washington County (Pa.) militia destroyed remaining Delaware towns on Tuscarawas River, Ohio.

Mar., 1782 Williamson's militiamen killed 90 pacific Moravians who had returned from Upper Sandusky to Gnadenhutten to get stores abandoned previous fall.

June, 1782 Col. William Crawford, with Williamson as second in command, and 480 Westmoreland and Washington County (Pa.) militia assembled at Mingo Bottom to attack Wyandot and Delaware at Upper Sandusky, Ohio. During retreat, Crawford captured by Delaware and burned in revenge for "Gnadenhutten massacre."

Nov., 1782 Clark and 1,050 militia met at mouth of Licking; destroyed three Shawnee towns on Great Miami River in retaliation for the British and Indian victory in August at Blue Licks, Kentucky. Col. Benjamin Logan destroyed British supplies at Lorimer's Store.

Oct., 1786 Under instruction of Clark, Logan organized 800 men at Limestone, Kentucky, and made coordinated attacks on 7 Shawnee towns on upper Mad River, Ohio.

Sept., 1787 Kentuckians' final attack on Shawnee remaining at Old Chillicothe on Paint Creek, Ohio.

Aug., 1788 Patrick Brown and 60 frontiersmen attacked friendly Piankeshaw at Vincennes.

Aug., 1789 Maj. John Hardin and about 250 Kentuckians attacked Wea near towns on Wabash.

Oct., 1790 Gen. Josiah Harmar with 320 regulars and 1,100 Kentucky militia burned 5 towns of Miami, Shawnee, and Delaware at head of Maumee River, but were defeated with 270 casualties in two engagements.

May, 1791 Gen. Charles Scott and 700 mounted Kentucky militia burned 3 Wea and 2 Kickapoo villages on Wabash River.

Aug., 1791 Gen. James Wilkinson and 500 Kentucky militia attacked Miami town on Eel River and burned Wea towns for second time.

Nov., 1791 Gen. Arthur St. Clair's 1,400 troops were attacked and disastrously defeated at later site of Fort Recovery by 1,000 Indian confederates under Little Turtle; 600 U.S. soldiers killed, 300 wounded.

Aug., 1794 Gen. Anthony Wayne's Legion of 2,000 regulars and 1,000 Kentucky militia under Gen. Charles Scott achieved military victory over Indian confederates at Battle of Fallen Timbers; 9 towns and cornfields of Delaware, Shawnee, Miami, Wyandot, and Ottawa destroyed along Maumee River.

For Indians living in the eastern sector of the Great Lakes area, the key event of the period was the Revolutionary War. The Canadian side of both Lake Ontario and Lake Erie remained in a state of equilibrium until the middle years of the American Revolution. With the exception of some fur traders and the occasional isolated settler, it was exclusively Indian country, homeland of the Missisauga and Ojibwa who concentrated their summer camps along the river valleys from the Thames to the Trent, then scattered to smaller camps during the winter. They felt little pressure from either the Iroquois, from whom they had wrested these lands in the late seventeenth century, or from the British, who claimed it at the end of the Seven Years War in 1763.

In 1770, New York and Pennsylvania tribes were also living in stable communities, believing that the boundary established by the Treaty at Fort Stanwix in 1768 had set the western limit of white settlement. The American Revolution gravely altered their situation. By 1784, weakened by warfare, economic loss, and dissension, the Iroquois and , their allies were forced to accept new boundaries in the second Fort Stanwix treaty, by which they lost all their lands in Pennsylvania and opened their New York lands to further white settlement. Close to half the population chose to move to British territory in present Canada.

The Revolutionary War, which involved an imperial conflict between Great Britain and the American colonies and an internal struggle between Patriots and Loyalists, also drew the Iroquois tribes and their allies into partisan activity. The Revolution posed a perplexing problem for the Iroquois, who viewed their longstanding alliance with the English as a covenant chain, with the Iroquois holding one end and the English holding the other end of the chain of friendship. Following the division of the English into British and American antagonists, the Iroquois tribes had to decide which party held the other end of the friendship chain, and there was no general consensus on this point.

American Revolution Begins

Because the Iroquois country was an important intermediate zone through which both British and American forces moved, the Iroquois Confederacy was unable to maintain its neutrality after 1777. The British had been urging the Iroquois to join them from the start of the war. The Americans wished the Indians to remain neutral until the Continental Congress decided in May, 1776, to seek military alliance with the Indians. The Mohawk, whose lands were already dotted with white settlements, allied themselves with the British. They were joined by the Seneca, the Cayuga, and most Onondaga. The majority of the Oneida and Tuscarora became American allies, eleven of their leaders receiving commissions as officers in the Continental Army. An Oneida contingent spent the winter of 1776 with the army at Valley Forge, Pennsylvania. Tribal tradition retains the memory of three contributions of the Oneida to the American cause; providing General George Washington with a cook, making snow shoes for soldiers, and rescuing French General Lafayette from ambush.

Between 1777 and 1779, a series of raids, campaigns, and retaliatory counterattacks throughout Pennsylvania and central and western New York resulted in destruction of Indian villages as well as displacement of white settlers. In August, 1777, about seven hundred pro-British Indians took part in the battle of Oriskany, located between Forts Stanwix and Dayton, the beginning of the campaign in the Mohawk River valley in New York. The valley saw repeated conflict throughout the war, as Tories (Loyalists) and Indians attacked settlements providing supplies to the Americans. Similar raids occurred in southwestern Pennsylvania, beginning in the summer of 1777 and continuing throughout the war. Here a circle of forts including Ligonier, Crawford, and Hand provided defense against Indian attackers from the Ohio country and the upper Allegheny River. The campaigns of September, 1777, included an unsuccessful siege by British and Indian forces on Fort Henry on the Ohio River in present West Virginia.

From Niagara, Montreal, and Carleton Island, which was the military base established by British Governor Frederick Haldimand near present Kingston, Ontario, the Indians and Loyalists engaged in a series of raids against rebel settlements in the Mohawk and Susquehanna valleys of New York and Pennsylvania. Early in July, 1778, about one thousand men, including five hundred Seneca and Cayuga, destroyed the Wyoming valley settlements in the vicinity of Wilkes-Barre, Pennsylvania. That same month and in the fall, Joseph Brant, war leader of the Mohawk, led raids against Mohawk River white settlements. In retaliation, Patriot forces under Thomas Hartley destroyed Queen Esthers, Tioga, and other Indian towns along the Susquehanna River as well as Brant's base at Oquaga (or Onaquaga). Reprisal followed retaliation as Tory leader Walter Butler and Brant attacked the Cherry Valley settlements in New York in November. The Seneca leader Sayengaraghta or "Old Smoke" was also active in this war theatre.

The following year, the Americans succeeded in destroying the villages and crops of the pro-British Indians. In April, 1779, Colonel Goose Van Schaick's force from Fort Stanwix destroyed the Onondaga villages. A dual campaign, originating in Tioga and Pittsburgh during August and September,

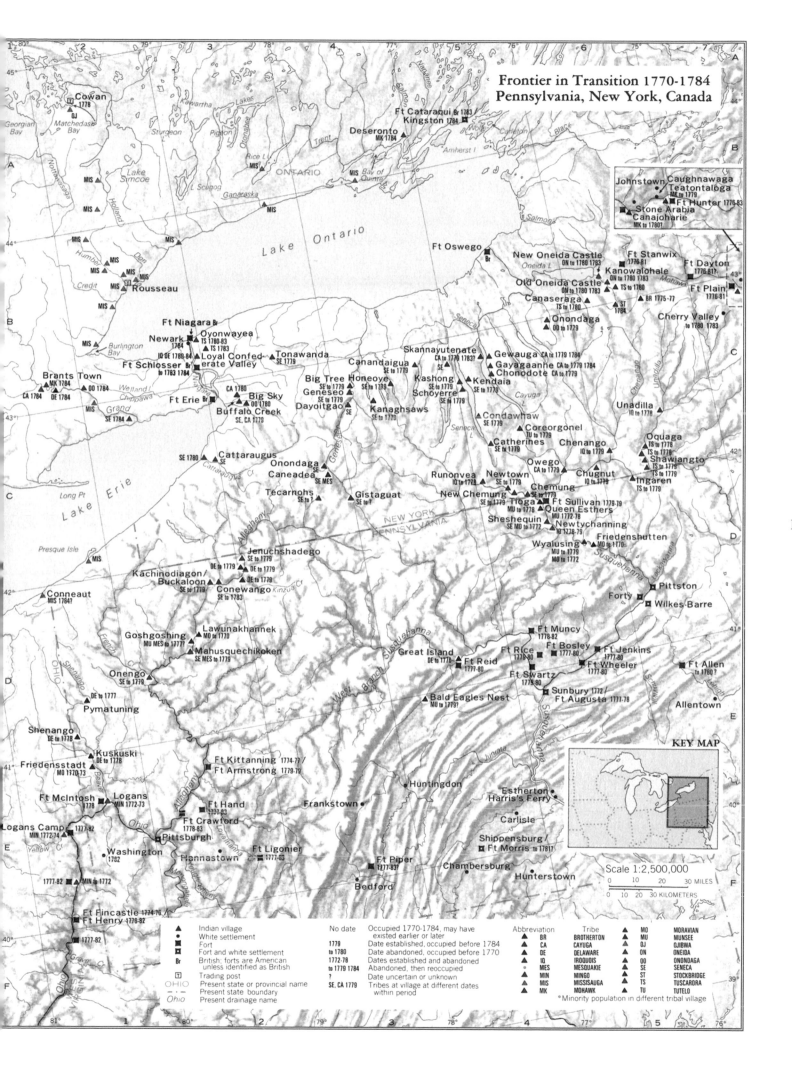

Frontier in Transition 1770-1784
Pennsylvania, New York, Canada

MAP
15

KEY MAP

Scale 1:2,500,000

0   10   20   30 MILES
0 10 20 30 KILOMETERS

▲	Indian village	No date	Occupied 1770-1784, may have existed earlier or later	Abbreviation	Tribe
●	White settlement	1779	Date established, occupied before 1784	BR	BROTHERTON
■	Fort	to 1780	Date abandoned, occupied before 1770	CA	CAYUGA
⊡	Fort and white settlement	1772-78	Dates established and abandoned	DE	DELAWARE
Br	British; forts are American unless identified as British	to 1779 1784	Abandoned, then reoccupied	IQ	IROQUOIS
⊤	Trading post	?	Date uncertain or unknown	MES	MESQUAKIE
OHIO	Present state or provincial name	SE, CA 1779	Tribes at village at different dates within period	MIN	MINGO
---	Present state boundary			MIS	MISSISAUGA
Ohio	Present drainage name			MK	MOHAWK

MO	MORAVIAN
MU	MUNSEE
OJ	OJIBWA
ON	ONEIDA
OO	ONONDAGA
SE	SENECA
ST	STOCKBRIDGE
TS	TUSCARORA
TU	TUTELO

*Minority population in different tribal village

Outlet of the Niagara River from the American shore, with British Fort Ontario on the left. By W. H. Bartlett. From Willis, American Scenery, vol. 1. The Newberry Library.

struck Iroquois villages in New York and the Seneca and Delaware towns along the Allegheny River in Pennsylvania. The eastern wing of five thousand soldiers and officers led by Major General John Sullivan, including fifteen hundred under Brigadier General James Clinton, left Tioga and moved slowly through Seneca and Cayuga territory. They burned forty towns and 160,000 bushels of corn, as well as a large quantity of other vegetables.

About five thousand Indians were forced to flee to the British for shelter at Fort Niagara. Meanwhile, the western wing of the American army under Colonel Daniel Brodhead ascended the Allegheny River from Pittsburgh with six hundred men, destroying twelve Delaware and Munsee towns and their crops (see map 14).

Despite the ravaging of Iroquois towns and standing crops, the pattern of raids against American settlements by Indians and Tories from New York and Pennsylvania continued. Brant led his Indian forces against the Oneida in the spring of 1780, destroying their settlements and forcing them and their Tuscarora allies to seek shelter around Schenectady, New York. That same year two Oneida, Good Peter (Agwelentorgwas) and John Skanadon, along with two Mohawk, Abraham (Tigoransera) and Hans Cryne, went to Niagara on a non-partisan peace mission but were arrested by the British. Although Abraham died in jail, the other three were freed on condition they accompany the British expeditions as scouts.

Mohawk valley settlements were again attacked and burned between May and October, 1780, and in the early

months of 1781. At the peak of military activity in 1780, reports indicated that 64 Indian war parties with 2,945 warriors were out on the frontiers of New York, Pennsylvania, and Ohio. The last British attack in central New York occurred in October, 1781, when American resistance forced the raiders to retreat from Johnstown. Seneca warriors devastated southwestern Pennsylvania settlements in July, 1782, almost totally destroying Hannastown, the northern frontier of American settlement in the region.

As it became increasingly possible that the rebellion of the American colonies could evolve into a successful revolution, many of those who had cast their lot with the British began to leave the colonies. As early as 1779, Loyalists began farming on both sides of the Niagara River in the vicinity of Fort Niagara, where Colonel John Butler headquartered his rangers after 1775. Others had followed Sir John Johnson, the son of Sir William and a future Superintendent General of Indian Affairs, to Montreal in 1776. Among those who followed Johnson, and who visited Butler, was Mohawk leader Joseph Brant, who carried a substantial portion of the Iroquois Confederacy with him into war on the British side.

When the Revolutionary War ended, the Iroquois and other Indians who had supported the British had lost homes and crops but had not experienced military defeat. Yet, at the end of the war, the Treaty of Paris stipulated that the lands of the Iroquois Confederacy lay within the boundaries of the new republic, and thereby Britain recognized the political sovereignty of the Americans over lands that the British had

Last home of Joseph Brant (1742-1807), Mohawk leader of the Revolutionary War era, on Burlington Bay at the head of Lake Ontario. By E. Walsh. Clements Library.

recognized as Indian territory since the Treaty of Fort Stanwix in 1768. American authorities had acknowledged the same territorial boundary by treaties at Pittsburgh in 1775 and 1776. By the end of the war, the Iroquois people were dispirited. While some Cayuga and Oneida returned to their homes in 1783 and 1784, pro-British Seneca and Cayuga and some Tuscarora preferred to establish villages in the vicinity of Buffalo Creek, near British protection at Niagara.

Although peace prevailed in 1783, it was clear that the Loyalists who had come to the Province of Quebec during the wars and attacked the frontiers of New York and Pennsylvania could not return to their former communities. Many of the Indians felt a similar misapprehension about reoccupying their tribal lands. These groups and the Loyalists who followed after the peace required accommodation within the remnants of British North America.

For a variety of reasons, Governor Haldimand decided to provide that accommodation along the northern and western shores of Lake Ontario. Accordingly, he authorized a series of treaties with the Missisauga Indians in order to secure lands for the settlement of the Loyalists who had come, and would come, to Canada (see map 30). The arrangements for the white Loyalists were made fairly easily, and in the years 1783-85 about 6,000 moved via Johnstown (Cornwall) and Niagara into the townships that were organized for them on the Niagara peninsula and the north shore of Lake Ontario. The first settlements included Newark on the Niagara River, and Kingston, the site selected for a military base when it appeared that Carleton Island lay within American territory. The Indian Loyalists presented a more serious problem.

Reserves for Indian Loyalists

The Indians felt deceived and abandoned by the British when the terms of the peace became known. Because he feared that these passions might be translated into hostile actions against the diminished British troops and against the white Loyalists, Governor Haldimand took several steps to placate the Iroquois. These included a generous hand in distributing presents, constant verbal assurances at special Indian councils of the King's love for his "red children," and the physical retention of the western posts, including Niagara, Detroit, and Michilimackinac. Continued possession of the western posts did preserve a British presence in the west, but was an act in direct contravention of the Treaty of Paris and a source of Anglo-American friction until provisions of the Jay Treaty were carried out in 1796 (see maps 12c and 12d). Finally, to compensate for lands that might be lost in New York, Haldimand offered land in Canada to any Indians who wished to settle in British North America. Two groups of Iroquois led by John Deseronto and Joseph Brant availed themselves of this open opportunity.

John Deseronto accepted a tract of 92,700 acres of land bordering on the Bay of Quinte on Lake Ontario on the

Susquehanna River, east branch, above Owego, New York, about 1840. The river was a main artery of war and trade for centuries. From Willis, *American Scenery,* vol. 2, p. 81. The Newberry Library.

grounds that this refuge in a relatively remote area would permit him and his Mohawk to live undisturbed by the Americans. Joseph Brant also inspected the Bay of Quinte site, but rejected it because of this isolation. Instead he selected a tract of land extending six miles on each side of the Grand River from its mouth on Lake Erie to its source (see maps 30 and 31). It would keep them closer to the rest of the confederacy, who remained in the United States, he argued, and would also provide a connection with the "Western Nations." In 1784 about two thousand Mohawk and other British allies among the Iroquois moved to the Grand River Reserve. From his new base at Grand River, Brant continued to be active in the affairs of the Iroquois of New York and also with the western confederacy until after the 1 794 Battle of Fallen Timbers and the 1795 Treaty of Greenville.

These Indian Loyalists very quickly became a dominant force in the western part of the Province of Quebec (Upper Canada after 1791). The Missisauga, from whom the British had purchased the Bay of Quinte and Grand River lands on behalf of the Six Nations, accepted the leadership of the newcomers. Further, Brant for several years kept the British authorities in a state of anxiety because of his connections with the western Indians and because of the size of the Indian population compared to the white settlements.

Principal Sources: Cappon 1976; Donehoo 1928; Espenshade 1925; Fenton 1940; Graymont 1972; Hagan 1976; Hinman 1975; Johnston 1963; Kent 1974; Lemon 1972; Montgomery 1916 ; Vrooman 1943.

At first glance the map of the Ohio country for 1772-81 creates the impression of more even settlement than was the actual case at any given time, because two consecutive locations are shown for a dozen Indian towns and three for the Shawnee most often displaced by attacks from West Virginia and Kentucky. If the map were restricted to the pre1774 years, west central Ohio would still be a blank, since no Indians had yet settled on the upper Mad and Great Miami rivers. By 1781, however, these rivers had become the new centers of population, while eastern and southern Ohio were devoid of Indian towns except for a few Shawnee who remained at Old Chillicothe on Paint Creek until 1787. These radical changes in the population concentration over the course of a decade are more easily perceived by comparing this map of the Ohio country in the 1772-81 period with map 17 for the years 1782-86.

In 1772, Indian people were distributed throughout the Ohio country substantially according to the pattern portrayed on the map for 1768 with two differences, the addition of the' Moravians and withdrawal of the Mingos from the Ohio River. Moravian communities established in 1772 on the Tuscarawas River were Shönbrunn and Gnadenhütten, the former principally Delaware and the latter mainly Mahican. These Christian missionary settlements moved from Freidenstat on the Beaver River and Wyalusing on the Susquenhanna River of western Pennsylvania at the invitation of the Delaware council, a decision formally approved by Wyandot leaders. Also in 1772, the Mingo located two new towns in the upper Scioto River valley north of the Shawnee settlements. The formidable Mingo warrior, Pluggy, settled on the Olentangy, and other Mingo at the Old Shawnee Salt Licks. These Mingo moved from Mingo Bottom on the north bank of the Ohio River near modern Steubenville (map 15).

Dunmore's War, 1774

First casualties among the Indian towns of the Ohio country were Wakatomica and four other Shawnee villages of the upper Muskingum valley burned by McDonald's Virginians in August, 1774, at the beginning of Dunmore's War. To understand why the Shawnee were the first target for destruction, it is necessary to follow the confrontations that preceded McDonald's expedition. Organized violence was the outcome of five previous years of Indian-white friction in the area between Pittsburgh and Wheeling where Fort Fincastle was established in 1774 (map 15). The Shawnee had never accepted the Six Nations' action ceding their Kentucky hunting grounds at the Treaty of Fort Stanwix in 1768, and insisted that Virginians limit settlement in line with the boundary pre-

scribed earlier by the British. They protested the Ohio valley surveying activities of men like the land speculator William Crawford, agent for George Washington and other Virginians, and the settlement projects near Wheeling promoted by George Rogers Clark. Such men, their friends and followers, became the personal adversaries of Indians on the Great Lakes frontier in all the hostilities from the 1770s through 1794. These animosities persisted until the War of 1812.

In 1774, the initial militants among the Ohio Indian population were not the Shawnee but the Mingo. During the spring there were skirmishes along the Ohio River and the expectation of war throughout Virginia, but the precipitating event in April was the unprovoked killing of the relatives of the Mingo leader Captain John Logan at a settler's cabin opposite the mouth of Yellow Creek (map 15). Logan was a well-respected man of French and Cayuga heritage who had lived in Philadelphia during part of the French and Indian War. The Shawnee council meeting at Wakatomica urged preservation of peace despite this atrocity, but some of the Shawnee joined Logan in revenging the deaths of thirteen Indians killed locally that spring. As tension mounted, the Shawnee leader Cornstalk sent his brother to guide Pennsylvania traders in the Scioto Valley safely back to Pittsburgh. There the Shawnee rescue mission narrowly escaped assassination by Virginians. In 1774, the atmosphere was volatile in Pittsburgh where British troops had been evacuated in 1772, and Pennsylvania and Virginia authorities were in contention over the Indian trade and a colonial boundary not settled until 1779.

Late in August, 1774, Lord Dunmore, royal governor of Virginia, went to Pittsburgh hoping to avert more general war by councilling with the Delaware, Shawnee, and Mingo. The Shawnee refused to attend but indicated some possibility of meeting the governor farther down the Ohio River. Dunmore then led an expedition to the Lower Shawnee towns on the Scioto River. He had ordered a second body of militia to fortify the mouth of the Kanawha River, former site of the Upper Shawnee town (map 9).

When Dunmore was about six miles from Cornstalk's town, he established "Camp Charlotte" and waited to have a council with the Shawnee leaders. Meanwhile, the Shawnee warriors had all left to attack the new fort on the Kanawha River. Here occurred the only major engagement of Dunmore's War, the Battle of Point Pleasant, lasting from dawn. to noon on October 10, 1774. After an unsuccessful assault on the fort, Cornstalk took the lead in proposing peace to Dunmore. In the provisional treaty, Dunmore demanded hostages and a promise that the Shawnee and Mingo would cease hunting on "our side," or the south side of the Ohio River. In turn Dunmore promised that Virginians would

Frontier in Transition 1772-1781
The Ohio Country and Canada

Legend (symbols):

- ▲ Indian village
- ● White settlement
- ■ Fort
- ⊡ Fort and white settlement
- ⊤ Trading post
- Br British. Unidentified forts and trading posts are American.
- OHIO Present state or provincial name
- – · – Present state or provincial boundary
- *Ohio* Present drainage name

Dates:

- No date — Occupied 1772-81, may have existed earlier or later
- 1780 — Date established, occupied beyond 1781
- to 1774 — Date abandoned or destroyed by military action, established before 1772
- 1772-79 — Dates established and abandoned or destroyed by military action
- 1775* — Occupied at that date, earlier or later dates between 1772 and 1781 unknown
- ? — Date uncertain or unknown
- ⬭ Villages occupied to approximately same date

Scale 1:2,500,000

0 10 20 30 MILES
0 10 20 30 KILOMETERS

Abbreviation / Tribe

Abbreviation	Tribe
▲ DE	DELAWARE
▲ KI	KICKAPOO
▲ MI	MIAMI
▲ MIN	MINGO
▲ MO	MORAVIAN
▲ MU	MUNSEE
▲ OJ	OJIBWA
▲ OT	OTTAWA
▲ PO	POTAWATOMI
▲ SE	SENECA
▲ SH	SHAWNEE
▲ WE	WEA
▲ WY	WYANDOT

MAP
16

Map labels:

Ft Sinclair Br · Walpole · L Huron · St Clair · Pine · Black · OJ
Lake St Clair · Thames · Pt aux Pins · Lake Erie · Grand · Chagrin · Kettle
OJ · PO OJ · Rouge · PO OJ
Detroit Br · Canard · WY to 1778
Maguagua PO · Huron · Bois Blanc I · Pelee I · Bass Is · Pt Pelee
PO · Sulline Cr
Brownstown WY 1778 · OJ
Raisin
Agushawas OT 1778 · Swan Cr · Sandusky Bay · Tinkers Cr · Cuyahoga
McKees Br 1781 · Portage · Br T 1775-78
Roche de Bout OT · Maumee · Lower Sandusky WY · Rocky · Black · Capt Pipes DE 1777-78
St Joseph · Coldwater · Bean Cr · Huron
Ft St Joseph Br to 1781 · MICHIGAN / OHIO · INDIANA
Parc aux Vaches PO · Little Elkhart · Auglaize · Blanchard
Petit Fort Br to 1780 · Terre Coupee PO · Elkhart MI PO 1781 · OT 1780? · OT to 1779
Kankakee · St Joseph · Eel · St Marys
Yellow · Tippecanoe · Kekionga MI / MI · Ft Miami Br · OT 1780
Snipes 2 WY 1780 · Mohican Johns DE to 1778
Capt Pipes 2 DE 1780 · Half Kings / Upper Sandusky 2 WY 1781 · DE 1781 · Ft Laurens 1778-79
Upper Sandusky WY to 1781 · Darbys 1 MIN to 1780 · New Hell MIN 1776* · Schonbrunn MO to 1777
Captives MO 1781 · WY to 1779 · Snipes 1 WY 1779 · Hell 1 MIN to 1775 / DE MU 1777 · New Schonbrunn
Gnadenhutten MO 1772 · Salem MO
Kenapacomaqua MI · Wabash · Salamonie · Scioto · Kokosing · Coshocton · Newcomers · White Eyes · Lichtenau
Buckongahelas 1 DE 1778 · Solomons MIN 1778 · Zanes WY MIN 1778 · Pluggys MIN to 1779 · Little Shawnee Womans · Walhonding · Tuscarawas
Blue Jackets 2 SH 1778 · Wakatomica 2 SH 1778 · Snakes SH · Conners 1772* SH · Wakatomica 1 SH
Loramies Br · Mequashake SH 1778 · Darbys MIN 1780 · Shawnee Womans SH · to 1774
Deer Cr · Pipe Cr · Wildcat · Wapakoneta 1778 SH
Ouiatenon KI / WE · Piqua 3 SH 1780 · Salt Licks MIN to 1774 · Beavers / Assinink DE
Chillicothe 3 SH 1780 · Big Darby Cr · Olentangy · Muskingum
White R · Stillwater · Mad R · Piqua 2 SH 1777 to 1780 · Mequashake 1 SH
Chillicothe 2 SH 1774 · Lower Shawnee / Kispoko SH · Cornstalks SH
Sugar Cr · Fall Cr · Blue R · Brandywine Cr · Blue Jackets SH · Grenadier Squaw SH
Piqua SH 1773 · Waccachalla SH 1773 · Chillicothe 1 SH · to 1777-78
Great Mm · Little Mm · Paint Cr · Rocking
East Fk · West Fk · Flatrock Cr · Whitewater R · Deer Cr · Scioto Brush Cr
Ohio · Pt Pleasant 1774-75 · Ft Randolph 1777 · VIRGINIA
Horsehead Bottom MIN 1774* · Little Scioto · Guyandotte
DE 1776-81? · Muscatatuck · Eagle Cr · North Fk · Kanawha
KEY MAP
Ruddles Station 1779-80 · KENTUCKY · Big Sandy
Martins Station 1779-80 · Elkhorn · Licking
McClelland's Station 1775-77 · Twin Cr
Squire Boones Station 1775-77 · Leestown 1781 · Bryans Station 1779
Louisville 1779 · Bears Cr · Lexington 1779 · Boonesborough 1774 · Red R
Bashears Station 1779 · McAfees Station 1780 · Kentucky R · Estills Station 1781
Bardstown · Goodwins Station 1780 · Harrodsburg 1774 · Salt R · Dix R
St Asaphs / Logans Fort 1775

cease encroachment on the Indian shore north of the river. Logan, the Mingo leader, refused to attend Dunmore's council and on this occasion delivered an eloquent reply citing the recent loss of his entire family. To punish the Mingo, Dunmore dispatched a small force to attack Salt Lick Town, where five Indians were killed and fourteen prisoners taken, chiefly women and children.

As a consequence of Dunmore's War, Shawnee population distribution in Ohio began to change. The inhabitants of the burned Wakatomica towns left the Muskingum Valley to live in other Shawnee communities of the Scioto River region, and some may have been the first Shawnee on the Mad River where a Wakatomica town was in existence three years later. Chillicothe 1 in the Scioto Valley was partially evacuated by the establishment of Chillicothe 2 near present Xenia, Ohio. Logan joined the militant Mingo at Pluggy's town. Only the Delaware and Moravians were left in eastern Ohio.

The background and details of Dunmore's War have been recounted in order to point out the origin of strife in the Ohio country. Warfare justified on the one hand by white encroachment and on the other by Indian depredations, a recurrent theme in North American history, entered a new geographic area in 1774, the upper Ohio Valley. The first two settlements in Kentucky, Boonesborough and Harrodsburgh, were established the same year, foretelling the future direction of Indian-white hostilities in the Ohio country.

With the confusion at the outbreak of the American Revolution, the preliminary peace at Camp Charlotte was not completed until the Treaty of Pittsburgh was signed in October, 1775. Commissioners from the new Revolutionary government of Virginia and the Continental Congress, along with representatives of the Shawnee, Delaware, and Six Nations, agreed to the Ohio River as the line separating regions of Indian and white settlement, in effect ratifying the boundary established by the British treaty at Fort Stanwix in 1768.

The Delaware Quandary

The Delaware of the upper Muskingum valley, the Indians living closest to the American district command at Pittsburgh, were the first Ohio towns to react to the strains of the American Revolution. Like the Iroquois and Delaware of New York and Pennsylvania, who also lived in a military theatre, these Delaware could not avoid the American Revolution. Although individual choice was evident throughout the Delaware population, some general statements can be made about the varying decisions of the three Delaware divisions. White Eyes and Killbuck of the Turtle division were the most pacific and pro-American Delaware during the Revolutionary War; the Wolf division under Captain Pipe became militant and pro-British; while the Turkey division avoided immediate involvement by migrating westward to the White River region of southern Indiana.

In 1775, Newcomer, leading chief of the Delaware and head of the Turtle division, along with the more martial element left Newcomerstown to establish a new headquarters called Coschocton across the Tuscarawas River from the former site of Wyandot Conchake (see map 9). Newcomers-town

had been an impressive sight in 1772, with sixty or more long houses and some log residences two stories high with cellars, brick fireplaces, and glass windows. Killbuck and a pacifist contingent remained at Newcomerstown, but the community dwindled to twenty houses by 1776.

Custaloga headed the Wolf division hamlets on the Walhonding River until he returned in 1773 to Kuskuskies, Pennsylvania, where he died in 1776. His successor, Captain Pipe or Hopocan, and a Delaware and Munsee following left the Walhonding River in 1777, spending a year at the Cuyahoga Town site before settling near Wyandot, Upper Sandusky. The Wyandot in 1776 had already sent a message to the Delaware urging them to move nearer to Sandusky, where they "had prepared a bed for them." This invitation, or the independent inclination to live at a greater distance from a potential war zone, probably accounts for the movement of other Delaware and some Mingo to watercourses in north central Ohio. The new name "Hell" town was taken from the German word for "light" and had no fiery religious connotation.

In 1776 the future head of the Turkey division, Welandwecken, was already somewhere on the White River of southern Indiana. His group very likely came from Assinink, westernmost Delaware town in the Ohio country, located at the head of the Hocking River (present Lancaster, Ohio) where Turkey clan leader Beaver had settled in 1764. Assinink was probably vacated in 1777 when Captain Johnny, new head of the Turkey clan, returned to the Tuscarawas River and joined the Moravian community. Delaware camps on the lower White River were attacked by George Rogers Clark in March, 1779, after he had taken Vincennes (see map 19). In June, 1779, these Delaware were planning to resettle farther east in Indiana on the Muskatatuck or Driftwood Fork, called by the French the "Embarras."

With the intensification of the American Revolution in 1777, Ohio Indians were caught between the appeals of the British at Detroit and Americans at Pittsburgh and were soon forced out of a neutral stance. Supplied and encouraged by the British at Detroit, the "Lakes Indians" during the summer of 1777 spent their first season of universal warfare against the new Kentucky stations, with followup raids in 1778 netting Daniel Boone as one of their captives. Emotions had been further inflamed in 1777 by the murder of Cornstalk, Mequashake leader of the Shawnee, who with his sister the Grenadier Squaw had shown an unusually friendly attitude toward Americans ever since the peace conference at Camp Charlotte. His death at the hands of mutinous troops during a visit to Fort Randolph outraged many American leaders as well as Indian communities.

In 1777 and 1778 there was also a general exodus of Shawnee towns from the Scioto River valley, mainly toward the upper Mad River region. Piqua 2, however, located on the lower Mad River directly north of Chillicothe 2, established in 1774 at the time of Dunmore's War. One group of pacific Mequashake moved back to the Muskingum Valley temporarily in 1778, a detail omitted from the already complex map, but by 1779 were also on the upper Mad River. A definite time for some of these transfers is difficult to assign. An advance party usually set out to establish a new base and people left one town and settled in a new town

The Ohio River near Fort Randolph. From Schoolcraft, History of the Indian Tribes of the United States, pt. 6, p. 312. The Newberry Library.

by stages, so probably there was some time overlap. They also might return to a vacated town to plant corn.

Partisan Action and Reaction

In the spring of 1778 the Ohio Indians acquired further attachment to the British regime in Detroit when Alexander McKee, already suspected of Loyalist sympathies, and two other former members of the British Indian service secretly left Pittsburgh for Detroit. The changing allegiance of these influential people had a significant impact on the attitude of Indians in this section of the Great Lakes frontier. Alexander McKee, who immediately took over the direction of the British Indian service in Detroit, had family ties with the Kispoko, most conspicuously militant division of the Shawnee. His companion Matthew Elliott had traded in the Piqua town and fought with the Shawnee at the Battle of Point Pleasant.

Simon Girty, third member of the party leaving Pittsburgh in March, 1778, was one of three brothers who had been Indian captives as children during the French and Indian War-Simon with the Seneca, James with the Shawnee, and George with the Delaware. They brought a thorough familiarity with Indian life and knowledge of several Indian languages to the British headquarters at Detroit. The trio from Pittsburgh picked up James Girty in the Shawnee country on their way to Detroit and secured for him an appointment as British interpreter before he returned to his Shawnee family. George, the third Girty brother, was still on the side of the Continental cause dur-

ing the summer of 1778 as part of the Willing expedition that descended the Mississippi River to attack British plantations in the Natchez District of Louisiana. During the return trip, he took off and joined his Delaware family among the pro-British Indians.

By 1778, Indian population movements closer to Detroit gave further evidence of the increasing war posture. Wyandot moved from the Ontario side of the Detroit River to the Michigan shore south of fortified Detroit. Part of the Ottawa transferred to Ouiatenon, temporarily joining Wea and Kickapoo on the Wabash River. In northwestern Ohio, Ottawa advanced south on the Auglaize River to occupy a strategic site at the northern end of the portage route to the Great Miami River. At the other end of the portage stood Lorimer's trading post, established in 1769 by a member of an old French-Canadian trading family. In northeastern Ohio the British set up a trading base on the lower Cuyahoga River.

The first Kentucky retaliation against the punishing attacks of the "Lakes" Indians came in 1779 with Bowman's rather ineffective raid on Chillicothe 2, the Indian town most accessible to Kentuckians who generally rendezvoused at the mouth of the Licking River. After the Henry Bird expedition of Indians and British Rangers into Kentucky in 1780, carrying away 305 prisoners, George Rogers Clark brought cannon against both Chillicothe 2 and Piqua 2. These towns, usually located within easy communication distance of each other, moved next to third locations in Ohio on the Great Miami River near present Piqua.

Meanwhile, in 1778 the Delaware nation still looked chiefly to the American revolutionary government for protection and supplies of the kinds of goods usually acquired through normal Indian trade. American authorities were in a position to intensify war efforts after one of Clark's personal lieutenants made his way up the Ohio River to Pittsburgh in the spring of 1777 with military supplies made available by the Spanish governor in New Orleans the previous fall. At the fourth Treaty of Pittsburgh in 1778, the Delaware entered into a formal American alliance, looking forward to a joint march on British-held Detroit and the establishment of a Delaware state within the American confederation. They permitted the erection of American-garrisoned Fort Laurens near the former site of Tuscarawas town and within the Indian country, a step particularly opposed by the Wyandot, who harassed and virtually isolated the post. Troops were withdrawn the next year, 1779, for Brodhead's campaign into Pennsylvania during a momentary high tide of American status (see map 14). Even the Wyandot seemed inclined toward a pro-American position, but still would not permit Continental troops to march overland across Ohio to attack Detroit.

The Delaware-American alliance was weakened by the death of the friendly leader White Eyes in 1778, actually a murder concealed by official reports of "small pox." Furthermore, American authorities never were able to furnish the requisite supplies for the Delaware. The situation became more difficult after Simon Girty and an Indian party captured the second Spanish shipment of supplies destined for Pittsburgh by waylaying the leaders near present Cincinnati in July, 1779. By 1781 the majority of the Delaware felt forced to make their peace with the British because Americans could not provide them with necessary goods. Captain Pipe, who had signed the treaty of alliance in 1778, was living near the Wyandots at Upper Sandusky by 1780. Though Brodhead had received an honorary title from the Delaware in 1778, he led the expedition, including a persistently pro-American Delaware faction, against Delaware living at Coshocton and Lichtenau in April, 1781 (see map 14). Lichtenau had been a Moravian settlement initially, but was taken over by Delaware after the Moravians returned to New Schonbrun on the Tuscarawas in 1780.

Brodheads' expedition brought about the final evacuation of the Muskingum Valley. In the spring of 1781, Delaware either joined the Wyandot settlements at Upper Sandusky or augmented the Delaware population of Buckongahelas town on the headwaters of the Mad River, often

called "New Coshocton." The long and circuitous odyssey of the Moravians began again in 1781. Feeling that disadvantageous information was reaching American authorities at Pittsburgh by way of the Moravian missionaries' leaders, the Wyandot and Captain Pipe determined to take the Moravians under their protection. The Moravians were precipitously escorted to Upper Sandusky and assigned a location they called Captive Town, where they remained only a year before moving to Michigan (see chart no. 1). As a result, all the Delaware and Moravians of eastern Ohio had found new homes before Williamson led an expedition to burn their vacated towns in the fall of 1781.

The northwest corner of the map includes action in the country of the St. Joseph River Potawatomi. Here antipathies were more concerned with domination of the Indian trade than the issues of the American Revolution. The community at Fort St. Joseph (present Niles) consisted of a British military post and about ten houses belonging to French families engaged in agriculture and the Indian trade, maintaining traditional trading connections with French merchants in Cahokia. After the Franco-American alliance in 1779, the British general at Mackinac ordered the removal of the French traders in St. Joseph. In December of 1780, a British and Potawatomi party overtook a French contingent from Cahokia that had recently sacked Fort St. Joseph. The Cahokians suffered heavy losses at the small fortification erected at the mouth of Trail Creek. Two months later, a larger expedition sponsored by the Spanish commandant at St. Louis drove the British from Fort St. Joseph, holding this military position for a day before returning to St. Louis. Guide for the expedition was Louis Chevalier, Jr., a member of the Spanish militia in St. Louis and son of the principal trader at Fort St. Joseph. Later in 1781, Miami and Potawatomi established the important village of Elkhart farther upstream on a tributary of the St. Joseph River near present Waterford, Pulaski County, Indiana.

Principal Sources: Bushnell 1919; Butterfield 1890; Crevecoeur 1787; De Peyster 1888; Downes 1940; Hanna 1911; Heckewelder 1820; Hildreth 1848; James 1912; Jones 1865; Kellogg 1916, 1917; Morgan MSS 1776-1778; MPHC (10) 1888; Smyth 1784; Stone 1974; Talbert 1962; Thwaites and Kellogg 1905, 1908, 1912; Voegelin 1941, 1962, 1974c; Zeisberger 1885.

FRONTIER IN TRANSITION 1782-1786:
THE OHIO COUNTRY AND CANADA, Map 17

Highlights of the five-year period covered by this map are: (1) movement in and out of the Upper Sandusky region, (2) destruction of the Shawnee towns, and (3) population expansion north and south of Detroit and down the Ohio River.

Two more moves were plotted for the frequently dislodged Moravians brought to Captives Town on the Sandusky River in 1781 (map 16). Their numbers decreased in the spring. of 1782 when about ninety, who had returned to the Tuscarawas River to collect food stores, were surprised and killed by Colonel David Williamson's militia party in the incident known as the "Gnadenhütten Massacre" (map 14). Most of the remaining Moravians were escorted to Detroit under British protection. They next established New Gnadenhütten on the Clinton River near present Mount Clemens, Michigan, with permission of the local Ojibwa. By 1786, however, they were no longer welcome and moved back south of Lake Erie in July, remaining ten months at Pilgeruh on the Cuyahoga River, site of an Ottawa town in the 1740s (map 9).

A few Mahican from Captives Town split off and established a small settlement known as Mahican Town, and later as Stephenstown, on the north bank of the St. Marys River opposite Rockford in Mercer County, Ohio. The Moravians had all left the Upper Sandusky region before the Wyandot towns became the target of a Kentucky expedition led by William Crawford with Williamson as second in command in June, 1782. Captured by Delaware during a confused retreat, Crawford was burned at the stake in retaliation for the Gnadenhütten Massacre.

The Wyandot community at Upper Sandusky, already reinforced by Captain Pipe's Delaware and Munsee following, added a Turkey division Delaware town near Captain Pipes in 1782. Lower Sandusky (present Fremont), chief Wyandot town in Ohio during the American Revolution, became an important center for British traders. Here in September, 1783, a meeting was held to form a general Indian confederacy with representation of all the nearby "Lakes" tribes, the Six Nations, and delegates from the Creek and Cherokee.

A prominent feature of this stage of Indian population movement in the Ohio country is the cluster of towns on the headwaters of the Great Miami and Mad rivers hit by Kentucky expeditions in 1782 and 1786. Although the principal formation was away from the main thoroughfares, Piqua 3 and Chillicothe 3 and their associated settlements lay on the well-traveled Miami River course. This configuration had developed during the previous five years with Waketamica 2, two miles south of present Zanesfield, as the headquarters.

The attack on the Great Miami towns in November, 1782, was a response to the defeat of Kentuckians earlier in the year at Blue Licks (see map 14). The area vacated included about half a dozen Shawnee settlements, of which three are mapped, and Lorimer's Post, the major supply depot established in 1769 at the south end of the portage to the Auglaize and St. Marys rivers (map 9). Chillicothe 3 or Standing Stone village, occupying the 1752 site of Pickawillany (present Piqua), moved north to the portage point on the St. Marys River (present St. Marys). This town was sometimes called "New Chillicothe," but became better known as Girty's Town, residence of the trader James Girty.

The remaining population from the Great Miami region enlarged the Shawnee component on the upper Mad in southern Logan and northern Champaign counties. Piqua 3 located at present West Liberty. The Mequashake division had a double town straddling Mequaschaik Creek east of present West Liberty. Kispoko 2, also Alexander McKee's Town, was situated on present McKee's Creek; Blue Jacket lived at present Bellefontaine. The single Delaware town in this complex was headed by Buckongahelas of the Wolf division, son of Wandochale who had lived briefly on the Scioto in the 1750s before joining other Delaware on the Walhonding (map 9).

Zanestown (present Zanesfield) belonged to Isaac Zane, who had been captured about 1760 and had married the daughter of a Wyandot chief. Solomon's town had originally been founded by Mingo, but became a predominantly Wyandot settlement, reported headquarters of Simon Girty of the British Indian department in Detroit. Beginning in 1782, the military strength of the Ohio Indian frontier was augmented by Cherokee warriors of the Chicamauga district who joined the Shawnee at Old Chillicothe on Paint Creek and the mixed population around Zanestown.

Several population movements of this five-year period were based on reactions to the outcome of the American Revolution. The British retained Detroit despite the terms of the Treaty of Paris in 1783. As a consequence, many French families left the immediate vicinity of Detroit, spreading northward along the St. Clair River and south around the western end of Lake Erie. The narrow French "ribbon farms," with orchards and windmills, had lined the riverbanks for decades, but this migration produced new population concentrations. Frenchtown (present Monroe) at the mouth of the Raisin River developed into a significant community by 1785.

Ogontz, a northern Michigan Ottawa trained in Quebec as a priest, led a movement from the Canadian shore to Sandusky Bay in 1784, remaining until 1811. Ogontz located at the site of present Sandusky, Ohio. His Ottawa following

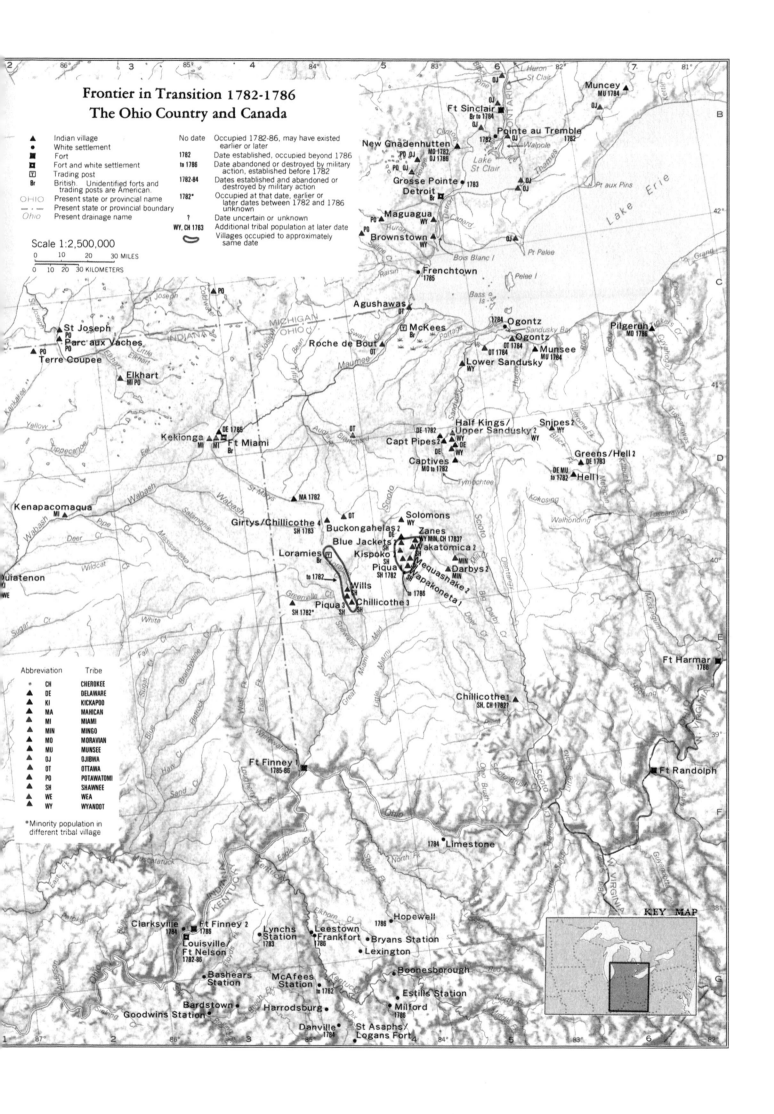

Frontier in Transition 1782-1786
The Ohio Country and Canada

▲	Indian village
●	White settlement
■	Fort
⬟	Fort and white settlement
T	Trading post
Br	British. Unidentified forts and trading posts are American.
OHIO	Present state or provincial name
—·—·—	Present state or provincial boundary
Ohio	Present drainage name

No date	Occupied 1782-86, may have existed earlier or later
1782	Date established, occupied beyond 1786
to 1786	Date abandoned or destroyed by military action, established before 1782
1782-84	Dates established and abandoned or destroyed by military action
1782*	Occupied at that date, earlier or later dates between 1782 and 1786 unknown
?	Date uncertain or unknown
WY, CH 1783	Additional tribal population at later date
⌣	Villages occupied to approximately same date

Scale 1:2,500,000

0 10 20 30 MILES

0 10 20 30 KILOMETERS

Abbreviation / Tribe

Abbreviation	Tribe
CH	CHEROKEE
DE	DELAWARE
KI	KICKAPOO
MA	MAHICAN
MI	MIAMI
MIN	MINGO
MO	MORAVIAN
MU	MUNSEE
OJ	OJIBWA
OT	OTTAWA
PO	POTAWATOMI
SH	SHAWNEE
WE	WEA
WY	WYANDOT

*Minority population in different tribal village

MAP
17

KEY MAP

Alexander McKee, Shawnee trader and Indian agent, who supported allied Indian attacks on Kentucky frontiersmen after he joined the British service in Detroit in 1778. Oil portrait. Clements Library.

extended along the south side of Sandusky Bay as far west as Pickerel Creek, site of Wyandot Sunyeneand in 1755 (see inset, map 9). The twenty to thirty French families accompanying Ogontz settled on the peninsula north of Sandusky Bay.

Toward the end of the American Revolution and immediately after the announcement of peace with Great Britain, frontier people swarmed into Kentucky and squat-ted on Indian land north of the Ohio. George Rogers Clark's people moved north of the Ohio River to found Clarksville in Indiana in 1784. The same year, Limestone (present Maysville) became the Ohio River port of entry for settlers arriving by boat rather than the overland trail to establish new stations in northern Kentucky.

Fort Harmar at the mouth of the Muskingum River, completed in 1786, marks the tentative beginning of future American control of the Ohio country. Fort Finney 1 at the mouth of the Great Miami River had a brief existence to accommodate Shawnee and American delegations holding a treaty in January, 1786, subsequently declared invalid by the Indian confederacy. Later in the year Major Finney moved down the Ohio River to the site of present Jefferson-ville, Indiana, establishing a second Fort Finney officially named Fort Steuben in 1787, not be confused with the development of present Steubenville, Ohio.

Most of the Shawnee appeared inclined toward peace in 1786 despite the coercion evident during treaty negotia-tions at Fort Finney 1, yet attacks on the Kentucky stations continued, principally from the direction of the Wabash River. Nevertheless, Logan's expedition in November struck the Shawnee towns at the head of the Mad River while their warriors were absent defending Indian towns on the Wabash against an expected attack by Clark that did not materialize. The peaceable Mequashake chief Melunthe, leader of the Shawnee at the Fort Finney council, was cap-tured and killed. The prisoners, principally women and children, were taken back to Kentucky. The Indian confed-eracy meeting in Detroit in December, 1786, sent a renewed demand that the United States respect the Ohio River boundary line. The new military headquarters for the confederacy became the Miami Towns at present Fort Wayne, Indiana. Some Shawnee, however, went to south-ern Indiana. Other Shawnee who had conferred with Span-ish authorities in St. Louis in 1784, began to carry out plans to move into Spanish Louisiana (see map 19).

Principal Sources: Askin 1931; Burnett 1967; Butterfield 1873; Dillon 1859; Dodge 1859; MPHC (10) 1888, (11) 1888, (20) 1892, (24) 1895, (25) 1896; Talbert 1972; Tan-ner 1974b, c; Voegelin 1974c, d; Zeisberger, 1885.

The line of American forts marching northward in western Ohio is the most eye-catching feature of this map emphasizing the Indian War (1791-94) leading up to the Treaty of Greenville in 1795. Through the year 1791 the chief military objective of these forts was the "Miami Towns" (present Fort Wayne, Indiana) at the head of the Maumee River, where Delaware and Shawnee joined the Miami between 1785 and 1790. In 1792, following the expeditions of Harmar in 1790 and St. Clair in 1791, headquarters for the Indian confederacy transferred downstream about forty-five miles to the mouth of the Auglaize River (Defiance, Ohio). This later grouping of Indian towns, along with allies assembled lower on the Maumee near the rapids, became the target of General Anthony Wayne's successful campaign in 1794. The climactic engagement, the Battle of Fallen Timbers, occurred August 24 immediately west of the second Fort Miami built by the British in 1794 near present Maumee, Ohio (see also map 14).

The chronology of events preceding this final stage of warfare over the Ohio country began in the spring of 1787 with peaceful overtures for the exchange of prisoners between Kentuckians and the Shawnee. Daniel Boone initiated contacts leading to a festive council with music and dancing at his tavern in Limestone (Maysville), Kentucky, in August. Speeches made by Captain Johnny, leader of the peace faction among the Shawnee towns, and Benjamin Logan, leader of the 1786 Kentucky expedition against the Shawnee towns on the Mad River were reported in the *Kentucky Gazette*.

Captain Johnny had spent about two months early in 1787 traveling over an unknown route to Shawnee camps scattered throughout the Wabash country of Indiana in order to collect white prisoners. At the Limestone council he stated that all of his Mequashake towns and about half of the Chillicothe, Piqua, Kispoko, and Wakatomica towns looked forward to returning where their homes had been burned (i.e., the Mad River) and living in peaceful trade with the "Big Knives." Their five towns would be distinct from the hostile element remaining on the Wabash River. Benjamin Logan promised that if they lived in peace, no Kentucky expedition would be sent against the Shawnee.

Shawnee Dispersal

Despite these pacific announcements, Chillicothe 1 on Paint Creek was attacked late in the fall of 1787, and the inhabitants fled to the lower White River (see map 19). At the evacuation of Paint Creek, southern Ohio was cleared of stable Indian communities, but was still used for hunting and planting in support of war parties patrolling the Ohio River in an effort to prevent further white settlement. Indian raids on isolated Kentucky homes and riverboats continued; captives in 1788 included Thomas Rideout, subsequently surveyor-general of Canada. Captain Johnny by 1789 had established a town at "The Glaize," the term identifying an ancient buffalo wallow, at the juncture of the Maumee and present Auglaize rivers in northwestern Ohio. His town was the nucleus of the multi-tribal cluster that became prominent in 1792 after the desertion of the Miami Towns locale.

The movements of other Shawnee dispersed following Benjamin Logan's expedition of 1786 can be partially traced. Some of the Kispoko division lived several years with the Chicamauga Cherokee on the Tennessee River near the Alabama-Georgia border. Part of the Shawnee who had maintained frequent communication with Spanish authorities in St. Louis since 1784 crossed the Mississippi to the Cape Girardeau region of Spanish Louisiana. Although Captain Johnny stated at Limestone that it took him two months to make contact with the scattered Shawnee in the Wabash country, only two towns on the lower White River can be definitely located; one, already cited, composed of refugees hum Chillicothe 1 on Paint Creek (see map 19). In 1788 Shawnee, probably from the White River country, emerged to establish Chillicothe 5 on the Maumee River a few miles east of Fort Miami. Piqua 5 followed in early 1790. These were the last towns added to the Miami Towns complex that had grown from two to seven towns since 1785.

The Miami Towns

Central to the Miami Towns complex were the two Miami villages located on the east and west banks of the St. Joseph River where it joins with the St. Marys to form the Maumee River. Kekionga, on the west bank, the oldest Miami town, had long been the home base for Pacanne, while the younger Le Gris was leader at the town on the east bank identified on the map by an arrow adjacent to Fort Miami. The town named "Le Gris" on the map is a newer settlement established by Le Gris in 1792 when the neighboring communities left the area. Although Kekionga was considered Pacanne's town, in 1790 the principal figure was Richardville, son of a deceased Three Rivers, Quebec, merchant and a Miami woman who took over management of his Indian trade. Since Pacanne himself favored peaceful relations with the Americans, he moved to Vincennes in 1784, beginning a period of oscillation between the Wabash and Mississippi rivers (see map 19). Situated next to Le Gris's town, Fort Miami in 1790 contained about a dozen homes of French families and a few British with trading connections in Detroit, all guarded by a contingent of Canadian volunteers. In a convivial atmosphere, traders often entertained Indian

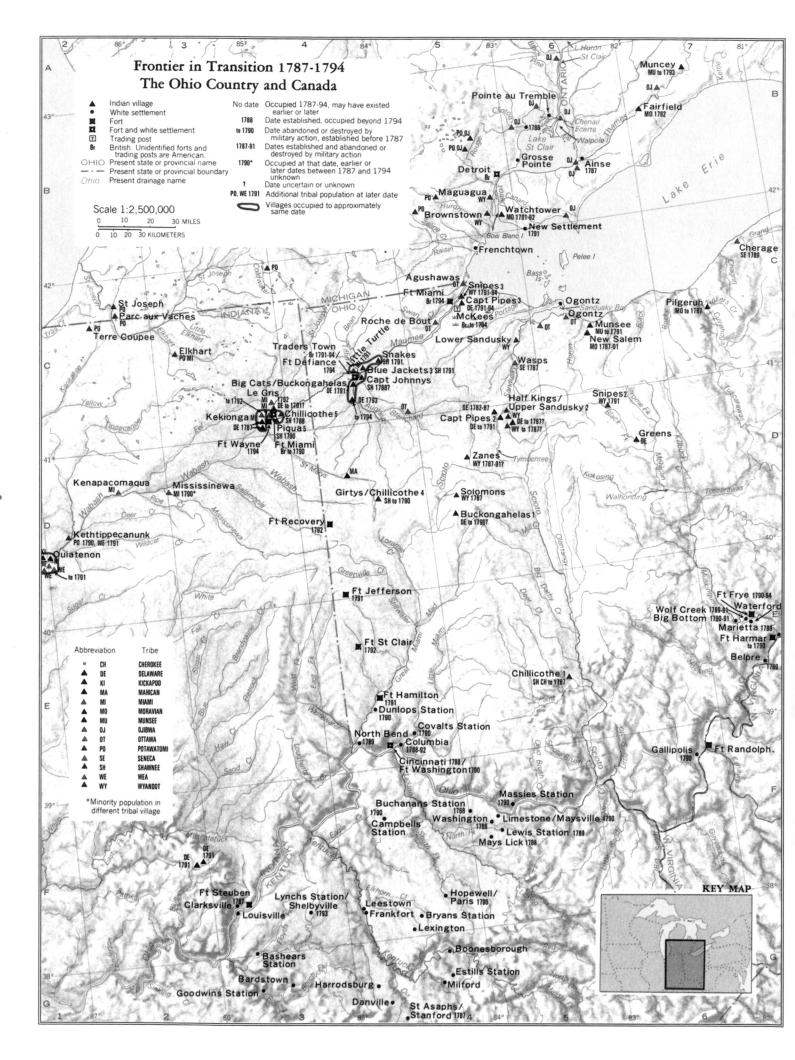

Frontier in Transition 1787-1794
The Ohio Country and Canada

▲ Indian village
● White settlement
■ Fort
⊞ Fort and white settlement
⊡ Trading post
Br British. Unidentified forts and trading posts are American.
OHIO Present state or provincial name
— · — · — Present state or provincial boundary
Ohio Present drainage name

No date Occupied 1787-94, may have existed earlier or later
1788 Date established, occupied beyond 1794
to 1790 Date abandoned or destroyed by military action, established before 1787
1787-91 Dates established and abandoned or destroyed by military action
1790* Occupied at that date, earlier or later dates between 1787 and 1794 unknown
? Date uncertain or unknown
PO, WE 1791 Additional tribal population at later date
⬭ Villages occupied to approximately same date

Scale 1:2,500,000

0   10   20   30 MILES
0   10   20   30 KILOMETERS

MAP
18

Abbreviation	Tribe
● CH	CHEROKEE
▲ DE	DELAWARE
▲ KI	KICKAPOO
▲ MA	MAHICAN
▲ MI	MIAMI
■ MO	MORAVIAN
▲ MU	MUNSEE
▲ OJ	OJIBWA
▲ OT	OTTAWA
▲ PO	POTAWATOMI
▲ SE	SENECA
▲ SH	SHAWNEE
▲ WE	WEA
▲ WY	WYANDOT

*Minority population in different tribal village

KEY MAP

Muncey MU to 1793
Fairfield MO 1792
Cherage SE 1789
Pointe au Tremble
Grosse Pointe
Ainse 1787
Detroit Br
Maguagua WY
Watchtower MO 1791-92
New Settlement 1791
Brownstown WY
Frenchtown
Agushawas
Ft Miami Br 1794
Snipes 3 WY 1791-94
Capt Pipes 3 DE 1791-94
McKees Br to 1794
Roche de Bout OT
Lower Sandusky WY
Ogontz
Ogontz
Munsee MU 1791
New Salem MO 1787-91
Pilgeruh MO to 1787
St Joseph PO
Parc aux Vaches PO
Terre Coupee PO
Elkhart PO MI
Traders Town Br 1791-94
Ft Defiance 1794
Little Turtle ? 1790
Snakes SH 1791
Blue Jackets 3 SH 1791
Capt Johnnys SH 1788?
Wasps SE 1787
Snipes 2 WY 1791
Big Cats/Buckongahelas DE 1791
Le Gris MI to 1792
Kekionga DE 1787
Chillicothe 5 SH 1788
Piqua 5 SH 1790
Ft Wayne 1794
Ft Miami Br to 1790
Half Kings/Upper Sandusky 2 WY
Capt Pipes 2 DE 1782-87, DE 1791
Greens DE
Zanes WY 1787-91?
Kenapacomaqua MI
Mississinewa MI 1790*
Girtys/Chillicothe 4 SH to 1790
Solomons WY 1787
Buckongahelas 1 DE to 1790?
Ft Recovery 1792
Kethtippecanunk PO 1790, WE 1791
Ouiatenon to 1791
Ft Jefferson 1791
Ft Frye 1790-94
Waterford
Wolf Creek 1789-91
Big Bottom 1790-91
Marietta 1788
Ft Harmar to 1790
Belpre 1789
Ft St Clair 1792
Chillicothe 1 SH CH to 1787
Ft Hamilton 1791
Dunlops Station 1790
Covalts Station 1790
North Bend 1789
Columbia 1788-92
Cincinnati 1788/Ft Washington 1790
Gallipolis 1790
Ft Randolph
Massies Station 1790
Buchanans Station 1790
Washington 1788
Limestone/Maysville 1790
Campbells Station
Lewis Station 1789
Mays Lick 1788
DE 1791
DE 1791
Hopewell/Paris 1790
Ft Steuben 1786
Clarksville
Louisville
Lynchs Station/Shelbyville 1793
Leestown
Frankfort
Bryans Station
Lexington
Boonesborough
Bashears Station
Bardstown
Harrodsburg
Estills Station
Milford
Goodwins Station
Danville
St Asaphs/Stanford 1787

leaders at breakfast, and danced, sang, and played card games in the evening.

The increase in the Miami Towns began in 1785 when the Delaware sought refuge with the Miami, establishing their first town north of Fort Miami on the east bank of the St. Joseph River. In 1787, two more Delaware towns located nearby on the St. Marys River, one new group being the Turkey division that had been living near Captain Pipe's village at Upper Sandusky. The Miami were already feeling crowded before the addition of segments of two Shawnee divisions, the Chillicothe in 1788 and Piqua in 1790.

Seneca and Loyalist Immigrants

While the population concentration at the Miami Towns was under way between 1787 and 1790, notable developments were in progress in other sections of the Ohio country and in Canada. Seneca under the leadership of the Wasp came west to establish a new town on the Sandusky River midway between the Wyandots at Lower and Upper Sandusky. Two years later, 1789, another Seneca community was in existence at the mouth of the Grand River near the present Ohio-Pennsylvania border. By 1787, twenty-eight families of English, German, French, and Indian heritage were settled at the site of modern Chatham, Ontario, in a community called Sally Ainse's, or, less accurately, Sally Hand's. Widow of a British Indian interpreter, Sally Ainse was a member of the influential Montour family, with relatives among the Iroquois and Delaware. Other families settled at intervals along the Thames River. The first authorized town in this region of Ontario was the New Settlement (Colchester) formed in 1791 by a group of British Loyalists granted new homesites in an area surrendered to the British government by the Missisauga and Ojibwa in 1790 (see map 30). Here the Loyalists were near the farms of members of the British Indian department who in 1784 had acquired Indian land on the east bank of the Detroit River near the entrance to Lake Erie. This small white population lived in harmony with Indians of the region.

Land and Treaty Projects

More disturbing to Indian people were the organized efforts of the American government and land speculators to take over Indian land between the Muskingum and Great Miami rivers. Presuming that the Treaty of Fort McIntosh in 1785 was a valid Indian land cession, Congress enacted the Northwest Ordinance in 1787. Settlement began the following year at Marietta, across the Muskingum River from Fort Harmar. Arthur St. Clair, governor of the Northwest Territory, proclaimed the organization of Washington County on July 26, 1788. Yet, em July 2, Congress appropriated funds to negotiate with the Indians for purchase of the Ohio district from which Washington County was created. In June, supplies had been sent sixty miles up the Muskingum (present Duncan Falls) for new treaty and boundary discussions necessitated by revised federal policy acknowledging Indian "rights to the soil."

Surrounded by evidence of hostility, the negotiators had made little progress at the falls of the Muskingum by August, 1788. In September, Cornstalk and a Six Nations delegation more amenable to a land cession came to Fort Harmar with an escort of soldiers from Fort Pitt; yet Brant and a more resistant Six Nations faction insisted in November on holding councils at the original site. Finally, in mid-December, about two hundred Indians came to Fort Harmar, and on January 9, 1789, two treaties were signed, one by the Six Nations representation and the other by Ohio Wyandot and Delaware along with some Ottawa, Chippewa, and Potawatomi.

The Fort Harmar treaties were intended to legalize land sales already completed and settlements already in existence. The Marietta community of 52 families and 157 single men, the first American town in the Northwest Territory, was the population center for the Ohio Company, organized by New Englanders who contracted with Congress for almost a million acres of land between the Muskingum and Hocking rivers, at two-thirds of a dollar per acre. Closely following this project, John Cleves Symmes and associates planned to develop a million acres of land between the Great and Little Miami rivers in southwestern Ohio. In late December, 1788, the first party arrived at the site of Cincinnati, temporarily called Losantiville.

The advance of white settlement north of the Ohio River brought easterners into the region, but also represented the expansion of population from northern Kentucky. The federal census for 1790 reported seventy-three thousand people in the Kentucky district that had counted barely four hundred in 1774. By 1790, additional settlements existed up the Muskingum and down the Ohio. In October, French emigrants founded Gallipolis.

Indian War Renewed

When the western Indian confederacy as a whole refused to give up land northwest of the Ohio River, Americans turned again to military force in the fall of 1790. From Ft. Washington, the new post at Cincinnati, General Josiah Harmar marched to the Miami Towns occupied by Miami, Delaware, and Shawnee who had refused to attend the treaty negotiations at Fort Harmar in 1788-1789 (see map 14). Before his arrival, residents fled temporarily toward the Elkhart River, but returned to rebuild some of the homes. The beginning of the permanent evacuation of the Miami Towns at the head of the Maumee River is observable on the map with the appearance of a new community at the mouth of the Mississinewa River. The Indian confederacy's reaction to military force was general warfare that erupted in the spring of 1791 and continued until Indian defeat in 1794.

The onset of the Indian War (1791-94) is reflected in all sections of the map. Delaware and probably Shawnee began to move out of the Miami Towns. Delaware on the White River in southern Indiana in 1791 were probably at the first stage of further migration to Spanish Louisiana, though Delaware were consistently reported in the White River region in the 1790s. The Moravians at New Salem, alarmed over the state of warfare, crossed Lake Erie to the mouth of the Detroit River, remaining one winter at Watch-

Striking the Warpost, preparatory to going into battle. From Schoolcraft, *History of the Indian Tribes of the United States,* pt. 3, p. 64. The Newberry Library.

tower before moving to a more permanent location at Fairfield, near present Thamesville, Ontario. Zane's largely Wyandot community, shown on this map north of their 1786 location at a place called Beaver Dams, spent an interval of time during the war years at Upper Sandusky before returning to their Zanesfield site after 1794.

By the winter 1791-92, some Miami, Shawnee, and Delaware were moving downstream on the Maumee to new towns near Captain Johnny's at the mouth of the Auglaize River. Buckongahelas, whose town on the upper Mad River escaped Benjamin Logan's 1786 expedition, probably arrived at The Glaize about this time. At the new village, a sage councillor was Big Cat or Whingapuchees, one of the actively pro-American Delaware of the Muskingum valley during the early years of the Revolutionary War. The Snake had earlier headed one of the Shawnee Wakatomica towns destroyed by McDonald's expedition in 1774 (see map 16). War leaders of the three principal tribes at The Glaize were Little Turtle of the Miami, Blue Jacket of the Shawnee, and Buckongahelas of the Delaware. On the point of land at the west bank of the mouth of the Auglaize River, traders from Fort Miami set up their homes and storehouses near a stockade protecting the British supply depot.

Contemporary records refer to additional Delaware as well as Nanticoke, Conoy (Piscataway), Mingo, Cherokee, Creek, and a number of white captives at The Glaize in 1792. No other towns can be mapped except for the Delaware town about 15 miles from the mouth of the

Auglaize that appeared shortly before Wayne began to advance north from Fort Recovery, an outpost reported under construction in 1792 but not significantly used until late in 1793. In the light of evidence discovered by the first settlers at Van Wert, Ohio, it seems likely that a hidden town existed at that location for several years about 1790 (see map 33).

In conjunction with the new concentration of Indian population at The Glaize, a secondary line of defense was assembled near the Ottawa at the mouth of the Maumee River. Captain Pipe, who had been present at the Fort Harmar treaty, brought his people from Upper Sandusky. The Snipe's Wyandot and Mingo following moved from the Mohican River east of Upper Sandusky. On the lower Maumee, allied Indians were close to the trading post at "the Rapids" maintained by Alexander McKee of the British Indian department. These moves were part of military defense strategy.

Actual warfare accounts for other changes recorded on the map for the years 1791-94. Indian attacks such as the "Big Bottom massacre" on Wolf Creek forced the abandonment of isolated stations and the "forting up" of all settlements north of the Ohio River. Inhabitants of Marietta were confined behind palisades until the conclusion of the war. During 1791, Fort Hamilton and Fort Jefferson were erected, advancing the line of military posts north of Cincinnati. In June and August, Charles Scott and James Wilkinson led expeditions against the Wabash Indian towns. Although both expeditions missed the Mississinewa town of Miami, and the Wea reoccupied their traditional site, the Kickapoo left Ouiatenon permanently in 1791 and were found lower on the Wabash near the mouth of the Vermilion River (see map 19). The defeat of General Arthur St. Clair in November, the worst ever experienced by American forces, marked the high point of Indian military success during the war.

Directing the overall campaign from Philadelphia, Secretary of War Henry Knox utilized diplomatic as well as military strategy as means to achieve peace and more Indian land on the northwest frontier. He called to Philadelphia for consultation Colonel Lewis Cook, Mohawk leader of Black and Abenaki heritage, who had been commissioned in the American service during the Revolutionary War. Joseph Brant also came for a conference, and was persuaded that a sacrifice of already-settled land east of the Muskingum might solve conflicting demands of the equally adamant American republic and Indian confederacy. American peace commissioners from 1791 to 1793 circuited north of the contested area, traveling first to the Six Nations community at Buffalo Creek, New York (map 20), then across Lake Erie to the mouth of the Detroit River in territory still under Indian and British control.

The Indian confederacy conducted independent diplomatic negotiations. In October of 1792, The Glaize was the scene of a crucial inter-tribal council preceded by preliminary missions among Great Lakes and southern Indian villages and a further defense buildup. One hundred canoes of Ojibwa and Ottawa Indians came down across Lake Huron to Detroit. Another canoe appeared, carrying members of an unknown tribe still ignorant of the use of firearms who had come "three moons" distance from the northwest. The British Indian agents prevented American emissaries from ever meeting the Indian confederacy leaders, though correspondence was exchanged locally. The ultimate decision of the confederacy was to retain their demand for the Ohio River boundary. Leaders suggested that the American government use its money to pay poor settlers to leave the land rather than trying to buy land from Indians who had no need for money.

American diplomatic missions did not impress the Indians as much as the new army mobilizing in the fall of

1792 at Pittsburgh, under the command of Major General Anthony Wayne. A year later, Wayne's legion advanced to a headquarters camp called Greenville six miles north of Fort Jefferson. His rapid descent of the Auglaize River in the summer of 1794, aided by Chickasaw and Choctaw scouts, gained him the name "Big Wind" among the Indians. On the site of the traders' town at The Glaize he built Fort Defiance. His army then pursued the inter-tribal force of wavering numbers down the Maumee. The gates of Fort Miami, newly-built by the British, were closed against the Indian warriors and they received no last-minute British military support. Following the Battle of Fallen Timbers on August 20, 1794, the Indian people retreated to the mouth of Swan Creek (present Toledo). General Wayne reversed his direction and ascended the Maumee to the former Miami towns site, where he built Fort Wayne, the new advance post for American control of the Great Lakes Region.

The success of the combined American army and Kentucky militia, along with the knowledge that the British would have to evacuate Detroit by terms of the Jay Treaty (map 12D) gradually convinced individual Indian leaders to make preliminary peace. The next summer, 1,130 Indian people gathered at Wayne's former army headquarters, Greenville, Ohio, for the formal treaty ceding two-thirds of Ohio, territory long desired by American land promoters. On August 8, 1795, the Treaty of Greenville ending the Indian war was signed by representatives of the Wyandot, Shawnee, Delaware, Chippewa, Ottawa, Potawatomi, Miami, Wea, Piankeshaw, Kickapoo, and Kaskaskia. In addition to the principal cession, the Indians surrendered sixteen tracts at strategic locations in the remaining unceded territory of the Great Lakes Region (see map 30).

Principal Sources: American State Papers 1832; Askin 1928; Aupaumut 1827; Brickell 1842; Carter 1934; Fliegel 1970; Heckewelder 1884; Hildreth 1848; Kentucky Gazette 1787; Lindley 1892; Morgan 1778; MPHC (17) 1892, (24) 1895; Mueller 1963; Putnam 1903; Rideout 1890; Roads 1888; Simcoe 1923-31; W. Smith 1882; Spencer 1968 ; Tanner 1974b, 1978;]. Tanner 1956; Voegelin 1974c, d; Wayne 1940; Whittlesey 1867.

Although clearly a part of a larger "frontier in transition," the Illinois Country differed from the more easterly regions mapped in this series. While the tribes of present New York, Pennsylvania, and Ohio were caught in the new British-American imperial struggle, in the Illinois country the old British-French rivalry was replaced by a three-way contest between Great Britain, America, and Spain. In contrast to the eastern focus of upper Ohio Valley tribes toward British Montreal and American Philadelphia, the Illinois tribes looked south and west to St. Louis, where the Spanish governor was a friendly substitute for the previous French administration and where French traders continued in business. The migration and founding of new villages by the Sauk, Mesquakie, Kickapoo, Potawatomi, Piankeshaw, and the Illinois tribes, as well as by bands of Shawnee and Delaware from present Indiana and Ohio, illustrate this southwesterly orientation of Indians in the Illinois country.

Spanish Aims

Among the immediate aims of the Spanish administration in upper Louisiana was the building of new towns and posts on the west bank of the Mississippi to thwart British influence. Following the British occupation of Fort Chartres in 1765, the old French population of the Kaskaskia and Cahokia region, numbering about 2,000, began a wholesale migration to the Spanish shore. There they concentrated in two settlements. St. Louis (Pain Court), established in 1764, and Ste. Genevieve (Misere), in existence since 1739. Indian allies of the French followed, partly in response to Spanish offers of patronage. The Peoria from Cahokia migrated to a site south of St. Louis, where they remained until attacked by a party of enemy Sauk in 1777. A band of Kickapoo and Mascouten who had earlier settled on the west bank of Missouri were to serve as mercenaries in Spain's battles against the Chickasaw and Osage.

Seeking Spanish protection from hostile Indian attacks, the Kaskaskia chief Duquoin led 80 warriors and their families from their villages near Kaskaskia and Fort Chartres in late fall, 1774. Duquoin found temporary asylum at the mouth of the Arkansas River among the Quapaw who earlier had taken in the majority of Michigamea. He finally received Spanish permission to establish a separate Illinois village on the White River in present Arkansas, but the onset of the American Revolution interfered, and he brought his band back to Kaskaskia in 1777. In the same year, many Peoria returned to Black Dog's village near Cahokia, and some Kaskaskia and Peoria settled in a village halfway between Ste. Genevieve and the mouth of the Ohio. Whether this village persisted after 1777 is unknown, although its probable location at the mouth of Apple River was near the site of a larger congregation of migrant Delaware, Shawnee, Miami, and Piankeshaw.

Unlike Indians in the northern Great Lakes Region and Ohio Valley, who almost universally supported the British during the American Revolution, the tribes of the Illinois country were influenced by their own pro-French background and new Spanish ties to favor a neutral, if not a forthrightly anti-British, attitude. Spanish partisan groups like the Missouri and Illinois River Kickapoo and Duquoin's Kaskaskia, as well as groups of Potawatomi, actively harassed British traders before 1777. The French declaration of support for the Americans in 1778 and entry of Spain into the war against the British in 1779 strengthened this stance. George Rogers Clark's bloodless conquest of inadequately garrisoned British posts at Kaskaskia, Cahokia, and Vincennes in 177879 and his display of diplomatic bravado in council temporarily impressed the Illinois remnant bands and Tobacco's Piankeshaw at Chippekoke on the lower Wabash.

Thus, in contrast to their tribesmen in Michigan and eastern Indiana, many Indians in the Illinois country acted in the American interest at least between 1778 and 1781. These included Potawatomi of the Illinois River and Chicago, Siggenauk's band at Milwaukee, the Wea and Piankeshaw of the Wabash, and the Kickapoo and Illinois. Some members of these groups sided with Clark in the capture of the British governor of Detroit, Henry Hamilton, at Vincennes in 1779; provided intelligence or helped to protect St. Louis and American Illinois settlements against British-Indian attack in 1780; and aided the French LaBalme expedition of 1780 and the Spanish-Indian expedition against Fort St. Joseph in 1781 (see map 14).

The short foray from St. Louis to the St. Joseph River in Michigan was principally a protest against the British removal of French traders at the fort in 1780 and the installation of British traders. Local Michigan Potawatomi shared the spoils of British trade goods seized by the Spanish force. Louis Chevalier, Jr., guide for the expedition, was a member of the Spanish militia at St. Louis and son of the leading French trader on the St. Joseph River (see map 16). The apparently pro-American position of certain Potawatomi and Miami bands did not cause conflict with other bands supporting the British interest.

Tribal Expansion

The Sauk, Mesquakie, and Winnebago, occupying the northwest corner of Illinois country and southwestern Wisconsin, also expanded in a southwesterly direction during the years 177 4-94. Supplied by British traders from Michilimackinac

Frontier in Transition
1774–1794
The Illinois Country

Legend:

▲ Indian village
● White settlement
■ Fort
⊠ Fort and white settlement
⊡ Trading post
Am American
Sp Spanish
Br British

ILLINOIS   Present state name
— ‐ — Present state boundary
Illinois   Present drainage name
No date   Occupied 1774-1794, may have existed earlier or later
1776   Date established, occupied beyond 1794
to 1791   Date abandoned, occupied before 1774
1776-81   Dates established and abandoned
1776*   Occupied at that date, earlier or later dates between 1774 and 1794 unknown
to 1780 1784   Abandoned, then reoccupied
?   Date uncertain or unknown
SE,MES 1781   Tribes at village at different dates within period

Abbreviation	Tribe
DE	DELAWARE
IL	ILLINOIS
IO	IOWA
KA	KASKASKIA
KI	KICKAPOO
MC	MASCOUTEN
MES	MESQUAKIE
MI	MIAMI
OJ	OJIBWA
OT	OTTAWA
PE	PEORIA
PI	PIANKESHAW
PO	POTAWATOMI
SA	SAUK
SH	SHAWNEE
WE	WEA
WI	WINNEBAGO

Scale 1:2,500,000

0 10 20 30 MILES
0 10 20 30 KILOMETERS

MAP 19

KEY MAP

INSET MAP

Map labels:

Grey-Headed Decorah WI 1793
Nibakoa SA MES OJ WI 1778*
Sauk Prairie SA to 1783
Iron Walker WI 1783
Onangeesay
PO 1785
Milwaukee
Siggenauk OT PO OJ SA
Koshkonong WI
Howink WI
L. Koshkonong
Prairie du Chien c. 1781
La Porte MES
MES to 1783?
MES 1783
Dubuques Mine 1788 MES
MES
WISCONSIN / ILLINOIS
Lake Michigan
Chicago
PO 1794
PO OJ OT SA to 1794
Petit Fort Br to 1780
PO 1793*
Wabenaneto PO 1790
PO OJ OT, MC KI 1779
Mesquakenuk MES
WI 1777-79
Saukenuk SA
SA c. 1780
SA MES c. 1780
Upper Iowa Town IO
MC 1774*
INDIANA / ILLINOIS
PO c. 1792
Peoria
KI MC, WE PI 1792 to ?
Grand Kickapoo Village KI 1792
Kesis PO 1794
KI to 1791
KI 1788*
KI c. 1780
PI to 1791, KI 1792
Montbruns Ft Sp 1780 to?
SA 1780
SA c. 1780
Lower Iowa Town IO
Vermilion River PI 1791
Raven KI MC 1776-81
Maillots Ft Sp 1780-81
KI?
Crooked Legs WE KI, PI 1786
WE 1791
Ft Sackville Br 1769-78
Ft Patrick Henry Am 1778-87
Ft Knox Am 1788
El Tander MC to 1787
KI to 1788 ?
Pacanne MI PI 1785-88
Chippikoke PI
Vincennes
KI MC?
SH 1788-89
SH 1788-89

Inset Map:

Salt Springs DE 1794*
Chillicothe 6 SH 1787
Pacanne MI PI 1793-94
PE 1777*
DE 1781 SH 1793
SH 1793
PI KI 1788-89*
Cape Girardeau 1793
Montgomerys Blockhouse
Ft Massac Am 1794
Ft Jefferson Am 1780-81
Tewapite
St Charles
Rogerstown SH 1777?
St Ferdinand c. 1785
St Louis PE to 1777
Cahokia
Carondelet PE to 1789
Ft Bowman Am 1778
Black Dog
PI 1786*
St Philip
Prairie du Rocher
IL to 1775
Duquoin
Ste Genevieve PE 1780
New Bourbon
Big Shawnee Springs SH DE 1784-94
Kaskaskia KA
Ft Gage Br 1772-78
Ft Clark Am 1778

See continuation on INSET MAP

Muscatine Prairie on the west bank of the Mississippi River about thirty miles below Saukenuk. From Lewis, *Das Illustrierte Mississipithal* p. 218. The Newberry Library.

and Green Bay, their movements into the Rock River valley and the west bank of the Mississippi actually represented British penetration into Spanish Louisiana. These groups provided the primary Indian support for the ill-fated British attack on St. Louis in May, 1780. In retaliation a month later, the American commandant at Cahokia, John Montgomery, led a force of about 300 Spanish and American militia against the principal Sauk town at the mouth of Rock River, burning the ripening corn crop and the gabled houses (see map 14).

The burning of Saukenuk was the only attack on an Indian village in the Illinois country during the Revolutionary War and left an anti-American legacy with the Sauk. In the aftermath of the British attack on St. Louis, the Spanish placed small garrisons of militia at the mouth of the Des Moines River and at the "Mauvais Terre" or Bad Lands on the Illinois River. Montbrun's Fort in particular drew a portion of the Sauk and Mesquakie into the Spanish trade system, and new Indian villages rose near the mouths of the Iowa and Des Moines rivers. British influence persisted among the Sauk and Mesquakie, however, reinvigorated by the concentration of British traders who settled at Prairie du Chien about 1781.

The enthusiasm of the tribes of the Illinois country for the Americans began to fade about 1781 as white settlers moved into southern Indiana and Illinois in the wake of Clark's army. Terms of the Treaty of Paris, 1783, fully unmasked American intentions to take over the Indian country west and north of the Ohio River. The end of the Anglo-American war did not stop the American-Indian war, a conflict more critical to the future of Great Lakes Indians than the fight for independence of the American colonies. In 1783, encouraged by British agents anxious to retain control of the Indian trade, a western Indian confederacy was formed to halt the westward spread of white settlement.

The tribes of the Illinois country aligned themselves with the confederacy, joining the Wyandot, Shawnee, Delaware, Miami, and other allies against the American settlements across the Ohio (see maps 17 and 18). For those groups occupying a sheltered position removed from the battle zone, such as the Potawatomi, these raids brought few losses and much booty. Increasingly, however, villages on the lower Wabash felt the impact of the war, since they were situated along the warpath for Miami and Kickapoo raids into Kentucky.

The Lower Wabash

Indian sentiment on the lower Wabash became locally more pacific following the arrival of Major John Francis Hamtramck in 1787, assigned to command the American garrison at Vincennes, renamed Fort Knox in 1788. Hamtramck was born in Quebec, spoke fluent French, and soon married into a prominent French family. These factors contributed to his influence in Vincennes, a town of about 400 bark and log cabins inhabited by 400 Americans and 900 French, about a third of whom left for Spanish Louisiana in 1791.

Diplomatic efforts of Major Hamtramck with the Wabash and Illinois tribes were all designed to bring peace and order to the Wabash Valley, but aggressive attacks by Kentuckians diminished American credibility. Although he protested to the War Department, Hamtramck was powerless to prevent incursions such as the surprise attack by 60 Kentuckians under Patrick Brown in August, 1778, on the villages of Kickapoo, Piankeshaw, and Miami under Pacanne on the Embarras River. Indian raids against American settlers resumed, and retaliatory attacks by Americans against Indian settlements in the lower Illinois country persisted, while both sides talked of peace.

Although the Wea under Crooked Legs had signed a peace treaty with George Rogers Clark when he arrived at Vincennes in 1778, and a band of 80 Wea warriors renewed the alliance with Hamtramck in 1798, even these tribesmen proved untrustworthy in the generally anti-American climate of the Wabash Valley. Warfare escalated during the next four years with the United States bearing the heaviest losses before finally defeating the Indian confederacy at Fallen Timbers in 1794 (see map 18). As a result of the Scott and Wilkinson raids in 1791 (map 14), most of the Wea and Piankeshaw retreated down the Wabash toward Chippikoke, while the majority of the Wabash Kickapoo abandoned their homeland as well. Some Kickapoo established new villages on the Vermilion River of Indiana and at the headwaters of Salt Creek, while others joined their kinsmen in Missouri or on the Illinois River. A small group of Piankeshaw and Kickapoo had already spent at least a winter and summer on the Spanish side of the Mississippi between 1778 and 1789.

As part of the United States efforts to achieve a peace with the northwest Indians during 1792, Rufus Putnam convened a treaty council in September at Vincennes, after he had been unsuccessful in arranging a council at Fort Jefferson near the Miami River. Although 247 men and 439 women attended, the treaty, which was never ratified, had only thirty-one signers, including Eel River Miami, Wea, Potawatomi, Mascouten, Kickapoo of the Wabash, Piankeshaw, Peoria, and a single Ottawa. Putnam's council took place at the same time that a larger anti-American congress of over 1,000 warriors was gathering on the Maumee River in Ohio to reaffirm their insistence on the Ohio River boundary limit for white settlement.

By this time, Delaware and Shawnee from the Ohio country were also congregating on the western bank of the Mississippi River. Delaware had been noted in the vicinity of Ste. Geneviève, opposite the mouth of the Kaskaskia River, building houses as early as the summer of 1775. There is no evidence that they remained at this site, then known as the Bois Brulé and later as Big Shawnee Springs. By 1784, however, both Shawnee and Delaware bands had villages in this locale. Three years later the concentration of Indians from Ohio increased following Logan's raid in 1786 on the confederated towns of the Mad River region.

The Spanish governor of Louisiana invited Louis Peter Lorimer, whose trading post at the head of the Miami River had been destroyed by Kentuckians in 1782, to move across the Mississippi and bring along his Indian clients (map 17). In 1787, about 1,200 Shawnee and 600 Delaware moved to Upper Louisiana, settling along the frontier of the Ste. Geneviève and Cape Girardeau Districts. About the same time that Roger's Band of Shawnee located farther north near the French Creole community of St. Charles, Lorimer was appointed interpreter on the staff of the Spanish Indian administration.

Summary

By 1794, closing date for this map, the Shawnee and Delaware towns of Upper Louisiana stretched from the Apple River in the north to New Madrid on the south. Joining them on the west bank of the Mississippi were bands of Piankeshaw, Miami, and Kickapoo, and the majority of the forty-six remaining Illinois Indian families. Only twenty families of Kaskaskia remained on the east bank of the Mississippi by 1789.

As had been the case during the Revolutionary War years, the tribes of the Illinois country were relatively immune from attack between 1783 and 1794. During this interval the Potawatomi, Sauk, and Prairie Kickapoo further enlarged their territorial domains at the expense of the remnant Illinois tribes, the Potawatomi extending southward on the Illinois River to Peoria. These were the tribal people left to bear the responsibility for maintaining Indian control of the Illinois country as the nineteenth century loomed.

Principal Sources: Alvord 1922; Anson 1970; Barnhart 1951; Clifton 1977; Ferguson 1972; Higginbotham 1971; Houck 1909; James 1912; Kinnaird 1932, 1946; MacLeod 1978; Musick 1941; Nasatir 1928, 1952, 1976; Peterson 1978; Temple 1958; Voegelin 1974e.

War Dance of the Sauk and Mesquakie. The collection of C. J. Hambleton.

The purpose of this map is to portray the distribution of Indian and white communities in the Great Lakes Region just before the War of 1812. The population picture in 1810, when compared to the situation in 1768 (map 13), shows a proliferation of Indian village sites as well as the advance of new settlers into former Indian territory, with the largest population bulge occurring in the Ohio country. The appearance of additional Indian villages is partially the consequence of more extensive information available for the western area, as well as the result of an actual increase in the number of tribal communities.

Indian population by 1810 had achieved a stable pattern of distribution in the northern part of the Great Lakes, where the British fur trade was near peak productivity. On the other hand, an unstable situation was redeveloping to the south and west, where reactions to the teachings of the Shawnee prophet reached highest intensity in the Wabash and Illinois River region by 1807.

On the leading edge of the American frontier northwest of the Ohio River, Indian people were still subject to the , interrelated strains of accelerating white settlement, successful demands for additional land cessions, and the formation of new states and territories. In 1810, the white population of recently established American and British governmental districts within the Great Lakes Region exceeded 345,000 divided as follows:

Geographical District	Date Established	Approximate Population
Province of Upper Canada	1791	75,000
Indiana Territory	1800	24,000
State of Ohio	1803	230,000
Michigan Territory	1805	4,800
Illinois Territory (including Wisconsin)	1809	12,000

This map records other post-1768 developments such as the westward shift of the Ojibwas from Lake Superior and the establishment of reservations in the eastern Great Lakes Region. By 1810, British and American military posts were in new locations determined by provisions of three American agreements with Indian and European nations: (1) Greenville Treaty of 1795, signed by thirteen allied Indian nations, (2) Jay Treaty of 1794 with Great Britain, and the (3) purchase of Louisiana Territory west of the Mississippi River from France in 1803, after it had been retroceded by Spain in 1802 (map 12).

In the southern Great Lakes Region, stages in the overall changes between 1768 and 1794 have been traced in the "Frontier in Transition" series (maps 15-19). The 1810 map reflects further readjustments in the same transitional area as a result of the Greenville land cession and additional land cessions from 1803 to 1809 in Ohio, Indiana, and Michigan. Since the distribution of Indian and white communities was affected by different factors in different parts of the Great Lakes Region, comments on the map data are grouped with reference to three sections of the map: northern, western, and southeastern. Discussion begins with coverage of present Canadian territory spanning the northern section of the map.

Northern Section

By 1810, the pattern of relations between whites and Indians and among Indians had been set in present eastern Canada. About 75,000 whites occupied land west of Montreal in the British province of Upper Canada, with administrative headquarters at York (Toronto). New communities radiated out from pockets of settlement begun between 1784 and 1795 in three areas: at Amherstburg on the Detroit River and in the lower Thames Valley, at York on Lake Ontario and along the Niagara peninsula between Lakes Ontario and Erie, and at Kingston and the Bay of Quinte at the eastern end of Lake Ontario. Ranging around and among these pockets were reservation communities of Wyandot, Six Nations, and Missisauga. Close to white settlements on the lower Thames and St. Clair rivers were villages of Moravians, Munsee, and Ojibwa. The small white population of a thousand in the vicinity of York was isolated from the larger centers at the head and foot of Lake Ontario. Although the neighboring Missisauga were quiescent in 1810, during the 1790s unpleasant Indian-white friction had occurred, leading to the threat of an uprising in 1798 despite the weakness of the Missisauga population following a smallpox epidemic in 1793.

Among the Indians themselves, relations in present southeastern Ontario were peaceful, if not always cordial. Spheres of influence existed, but these seem to have been less rigidly enforced than in the past. Mississauga who had fought the Iroquois for control of the territory in the late seventeenth century now reluctantly recognized the Iroquois leadership in Upper Canada. Mississauga were visited in Six Nations territory on the Grand River, where fragments of the Delaware also resided. Moravians and Munsee peacefully continued to occupy land within the Missisauga-Ojibwa country along the Thames River.

In Lower Canada adjoining the St. Lawrence River a much larger white population of 225,000 totally overshadowed the settled Indian population of about 3,000 at St. Regis, at Caughnawaga south of Montreal, at Oka on the Lac des Deux Montagnes, and at Lorette near Quebec. Although accomplishments of the settled Indians were applauded by

British administrators, they did not consider it possible or even desirable for the settled life to become general among the Indian population. That concept began to take hold a decade later. Still viewing the Indian principally as a hunter and warrior, the British reorganized and revitalized the Indian branch after 1807 in order to solicit stronger Indian support. The prospect of another war with Americans already seemed real.

Near Georgian Bay, the northern shore of Lake Huron, and Lake Superior, the Ojibwa remained largely unmolested by white settlement, as was the case with the Algonquin to the north and east of the Ottawa River. Still, there was some white influence on these two tribes through contact with traders who were scattered across the fur-producing areas. Trading posts mapped in present northern Ontario infer an Indian population composed of small and mobile bands distributed throughout this sparsely inhabited area.

Terms of the Jay Treaty, which went into effect in 1796, brought about readjustments in the crossroads region where the waters of Lakes Huron, Michigan, and Superior join. After the British vacated Fort Mackinac and Americans first occupied the island in 1796, British traders established Fort St. Joseph on the large island at the mouth of the St. Mary River in Lake Huron. The North West Company trading post established at the outlet of Lake Superior marks the beginning of British settlement on the Canadian bank of the St. Marys River.

The 1810 map is the first to show Ojibwa villages on the northeast shores of Lake Michigan in a region principally occupied by the Ottawa. Early Ojibwa locations tentatively identified are Stony Point on the western shore of Grand Traverse Bay and Wequagemog on the eastern side of the bay at the north end of Elk Lake. According to traditional history, the Ojibwa of the Upper Peninsula of Michigan were given hunting rights in a corridor extending from the Lake Michigan shoreline northeast of Grand Traverse Bay to the head of the Muskegon River. These hunting lands were granted in recompense for a murder committed by an Ottawa in a quarrel over fishing nets.

North and west of Lake Superior, the spread of Indian villages after 1768 was tied to the exponential growth of British fur trade activity. The earlier rigid licensing system gave way to open competition, and ultimately to the growth of partnerships and monopoly companies. By the 1780s, scarcity of game in northern Wisconsin and eastern Minnesota led to a joint Indian-trader search for richer hunting grounds. Striking out from bases at Fond du Lac and Sandy Lake, North West Company traders established posts at Leech Lake by the 1780s and were at Pembina on the Red River of the North by 1800. Posts along the Rainy River, at Fort William, and along the north shore of Lake Superior seriously challenged the Hudson's Bay Company monopoly in those districts. Fort William was founded in 1804 when the discovery was made that Grand Portage, location of Fort Charlotte, lay in American territory.

Western Section

In conjunction with the establishment of new British trading posts, Ojibwa bands from Wisconsin and Michigan's Upper

Tenskwatawa, Shawnee religious leader, who reached the height of his influence between 1807 and 1811. Indians of many tribes gathered at Prophetstown, his village on the Wabash River in Indiana. From McKenny and Hall, *History of of the Indian Tribes of North America*. The Newberry Library.

Peninsula made a major westward move beginning about 1770, successfully wresting the Mississippi headwaters above the Crow Wing River from the Dakota. By 1810, the Ojibwa were securely located at Sandy Lake, Pokegama Lake, Cass Lake, Leech Lake, Lake Winnebigoshish, Red Lake, and the Red River of the North. These new Ojibwa village sites on lakes in present Minnesota and on the upper Chippewa, Red Cedar, and St. Croix rivers of Wisconsin were still subject to Dakota raiding parties. The war zone, about one hundred miles wide, stretched over four hundred miles from the forks of the Red Cedar and Chippewa rivers northwest to Pembina. Lands north of Mille Lacs Lake and Crow Wing River at this date were occupied exclusively by the Ojibwa, while lands south of the Minnesota River within the present state of Minnesota were the domain of the Dakota.

By 1810, the Dakota likewise had moved westward and were forming new bands. Teton, who had been noted at Lake Traverse around 1768, and part of the Yankton transferred their bases to the plains of present North and South Dakota beyond the Great Lakes Region. Incorporating the use of horses into their buffalo-hunting society, the western bands diverged in their life style from the Dakota remaining in present Minnesota. Villages of eastern Dakota including the Mdewakanton, Wapekute, Sisseton, and Wahpeton, stretched along the Minnesota River valley, with prairie-oriented bands

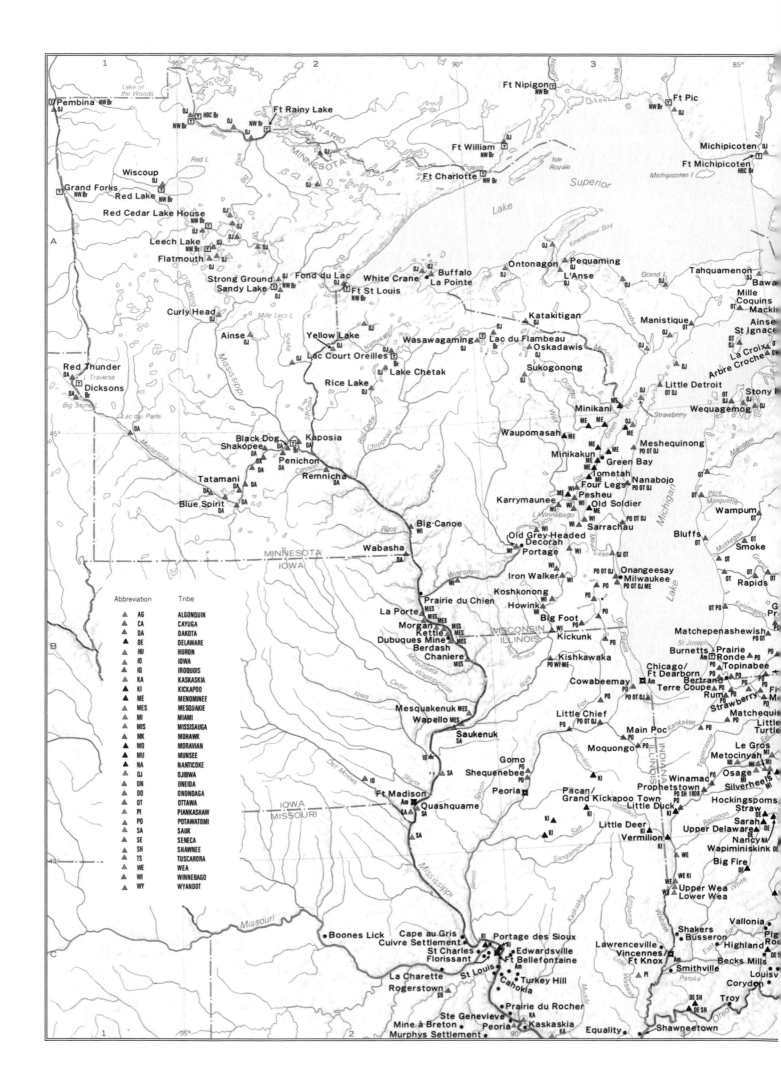

Pembina NW Br
OJ

HBC Br
NW Br
OJ
Ft Rainy Lake
NW Br
OJ
T
ONTARIO
MINNESOTA
Ft Nipigon
NW Br
Ft Pic
NW Br
OJ

Lake of the Woods

Red L

Wiscoup
T
Ft William
NW Br
Ft Charlotte
NW Br
OJ
Pigeon
Isle Royale
Michipicoten
OJ
Ft Michipicoten
HBC Br
Michipicoten I
Superior

Grand Forks
NW Br
T
Red Lake
NW Br
T
Red Cedar Lake House
NW Br
T
OJ

Leech Lake
NW Br
T
Flatmouth
OJ

Lake

Kawaenaw Bay
Grand I

Ontonagon
OJ
OJ
Pequaming
OJ
L'Anse
Tahquamenon
OJ

Bawa

Strong Ground
OJ
Fond du Lac
OJ
White Crane
Buffalo
La Pointe
OJ
Mille Coquins
Macki
Sandy Lake
NW Br
OJ
Ft St Louis
NW Br
OJ
St Louis
Ainse
St Ignace

Curly Head
Mille Lacs L
Katakitigan
OJ
Manistique
OT
OJ
La Croix
OJ

Ainse
OJ
Yellow Lake
OJ
Lac Court Oreilles
Br
OJ
Lake Chetak
Wasawagaming
OJ
Lac du Flambeau
OJ
Oskadawis
OJ
Sukogonong
OJ
Little Detroit
OT OJ
Arbre Croche
Stony
OJ

Rice Lake

Red Thunder
DA
T
L Traverse
Dicksons
DA
Br
Big Stone L
Minikani
ME
Wequagemog
OJ

Lac qui Parle

Waupomasah
ME
ME
Strawberry

Minikakun
ME
ME
ME
ME
Green Bay
Meshequinong
PO OT OJ
Nanabojo
PO OT OJ
Père

DA
Black Dog
DA
Br
Kaposia
Shakopee
DA
DA
DA
Penichon
DA
Br
Remnicha
DA
Tatamani
DA
DA
DA
Blue Spirit
DA

Four Legs
ME
ME
Tometah
Pesheu
WI
Karrymaunee
WI
WI
Old Soldier
WI
Sarrachau
WI
L Winnebago
Marquette
Wampum

Michigan

Big Canoe
WI
Wabasha
DA
MINNESOTA
IOWA

Old Grey-Headed
Decorah
WI
Portage
WI
WI
Iron Walker
WI
Koshkonong
WI
Howink
WI
Big Foot
WI
Onangeesay
Milwaukee
PO OT OJ ME
PO OT OJ
Rapids
OT
Bluffs
OT
Smoke
OT
Muskegon
Grand

Abbreviation   Tribe
▲ AG   ALGONQUIN
▲ CA   CAYUGA
▲ DA   DAKOTA
▲ DE   DELAWARE
▲ HU   HURON
▲ IO   IOWA
▲ IQ   IROQUOIS
▲ KA   KASKASKIA
▲ KI   KICKAPOO
▲ ME   MENOMINEE
▲ MES MESQUAKIE
▲ MI   MIAMI
▲ MIS MISSISAUGA
▲ MK   MOHAWK
▲ MO   MORAVIAN
▲ MU   MUNSEE
▲ NA   NANTICOKE
▲ OJ   OJIBWA
▲ ON   ONEIDA
▲ OO   ONONDAGA
▲ OT   OTTAWA
▲ PI   PIANKASHAW
▲ PO   POTAWATOMI
▲ SA   SAUK
▲ SE   SENECA
▲ SH   SHAWNEE
▲ TS   TUSCARORA
▲ WE   WEA
▲ WI   WINNEBAGO
▲ WY   WYANDOT

Prairie du Chien
La Porte
MES
MES
Morgan
MES
Kettle
MES
MES
Dubuques Mine
MES
Berdash
Chaniere
MES

Kickunk
PO
Matchepenashewish
PO
G
Pr
Burnetts
Prairie
Ronde
T
Am
Topinabee
PO OT OJ
Chicago/
Ft Dearborn
Am
Bertrand
Terre Coupe
Rum
Strawberry
M
Matchequis
Little
Turtle

Kishkawaka
Cowabeemay
PO
PO OT OJ

Mesquakenuk
MES
Wapello
MES
Saukenuk
SA
IO

Little Chief
PO OT OJ
Main Poc
PO
Moquongo
PO
Le Gros
Metocinyah
MI
MI
MI
Osage
MI
Silverheels
MI

Ft Madison
Am
SA
Quashquame
SA
SA

Gomo
PO
Shequenebee
PO
Peoria
T

Pacan/
Grand Kickapoo Town
PO SH 1808
Prophetstown
Winamac
PO
Hockingspoms
Straw

Little Duck
KI
Little Deer
KI
Vermilion
KI

Upper Delaware
DE
Nancy
NA
Wapiminiskink
DE
Big Fire
DE

Upper Wea
WE
Lower Wea
WE

IOWA
MISSOURI

INDIANA
ILLINOIS

WISCONSIN
ILLINOIS

Boones Lick
Cape au Gris
Cuivre Settlement
KI
Portage des Sioux
St Charles
Edwardsville
Florissant
Ft Bellefontaine
La Charette
St Louis
Turkey Hill
Rogerstown
SH
Cahokia
Prairie du Rocher
Ste Geneviève
KA
Mine à Breton
Peoria
Kaskaskia
Murphys Settlement
KA
Equality

Lawrenceville
Vincennes
Ft Knox
Am
Smithville
Corydon
DE SH
DE SH

Shakers
Busseron
Pig
Highland
Vallonia
Pi

Shawneetown
Troy

Missouri

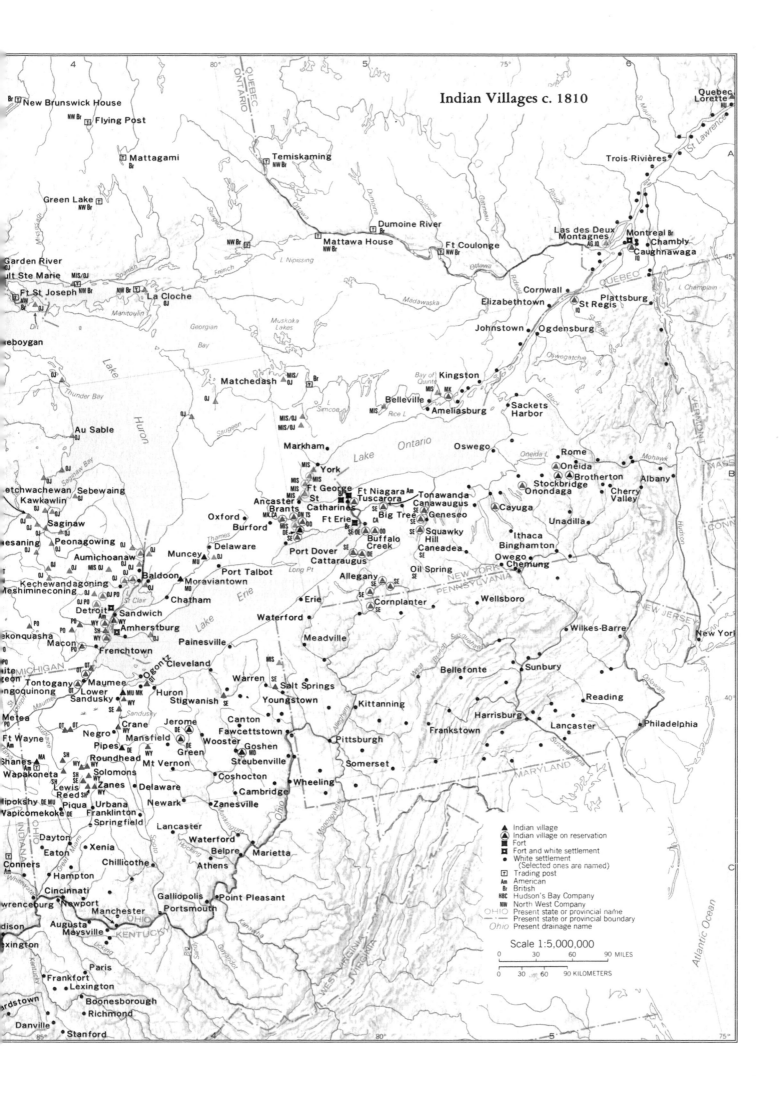

Indian Villages c. 1810

MAP
20

Indian village
Indian village on reservation
Fort
Fort and white settlement
White settlement
    (Selected ones are named)
Trading post
Am   American
Br   British
HBC   Hudson's Bay Company
NW   North West Company
——— Present state or provincial name
 - - Present state or provincial boundary
Ohio Present drainage name

Scale 1:5,000,000

0   30   60   90 MILES

0   30   60   90 KILOMETERS

of northern Yankton (Yanktonnai) and Upper Sisseton occupying the headwaters district between Big Stone Lake and Lake Traverse. Most southwesterly of the British trading posts, Dickson's, was established at the head of Big Stone Lake in 1789.

The rich game reserves of the Ojibwa-Dakota war zone were safely exploited by the Menominee, who were friendly to both tribes. In winter, Menominee hunters ranged from the lower Chippewa River to the mouth of the Crow Wing, returning in spring to their villages on the Wolf and Oconto rivers flowing into Green Bay, the western arm of Lake Michigan. While most Menominee villages still clustered near the bay, a few Menominee were living among Ojibwa bands on their northern fringe and within the composite Ojibwa, Ottawa, and Potawatomi villages lining the western shore of Lake Michigan, most notably at Milwaukee. Villages of the Winnebago stretched from Lake Winnebago to the Rock River near the present Illinois-Wisconsin state line. In southwestern Wisconsin, there were also Winnebago along the Wisconsin River and at present-day LaCrosse on the east bank of the Mississippi River near the mouth of the Black River.

In present Wisconsin, the only white settlements in 1810 were the Indian trading centers at Green Bay, Milwaukee, Portage, and Prairie du Chien. The local inhabitants of French heritage, more accurately designated Metis, were the conspicuous population element in these communities and also at Fort Mackinac (Michilimackinac), St. Ignace, and Sault Ste. Marie on the eastern tip of the Upper Peninsula of Michigan. Smaller fur trading companies that had been operated by British subjects at Green Bay, Prairie du Chien, and Michilimackinac (Fort Mackinac} were merged into John Jacob Astor's South West Company in 1810. Despite Zebulon Pike's expedition up the Mississippi in 1805 and the joint expedition of Meriwether Lewis and William Clark up the Missouri 1804-1806, few signs of American influence north or west of Fort Dearborn at Chicago could be seen in 1810.

The Sauk and Mesquakie by 1810 had abandoned their earlier territory in western Wisconsin and instead occupied a string of villages along the Mississippi River extending from Prairie du Chien south beyond the mouth of the Des Moines River. Although increasingly a prairie people, the Sauk and Mesquakie enjoyed a uniquely advantageous commerce with the non-Indian trading communities at Prairie du Chien and St. Louis. The Mesquakie living south of Prairie du Chien mined lead ore that was traded for supplies, while the Sauk farmers of Saukenuk at the Rock River mouth provided corn for the British fur trade of the northwest that operated out of Prairie du Chien.

South of Saukenuk, the Sauk and Iowa jointly utilized the Des Moines River drainage. The proximity of these villages to American-occupied St. Louis and to Fort Madison, erected in 1809, drew their leaders from the British into the American orbit, forecasting a split in the Sauk ranks.

In the Illinois River valley, the southernmost summer villages of the Potawatomi clustered about Peoria. Along with hunters from the villages of the "United Bands" around Chicago and Milwaukee, the Illinois River Potawatomi ranged in their hunting expeditions across the Mississippi and, like the Sauk, engaged in periodic raids

against the Osage. In regional tribal affairs, the gradual emergence of the so-called "United Bands" of Chippewa, Ottawa, and Potawatomi by 1810 had resulted in the creation of new village leaders who were independent of the traditional Potawatomi leadership on the St. Joseph River.

The Kickapoo, close neighbors of the Potawatomi, had a large community at the Grand Kickapoo Town in the Illinois prairie lands at the head of the Sangamon River. They also occupied the valleys of two Vermilion rivers, flowing into the Illinois and Wabash rivers, with part of the population still on the middle Wabash. Across the Mississippi River in Missouri, the two small Kickapoo communities near Portage des Sioux had absorbed the remaining Mascouten by 1810.

The patterns of territorial expansion and population growth characteristic of most tribes in the western section of the 1810 map were in sharp contrast to the situation of tribal remnants in the southern parts of Illinois and Indiana. Here Indian people were existing in one of three conditions. Either they had been reduced to a fraction of their former population and encapsulated on a reservation, like the Kaskaskia; or were soon destined for removal or absorption, like the Wea and Piankeshaw; or were already refugees temporarily sequestered during their migration to the west bank of the Mississippi, like the Shawnee and Delaware living close to the Ohio River in southwestern Indiana.

In Illinois, white settlement was still limited to the river valleys of the southern quarter of the present state. On the northern frontier of white settlements, Edwardsville, founded in 1805, became the seat of government when Illinois Territory was established in 1809.

Southeastern Section

South of Lake Ontario and Lake Erie, the distribution of Indian population in 1810 indicated a continued retreat in the face of advancing agricultural settlements and speculative land enterprises. In New York and Pennsylvania, new lands had been thrown open to aspiring farmers by treaty with the Six Nations in 1794 and the purchase of Seneca land by the Treaty of Big Tree in 1797.

The Oneida, Onondaga, and Cayuga living on reservations in eastern New York, along with the Brotherton and Stockbridge of New England origin, were surrounded by white farmers who moved into New York by way of the Mohawk Valley. Ascending the Susquehanna River through Pennsylvania, settlers by 1810 had taken over former Iroquois townsites at Owego, Chemung, and Unadilla. Inroads were beginning toward reservations of Cornplanter and other Seneca on the upper Allegheny. Seneca towns along the Genesee River occupied the most remote district of the former Iroquois country.

The Seneca, major Iroquois or Six Nations division remaining in the United States, became dispirited and further weakened by almost universal dipsomania during their initial reservation years. Nevertheless, in 1799 they initiated a temperance movement and adopted a farming, lumbering, and domestic arts economy that produced marketable surpluses before 1810. A significant factor in their rapid change from a traditional economy was the example of a model farm and educational project commenced by the Society of Friends

American Fur Company Buildings at Fond du Lac, head of Lake Superior. From McKenny, *Tour to the Lakes*. The Newberry Library.

(Quakers) in 1789 nine miles upstream from Cornplanter's village. Cabins were soon replaced by houses with shingled roofs, glass windows, and paneled doors often superior to those of pioneer white establishments. In the local labor exchange, Indians hired white blacksmiths and carpenters, and in turn worked for white farmers.

Northeastern Ohio in 1810 was an intermingled frontier with small communities of Seneca and Missisauga still part of the population. Cleveland, founded in 1796, became the launching point for American expansion across north central Ohio. At that time, 1796, the entire white population of present Ohio was only 5,000 people who all lived within fifty miles of the Ohio River. Land westward to Sandusky Bay became available after a treaty was concluded in 1805 (map 30). Antipathy toward Indian people occasionally sparked incidents in northern Ohio where Indians became subject to the jurisdiction of local authorities.

The three Indian reservations in Ohio at this time were special cases (map 36). Goshen, a dwindling Moravian settlement near present New Philadelphia, occupied land granted by Congress in 1788, principally to atone for losses of the Gnadenhütten massacre of 1782 (see pp. 72, 85, and map 17). The Delaware of J Jerometown and Greentown, given reservation status in 1807, had returned to their former homes following warfare that ended in 1794. Jerometown was approximately the same site as Mahican Johns Town of the 1760s (map 9).

Pioneers at Mansfield and Wooster were friendly neighbors of the nearby Indians. By 1810, American settlers had spread through most of Ohio, confining Indians to the northwest part of the state, the only unceded area (map 30). Among the white towns occupying former Indian sites in Ohio were Coshocton, Lancaster, Piqua, and Chillicothe, the state capital.

In this central part of the map, the Great Lakes Indian country began in northwest Ohio and extended across central and northern Indiana as well as across all of Michigan except the vicinity of Detroit. Tribal communities of northwest Ohio, re-stabilized since the war period of the 1790s, presented a distribution pattern similar to maps of the same area in the late eighteenth century (maps 17, 18). Wyandot on the upper Sandusky River still had Pipe's Delaware allies nearby and an associated Negro hamlet, both communities in existence since the American Revolution. Just north of the Greenville Treaty line, Wyandot, Seneca, and Shawnee clustered as close as possible to the headwaters of the Great Miami River, locale of the confederated Indian villages destroyed in 1786 (map 17). New headquarters for the Shawnee remaining east of the Mississippi River was Wapakoneta, established by 1798 on the upper Auglaize River at a place inhabited by Ottawas in the 1780s. Ottawa were located at familiar points on the Maumee River, as well as newer sites on Blanchard's Fork of the Auglaize River (see also Map 21, Detroit Region inset). In the midst of their settlements in 1810, Maumee City occupied a block of land at the rapids reserved for American use by the Greenville Treaty.

Detroit in 1810 was a town of about 700 principally French inhabitants, with an American garrison. The town was situated in the midst of twenty miles of riverfront farms, with unbroken forests commencing a few miles back from the shoreline. Outlying communities and a few isolated French homes were spread northward to the St. Clair River shores and southward around the western end of Lake Erie as far as Sandusky Bay. South of Detroit, the Wyandot at Monguagon and Brownstown lived in communities with

Shingabawossin, Ojibwa leader of St. Marys River and northwestern Lake Huron district. From McKenny and Hall, *History of the Indian Tribes of North America*. The collection of C. J. Hambleton.

farms and orchards like their non-Indian neighbors. The home of Adam Brown, son of a white captive, regularly offered hospitality to travelers on the road to Detroit from the Ohio country.

Despite the evidences of continuity and stability, a changed picture around the western end of Lake Erie in 1810 had been evolving since the Greenville peace treaty and land cession of 1795. The 1810 map shows the results, but not the sequential steps in this change. The first step was the British evacuation of Detroit and Fort Miami on the lower Maumee River in 1796, carrying out terms of the Jay Treaty (map 12D). In July, 1796, the British garrison and Indian staff crossed the Detroit River and established a new base at Fort Malden in Amherstburg. With the arrival of American troops in Detroit, a number of loyal British families also changed residence to the Canadian shore.

At the same time, Indians who had received subsistence and protection from the British since 1794 on the lower Maumee moved to Walpole Island on the Canadian side of Lake St. Clair near a long-existing Missisauga-Ojibwa community. The British agent set up a refugee camp on an eastern channel of the St. Clair River called Le Chenail Ecarte, the French "Chenail" later corrupted to "The Sny" (map 18). The community temporarily accommodated from a thousand to perhaps 3,000 Indians, the majority Ottawa from the Maumee along with Missisauga-Ojibwa from Saginaw. After American troops abandoned Fort Defiance, at the juncture of the Auglaize and Maumee rivers, in 1797, most of the Ottawa and Shawnee drifted

back to the Maumee River region. Blue Jacket's family relocated on the Detroit River by Brownstown, where they were also near French relatives in Detroit (map 21, Detroit Region inset).

A second step producing further change around Detroit was the creation of Michigan Territory in 1805, the year the town was virtually destroyed by fire. To acquire land for anticipated population expansion, Governor William Hull in 1807 secured an Indian land cession extending from the middle of the "thumb" district north of Detroit to the Maumee River. The treaty set aside reservations at nine Chippewa, Potawatomi, and Ottawa townsites in the ceded area (map 31). The country north of Detroit belonged to Missisauga-Ojibwa bands of the Saginaw Valley and headwaters of the Grand River, who opposed American intrusion. Reservations for the Wyandot living south of Detroit were created in 1808 as one provision of a treaty permitting a public road through the Indian country of northwest Ohio (map 30).

The advent of the American regime in Detroit promoted new Indian trading enterprises among the Potawatomi at the southern end of Lake Michigan. The St. Joseph River, never a region sympathetic to the British, was chiefly the trading zone of an American, William Burnett, whose post stood at the river mouth from the end of the Revolution until his death in 1814.

Old French inhabitants remaining on the upper course of the St. Joseph River are represented on the map by Bertrand, a settlement between present Niles, Michigan, and South Bend, Indiana. John Kinzie, a silversmith on the upper Maumee until the 1790 war era, carried the Detroit-linked Indian trade farther west to Chicago in 1804. There he replaced a black trader of Haitian origin who had retired to St. Louis. Building Fort Dearborn at Chicago in 1803, on land reserved by the Greenville Treaty, marked a bold American advance to the edge of territory dominated by British traders.

The Delaware villages in central Indiana fill an area on the 1810 map that is blank on maps of the Great Lakes Region for earlier dates. The Delaware began moving from the Muskingum River in Ohio to hidden retreats of the White River country during the American Revolution. Connor's trading post on the Whitewater River in southeastern Indiana was operated by a family that had traded on the Muskingum during the 1770s (map 16). The Delaware concentration in Indiana, observable in 1810, had developed as villages relocated following warfare of the 1790s. The single Nanticoke village represents a refugee group originally from the Potomac River region that reached the upper Susquehanna River by the mid-eighth century and by 1792 joined the Delaware on the Auglaize River of northwest Ohio.

White population in Indiana had expanded around Vincennes, administrative center for Indiana Territory, established in 1800 with William Henry Harrison as first governor. The Busseron settlement was founded by one of the old French families of Vincennes, while the Shakers, who arrived in 1805, were a new religious sect originating in New York. In Indiana, the tide of American settlement in 1810 was still in the extreme southern part of the present state, where a pioneer population principally from Kentucky was moving into land ceded in 1803. An additional Indian cession secured by Governor Harrison in 1809 opened the southern third of Indiana to settlement, forecasting a white population surge northward and consequent pressure on Indian communities. At an early stage in Harrison's regime, Eel River Miami living on the Eel River in southwestern Indiana moved north, where a more prominent stream, entering the Wabash at modern Logansport, was named for their presence. Both Eel rivers are on contemporary maps.

Religions, Factions, Re-alliances

Clashes of competing religions added to the atmosphere of dissension created by continued white encroachment in the lower Great Lakes Region. Beginning at the turn of the nineteenth century, a wave of religious fervor arose in northern New York and swept westward, affecting both white and Indian communities. New expressions of Indian religion were advocated by prophets appearing among the Seneca on the Allegheny River, Onondaga of New York, Mohawk on the Six Nations Reserve in Canada, and Shawnee in Ohio and Indiana.

Before the Indian prophets gained popularity, Protestant missionaries established firm bases among the New England Indians at Stockbridge and Brotherton reservations and among the Oneida where the Mohawk Prophet also acquired a following. Miami, Potawatomi, and Shawnee invited the Society of Friends, who had been accepted by the Allegheny Seneca, to come to their tribes in 1801. Although missions for Five Medals's Potawatomi and Little Turtle's Miami did not materialize, a Quaker agricultural project began at the Shawnee center, Wapakoneta, in 1807. A Presbyterian minister took up residence in Lower Sandusky in 1803, across the river from the Wyandot town. Moravians, long active among the Delaware, established a mission on the White River of Indiana in 1801, but the project came to an end in 1806, at a time when the Shawnee Prophet exerted a powerful force.

These tenuous missionary ventures impinged upon more traditional forms of Indian religious observance, and the limited activity of Catholic priests commenced in the seventeenth century (see map 8). The Catholic priest in Detroit, the only resident cleric, ministered to Indians as well as to the predominantly French inhabitants and made periodic visits to Mackinac and Illinois.

In the early years of the nineteenth century, the two new Indian religious leaders with the most widespread followings were the Seneca herbalist, Handsome Lake, and the Shawnee Prophet, Tenskwatawa. The two religions became competing influences among the Seneca and Wyandot of Ohio. Both leaders made accusations of witchcraft, occasionally enforcing death sentences, but they differed radically in their attitudes toward white society. While Handsome Lake advocated adoption of the technologically advanced farming economy taught by the Quakers, Tenskwatawa rejected white society and urged a return to the traditional Indian way of life. Shakers in Indiana defended the Shawnee Prophet, claiming him as a respected member of their congregation.

The new Indian religions had disruptive effects on tribal society, reaching a peak in 1807. In New York, Handsome Lake's actions were based on visions, the first revealed in 1799. He subsequently leveled witchcraft charges against the Delaware, who, in protest, left Cattaragus for Buffalo Creek Reservation, then later moved to the Six Nation Reserve in Canada. Handsome Lake's personal followers established a separate community at Coldspring on the upper Allegheny River, where visitOrs included Seneca, other Iroquois, and eventually Wyandot, all from the Sandusky River in Ohio. Tenskwatawa, who with his brother Tecumseh lived among the White River Delaware from 1798 to 1801, came into contact with a long tradition of Delaware prophets. The two brothers made Greenville, Ohio, their next base from 1802 to 1807, but the Prophet returned to the White River to begin active preaching in 1805. He brought about the death of Tetepachsit, first chief of the Delaware who lived at Telipokshy, his nephew and two other Delaware, and elderly Seneca in Ohio. Although he also sentenced four Wyandot women accused of witchcraft, their lives were saved through the interference of the Presbyterian missionary at Lower Sandusky. The Shawnee Prophet's message aroused his followers, and drew potential converts from tribes living hundreds of miles distant on both sides of Lake Michigan.

Despite the religious strains within the tribes of the lower Great Lakes Region, there was strong motivation toward cooperative alliances to strengthen the Indian position in the face of the overwhelming growth of white population. During 1807, meetings took place across the lower Great Lakes Region from New York to Illinois, at a time when both an Indian war and a British-American war seemed imminent. A well-attended Six Nations council met at Buffalo Creek to revitalize the confederacy with pledges of unity that suppressed the political influence of Handsome Lake.

Runners were out in July with notices of a council planned for August at Greenville, headquarters for Tenskwatawa and Tecumseh. Although eastern tribes were invited, none came. British authorities dissuaded the Seven Nations of Lower Canada from attending western councils. The appeal to join the new alliance was rejected by the Six Nations on Grand River and later by New York Iroquois. In September, 1807, a great inter-tribal council convened at the Grand Kickapoo Town on the headwaters of the Sangamon River. Delegations included Illinois River Potawatomi, Shawnee, Kickapoo, Miami, and Delaware. The following year, 1808, Prophetstown on the Wabash River became the base for an increasingly martial western confederacy. As a counterinfluence, Handsome Lake Came to the Sandusky River in the fall of 1808 to urge maintenance of peace.

The Miami's cession of land south of the Wabash River, procured by Governor Harrison in the Treaty of 1809 through divisive tactics, pressure, and intimidation, proved to be a catalyst. The ceded land was a joint concern of neighboring tribes, particularly the Shawnee and Delaware. This cession consolidated western Indian opposition, under Tecumseh's leadership, to relinquishing further land for white settlement. Tecumseh took Pontiac as his model, hoping to succeed where the Ottawa leader had failed in 1763 (map 10). Apprehension mounted in American communities along the Mississippi River, as well as in southern Illinois and Indiana and throughout Ohio. Many settlers retreated in flight toward the Ohio River or into Kentucky. In this climate, young men from other tribes flocked to Tecumseh's standard. Harrison became aware of Tecumseh's strength and potential during an oratorical confrontation in Vincennes in August, 1810. Present with him, and perfectly 'comprehending Tecumseh's tirade, was John Gibson, former Indian trader now secretary-treasurer of Indiana Territory, whose first public service had been as Lord Dunmore's interpreter in 1774 (maps 14 and 16). Henceforth the Shawnee war leader superseded his brother the religious leader in inter-tribal affairs, and thereby received increasing attention from American and British officials.

Principal Sources: Andreas 1884; Anson 1970; Bardon 1943; Barnhart 1953; Bauxar 1959; Beckwith 1880, 1884; Bigsby 1850; Blair 1911; Brisbois 1882; Brown 1979; Burnett 1967; Canada 1923; Carter 1939, 1942, 1948; Clench 1810; Claus n.d.; Clifton 1977, 1978; Coleman 1978; Coues 1897, 1965; Dean 1969; Dillon 1859, 1897; Drake 1852; Edmunds 1979; Edwards 1870; Esarey 1922; Ferguson 1972; Finley 1840; Forsyth 1812; Fulkerson 1915; Gates 1933; Gibson 1963; Gray 1956; Gray 1954; Greeley 1847; Guernsey 1932; Hagan 1958; Hamil 1939, 1951; Hickerson 1956, 1974 a, c, d; Howe 1898; Jackson 1964; Jenks 1912; Johnston 1964; Johnston 1960; Kay 1977, 1979; Keating 1825; Keesing 1939; Knapp 1872; Lurie 1980; McLoughlin 1807; Martindale 1888; Masson 1980; Montour 1973; Ourada 1979; Perrault 1910; Schmalz 1977; Scott 1966; Smyth 1799; Spector 1974; Temple 1958; Thomas 1819; Thompson 1937; Thornbrough 1961; Tipton 1942; Tohill1926; Tyrell 1916; Voegelin 1962, 1974 c, g; Voorhis 1930; Wallace 1972; Warren 1885; Wilson 1946; Winter 1917; Woodford 1958.

Explanation of Map Data and Chronological List

The geographic range and frequency of Indian hostilities is the particular emphasis of this mapping of the War of 1812 era in the Great Lakes Region. Except for a distribution of geographic reference points, the only place names are those necessary to locate engagements in two separate but concurrent conflicts, an American-British war and an American Indian war.

The map records the locations and dates of 150 incidents in the dual warfare, some involving multiple action such as the destruction of a group of Indian villages in central Indiana (see also map 20). These incidents are divided into six classes, identified by four kinds of "x" marks and two sizes of red dots explained at the end of the map legend. The accompanying "Chronology of Hostile Actions" numbers each incident by date and gives brief explanatory remarks.

In, the American-British war, 16 sites of major action are shown on the map in two colors. Large red "X" marks, signifying important Indian participation, note four major events: British capture of Fort Mackinac in July, 1812 (no. 10), American surrender of Detroit in August, 1812 (no. 18), victory of the Caughnawaga Mohawk and allies over Americans in June, 1813 (no. 70), and American victory at Moraviantown, Ontario, when Tecumseh was killed in October, 1813 (no. 93). There are 12 large blue "X" marks showing battles without significant Indian participation. These include the American naval victory in western Lake Erie in September, 1813 (no. 88), as well as engagements numbered 39, 60, 65, 67, 82, 96, 97, 102, 120, 125, and 140. In the class of minor actions, there are 23 with significant Indian participation shown by small red "x" marks, and 55 shown by small blue "x" marks. Incidents such as evacuations of forts carry dates but no symbol.

In the conflict between Americans and Indians during the War of 1812 era, the four major events shown by large red dots were the Battle of Tippecanoe, when General William Henry Harrison attacked Prophetstown in November, 1811 (no. 2); Fort Dearborn massacre, when Potawatomi ambushed the evacuating garrison in August, 1812 (no. 17); attack on Indian villages near Peoria, October, 1812 (no. 36); and Indian victory over Americans near Saukenuk in July, 1814 (no. 124). The additional 45 red dots on the map probably are not a complete record of all Indian and white hostilities during the War of 1812 era; they represent only those that were mentioned in accounts and located. The line of blockhouses erected during the war approximates the white population frontier that can be seen on the 1810 map (map 20). Only selected blockhouses were mapped, for most of the frontier farms were forti-fied. The largest center of defense, Fort Vallonia in southern Indiana, covered an acre of land with blockhouses at all four corners.

The progress of the American-British war at strategic locations is concisely summarized on the map by listing battle dates and times when a fort changed hands. For example, Fort Erie, on the inset map of the Niagara Region, was a focal point of action six times during 1813 and 1814. The "Br" abbreviation heading the list of dates referring to Fort Erie shows that the fort was initially British. Subsequently, Fort Erie was occupied by Americans in May, 1813 (no. 64), and returned to the British in June (no. 68), both incidents without battle. In four battles the following year, Americans conquered the fort in July (no. 117) and repulsed attacks in August (no. 129) and September (no. 139), but the British regained Fort Erie in November, 1814 (no. 143).

Shifting concentrations of partisan Indian population during the war can be followed by noting the dates beside the eight small red-tinted areas and the single green-tinted area on the map:

(1) Prophetstown, near the juncture of the Tippecanoe and Wabash Rivers in Indiana, was the main center for anti-American Indians from its founding in 1808 until after the American declaration of war in 1812. Then both Tecumseh and the Prophet went to Canada.

(2) Potawatomi towns on the Illinois River were joined by Kickapoo, Piankeshaw, Ottawa, and Ojibwa militants by 1812. For comparison, see 1810 situation (map 20).

(3) During 1812 and 1813, Indians cooperating with the British concentrated on both sides of the Detroit River in the international war zone under British control, until evacuation in late September, 1813.

(4) The green-shaded area in Ohio indicates a region occupied by pro-American Indians during 1812 and 1813. The single village symbol near Fort Piqua represents several temporary refugee camps containing about 3,000 Indians under American protection.

(5) In 1814 and 1815, militant pro-British Indians were in three locations. One contingent accompanied the British army retreating up the Thames River to the western end of Lake Ontario, present Burlington Bay and Hamilton (see also map 15). Hostile Potawatomi retired to the mouth of the St. Josephs River in Michigan. A third pro-British faction gathered around the Sauk stronghold at the mouth of the Rock River in Illinois.

(6) Throughout the war era, loyal British Indians were in the vicinity of Kingston, Ontario.

An examination of the main map reveals two distinct theatres in the dual conflict of the War of 1812. In simplest terms, there was an international war in the east reaching down the St. Lawrence Valley, and an Indian war in the

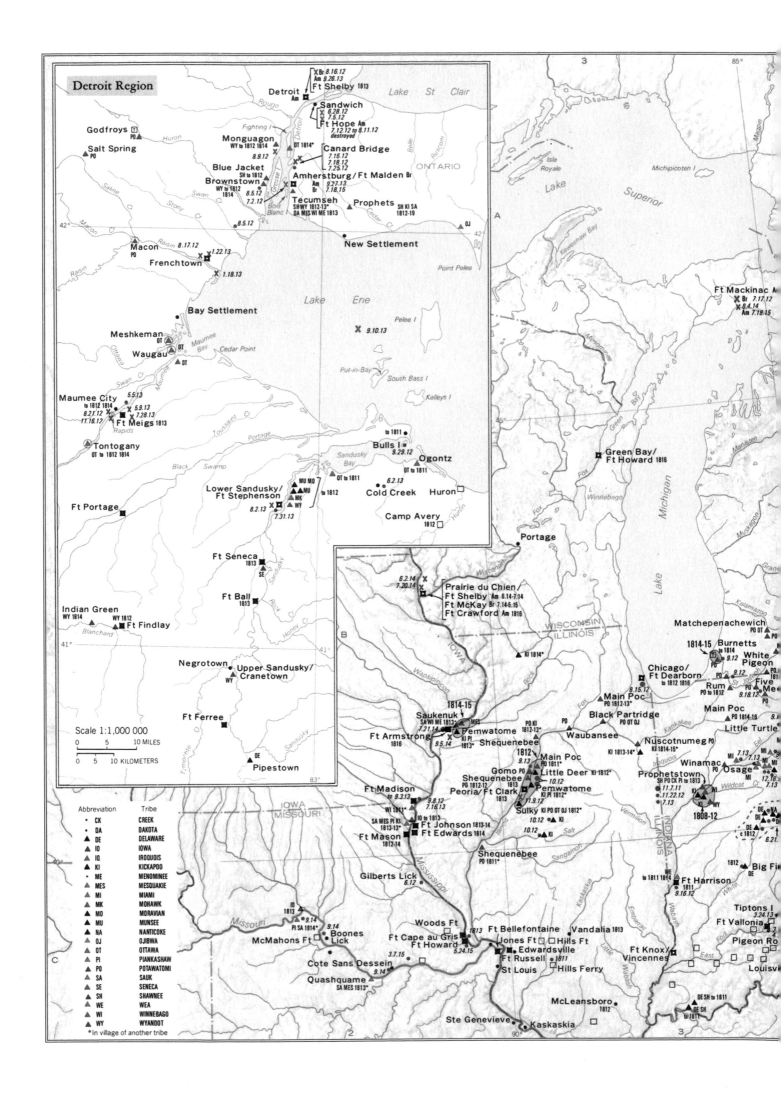

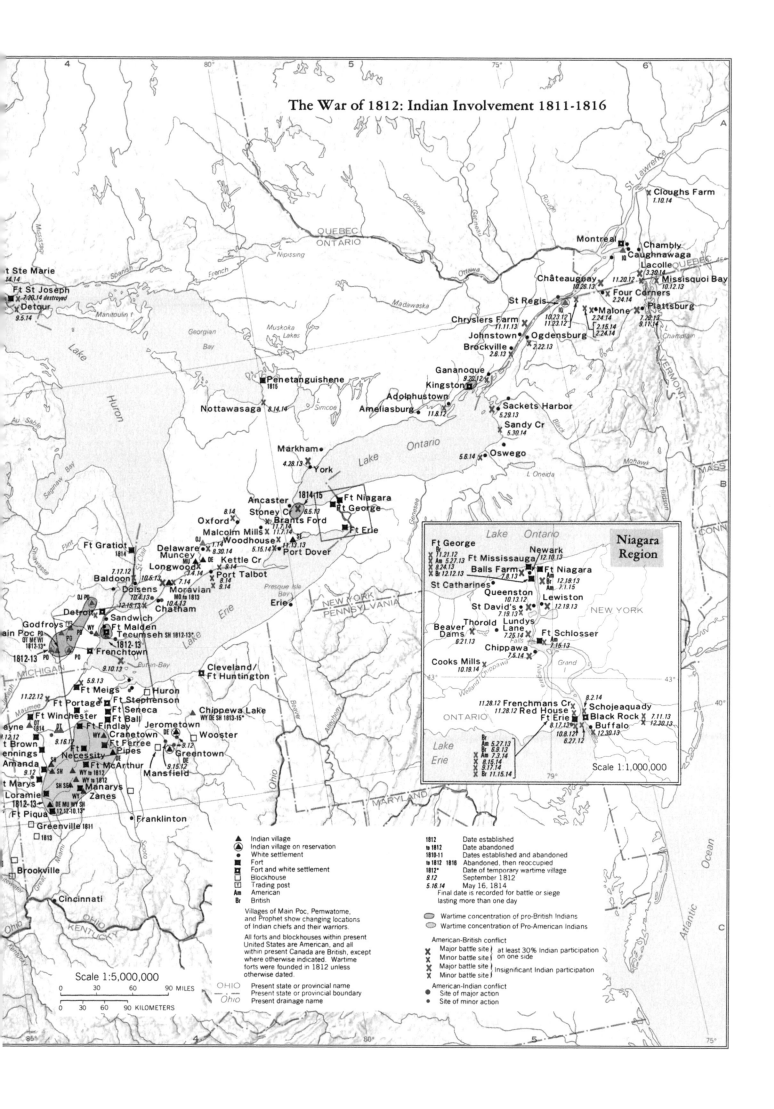

The War of 1812: Indian Involvement 1811-1816

MAP
21

Niagara Region

Scale 1:1,000,000

Ft George
11.21.12
Am 5.27.13 Ft Mississauga
8.24.13
Br 12.12.13
St Catharines
Newark
12.10.13
Ft Niagara
Br 12.19.13
Am 7.1.15
Balls Farm
Queenston
10.13.12
Lewiston
12.19.13
St David's
7.19.13
NEW YORK
Thorold
Beaver
Dams
6.21.13
Lundys
Lane
7.25.14
Ft Schlosser
Am
7.15.13
Chippawa
7.5.14
Cooks Mills
10.19.14
ONTARIO
Lake
Erie
8.2.14
Schojeaquady
Frenchmans Cr
11.28.12
11.28.12 Red House
Ft Erie
8.17.13*
10.8.12
6.27.12
Black Rock
7.11.13
Buffalo
12.30.13
12.30.13
Br
Am 5.27.13
Br 6.9.13
Am 7.3.14
8.15.14
9.17.14
Br 11.15.14

Cloughs Farm
1.10.14
Montreal
Chambly
Caughnawaga
Lacolle
Châteauguay 11.20.12 3.30.14 Missisquoi Bay
10.26.13 10.12.13
St Regis Four Corners
2.24.14
Chryslers Farm 10.23.12 Malone Plattsburg
11.11.13 11.23.12 2.24.14 7.20.13
Johnstown Ogdensburg 2.15.14 9.11.14
Brockville 2.22.13 2.24.14
2.6.13
Gananoque
9.20.12
Kingston
Adolphustown Sackets Harbor
Ameliasburg 5.29.13
11.8.12 Sandy Cr
5.30.14
Markham Oswego
4.28.13 York 5.6.14
Ancaster Ft Niagara
1814-15 Ft George
Stoney Cr 6.5.13
Oxford 8.14 Brants Ford Ft Erie
Malcolm Mills 11.7.14
Woodhouse 11.7.14
Delaware Kettle Cr SE
Muncey 8.30.14 5.15.14 11.13.13
Longwood 8.14 Port Dover
Ft Gratiot Baldoon 3.4.14 Port Talbot Erie
1814 Dolsens 10.5.13 7.14 8.14
10.4.13 Moravian 9.14
Detroit Chatham 10.4.13
Godfroys Sandwich
ain Poc Ft Malden
Tecumseh SH 1812-13*
1812-13
Frenchtown
9.10.13 Put-in-Bay Cleveland/
Ft Huntington
5.9.13 Huron
11.22.12 Ft Meigs
Ft Portage Ft Stephenson
Ft Winchester Ft Seneca Chippewa Lake
ayne Ft Ball WY DE SH 1813-15*
Ft Findlay Cranetown Jerometown
Brown Ferree Wooster
nnings Pipes
Amanda Ft McArthur Greentown
St Marys Mansfield
Loramie Manarys
Zanes
Ft Piqua
Greenville 1811
1813
Brookville
Cincinnati

Penetanguishene
1815
Nottawasaga 8.14.14

St Ste Marie
14.14
Ft St Joseph
7.20.14 destroyed
Detour
9.5.14

Scale 1:5,000,000

| 0 | 30 | 60 | 90 MILES |

| 0 | 30 | 60 | 90 KILOMETERS |

▲ Indian village
◮ Indian village on reservation
• White settlement
■ Fort
⊡ Fort and white settlement
□ Blockhouse
⊤ Trading post
Am American
Br British

1812 Date established
to 1812 Date abandoned
1810-11 Dates established and abandoned
to 1812 1816 Abandoned, then reoccupied
1812* Date of temporary wartime village
9.12 September 1812
5.16.14 May 16, 1814
Final date is recorded for battle or siege
lasting more than one day

Villages of Main Poc, Pemwatome,
and Prophet show changing locations
of Indian chiefs and their warriors.

All forts and blockhouses within present
United States are American, and all
within present Canada are British, except
where otherwise indicated. Wartime
forts were founded in 1812 unless
otherwise dated.

OHIO Present state or provincial name
Ohio Present state or provincial boundary
Ohio Present drainage name

⬭ Wartime concentration of pro-British Indians
⬭ Wartime concentration of Pro-American Indians

American-British conflict
✕ Major battle site
✕ Minor battle site at least 30% Indian participation on one side
✕ Major battle site
✕ Minor battle site Insignificant Indian participation

American-Indian conflict
● Site of major action
• Site of minor action

west extending to central Missouri. The two conflicts merged at the western end of Lake Erie, and along the Detroit River and the lower Thames valley east of Lake St. Clair (see also map 20). The American-British war developed a secondary line of action on and near the St. Marys River, as well as on a sector of the Mississippi River where similar action had occurred during the American Revolution (map 19). Indians were major protagonists in the west and served in a supporting capacity in the eastern war zone.

Two further comments should be added concerning apparent exceptions to the dominant pattern of symbol dis-

tribution on the 1812 map. The red dots east of the Detroit River shore indicate two encounters between Indian war parties and American troops on the lower Thames River. Although no British troops were involved, these skirmishes were preliminary to the Battle of Moraviantown, a major event in the international war. The only blue "x" mark west of Detroit identifies an American attack on an Illinois River community suspected of aiding Indians. No Indians were directly involved, but the action was an aspect of the frontier Indian war.

WAR OF 1812 IN THE GREAT LAKES REGION: CHRONOLOGY OF HOSTILE ACTIONS, 1811-1815

No.	Date	Symbol	Location	Indian Participation	Map	Remarks
(1)	1811		Hills Ferry, Ill.	100%	Main	At present Carlyle on Kaskaskia River, one of several 1811 Indian actions that inspired Harrison to move toward Prophetstown.
(2)	11.7.11 (Nov. 7,1811)		Prophetstown, Ind.	100%	Main	Gen. Harrison (Am) led attack on joint Indian force in Battle of Tippecanoe at present Battleground.
(3)	6.12 (June, 1812)		Gilbert's Lick, Mo.	100%	Main	Over a dozen settlers killed near present Palmyra, probably by Sauk.
(4)	6.27.12		near Black Rock, N.Y.	—	Niagara	Canadians captured the *Commencement*. First encounter after the United States declared war.
(5)	6.28.12 (June 28, 1812)		Sandwich, Ont.	—	Detroit	Canadian militia detained ferry boats on Detroit River at present Windsor.
(6)	7.2.12 (July 2, 1812)		near Grosse Isle, Detroit River	—	Detroit	British captured the *Cuyahoga*, which carried Gen. Hull's (Am) papers.
(7)	7.5.12 (July 5, 1812)		Sandwich, Ont.	—	Detroit	American artillery barrage on Sandwich, present Windsor.
(8)	7.16.12 (July 16, 1812)		Canard River, Ont.	35%	Detroit	Minor action.
(9)	7.17.12 (July 17,1812)		Baldoon, Ont.	—	Main	American raid for forage.
(10)	7.17.12 (July 17, 1812)		Fort Mackinac, Mich.	75%	Main	British captured fort on Mackinac Island with aid of Dakota, Menominee, Winnebago, Ottawa and Ojibwa.
(11)	7.18.12 (July 18, 1812)		Canard River, Ont.	35%(?)	Detroit	Skirmish.
(12)	7.25.12 (July 25,1812)		Canard River, Ont.	100%	Detroit	Menominee routed an attempted American ambush.
(13)	8.5.12 (Aug. 5, 1812)		Brownstown Creek	100%	Detroit	Tecumseh's Indian force ambushed and routed American force near present Gibralter, Mich.
(14)	8.5.12 (Aug. 5, 1812)		Swan Creek, Mich.	100%	Detroit	Indians captured mail and killed most of the 20-man escort.
(15)	8.9.12 (Aug. 9, 1812)		Monguagon, Mich.	50%	Detroit	At present Wyandotte, Gen. Muir (Br) and Tecumseh (Shönbrunn) prevented Americans from opening road to Raisin River.

No.	Date	Symbol	Location	Indian Participation	Map	Remarks
(16)	8.11.12 (Aug. 11, 1812)	Destroyed	Sandwich, Ont.	—	Detroit	Fort Hope at present Windsor, built by Americans in July, 1812, destroyed at time of Gen. Hull's evacuation.
(17)	8.15.12 (Aug. 15, 1812)		near Fort Dearborn (Chicago, Ill.)	100%	Main	About 400 Potawatomi massacred most of garrison being evacuated by Wm. Wells, adopted son of Little Turtle (MI). Trader John Kinzie and family rescued.
(18)	8.16.12 (Aug. 16, 1812)		Detroit, Mich.	35%-40%	Detroit	Gen. Hull (Am) surrendered Detroit, capital of Michigan Territory, to Gen. Brock (Br).
(19)	8.17.12 (Aug. 17, 1812)		Raisin River, Mich.	—	Detroit	American outpost given up as part of the Detroit surrender terms.
(20)	8.21.12 (Aug. 21,1812)		Rapids of the Maumee River, Ohio	—	Detroit	American outpost also surrendered.
(21)	9.12 (Sept., 1812)		Lower St. Joseph River, Mich.	100%	Main	After Fort Dearborn massacre American raids destroyed the cornfields of Potawatomi near present St. Joseph.
(22)	9.12 (Sept., 1812)		St. Joseph River near Mich.-Ind. border	100%	Main	Potawatomi's crops destroyed near present Niles, Mich.
(23)	9.12 (Sept., 1812)		Jerometown and Greentown, Ohio	100%	Main	Delaware reservation town evacuated by American troops; 45 Greentown Indians return and kill nearby settlers.
(24)	9.12 (Sept., 1812)		Fort St. Mary's Ohio	100%	Main	Indians fired on fort.
(25)	9.3.12 (Sept. 3, 1812)		Pigeon Roost, Ind.	100%	Main	Shawnee led by Missilimeta ravaged the settlement; killed 20.
(26)	9.8.12 (Sept. 8,1812)		Fort Madison, Iowa	100%	Main	Winnebago attacked fort for 3 days, were beaten off.
(27)	9.12.12 (Sept. 12, 1812)		Fort Wayne, Ind.	100%	Main	Gen. Harrison (Am) relieved Fort Wayne from Tecumseh's (Shönbrunn) 6-day siege.
(28)	9.15.12 (Sept. 15, 1812)		near Mansfield, Ohio	100%	Main	Three actions along Black Fork of Mohican River, near Mifflin 9 miles from Mansfield.
(29)	9.16.12 (Sept. 16, 1812)		Fort Harrison, Ind.	100%	Main	Col. Russell relieved fort from a 2-week siege.
(30)	9.16.12 (Sept. 16, 1812)		on Wabash River, Ind.	100%	Main	Deserted Miami villages burned by Americans.
(31)	9.16.12 (Sept. 16, 1812)		Blanchard River, Ohio	100%	Main	Two Ottawa towns destroyed.
(32)	9.17.12 (Sept. 17, 1812)		Little Turtle's Village, Ind.	100%	Main	American raid on deserted Miami village northwest of Fort Wayne.
(33)	9.18.12 (Sept. 18, 1812)		Five Medals Towns, Ind.	100%	Main	American raid destroyed Potawatomi villages on Elkhart River near present Benton and Waterford.
(34)	9.20.12 (Sept. 20,1812)		Gananoque, Ont.	—	Main	American raid on town.
(35)	9.29.12 (Sept. 29, 1812)		Bull Island, Sandusky Bay, Ohio	100%	Detroit	Eight killed in skirmish.

No.	Date	Symbol	Location	Indian Participation	Map	Remarks
(36)	10.12 (Oct., 1812)	●●	near Peoria, Ill.	100%	Main	Three Potawatomi, Kickapoo, and Piankeshaw villages destroyed at Peoria and northeast at Spring Bay.
(37)	10.12 (Oct., 1812)	●●	north of Salt River, Ill.	100%	Main	Two Kickapoo villages destroyed at present Lincoln and McLean.
(38)	10.8.12 (Oct. 8, 1812)	x	near Fort Erie, Ont.		Niagara	Naval actions. Americans captured the *Caledonia* and sank the *Detroit* carrying papers of Gen. Hull (Am) and Gen. Brock (Br).
(39)	10.13.12 (Oct. 13, 1812)	X	Queenston, Ont.	10%	Niagara	British repulsed invasion by American force of 4,000; Gen. Brock (Br) killed.
(40)	10.23.12 (Oct. 23, 1812)	x	east of St. Regis in N.Y.	—	Main	Americans captured British post on Salmon River, by present Fort Covington.
(41)	11.8.12 (Nov. 8, 1812)	x	near Adolphustown, Ont.	—	Main	Minor naval action in Bay of Quinte.
(42)	11.9.12 (Nov. 9, 1812)	x	Peoria, Ill.	—	Main	French population suspected of assisting hostile Indians. American raid destroyed half the town, carried inhabitants to St. Louis.
(43)	11.16.12 (Nov. 16, 1812)	x	Rapids of the Maumee River, Ohio	75%	Detroit	Americans forced a British and Indian force to withdraw.
(44)	11.20.12 (Nov. 20, 1812)	x	Lacolle, Quebec	—	Main	Minor action.
(45)	11.21.12 (Nov. 21, 1812)	x	Fort George and Fort Niagara, N.Y.	—	Main	Artillery duel.
(46)	11.22.12 (Nov. 22, 1812)	x	Maumee River, Ohio	100%	Main	Capt. Logan (Shönbrunn), American scout, mortally wounded in action with British-Indian patrol.
(47)	11.22.12 (Nov. 22, 1812)	●	Prophetstown and Wild Cat Creek, Ind.	100%	Main	Prophetstown and deserted Winnebago and Kickapoo villages destroyed in brief engagement on Wild Cat Creek. 16 Americans killed.
(48)	11.23.12 (Nov. 23, 1812)	x	East of St. Regis, in N.Y.	—	Main	British recaptured post on Salmon River by present Fort Covington.
(49)	11.28.12 (Nov. 28, 1812)	x	Red House, Ont.	10%	Niagara	American attack repulsed, 30 taken prisoner.
(50)	11.28.12 (Nov. 28, 1812)	x	Frenchman's Creek, Ont.	10%	Niagara	Minor action.
(51)	12.18.12 (Dec. 18, 1812)	●	northeast of Wild Cat Creek, Ind.	100%	Main	Three Miami and Delaware towns on Mississinewa River destroyed. Miami attacked Americans at Silver Heels town.
(52)	1812	●	Big Fire, Ind.	100%	Main	Mistaken for Shawnee, Delaware village near Waverly destroyed by Americans; Upper Delaware village also struck.
(53)	1.18.13 (Jan. 18, 1813)	x	Raisin River, Mich.	80%	Detroit	Americans forced British and Indians to withdraw.

No.	Date	Symbol	Location	Indian Participation	Map	Remarks
(54)	1.22.13 (Jan. 22,1813)	x	Frenchtown, Mich.	50%	Detroit	Gen. Winchester (Am) surrendered; Indians prominent in fighting; 100 Americans killed in massacre after the battle.
(55)	2.6.13 (Feb. 6,1813)	x	Brockville, Ont.	—	Main	Americans raided town on St. Lawrence River.
(56)	2.22.13 (Feb. 22,1813)	x	Ogdensburg, N.Y.	—	Main	British raided town.
(57)	3.18.13 (Mar. 18, 1813)	•	Fort Vallonia, Ind.	100%	Main	Indians raided fort and inflicted 4 casualties.
(58)	3.24.13 (Mar. 24,1813)	•	Tipton's Island Ind.	100%	Main	Skirmish, 1 Indian killed on East Fork of White River.
(59)	4.16.13 (Apr. 16, 1813)	•	near Fort Vallonia, Ind.	100%	Main	Indian raid, 2 settlers killed at "The Forks," juncture of Muscatatuck and East Fork of White River.
(60)	4.28.13 (Apr. 28, 1813)	X	York, Ont.	—	Main	Americans burned York (Toronto), capital of Upper Canada.
(61)	5.5.13 (May 5,1813)	•	near mouth of Maumee River, Ohio	50%	Detroit	British-Indian victory at Fort Miami site near modern Toledo followed by massacre of 40 Americans.
(62)	5.9.13 (May 9,1813)	x	Fort Meigs, Ohio	50%	Detroit & Main	British siege at present Perrysburg begun May 1 was lifted May 9.
(63)	5.27.13 (May 27,1813)	x	Fort George, Ont.	—	Niagara	Americans captured Fort George.
(64)	5.27.13 (May 27,1.813)	x	Fort Erie, Ont.	—	Niagara	Americans captured Fort Erie.
(65)	5.29.13 (May 29,1813)	X	Sackets Harbor, N.Y.	—	Detroit	Americans beat off a British attack.
(66)	6.2.13 (June 2, 1813)	•	Cold Creek, Ohio	100%	Detroit	Indian raid; 3 families killed or captured.
(67)	6.5.13 (June 5,1813)	X	Stoney Creek, Ont.	—	Main	British forced American retreat.
(68)	6.9.13 (June 9, 1813)	x	Fort Erie, Ont.	—	Main	British recaptured Fort Erie.
(69)	6.21.13 (June 21,1813)	••• •••	Along upper White River, Ind.	100%	Main	Americans raided 9 Delaware, Munsee and Nanticoke towns.
(70)	6.24.13 (June 24,1813)	X	Beaver Dams, Ont.	Almost 100%	Niagara	Six Nations and Caughnawaga under their own command forced American surrender to the British.
(71)	Summer, 1813	•	Opposite Cape au Gris, in Ill.	100%	Main	Twelve Americans killed in Indian attack on fort.
(72)	7.13 (July, 1813)	•	Miami villages on Eel River, Ind.	100%	Main	These 3 sets of villages were attacked and though largely empty, destroyed during Col. Russell's (Am) 4-week campaign in July, 1813.
(73)	7.13 (July, 1813)	•	Miami villages on Wabash River, Ind.	100%	Main	
(74)	7.13 (July, 1813)	•	Miami villages on Mississinewa River, Ind.	100%	Main	
(75)	7.13 (July, 1813)	•	Prophetstown, Ind.	100%	Main	Third American raid on Wabash River near mouth of Tippecanoe, present Battleground.

No.	Date	Symbol	Location	Indian Participation	Map	Remarks
(76)	7.13 (July, 1813)		Fort Schlosser, N.Y.	—	Niagara	British raid on fort. Some prisoners taken.
(77)	7.8.13 (July 8, 1813)		Balls Farm, Ont.	50%	Niagara	Brief engagement, British victory.
(78)	7.11.13 (July 11, 1813)		Black Rock, N.Y.	—	Niagara	British destroyed barricades at garrison.
(79)	7.16.13 (July 16, 1813)		Fort Madison, Iowa	100%	Main	Indian raid on fort.
(80)	7.19.13 (July 19, 1813)		St. Davids, Ont.	—	Niagara	Engagement after British moved headquarters to St. Davids.
(81)	7.28.13 (July 28, 1813)		Fort Meigs, Ohio	80%	Detroit	British and Indian siege of fort, July 21-28
(82)	7.29.13 (July 29, 1813)		Plattsburg, N.Y.	—	Main	British raid destroyed American barracks and stores.
(83)	7.31.13 (July 31, 1813)		near Lower Sandusky, Ohio	100%	Detroit	Eleven Indians killed near present Ballsville, south of Fremont.
(84)	8.2.13 (Aug. 2, 1813)		Fort Stephenson, Ohio	80%	Detroit	Americans beat back British-Indian attack at present Fremont.
(85)	8.17.13 (Aug. 17, 1813)		south of Fort Erie, Ont.	—	Niagara	Skirmish near shore.
(86)	8.24.13 (Aug. 24, 1813)		Fort George, Ont.	—	Niagara	Minor action. American party forced to retire into fort.
(87)	9.13 (Sept., 1813)		Gomo's, Ill.	100%	Main	Deserted Potawatomi village at Chillicothe and 2 others burned by Americans from St. Louis.
(88)	9.10.13 (Sept. 10, 1813)		north of Put-in-Bay, Lake Erie	—	Detroit & Main	American naval victory gave United States control of Lake Erie.
(89)	9.26.13 (Sept. 26, 1813)		Detroit, Mich.	—	Detroit	British evacuated Detroit.
(90)	9.27.13 (Sept. 27, 1813)		Fort Malden, Ont.	—	Detroit	British evacuated Fort Malden.
(91)	10.4.13 (Oct. 4, 1813)		Dolsen's Farm Ont.	100%	Main	Indians skirmished with Gen. Harrison's (Am) army advancing up the Thames River.
(92)	10.4.13 (Oct. 4, 1813)		near Chatham, Ont.	100%	Main	Another skirmish at McGregor's Creek.
(93)	10.5.13 (Oct. 5, 1813)		Moraviantown, Ont.	35-50%	Main	Gen. Harrison routed British and Indians under Gen. Proctor. Tecumseh killed. Indian town destroyed.
(94)	10.13 (Oct., 1813)		Fort Clark, Ill.	—	Main	Americans from St. Louis establish fort to keep Potawatomi in check.
(95)	10.12.13 (Oct. 12, 1813)		Mississquoi Bay, Quebec	—	Main	American raid at head of Lake Champlain, 100 prisoners taken.
(96)	10.26.13 (Oct. 26, 1813)		Châteaugüay, Quebec	—	Main	British defeated invading American army.
(97)	11.11.13 (Nov. 11, 1813)		Chrysler's Farm, Quebec	5%	Main	British defeated invading American army.
(98)	11.13.13 (Nov. 13, 1813)		Woodhouse, Ont.	—	Main	American raiding party dispersed.
(99)	12.10.13 (Dec. 10, 1813)		Newark, Ont.	—	Niagara	Americans burned town.

No.	Date	Symbol	Location	Indian Participation	Map	Remarks
(100)	12.12.13 (Dec. 12, 1813)	x	Fort George, Ont.	—	Niagara	British occupied Fort George after Americans evacuated.
(101)	12.15.13 (Dec. 15, 1813)	x	mouth of Thames River, Ont.	—	Main	British captured American party at McCrae's Farm.
(102)	12.19.13 (Dec. 19, 1813)	X	Fort Niagara, N.Y.	—	Niagara	British captured Fort Niagara.
(103)	12.19.13 (Dec. 19, 1913)	x	Lewiston, N.Y.	—	Niagara	British and Indians burned Lewiston; retaliation for burning of Newark.
(104)	12.30.13 (Dec. 30, 1813)	x	Black Rock, N.Y.	—	Niagara	British and Western Indians burned village.
(105)	12.30.13 (Dec. 30,1813)	x	Buffalo, N.Y.	—	Niagara	British burned Buffalo.
(106)	1.14 (Jan., 1814)	x	Delaware, Ont.	—	Main	Americans raid Canadian town on Thames River.
(107)	1.10.14 (Jan. 10, 1814)	x	Clough's Farm, Quebec	—	Main	Skirmish near present Yamaska.
(108)	2.15.14 (Feb. 15, 1814)	x	near Malone, N.Y.	—	Main	British raid on Salmon River below Malone.
(109)	2.24.14 (Feb. 24, 1814)	x	near Malone, N.Y.	—	Main	British again raid Salmon River area.
(110)	2.24.14 (Feb. 24, 1814)	x	Malone, N.Y.	—	Main	British raid at Salmon River town.
(111)	2.24.14 (Feb. 24, 1814)	X	Four Corners, N.Y.	—	Main	British raid.
(112)	3.4.14 (Mar. 4, 1814)	x	Longwood, Ont. River.	10%	Main	American victory on upper Thames
(113)	3.30.14 (Mar. 30, 1814)	x	Lacolle, Quebec	5%	Main	Minor action, British victory.
(114)	5.6.14 (May 6, 1814)	x	Oswego, N.Y.	—	Main	British victory on eastern Lake Ontario.
(115)	5.15.14 (May 15, 1814)	x	Port Dover, Ont.	—	Main	Americans burned town on Lake Erie.
(116)	5.30.14 (May 30, 1814)	x	Sandy Creek, N.Y.	—	Main	Americans ambushed British on eastern shore of Lake Ontario.
(117)	6.2.14 (June 2, 1814)	x	Prairie du Chien, Wis.	35%	Main	Americans occupied town; 20 Winnebagos captured.
(118)	7.14 (July, 1814)	x	Moraviantown, Ont.	—	Main	American raid, skirmish with British.
(119)	7.3.14 (July 3, 1814)	x	Fort Erie, Ont.	—	Niagara	British capitulated to Americans.
(120)	7.5.14 (July 5, 1814)	X	Chippawa, Ont.	20%	Niagara	American victory.
(121)	7.14.14 (July 14, 1814)	x	Sault Ste. Marie, Mich. and Ont.	5%	Main	Encounter along St. Marys River; Americans destroyed traders property and burned North West Co. warehouses.
(122)	7.20.14 (July 20, 1814)	x	Prairie du Chien, Wis.	70%	Main	British and Indians (Dakota, Menominee, Ojibwa, Winnebago) capture new American Fort Shelby and rename it Fort McKay.

No.	Date	Symbol	Location	Indian Participation	Map	Remarks
(123)	7.20.14 (July 20, 1814)	x	St. Joseph Island, Ont.	—	Main	Americans destroyed abandoned British fort, in northern Lake Huron.
(124)	7.21.14 (July 21, 1814)	•	near Saukenuk, Ill.	100%	Main	Sauk, Mesquakie, and Kickapoo ambush American forces near mouth of Rock River.
(125)	7.25.14 (July 25, 1814)	X	Lundy's Lane, Ont.	5%	Niagara	Americans withdrew from battle.
(126)	8.14 (Aug., 1814)	x	Oxford, Ont.	100%	Main	Indians with American army raided town, present Woodstock, on upper Thames River.
(127)	8.14 (Aug., 1814)	x	Port Talbot, Ont.	100%	Main	Indians with American army raided town.
(128)	8.2.14 (Aug. 2, 1814)	x	Schojeaquody Creek, N. Y.	—	Niagara	British forces stopped by Americans en route to attack Buffalo.
(129)	8.4.14 (Aug. 4, 1814)	x	Fort Mackinac, Mich.	50%	Main	British beat off American attack on Mackinac Island.
(130)	8.14.14 (Aug. 14, 1814)	x	Nottawasaga Bay, Ont.	—	Main	American raid at base of Georgian Bay destroyed British blockhouses and the *Nancy*. Gave United States control of Lake Huron.
(131)	8.15.14 (Aug. 15, 1814)	x	Fort Erie, Ont.	—	Niagara	British attack repulsed, siege begun.
(132)	8.30.14 (Aug. 30, 1814)	x	Delaware, Ont.	—	Main	Second American raid on settlement on Thames River.
(133)	9.14 (Sept., 1814)	x	Kettle Creek, Ont.	—	Main	American raid south of present St. Thomas.
(134)	9.14 (Sept., 1814)	x	Port Talbot, Ont.	—	Main	American raid.
(135)	9.14 (Sept., 1814)	•	Boones Lick, Mo.	100%	Main	Indian raid near present Boonesboro.
(136)	9.14 (Sept., 1814)	•	Piankeshaw and Sauk Village, Mo.	100%	Main	American raid on Indian fort at present Miami; prisoners taken to St. Louis.
(137)	9.14 (Sept., 1814)	•	Cote Sans Dessein, Mo.	100%	Main	Sauk-Piankeshaw raid on Missouri River settlement.
(138)	9.5.14 (Sept. 5, 1814)	x	Detour Point, Mich.	—	Main	British captured *Tigris* and *Scorpion*. Regained control of Lake Huron.
(139)	9.5.14 (Sept. 5, 1814)	X	near Saukenuk, Ill.	95%	Main	By Rock Island, 1,200 Sauk Mesquakie, and Winnebago, under Black Hawk, with 30 British, rout 430 Americans.
(140)	9.11.14 (Sept. 11, 1814)	X	Plattsburg, N.Y.	—	Main	American victory in major battle.
(141)	9.17.14 (Sept. 17, 1814)	x	Fort Erie, Ont.	—	Niagara	Americans repulse British attack.
(142)	10.19.14 (Oct. 19, 1814)	x	Cooks Mills, Ont.	—	Niagara	Skirmish between British and American forces.
(143)	11.7.14 (Nov. 7, 1814)	x	Brants Ford, Ont.	50%	Main	American raid and battle on Six Nations reserve, present Brantford.
(144)	11.7.14 (Nov. 7, 1814)	x	Malcolm's Mills, Ont.	—	Main	American raid at present Burford.

No.	Date	Symbol	Location	Indian Participation	Map	Remarks
(145)	11.15.14 (Nov. 15, 1814)	x	Fort Erie, Ont.	—	Niagara	British re-occupied Fort Erie after Americans withdrew.
(146)	3.7.15 (Mar. 7,1815)	•	northeast of Cote Sans Dessein, Mo.	100%	Main	Sauk and Mesquakie ambushed American militia at Loutre Creek settlement near present McKittrick.
(147)	5.24.15 (May 24,1815)	•	near Fort Howard, Mo.	100%	Main	Sauk raid and battle at Sinkhole, Old Monroe, at mouth of Cuivre River: 8 Americans killed.
(148)	7.1.15 (July 1, 1815)		Fort Niagara, N.Y.	—	Niagara	Fort returned to the United States, according to terms of Treaty of Ghent.
(149)	7.18.15 (July 18,1815)		Fort Malden, Ont.	—	Detroit	Fort returned to Great Britain, a treaty provision.
(150)	7.18.15 (July 18,1815)		Fort Mackinac, Mich.	—	Main	Fort returned to the United States, a peace treaty stipulation.

Great Lakes Indians and the War of 1812: Introduction

The Battle of Tippecanoe on November 7, 1811, opened a new round of hostilities between Great Lakes Indians and the constantly advancing American frontier. It was not unexpected, for Governor William Henry Harrison of the Indiana territory and Tecumseh, acknowledged war leader of the uniting Indians, had been squaring off for months. This new contest for control of the Old Northwest differed from that of the 1790s, for eight months later it coincided with the more general struggle known as the War of 1812. The American declaration of war against Great Britain was triggered principally by British impressment of American seamen on merchant vessels in the Atlantic Ocean. The existence of a state of war secured for the militant Indians more active cooperation and support from the British in Canada, a continuing source of trade and presents since 1783.

In the Great Lakes Region, the War of 1812 remained very much an Indian War. Indians began their fight against Americans before the British involved themselves, and they remained in the field for months after the British left. As in previous disputes with Americans, Indian people ultimately lost ground. Yet in the process, their presence dictated both strategy and tactics to the two white powers; and though tribal sympathies were divided, they gave greater assistance to the British. In particular, their presence explains the American failures and British successes in 1812, and the American reluctance to undertake bolder action against Upper Canada during campaigns of 1813 and 1814.

The *Atlas* account of the War of 1812 era is restricted to the Great Lakes theatre. Yet it is important to realize that while war was in progress in this American-Canadian borderland, naval engagements and military action took place along the Atlantic and Gulf coasts and within the present southeastern United States. During 1814, the British burned public buildings at Washington, D.C. For two years, 1813-14, the United States also carried on punitive war from Alabama to Spanish Florida against Creek and Seminole accused of cooperating with British traders or agents. Unaware of the preliminary peace treaty already signed, Americans fought and defeated the British at New Orleans, Louisiana, in January, 1815.

Detroit and the Western Theatre, 1811-1813

On the eve of the November 7, 1811, attack upon Prophetstown, the collected villages there could muster at least 700 warriors, largely representing Potawatomi, Kickapoo, Winnebago, and Sauk from present Illinois and Wisconsin, though there was also a group of dissident Wyandot from Ohio. General Harrison ordered the offensive action against the community at a time when Tecumseh was absent on an extended southern tour to the Creek, Choctaw and Chickasaw, winding up among the Shawnee and Delaware in Missouri. Tecumseh's mother was Creek, and Prophetstown had a small Creek contingent, most of whom had been in the area since the 1790s. During 1811, Tecumseh tried to unite northern and southern Indians in concerted action against American encroachment.

By 1811, Indians and whites were already moving to safer quarters as the expectation of general war in American territory increased. Ogontz and his French and Ottawa following left the shores of Sandusky Bay, some returning to Frenchtown on the Raisin River of Michigan (see also map 17). In Michigan and Ohio, frontier inhabitants reported that as war preparations became evident, Indians "just seemed to disappear." Greenville, Tecumseh's residence until 1808, was a fortified white settlement by 1811.

The Indian villages close to Lower Sandusky were all vacated early in the war era. The Wyandot and Mohawk moved up the Sandusky River, while most Munsee and Moravians crossed Lake Erie to Upper Canada. The Mora-

Chipaway, in the Niagara Peninsula war zone, May 17, 1804. By E. Walsh. Clements Library.

vians had remained at Pettquotting or New Salem (map 18) on the Huron River of Ohio until 1809, when they joined their former Munsee neighbors who had relocated north of Lower Sandusky in 1804. The abandoned Moravian mission became the site of a defense post, Camp Avery, in 1812 (see inset map of Detroit Region).

During the winter 1811-12, severe earthquake shocks at New Madrid, Missouri, with tremors extending to the shores of Lake Erie, seemed a portent of danger. In the spring of 1812, American troops and militia were organizing at Dayton, Ohio before General Hull arrived from Washington in May to take command of the expedition to strengthen Detroit. Wyandot, Shawnee, and Seneca leaders gave permission for the army to cut a road from Urbana across the virtually impassible Black Swamp to the place called the "Miami Rapids." At that time, the river name was in the process of changing from "Miami-of-the-Lakes," also known in abbreviated French as "Au Mi," to its present anglicized form "Maumee." Hull's trace is marked by Forts McArthur, Necessity, Findlay, and Portage (see main map and Detroit Region inset). At Frenchtown on July 1, before he reached Detroit, Hull learned of the American declaration of war on June 24.

Hull's fear of Indian attack was evident during his trek across northwest Ohio. At first, he hoped that diplomacy, combined with the defeat experienced at Tippecanoe, would promote Indian neutrality or confine hostilities to the small and sporadic raids that had hit western settlers over

the winter and spring. After he reached Detroit, he was less sanguine. Although he urged all tribes of the Old Northwest to attend a grand council at Piqua, Ohio, only Shawnee and Delaware had significant representation. When news of the fall of Detroit reached the gathering, it broke up.

The Miami and Potawatomi were split on issues involving the Prophet's message, Tecumseh's resistance movement, and the outbreak of war between the British and Americans. The Miamis lost the influence of Little Turtle, strongly pro-American leader, who died in 1812. Traditional Potawatomi like Kesis and Five Medals were unable to restrain their angry young men from gathering at Prophetstown. The community, temporarily dispersed following the Battle of Tippecanoe, again counted 700 to 900 warriors in 1812.

In June, 1812, Tecumseh shifted to the Canadian side of the Detroit River. He made his war-time headquarters south of Fort Malden on the farm of the British Indian agent, Matthew Elliott. The Prophet, his influence on the wane, moved with his most loyal followers to a well-hidden location on Cedar Creek east of Fort Malden, where they remained until several years after warfare ceased (see inset map of Detroit Region). Wyandot living south of Detroit under the leadership of Walk-in-the-Water were forced reluctantly into the British ranks.

Even before the American declaration of war, Indian troops from west of Lake Michigan were en route to Amherstburg to aid the British. First to arrive were the Menominee. These tribal contingents were organized and dispatched by British trader Robert Dickson, soon named Superintendent of Western Indians. Dickson operated out of Fort Mackinac as far west as the head of the Minnesota River (map 20). Although there was a potentially significant Indian force nearer to sites of conflict, these tribes resisted mobilization. It was estimated that the Six Nations of Upper Canada could easily field 400 warriors, a number that it was expected could be matched by the Missisauga and Ojibwa and by the Caughnawaga and others of Lower Canada.

During the summer of 1812, Indian opposition coalesced against the Americans, and with each successive action Hull's sense of isolation grew. Sometimes with substantial British support as at Canard bridge, sometimes with minor assistance as at Monguagon, and often on their own as at Brownstown and Swan Creek, the regional Indian alliance harassed Americans. They blockaded the road from the Raisin River to Detroit from the end of July on, killed messengers, and twice captured the United States mail. Beyond the Detroit region, Indians killed most of the garrison from Fort Dearborn and served heavily in the capture of Fort Mackinac. These actions left Fort Wayne as the only surviving major fort on the frontier of the Old Northwest, and it was under Indian siege by early September.

In the light of the foregoing events, Hull's surrender to General Isaac Brock at Detroit on August 16, 1812, is less surprising than many accounts have suggested. Hull was outnumbered-perhaps by as much as two to one-and was effectively isolated by surrounding British and Indian enemies. His medical supplies had been lost, his medical staff was reduced by over 50 percent and more than 400 of his garrison were ill. In addition, he faced a potential mutiny. Nevertheless, the surrender of Detroit to the British was the first great shock of the War of 1812 in the Great Lakes Region.

After the British occupied Detroit, Indian allies conducted offensive actions against Fort Wayne and Fort Harrison at Terre Haute, and against Fort Madison on the Mississippi River in Iowa. With support from the British, Indian soldiers moved into the lower Maumee valley in the fall of 1812, and patrols encountered American contingents from Fort Winchester, located at the former site of Fort Defiance (map 18). American forces advanced down the Maumee to camp at the rapids during the winter. In January of 1813, Indians clashed with Americans at the mouth of the Raisin River and again at Frenchtown, where massacre followed the surrender of American General James Winchester and his Kentucky troops.

General Harrison, who succeeded Hull as American commander in the district northwest of the Ohio, countered Indian aggression with expeditions against Indian towns in Indiana, southwestern Michigan, and Illinois. He realized that he had to subdue, or at least neutralize, Indians living south and west of Lake Erie before he could undertake an offensive campaign to regain Detroit and defeat the British on the battlefield. Toward this goal, destructive raids were launched in the fall of 1812 against Indian towns suspected of harboring anti-American warriors. Most were within reach of Fort Wayne or posts established by Hull in Ohio. Although an American contingent advancing from the Wabash River got lost in the Illinois prairies, Governor Ninian Edwards led a successful expedition against the Indian towns around Peoria Lake. Pemwatame's Kickapoo

and Piankeshaw moved to Sauk protection on the Rock River.

The concentration of about 800 warriors around Peoria was largely the work of the Potawatomi war leader, Main Poc, early convert of Tenskwatawa and strong supporter of Tecumseh. He gathered together members of the United Bands of Potawatomi, Piankeshaw from Indiana, and two bands of Kickapoo. Their combined influence overcame pleas for neutrality by the local Potawatomi leader, Gomo. Main Poc had established his village on Crow Prairie, north of Peoria, in 1811, but moved in 1812 to a more isolated location on the Fox River of Illinois. During 1812 and 1813 he coordinated allied Indian forces spread out in small detachments in southeastern Michigan between the Raisin and Huron rivers.

By early 1813, Harrison was situated at Fort Ferree, on the upper Sandusky River, poised for a new advance toward British-held Detroit. Only pro-American or passively neutral Indians remained in northwest Ohio (see inset map of Detroit Region). The pro-British Wyandot under Roundhead had left their village to join the British at Fort Malden. Shawnee headed by Black Hoof at Wapakoneta, like Tarhee (the Crane) at Upper Sandusky, adhered to promises of peace they had made at the Greenville Treaty. John Johnston had gathered non-belligerents from several tribes around his Indian agency headquarters at Upper Piqua, Ohio.

During 1813, the British gained additional Indian reinforcements from tribes west of Lake Michigan. Robert Dickson, following a mid-winter conference in Quebec in January of 1813, returned by way of Detroit and the overland route across Michigan to the mouth of the St. Joseph River. This location, as well as Chicago, was used by the British for distributing supplies to Indians during the War of 1812.

In southwestern Michigan, Potawatomi constructed a secret village of 600 people south of Matchepenachewich's town (present Kalamazoo), away from main routes of travel. Reports indicate that the British maintained a blacksmith there to repair weapons for Indians serving in the war. By June, 1813, Dickson collected more than 600 warriors at Mackinac Island, including large delegations of Menominee, Winnebago, and Ojibwa, as well as smaller numbers of Dakota, Mesquakie, and Ottawa. An additional 800 western Indians under Black Hawk, Sauk leader, went by way of Chicago. All were destined for the Detroit River war zone. At Fort Malden, the Indian military coalition exerted sufficient strength to dictate to their British ally. General Proctor agreed to a second siege of Fort Meigs in July, 1813, and to the siege of Fort Stephenson (present Freemont, Ohio) in August, only because Tecumseh and his warriors insisted.

Harrison's ability to advance against the British in the fall of 1813 rested more on Perry's naval victory near Putin-Bay (which gave control of Lake Erie to the United States) than on his own earlier successes against Indian opponents, for it was the naval defeat that caused Proctor to evacuate Detroit and Fort Malden. Protesting this cowardice, Tecumseh and a depleted Indian army nevertheless accompanied Proctor toward the Thames River. The British had concentrated 3,000 Indian warriors and their families near Fort Malden, along with an estimated 900 British troops. When

British post on St. Joseph Island, northern Lake Huron, a gathering point for Great Lakes Indians during the War of 1812. By E. Walsh. Clements Library.

Proctor retreated, more than 1,000 crossed the Detroit River to make preliminary peace with Americans.

In preparation for the invasion of Canada, Harrison was joined at Fort Seneca, Ohio, by 260 Wyandot, Shawnee, and Seneca. His total force was close to 5,000 men. American troops were transported across Lake Erie by way of Put-in-Bay to the Ontario shore of the Detroit River south of abandoned Fort Malden. Harrison pursued the retreating British and Indian forces until he caught them at Moraviantown on October 5, 1813, where he delivered a critical blow. Although Tecumseh was killed early in battle, he was survived by his second-in-command, Oshawanah, the Ojibwa leader from Ontario. Harrison's victory at the Battle of the Thames gave Americans control over the entire western peninsula of Upper Canada, yet he dared not advance far from reoccupied Detroit because of the continuing Indian threat. Following the battle, about 700 Indian warriors, with their families numbering more than 2,000 persons, accompanied Lieutenant Colonel Matthew Elliott and the British army eastward to the head of Lake Ontario. With age and exposure as factors, Elliott died there in May, 1814.

In Detroit, the American army immediately strengthened fortifications around the town. In 1814 they built Fort Gratiot at the outlet of Lake Huron to overawe regional Indians and restrict communication with the British. As late as 1816, American officers desired further action against the Potawatomi but dared not undertake an overland expedition to their towns.

Niagara Frontier and Eastern Theatre, 1812-1814

At the outset of the War of 1812, neutrality was the preference of Indian people living on both sides of the international border at the Niagara River and farther east along the upper St. Lawrence River. Canadian Indians had little to fear from the rather sparse white population of Canada, where the land question was not a dangerous issue; they also had little reason to risk the consequences of joining the British in war against the United States. On the American side of the border there was no prospect of hostilities between the Iroquois and settlers in New York and Pennsylvania.

The initial decision of the Six Nations of Upper Canada for neutrality may have been inspired partly by General Hull's proclamations of July 13 and 18, 1812, which first threatened destruction if they joined the British fighting forces; but it is also likely that they were influenced by news that the Iroquois of New York, urged by the Seneca leader Red Jacket, had decided at a council at Buffalo on July 6 to take no part in the war. The Six Nations' decision for neutrality tended to include most of the Mississauga, who were expected to follow their lead.

It was only through the special efforts of British Indian agents and a lavish generosity with presents, combined with the early victories of the allied Indians and British at Fort,

Mackinac and Detroit, that the Canadian Indians were willing to play even an ancillary role in the War of 1812. Across the Niagara border, Americans were successful through similar means in winning Iroquois support, largely from the Seneca, though some Tuscarora and Onondaga eventually participated in the conflict.

Of the sixty-three engagements east of the St. Clair River, only seven on the Ontario peninsula included a significant portion of Indians acting on either side. On only one occasion, at Beaver Dams on June 24, 1813, when the combined Iroquois nations from Upper and Lower Canada forced the surrender of an American contingent, did they contribute a dominant force. Indian participation was not prominent in any battle east of the Niagara River shores.

Although it was not the British practice to report Indian military action in joint operations, mention of Indian participation was recorded. There were at least a few Indians present at most encounters. Examples include the Six Nations force who acted decisively at Queenston Heights in 1812; Indian patrols of the Niagara frontier throughout 1813 and 1814; the fifty or more present when Americans attacked York in 1813; the Caughnawaga contingent at Chateaugeay; and the Indian troops in the British retreat from Fort Erie in 1813 and at Chippawa in 1814. Traditional accounts have expanded knowledge of Indian involvement in the War of 1812. Leaders of war parties from tribes surrounding Lake Michigan brought back tales of the burning of Buffalo and Black Rock, and the Indian sharpshooters perched in t,he rigging of British ships at the Battle of Lake Erie.

As military expeditions approached their reservations on both sides of the Niagara peninsula, Iroquois and Six Nations Indians were drawn into the fighting in support of American as well as British forces. Iroquois fighters accompanied American troops at Black Rock, Chippawa, Fort George, and other excursions on the Niagara frontier. Even limited involvement caused dismay in Indian ranks. At the Battle of Chippawa in July, 1814, some 500 American Iroquois found themselves fighting 300 Six Nations, Ojibwa, and western Indians who accompanied the British forces. Subsequently, Red Jacket and his Seneca did follow Americans on several raids against Canadian villages in the Niagara peninsula, but he had already begun to consider returning to the 1812 position of neutrality. To promote this view, a deputation of Iroquois from the United States attended a Six Nations council held in 1814 near Ancaster, present Burlington Bay. There they discovered that the Six Nations of Upper Canada were already disinclined to continue an aggressive war in behalf of the British, for they realized that Iroquois had been fighting Iroquois at Chippawa.

The British commander in the Burlington region at the western end of Lake Ontario, a center for Indian gatherings during the War of 1812, protested the attendance of the American Indians, claiming that they should have been arrested; but he could not prevent their presence, nor the decision of the council to restrict offensive actions. Although no longer as powerful as they had been a generation earlier, members of the Iroquois confederacy still felt themselves to be independent of any white commander. Few Indians fought on either side in subsequent battles at Lundy's Lane or Fort Erie later in 1814. Only in defense of

their Grand River reservation area, where the battle of Brants Ford was fought in November, 1814, were they present in substantial numbers.

Continuing War in the Mississippi Valley, 1813-1815

By the end of the 1813 campaign season, American military success had virtually subdued Indian opposition in the western theatre except for the Mississippi River region. Coincident with American victories on Lake Erie and the Thames River, General Benjamin Howard sent 1,400 men from St. Louis upriver to Peoria. They burned Gomo's vacant Potawatomi village on the Illinois River and by early October built Fort Clark to prevent further Indian raids on white settlements.

Along the Mississippi River, rifts had developed among the tribes since the outset of the War of 1812, creating neutral or pro-American divisions. By mid-1813, villages of supposedly "friendly" Iowa, Sauk, Mesquakie, Kickapoo, and Piankeshaw had congregated near the mouth of the Des Moines River. Doubtful of their loyalty, William Clark, governor of Missouri Territory, persuaded a group to relocate on the Missouri River above McMahons Fort in the vicinity of the mouth of the Grand River. By fall, about 1,500 Sauk and Mesquakie, along with Piankeshaw and Iowa, had formed villages on the advance Missouri frontier, within striking distance of their long-time enemies the Osage.

Meanwhile, the British adopted more northern channels for sending supplies from York or Kingston to their far western Indian allies. With the American army occupying both shores of the Detroit River, the British cut through a new road from Lake Simcoe to Nottawasaga Bay and made use of the canoe route via the Severn River, outlet of Lake Simcoe entering Matchedash Bay, an estuary of Georgian Bay unknown to Americans. Penetanguishene, established on the bay in 1815, became the new base on the British supply line to Lake Michigan, Green Bay, and Prairie du Chien.

Using these routes, anti-American Potawatomi continued to receive British goods by way of the St. Joseph River and the South Bend portage to the upper Kankakee. Main Poc, still leader of the Potawatomi militants, moved after Tecumseh's death to a sequestered site on the Yellow River in the swampy headwaters of the Kankakee. Chebanse and other Potawatomi from this area participated in the defense of Mackinac Island against American attack in August, 1814.

The last round of hostilities in the upper Mississippi Valley commenced with a strategic American offensive in the spring of 1814. Fearing a combined British-Indian attack on the Missouri settlements, Governor Clark led an expedition that on June 2 took unopposed possession of Prairie du Chien, westernmost base of British operations. The following month, the British captured a partially completed fort and held the position for the balance of the war. The Sauk and their allies decisively defeated American relief and retaliatory expeditions in July and September. Indian raids also forced the abandonment of Forts Mason and Johnson at and below the Des Moines River.

Spurred by British goods, power, and promises of sup-

Mackinac Island Fort and Trading Community. Beyond the harbor lies Round Island, used for Indian encampment, with the shoreline of the Lower Peninsula of Michigan in the distance. From Castlenau, *Vues et Souvenirs du L 'Amerique du Nord*, pl. 26. The Newberry Library.

port at the peace table, Sauk successes on the Mississippi emboldened the Indian villagers on the Missouri to abandon their "friendly" stance. Throughout 1814 and early 1815, small parties of warriors harassed white settlers west of St. Louis, stealing horses and killing at least 20 persons. In response, in September, 1814, mounted men with Shawnee scouts were sent to punish the hostile Piankeshaw near present Miami, Missouri. The captured band was sent to St. Louis, then transported back to Indiana. Although aware of the British-American peace, a Sauk war party in May, 1815, attacked soldiers from the garrison at Fort Howard northwest of St. Louis, with a few casualties on both sides. This "Battle of the Sinkhole" was the last battle of the war.

Ending the War on all Fronts, 1813-1817

Following the Battle of the Thames at Moraviantown, Ontario in October 1813, American authorities gradually made progress toward achieving Indian peace, a lengthy task completed after the American-British war ended. General Harrison signed a provisional armistice in October, 1813,

with Potawatomi, Wyandot, Miami, Ottawa, and Ojibwa who abandoned the British when General Proctor retreated from Detroit and Amherstburg. On July 22, 1814 a second treaty at Greenville, Ohio, established peace and friendship between the United States and the Wyandot, Delaware, Shawnee, Seneca, and Miami. This agreement also bound the 1,450 Indians at the council to fight for the United States and was an attempt to heal the breech between partisan factions that had developed because of the war.

On the international scene, the United States and Great Britain agreed to the Treaty of Ghent in December, 1814, with ratification completed on February 17, 1815. Final exchange of military posts in the western Great Lakes took place in July, when Fort Malden was returned to the British and Americans regained Fort Mackinac.

In 1815, the United States began rebuilding relations with tribes of the western Great Lakes and upper Mississippi valley, achieving peace by stages. The first series of seven treaties was signed July 18, 19, and 20 at Portage de Sioux on the Missouri River west of St. Louis, with the following Indian parties: Potawatomi in Illinois, Piankeshaw, four groups of Dakota, and the Omaha. The Kickapoo did not come in and make a treaty until September 2. They were followed shortly by the Osage, Mesquakie, and Iowa. In this same time interval, Harrison presided over a treaty council on September 8, 1815, at Spring Wells, south of Detroit, confirming peace with the Wyandot, Delaware, Seneca, Shawnee, Miami, Ojibwa, Ottawa, and Potawatomi of Indiana and Michigan Territory. In May and June of 1816, American commissioners in St. Louis made treaties with the more reluctant tribal divisions: Sauk of the Rock River, three additional Dakota bands, and a portion of the Win neb ago willing to come under the protection of the United States. The sixteenth and final War of 1812 peace treaty in the far western region was signed with the Menominee in March, 1817.

The United States followed up Indian peace councils by building additional military forts in the Indian country. During the spring of 1816, Americans reoccupied Fort Dearborn at Chicago and began constructing Fort Armstrong at Rock Island, Fort Crawford at Prairie du Chien, and Fort Howard at Green Bay.

Late in June, 1816, tribal leaders carried their objections to the British commander on Drummond Island, located by Detour passage, new post for troops evacuated from Fort Mackinac (see also map 24). More than 1,000 western Indians and local Ottawa and Ojibwa collected on the island for a two-day council. Speeches were made by staunch British supporters Wabasha and Little Crow of the Dakota, Tomah of the Menominee, LeMoite, representing

also Black Hawk of the Sauk, and Karrymaunee of the Winnebago. More critical to Indians than the question of new military posts was the American intention to cut off British Indian trade in American territory.

On this occasion, Lieutenant Colonel William McKay gave a farewell speech to the leaders and tribes who had served the British during the War of 1812. Also in June, 1816, the British Indian agent at Fort Malden ceased issuing special rations to more than 1,000 Indians, signifying an end to the wartime basis for provisioning, and dispersal of the last contingent of Indians receiving British military support. In recognition of their wartime service, Great Lakes Indians from American territory received annual presents at Fort Malden and British posts on Lake Huron until 1842.

Principal Sources: Aldrich 1889; Butterfield 1848; Chalou 1971; Cruikshank 1892, 1896, 1896-1908, 1902, 1913; Currie 1898; Edwards 1870; Esarey 1922; Forsyth n.d.; Gilpin 1958; Hill 1957; Howe 1898; Hunt 1979; Kappler 1972; Kinzie 1932; Klinek and Talman 1970; Lossing 1868; McAfee 1816; Mahon 1972; MPHC (15) 1889, (16) 1890; Peeke 1925; Quaife 1940; Richardson 1842; Roland 1979; Sarchet 1911; Stanley 1950,1963; Stevens 1904; Whickar 1921; Whittlesey 1867; Williams 1879; Wood 1920-28.

The distribution of Indian and white settlements in 1830 reflects the pressure a regional white population approaching 1,700,000 was exerting on a Great Lakes Indian population of about 72,000. In the overall population picture, a significant factor at this time is the disparity between total populations of 13,000,000 for the United States and 845,000 for Canada. Within the Great Lakes Region the differential is indicated by figures of 1,470,000 in the United States and 220,000 in Upper Canada. Approximate populations for governmental districts on the Great Lakes Indian frontier in 1830 are shown on the following table:

District	Date Established	Approximate Population
State of Ohio	1803	938,000
State of Indiana	1816	343,000
State of Illinois	1818	157,000
Territory of Michigan (Including Wisconsin)	1805	32,000
Province of Upper Canada	1791	220,000

Although all districts adjoining the Indian country of the Great Lakes Region had experienced continuous increases in white population, when compared with the 1810 figures the growth for the intervening years was most marked in Indiana and Illinois. The thinly spread population of Upper Canada had almost tripled in the previous twenty years, but was still confined to a border along the northern shores of Lakes Erie and Ontario, a continuation of the narrow band of inhabited area along the St. Lawrence River.

The year 1830 historically marks the threshold of rapid white population advance along a band west of Lake Erie as a consequence of the completion in 1825 of the Erie Canal, linking the Mohawk River with Buffalo, New York. The spurt in Great Lakes traffic, enhanced by the introduction of steam navigation in 1818, brought an influx of easterners as well as immigrant settlers from Europe into Upper Canada and the American Middle West in the 1830s.

The Indian population for the Great Lakes Region west of Montreal totaled about 12,000 in Canada and 60,000 in the United States in 1830. The six following maps of sections of the Great Lakes Region do not cover the entire area shown in this distribution map. The 1830 map series, at a larger scale, omits areas already taken over by white settle-

Fish Market at Toronto, on north shore of Lake Ontario, in 1838. By W. H. Bartlett. From Willis, *Canadian Scenery*, vol. 1, p. 83. The Newberry Library.

Dakota-Ojibwa boundary set by the Treaty of Prairie du Chien in 1825, surveyed in 1835, was ineffective in halting warfare. Southern boundary for the Dakota, contested west of the upper fork of the Des Moines River, became outdated in 1830 when a second treaty at Prairie du Chien ceded land on both sides of this line.

Scale 1:10,000,000

0   40   80   120 MILES

0   40   80   120 KILOMETERS

Distribution of Indian and White Settlements   c. 1830

MAP 22

ments: Canada and New York east of Lake Ontario, most of Pennsylvania and Ohio, and southern Indiana. Consequently, Canadian reserves in the St. Lawrence valley from St. Regis to Quebec City, representing a population of about 3,000, are not shown. Neither are four reservations in northeastern New York state. These can be found on maps 20 and 31.

Beyond the area mapped for 1830 there were also several thousand Great Lakes Indians who had already moved out of the region. A few hundred Iroquois, mainly Caughnawaga Mohawk, joined the western Canadian fur trade; some settled among the Cree in Alberta. Small numbers of Nipissing, Algonquin, and Abenaki also followed this path. Groups of Ojibwa people known as Saulteurs shifted from the southern side of Lake Superior to the country north of the height of land within the orbit of the Hudson's Bay Company.

The Iowa by 1830 had their principal focus in the Missouri rather than the Mississippi valley, along with the vanguard of the Sauk and Mesquakie. Before 1830 the advancing Sauk and Mesquakie had clashed with the Dakota in northern Iowa. American officials tried to settle this conflict, along with the continuing Dakota-Ojibwa antipathy, at an intertribal council held at Prairie du Chien,

Wisconsin, in 1825. The boundaries shown on the map, set by the 1825 Prairie du Chien treaty, were ineffective and soon superceded by land cessions.

Southwest of the Great Lakes Region, an estimated 7,500 Shawnee, Delaware, Wea, Piankeshaw, and Kickapoo were already beyond the Mississippi River where reservations were being blocked out. About 200 Shawnee and Delaware, along with their long-term Cherokee allies, had found refuge in the Caddo country south of the Red River on the Texas borderland. All these tribes had engaged in joint warfare against the Osage.

The 1830 series, maps 23 to 28, concentrates on the region of the Upper Great Lakes still occupied principally by Indian people. These six maps record the locations of 529 Indian villages, 58 in Canada and 471 in the United States. All Canadian and American towns along the frontier are also mapped. Since Indian removal was already under way in Ohio, Indiana, and Illinois as a result of post-War of 1812 treaties, the maps indicate the general status of tribal groups in transit or facing removal during the next decade.

In the larger field of Indian relations, the year 1830 is notable for the passage of the Indian Removal Act in the United States and the formulation of a new reserve policy in Canada (see also map 31). No longer considered necessary for

Galena, in the northwest corner of Illinois, center of the lead-mining district, as it appeared in the 1850s when mining was past the peak. The town had been platted in 1826. From Lewis, *Das Illustrierte Mississipithal*, p. 174. The Newberry Library.

Kaposia, Dakota village located below the site of St. Paul, Minnesota, in June, 1851. By Frank Blackwell Mayer. Sketchbook.

military support, Canadian Indians were transferred in 1830 from army to civilian administration. A similar change did not occur in the United States until 1849, when the Indian Office was placed under the newly created Department of Interior.

The period of the 1830s coincided with a new wave of religious conversion among Great Lakes Indians. The new missionary programs were carried on principally by Protestant denominations, but there was also a renewal of Catholic missionary work in the Upper Great Lakes. These efforts received continued resistance from traditionalists among the Indians, usually labeled the "pagan" element by missionaries. The same period also saw the revival of the religion of Handsome Lake among the Iroquois in New York (see also map 20).

The daily life and economic activities of tribal peo-ple varied considerably in different parts of the Great Lakes Region, a factor of continuing importance. In the east, for example, Indians living on reservations in Canada, New York, or Ohio harvested the products of farms and orchards like nearby white families. By contrast, Indians around Lake Superior were still locked into the seasonal demands of the fur trade. The year 1830 signals the rapid decline of the fur trade east of the Mississippi River. For Indian peo-ple, ceding land and receiving annuities became a new method of subsistence, in some cases indispensable for survival.

Principal Sources: Canada 1845; Cass 1835; Eaton 1829; Hicks MS 1978; Macaulay MS 1839; McKenney 1830; Morse 1822; Schoolcraft 1820, 1834, (3) 1854; United States 1832.

In terms of Indian distribution, the situation in Upper Canada in 1830 appeared remarkably stable. The rather extensive migrations of the eighteenth century were over. Six Nations settlements were confined to their lands in the United States or to those given to them in Upper Canada on the Grand River and the Bay of Quinte (see also maps 15, 31). Ojibwa bands had divided the rest of the province more or less into specific areas for different groups, outside those portions surrendered by treaty for reservations or for white occupancy.

The white population of Upper Canada stood at about 220,000 with only 2,800 residing in the provincial capital, York. This map is limited to the Ontario peninsula section of Upper Canada, an area covering the majority of Indian communities as well as the frontier of white settlement in the province. White towns were located at both ends of the Six Nations Reserve on the Grand River, and white farmers had acquired land within the original tract. North of Lake Ontario, the town of Peter borough denotes advancing settlement into the Otonabee River valley and farther along the waterway toward Lake Simcoe.

Penetanguishene, isolated on an arm of Georgian Bay, had been established as a naval base during the latter part of the War of 1812. Here a British Indian agency was located from 1828, when it moved from Drummond Island, until 1834, when another transfer was made to Manitoulin Island (map 24).

An Indian population of about 9,000 occupied the sections of Upper Canada shown on this and succeeding maps of the 1830 series. The region between Kingston and the mouth of the French River, the principal subject area for this particular map, accounts for about 6,300 of the total. The map shows the location of 41 Indian communities in Upper Canada, including four west from Whitefish Lake discussed in connection with map 24. Of the total, 25 are Ojibwa and Missisauga sites on lake shores and main rivers. The Missisauga continued to range the north shore of Lake Ontario from Kingston to the Credit River. One group of Ojibwa maintained a string of semipermanent villages in the Lake Simcoe region; another extended along the Thames River. The more itinerant Ojibwa spotted the north shore of Lake Huron and Georgian Bay. Tribal distinctions were becoming blurred, and a number of bands earlier termed Missisauga were called Ojibwa by 1830.

Among the preliminary signs of new currents in Indian affairs of Upper Canada was an experiment among the Credit River Missisauga, beginning in 1826, which achieved some success. The first Methodist mission was founded in 1827 at Grape Island in the Bay of Quinte. Peter Jones, a missionary of Ojibwa and British heritage, promoted conversion and establishment of agricultural settlements with special persistence, reaching both Canadian and American Indians. The new Canadian reserve policy enunciated in 1830 commenced with partially successful programs for Ojibwa at three locations: Cold water, "The Narrows" between Lake Simcoe and Lake Couchiching, and the upper St. Clair River near present Sarnia.

Aside from the groups of villages already discussed, there were individual villages of five different tribes located on the Thames River and near the Michigan border. Munsee refugees occupied a reserve adjacent to the Ojibwa west of St. Thomas. Farther down the Thames River, New Fairfield marks the Moravian community, rebuilt after destruction during the War of 1812, at a new site on the opposite side of the river. In addition to the longstanding Ojibwa or Missisauga community on Walpole Island, the map shows the location of later established Ottawa and Potawatomi villages on the eastern and southern sides of the island. A predominantly Ottawa settlement on the Chenail Ecarte, a narrow eastern channel of the St. Clair River, had been established as a refugee center by the British Indian Department in 1796. The number of Ottawa and Potawatomi refugees on Walpole Island, commencing as a trickle about 1828, became significant in the 1837-1839 period during the final phase of the American program to remove Indians from southern Michigan, Ohio, and Indiana to reservations in Kansas. This migration to Walpole Island was further encouraged by the British announcement in 1837 that Indians would have to be residents, not just visitors, in order to receive annual gifts from Canadian Indian agents.

The Huron or Wyandot village above Amherstberg on the Detroit River identifies a group that had been in the same region since the late seventeenth century. The Canadian Wyandot maintained contact with American Wyandot living at the Flat Rock Reservation on the Huron River southwest of Detroit, Michigan. They often sent their children to the school at Big Spring, a Wyandot reservation in northwestern Ohio (map 25).

Although the Indian communities of Upper Canada are the principal subject for this map, also included are most of the Six Nations reservations remaining in western New York, their traditional home country. Consequently, this map provides an opportunity to consider the overall distribution of Six Nations population, in 1830 totaling 7,200, with about 2,500 in Upper Canada and 4,700 in the United States in the present states of New York, Ohio, and Wisconsin.

The six reservation villages along the Grand River in Canadian territory accounted for about 2,000, including Delaware allies who had lived with the Six Nations Iroquois in Pennsylvania and New York before moving to Canada during the American Revolution. A separate Mohawk settlement, the village of Tyendinaga on the Bay of Quinte, had a population of about 300.

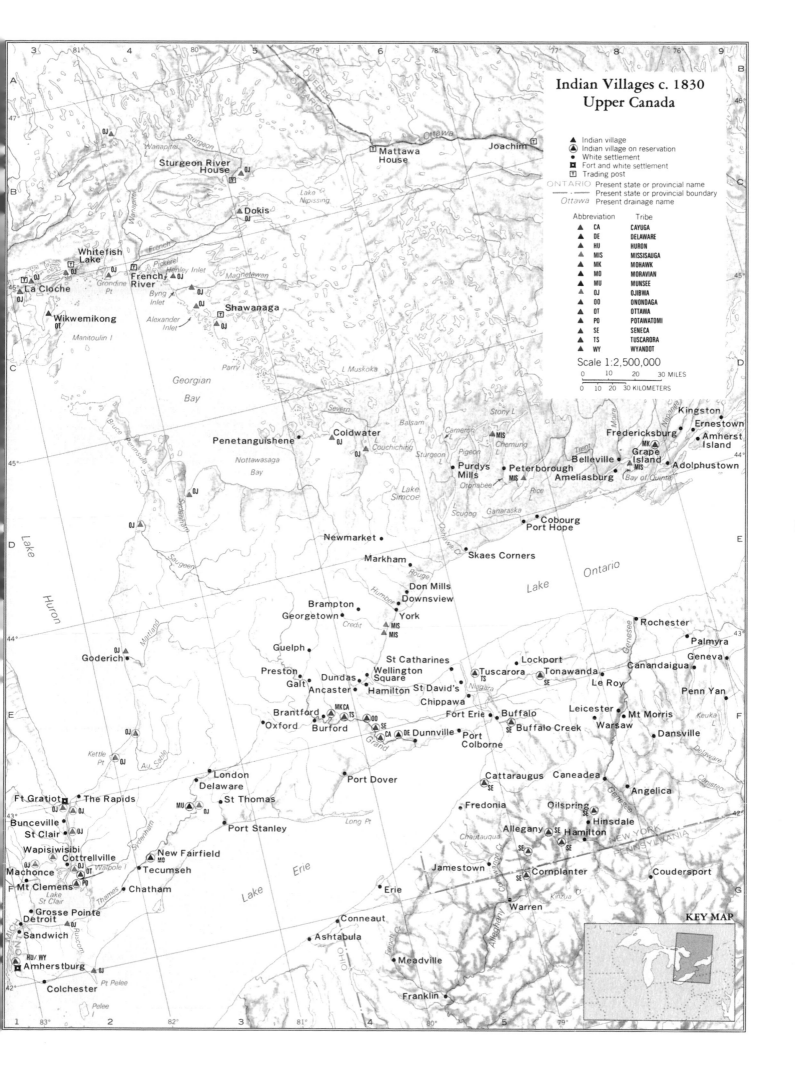

Indian Villages c. 1830
Upper Canada

▲ Indian village
⟁ Indian village on reservation
● White settlement
⊡ Fort and white settlement
Ⓣ Trading post
ONTARIO Present state or provincial name
———— Present state or provincial boundary
Ottawa Present drainage name

Abbreviation	Tribe
▲ CA	CAYUGA
▲ DE	DELAWARE
▲ HU	HURON
▲ MIS	MISSISAUGA
▲ MK	MOHAWK
▲ MO	MORAVIAN
▲ MU	MUNSEE
▲ OJ	OJIBWA
▲ OO	ONONDAGA
▲ OT	OTTAWA
▲ PO	POTAWATOMI
▲ SE	SENECA
▲ TS	TUSCARORA
▲ WY	WYANDOT

Scale 1:2,500,000

0 10 20 30 MILES

0 10 20 30 KILOMETERS

MAP
23

KEY MAP

Bay of Quinte, eastern Lake Ontario, location of Deseronto reserve and Grape Island mission established in 1827. By W. H. Bartlett. From Willis, *Canadian Scenery*, vol. 1, p. 105.

Timberslide at Les Chats, on the Ottawa River about thirty miles below Fort Coulange. Lumbermen advanced into the Indian country of the Great Lakes Region ahead of agricultural settlers. From Willis, *Canadian Scenery*, vol. 2, p. 4. The Newberry Library.

The Six Nations groups in the United States were in an unsettled state from 1818 to 1842 because of fluctuating plans to move from reservations in New York and Ohio. This map cuts off the eastern part of northern New York, location of reservations of the Onondaga and Oneida, as well as the Stockbridge and Brotherton, New England Indians accommodated on Oneida lands. In 1830 there were still in New York about 2,300 Seneca plus 1,600 Oneida, Onondaga, Tuscarora, and Cayuga, making a total Six Nations population of 3,900 in the state.

The Seneca reservation in Ohio had a population of more than 500 in 1830, mainly Seneca and Cayuga but also a small representation of other Six Nations divisions (map 25). The Oneida, who had been making arrangements to move to Menominee lands in Wisconsin since the 1820s, had moved about 300, more than a third of their tribal members by 1830, and that figure reached 600 by 1837 (map 27). Almost all of the 300 Stockbridge had also moved to Wisconsin by 1830, with an estimated 360 Brotherton temporarily remaining in New York. In 1839, following another removal treaty, a second group of 300 Oneida purchased land on the Thames River near present Delaware and became affiliated with the Six Nations in Canada (map 31).

A final comment should be made concerning the northern section of this map of Upper Canada. The large scale gives a more detailed view of part of the Ottawa River trade route branching off through the Mattawa River, Lake Nipissing, and the French River to Georgian Bay. The continuation of the route north of Manitoulin Island to the straits region can be followed on the next map in the series, map 24. This canoe route, shorter than the distance from Montreal through the lower Great Lakes by way of Detroit, was still in use to send supplies and trade goods to Lake Superior and posts farther west.

Principal Sources: Bauman 1949; Campbell 1966; Canada 1845,1858; Jameson 1838; Jones 1860; Lewis 1957; Lizars 1896; MacDonald n.d.; Macaulay MS 1839; Schoolcraft (3) 1854; Strickland 1853; Surtees 1969, 1971, 1982; Traill 1838.

INDIAN VILLAGES c. 1830: UPPER CANADA AND MICHIGAN TERRITORY,
Map 24

The crossroads of the upper Great Lakes, the region surrounding the hub of commerce on Michilimackinac island, is the area of concentration for this map. Only two tribes, the closely related Ottawa and Ojibwa, appear in this close-up view showing the locations of 52 population centers representing a total of about 4,700 Indians.

The non-Indian population lived or was based at two places, Michilimackinac and Sault Ste. Marie. The Michilimackinac district, including the island and mainland community of St. Ignace, numbered about 1,200 merchants, traders, and military personnel, including a number of families of Indian heritage. Sault Ste. Marie had a similar population of about 980. Michilimackinac was the largest population concentration in Michigan Territory outside the immediate vicinity of Detroit.

During the summer, visiting Indians from the west and south often increased the population temporarily to around 3,000 at "the Sault" and to 6,000 or more at Michilimackinac. In 1830 these Indian travelers usually continued their summer excursions to Penatanguishene (map 23), as they had to Drummond Island until 1828, to receive annual presents from British Indian agents. The year-round food supply of fish at the St. Marys rapids and in the Straits of Mackinac made these sites important for human habitation in an environment where starvation always was a possibility by late winter.

Indian village at St. Marys River Rapids, showing homes and burial houses over graves, with Canadian shoreline opposite. From Castlenau, *Vues et Souvenirs du L'Amerique du Nord*, pl. 31. The Newberry Library.

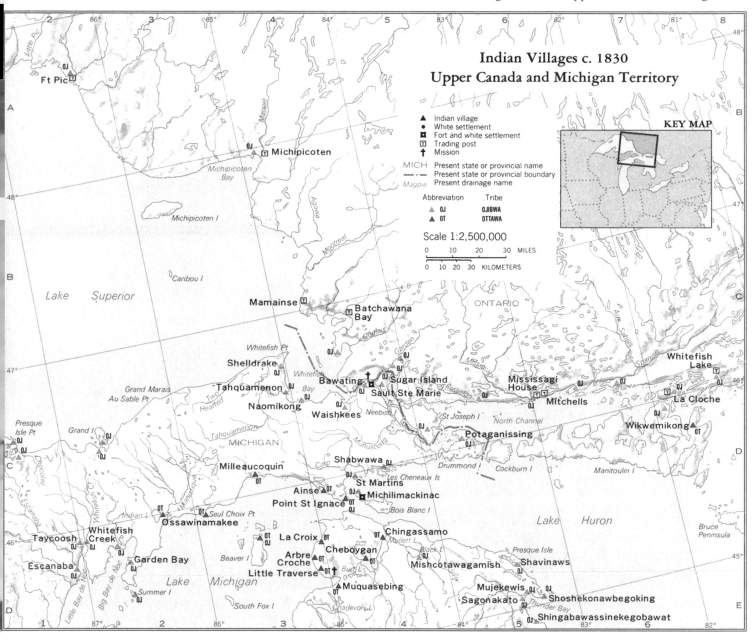

Indian Villages c. 1830
Upper Canada and Michigan Territory

The 14 widely dispersed villages and trading posts in the section of Upper Canada shown on this map represent a total Indian population of about 1,200, principally bands of Ojibwa. By 1830, however, the Ottawa had begun to reassert their ancient claim to Manitoulin Island, location selected by the British authorities in 1830 for promoting a concentration of Upper Canada's Ojibwa and Ottawa under the new reserve program (map 31).

The map covers the Upper Peninsula of Michigan as far west on the south shore of Lake Superior as present Marquette. This section of the Upper Peninsula displays sites of 25 Indian villages and fishing stations with an estimated population of 1,500 in 1830. At an earlier time the region had been more populous. All these villages were Ojibwa, with the exception of four Ottawa sites on the north shore of Lake Michigan between Point St. Ignace and the Manistique River.

The first effort to exert American sovereignty over the Upper Peninsula Ojibwa was the 1820 expedition to Sault Ste. Marie from Detroit, headed by Territorial Governor Lewis Casso At that time the British flag was still flying at the village of Bawating (The Rapids) adjacent to the trading center. The international border through the St. Marys River had been charted by the British in 1817.

The Americanization of the Upper Peninsula actually commenced with the founding of Fort Brady at Sault Ste. Marie in 1822, and the return of Henry Rowe Schoolcraft, mineralogist of the Cass expedition, as first American Indian agent for the district. Three years later he married Jane Johnston, daughter of the leading local Indian trader, John Johnston. Mrs. Johnston was a woman of consequence as daughter of Wabojig (White Fisher), famous warrior of the LaPointe, Wisconsin band.

The newest Ojibwa settlement on the map is found on present Waiska Bay east of Whitefish Point near the outlet from Lake Superior. This village had its beginning in 1826

131

John Johnston, trader at Sault Ste. Marie. Painted by Joseph Wilson in Belfast in 1787, when Johnston was twenty-seven. Original in Bayliss Library, Sault Ste. Marie. The collection of C. J. Hambleton.

Susan Johnston, Oshawguscodaywayqua, wife of John Johnston, was the daughter of Wabojig, a noted Ojibwa leader at LaPointe, Wisconsin, on the south shore of Lake Superior. From McKenny, *Tour to the Lakes*.

when Waishkee, Mrs. Johnston's brother, came from LaPointe with a large family to hunt in the vicinity. The relatives that Schoolcraft acquired by marriage, as well as his own writing and treaty-making projects, influenced the course of Indian affairs westward as far as the Minnesota country even after the end of his regime in 1841.

On the Canadian side of the St. Marys River the most prominent villages were two on Garden River, where the band was headed by Shingwakoonse (Little Pine). Sault Ste. Marie, Canada, was not yet in existence in 1830, but gradually formed a few years later. Michipicoten was the northernmost post on Lake Superior within the Sault Ste. Marie district.

The band resident on the south side of the St. Marys River rapids, whose French name "Saulteurs" accompanied them wherever they migrated, were accorded considerable deference by other bands. Shingabawassin, their leader up to the time of his death about 1830, hunted on Thunder Bay of Lake Huron, on Michigan's Lower Peninsula. On the southern end of the bay, his followers established a village incorporating his name. Mujekewis and Sagonakate were villages named for leaders of the Thunder Bay band. A newer settlement, Shavinaw's, had been founded by the son of a French trader from Michilimackinac. The Thunder Bay region had been Ottawa country in the seventeenth century.

In 1830, the Ottawa base was still L'Arbe Croche region on the northeast shore of Lake Michigan. Principal outlying Ottawa communities were located on Beaver Island, near the mouth of the Manistique River on the Upper Peninsula, and on Little Detroit Island in present Wisconsin at the northern end of Green Bay. The latter site is just beyond the edge of this map, south of Big Bay de

Noc, but can be found on map 25. Muquasebing (Bear River) marks an Ottawa and Chippewa settlement at the site of present Petoskey.

The Ottawa canoe trips across Lake Michigan brought them in contact with Ojibwa of the Bay de Noc region, some of whom came to Michigan villages. In the 1830s, the Ottawa and Ojibwa frequented traditional fishing sites on the islands and shoreline stations at river mouths, near shoals and offshore islets (map 3). With the fur trade declining, trading firms in alliance with these bands of the crossroads region were expanding commercial fishing operations from dried and smoked fish to the sale of fresh fish transported to Detroit and the Lower Great Lakes markets.

One last geographical observation concerns the important water routes that are more clearly shown on this map than on the double-page maps of the Atlas. The traditional route of the fur brigades ascending the Ottawa River, partially shown on map 23, continues on this map through the channel north of Manitoulin Island in Lake Huron, splitting at the mouth of the St. Mary River into one subsidiary route upstream to Lake Superior and a second to Michilimackinac Island and St. Ignace on the north side of the Straits of Mackinac leading into Lake Michigan. The St. Marys River bands dispersed for the fishing season to encampments as far south as the mouth of the Munuscong River, occupying also islands in the river and the shoals and islands of Whitefish Bay.

Principal Sources: Blackbird 1897; Jameson 1838; Johnston 1909; McKenney 1846; Sault n.d.; Schoolcraft 1821,1851; Strang 1894; Tanner 1974g; Trygg 1964-69; Verwyst 1900.

Featuring the 210 Indian villages in Michigan's Lower Peninsula, northwest Ohio, and northern Indiana, the entire map encompasses 272 Indian sites, about half the number plotted for the entire 1830 series. Discussion for this map is limited to the estimated 20,000 tribal people residing in the featured area in 1830, and highlights major developments during the next ten years. In this region, the decade was notable for the sudden rise in white population of southern Michigan and northern Indiana, construction of roads and canals, and a rapid series of Indian land cessions followed by removal of Indians from their briefly-held reservations.

Lower Peninsula of Michigan

The Indian population of Michigan's Lower Peninsula, approaching 14,000 in 1830, was concentrated in the southern section, where the majority of the 131 villages in this part of the state were located. Already covered in the discussion of the straits region are the 6 villages around Thunder Bay of northern Lake Huron and the 7 associated with the Little Traverse Bay region on the western tip of the Lower Peninsula (map 24). The remaining 118 villages in the Lower Peninsula were almost equally divided among the Ottawa on the western side of the present state, the Ojibwa in the east, and the Potawatomi in the south. Tribal populations became increasingly mixed toward the south central section of the Lower Peninsula. Members of all three tribes were found on the upper Thornapple River, a southern tributary of the Grand River, as indicated at a village east of present Hastings, Michigan, located on the map south of Bulls Prairie. The single Wyandot community remaining in Michigan in 1830 was situated at Flat Rock reservation on the Huron River, where the Wyandot of Brownstown and Monguagon moved after the War of 1812.

On the Lake Michigan shoreline, the next villages for discussion are those of the Ottawas and Ojibwa located southward from Grand Traverse Bay. On the east side of the bay, the northernmost village at present Eastport was the probable residence of the leading regional Ojibwa chief, Aishquagonabe. Ahgosa's village, at the end of the peninsula dividing the arms of the bay, became the location for a mission established in 1839. Chemogobing marked present Leland at the outlet of Leelanau Lake. Manistee and Muskegon were located close to the sites of the modern towns of the same names, while Nindebekatuning was the same site as present Ludington.

The densely populated Grand River valley sheltered Ottawa settlements where the Indians cared for more than 3,000 apple trees and cultivated close to 2,500 acres of corn and vegetable crops. In the eighteenth century, Ottawa had been a source of supply for traders and military personnel at Michilimackinac.

Principal villages on the lower Grand River were Nowaquakezick's (Noon Day's), in present central Grand Rapids, and Mukatasha's (Blackskin's), a few miles to the south near the foot of the rapids. A Protestant mission approved by Noon Day's family had been established in 1827, but still faced considerable opposition from other Ottawa in 1830.

South of the Grand River, a mixed Ottawa and Potawatomi population developed in the Kalamazoo River valley as increasing numbers of Ottawa came south from the straits region for winter hunting, settling close to Potawatomi camps. Marriages between the tribes occurred, and some Potawatomi in turn spent summer months near Michilimackinac. The area was profitable fur trading territory in the 1830s; a principal post was located about fifteen miles above the rapids of the Grand River at present Ada. The trade of the lower Grand and Kalamazoo rivers had been managed at this post by an Ottawa woman, Madame LaFramboise, from the death of her trader husband in 1806 until she sold her interest to the American Fur Company in 1821.

Upstream on the Grand River, the transition to the hinterlands of the Saginaw Valley Ojibwa country was indicated at the village of Coocoosh (present Lyons). This name was a shortened form of "Muckatycoocoosh" (Black Hog), a name the local Ojibwa and Ottawa gave to a black child captured during the War of 1812. By the 1830s the Indians accorded him a respected role as leader of the community. Interlocking head branches of the Grand and Saginaw river systems facilitated the spread of canoeing Ojibwa into the central part of the Lower Peninsula.

In the lower Saginaw valley, reservations surrounding a number of villages were established by treaty in 1819. The distribution of Indian settlements in the 1830s was closely correlated with present-day white towns: Kishkawkaw at the mouth of the Saginaw River (Bay City), Arbetchwachewan on the Tittabawassee River (Midland), Shingwakoosing on the Pine River (St. Louis), Otusson on the Cass River (Frankenmuth), and Muscatawaing at the "Grand Traverse" of the Flint River (Flint) (see map 31). The 1819 treaty also provided for a military fort, temporarily occupied in 1822, that gave rise to the trading settlement named Saginaw. Opposition to Americans made the region dangerous for American traders and early surveyors.

On the northern rim of Saginaw Bay, the Au Sable village (modern Oscoda) was the gateway to a water route across the peninsula. Resident trader was Louis Chevalier, Jr., who as a youth in 1781 had guided the Spanish expedition from St. Louis, Missouri, to attack the British post at St. Joseph (Niles, Michigan) (maps 14 and 15).

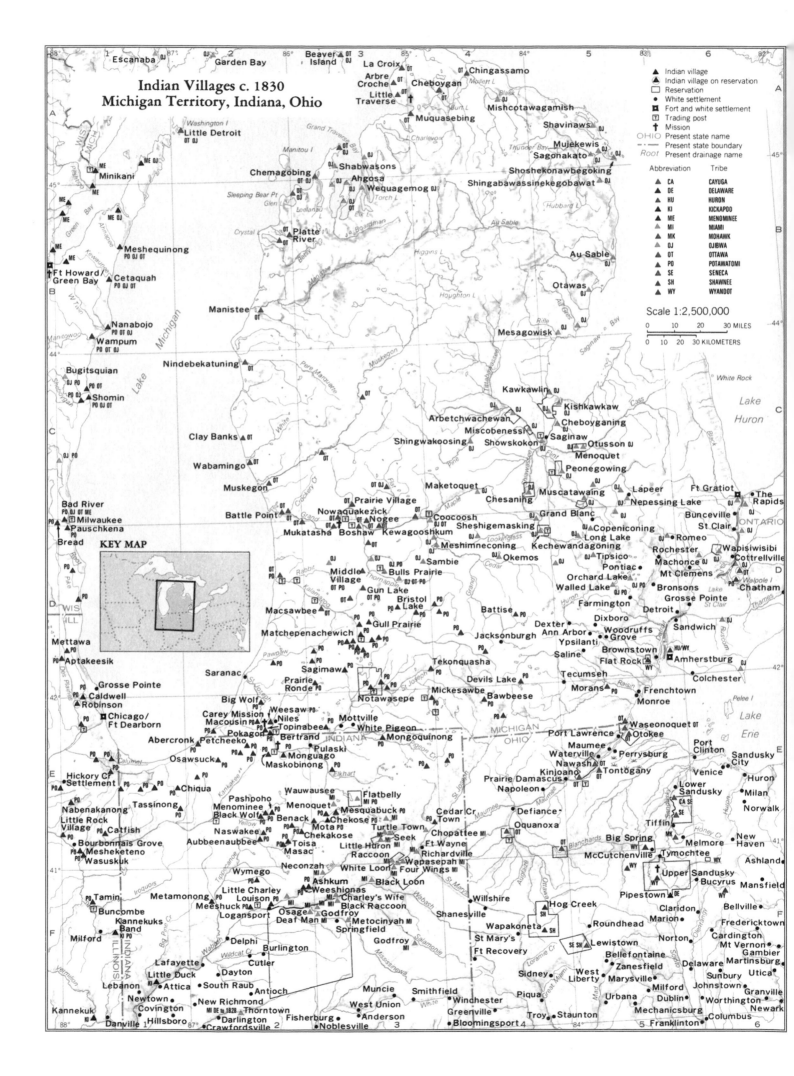

Indian Villages c. 1830
Michigan Territory, Indiana, Ohio

MAP
25

KEY MAP

Scale 1:2,500,000

▲	Indian village
▲	Indian village on reservation
◻	Reservation
●	White settlement
⊡	Fort and white settlement
Ⓣ	Trading post
✝	Mission
OHIO	Present state name
– – –	Present state boundary
Root	Present drainage name

Abbreviation	Tribe
▲ CA	CAYUGA
▲ DE	DELAWARE
▲ HU	HURON
▲ KI	KICKAPOO
▲ ME	MENOMINEE
▲ MI	MIAMI
▲ MK	MOHAWK
▲ OJ	OJIBWA
▲ OT	OTTAWA
▲ PO	POTAWATOMI
▲ SE	SENECA
▲ SH	SHAWNEE
▲ WY	WYANDOT

Fort Gratiot, Michigan, the outlet of Lake Huron, adjacent to Auminchaw reservation. On the opposite side of the St. Clair River are the Missisauga-Ojibwa communities in Ontario. From Castlenau, *Vues et Souvenirs du L 'Amerique du Nord*, pl. 18, fig. 4. The Newberry Library.

Closely allied to the Saginaw valley Ojibwa were the bands living on the Black River near present Port Huron and at Wapisiwisibi (Swan Creek) on northern Lake St. Clair. Reservations in this district had been established by treaty in 1807 and surveyed in 1810. As white settlement impinged on these people, they moved into the interior toward the Saginaw country or across the St. Clair River to British reserves near modern Sarnia.

The white frontier in this section of Michigan's Lower Peninsula was a loop around Detroit marked by the towns of Romeo, Pontiac, Jackson, and Tecumseh. Detroit had only 2,200 inhabitants. Grand Blanc, named for a local Indian leader, served as a way-station on the trail from Detroit to Saginaw; Lapeer was an outpost. The inland region northwest of Saginaw was unknown to non-Indians in 1837, when Michigan achieved statehood.

By 1830 the majority of the estimated 2,500 Potawatomi in Michigan were distributed in small communities in the southwestern interior of the Lower Peninsula. Nine towns existed in present Kalamazoo County, where the oldest settlement and trading post, present Kalamazoo, was named for Matchepenachewich, a signer of the Greenville Treaty. An easy portage route led south to Potawatomi congregated on the upper St. Joseph River at Notawasepe (Huron River) reservation, established in 1821 and enlarged in 1827 when the Potawatomi ceded reserves closer to Detroit. Main trading post for the reservation, present Mendon, attracted inhabitants of French heritage.

American settlers generally depended upon Indian people to supply their first needs for game, corn, berries, and medical treatment. They became well acquainted with Potawatomi leaders such as Bawbeese and Sagimaw, and Okemos, the Ojibwa leader who had his base on the Cedar River near present Lansing but circulated among the white communities of southeastern Michigan.

In the southwestern corner of the present state of Michigan, a group of Potawatomi villages identified the ancient tribal headquarters on the St. Joseph River. The Carey Mission, where a number of Potawatomi related to traders were educated, was established by the Reverend Isaac McCoy in 1822 when he moved from Fort Wayne. The closing of the mission in 1830 forecast a split in local Potawatomi society, since the younger Topinabee had supported the Baptist mission effort while his adopted brother, Pokagon, became a strong supporter of the Catholic mission introduced in 1831.

By 1830, the immediate vicinity of Niles and White Pigeon prairie was thinly settled by pioneers who made their way overland along the trail from Fort Wayne, following the Elkhart River. This pocket of white population is outlined on map 22. A few newcomers advanced to the mouth of the St. Joseph River and founded Saranac, a fledgling town that preceded later St. Joseph.

Potawatomi groups had not abandoned the southeastern section of the lower Peninsula, although reservations were ceded in 1827. Potawatomi continued to hunt in the relatively uninhabited region of southern Michigan and northwest Ohio

Quehmee, Potawatomi woman in group removed from Indiana in 1837. Sketch by George Winter. Tippecanoe County Historical Association.

until 1839. But two ancient village sites at present Ypsilanti and Saline were given over to incoming whites, who by 1830 had established settlements as far west as present Jackson.

Ohio Reservations

In Ohio, the northwestern part of the state was ceded by treaty in 1817, and the existing Indians were restricted to reservations soon to be ceded. Reservations of the Wyandot, Shawnee, and Seneca had a combined population of about 1,600 in 1830. The Wyandot, officially listed as 527 people, lived on farms distributed throughout the reserva-

tion areas. One Wyandot community is mapped southeast of Bucyrus, a white town built in a former Wyandot sugar grove. The small Wyandot reserve east of the "grand reservation" enclosed one of the several cranberry swamps, a valuable source of tribal income.

The Wyandot reservation at Upper Sandusky had made a considerable advance in agricultural production since the establishment of a mission in 1819. The grist mill and saw mill were the first in northwestern Ohio, and the farmlands and branded stock became the envy of nearby white residents.

The Wyandot had incorporated a number of white captives into their community, and individuals of dual heritage occupied positions of influence. Families of Negrotown still lived on the reservation, and some intermarriage had also occurred with this population. Wyandot in Ohio in the 1830s were torn by strife between the "Christian" and "Pagan" parties, for not all had accepted Protestant conversion.

On the south side of the Wyandot reservation, the small Delaware group of less than a hundred agreed in 1829 to move west of the Mississippi, but had not left in 1830. The Seneca reservation north of the Wyandot included more than 300 representatives of all five Iroquois nations, about half being Cayuga. An additional 200 Seneca lived at Lewistown with about a third of the 500 Shawnee whose main center was on the Wapakoneta reservation. These people also engaged in agriculture and stockraising.

On the Maumee River, white towns alternated with reservation villages of Ottawa totaling less than 500 population. A growing interest in the potential commercial development of the river channel foretold eviction of the Indian inhabitants. Port Lawrence was the customs station, one of several small settlements on the lower Maumee superseded by the founding of Toledo in 1837. The municipality took over the area where Ottawa reservations were established in 1807. Prairie Damascus was a name probably derived from the local geographic place name "Prairie des Mascoutin," an old landmark on the river course. The trading post near Oquanoxa's village indicated continued fur trading in the last general Indian hunting ground in Ohio.

With white population in Ohio pushing toward the one million mark, pressure was heavy to remove the 2,000 remaining Indians. Between 1831 and 1833, United States commissioners signed removal treaties with Ottawa, Seneca, and Shawnee living in Ohio. The Wyandot at Big Spring gave up their reservation in 1832 and moved to the "grand" reserve at Upper Sandusky, where Wyandot managed to withstand efforts to remove them until a treaty in 1842. The same treaty provided for removal of the Wyandot on the Flat Rock reservation in Michigan (map 31).

Northern Indiana

The northern part of Indiana in 1830 was the location of 36 Potawatomi and 23 Miami communities, as well as a single Kickapoo village on the Wabash River in the western part of the state. These 60 Indian communities represented populations of more than 1,000 Miami and about 2,500 Potawatomi and a small number of Kickapoo. Indian people

Catahecasa or Black Hoof, Shawnee leader who was present at Braddock's defeat near Pittsburgh, Pennsylvania, in 1755 and fought in frontier engagements until 1795. He died at Wapakoneta, Ohio, in 1831 (at an age estimated between 105 and 112), shortly before his people were removed to Kansas. From McKenny and Hall, *History of the Indian Tribes of North America*, vol. 1, p. 322. The Newberry Library.

River in 1826, trading interests joined the Indian leaders in trying to keep the area as a hunting preserve. Muskrat trapping in northern Indiana was a lucrative enterprise as a result of conditions affecting the European fur market at this time.

For an interval in the 1820s and 1830s, many Miami and Potawatomi enjoyed a relatively prosperous existence, acquiring the homes, farmlands and livestock valued by white society. Their choices of silken fabrics, ribbons, and silver jewelry were supplied by merchants specializing in Indian goods. Yet Miami leaders of French heritage, such as Francis Godfroy and Jean Bapiste Richardville, whose villages are shown on the map, identified themselves more firmly with Indian society. After the War of 1812 they gave up European dress and their use of French and English in conversation. Richardville, a trader and landowner as well as tribal leader, was considered the richest man in Indiana at the time of his death in 1841.

The white population north of the Wabash in Indiana increased tenfold during the decade, reaching a census figure of 36,400 in 1840. Hunting and trapping grounds were being drained and given over to agriculture. Potawatomi reservations of short duration were ceded by 1836, and tribal people

still maintained a tenuous balance in the region. The white population north of the Wabash, principally hunters and traders settled near the river banks, numbered 3,380 in 1830. The most populous town in Indiana in 1830 was Madison, a bustling port city on the Ohio River (map 20).

But the advancing tide of pioneers was moving northward. An initial spurt had occurred immediately after the War of 1812. By the early 1820s, Delawares had been removed from the White River region, including the sites of Muncie and Anderson shown on the map. A second rush occurred in 1826, when the land office opened in Crawfordsville, a town just within the map frame. Towns sprang up along the Wabash River; during high water season steamboats ascended as far as Lafayette, near the former sites of Fort Ouiatenon and the Wea villages. The Wea still living in Indiana on the middle Wabash River faced removal as a consequence of an 1820 treaty (map 26).

Spearheading the development of the upper Wabash, Indian Agent John Tipton in 1826 moved his headquarters from Fort Wayne to the mouth of the Eel River, site for the town of Logansport, laid out in 1828. That year, surveying was completed for the route of the Wabash-Maumee canal from Logansport to the Maumee Rapids in Ohio. Although the Miami and Potawatomi ceded land north of the Wabash

Tshusick, Ojibwa woman from Upper Great Lakes, on a visit to Washington. From McKenny and Hall, *History of the Indian Tribes of North America*. The collection of C. J. Hambleton.

were removed by 1840. Most resistant were the followers of the religious leader Menominee, who were taken to Kansas under army escort, long remembered as a tragic journey. The Miami signed a treaty in 1840 in preparation for removal, but only about half the tribe actually left Indiana five years later.

Westward Expansion and Potawatomi Removal

Drastic change was in store for Potawatomi living along the northern Indiana border and in southern Michigan as a consequence of construction of the road from Detroit to Chicago, a project commenced in 1825 when the Erie Canal opened. The route followed the main Indian trail passing through several points shown on this map: Ypsilanti, Saline, Mickasawbe (present Coldwater), and Niles, then struck west to Lake Michigan near the present Indiana state border.

A stage line from Detroit to Niles went into operation in 1831 and continued along the shore to Chicago in 1833. Although fears aroused by the Black Hawk War in 1832 (map 29) temporarily curtailed traffic across Michigan, by 1834 population surpassed 87,000 still confined to the Detroit hinterland, and reached 175,000 when Michigan joined the union. The population deluge, combined with final cessions of Potawatomi lands, precipitated the departure of Potawatomi from southern Michigan by flight or removal between 1837 and 1840. (see also maps 31 and 32).

During the period when plans for Indian removal were under way, armed confrontations, with arrests, gunfire and a few casualties, disrupted the state of affairs in the Detroit border region and western Lake Erie. Causes were the Michigan-Ohio boundary dispute and widespread demonstrations, principally by French inhabitants, against the government of Canada. Among the incidents, about a thousand Michigan militia marched south toward the mouth of the Maumee River in September, 1835, trying to prevent Ohio from incorporating the Maumee River area into the state boundaries. The problem was finally settled by assigning the "Toledo strip" to Ohio and adding Upper Peninsula territory to Michigan as compensation. Uprisings in Canada through 1837 and 1838 aroused a sympathetic American response, particularly from Michigan residents. They defied the officially proclaimed neutrality to launch invasions against Windsor and Fort Malden in support of local rebels. There was some concern that Indian people might take action under these circumstances.

Principal Sources: Alway 1838; Anson 1970; Atwater 1838; Baker and Carmony 1975; Baughman 1913; R. Bauman 1949; Berrien 1880; Berthrong 1974; Blois 1839; Carey 1822; Carter 1943a, b; Clifton 1975, 1977; Craig 1963; Cutler 1916; Dickens 1968; Dougherty n.d.; Durant 1877, 1880; Ellis 1879; Esarey 1915-1918; Everett 1878; Farmer 1830,1836; Farmer and Bromm 1834; Faulkner 1961; Finley 1853; Fox 1868; Gagnier 1918,1919; Guernsey 1932; Hill 1953; Hinsdale 1931; Historical Society of Michigan 1980; Jenkins 1837; Jenks 1912; Johnson 1880; Johnson 1919; Jones 1952; Kaatz 1955; Keating 1825; Lanman 1839; Leeson 1881; Lyon 1846; Maps 1968; McAllister 1932; McCord 1970; McCoy 1840; McDowell 1972; Melish 1819; Meyer 1954; Michigan Archaelogical Files; Mills 1918; Phillips 1926; Rafert 1982; Risdon 1825; St. Joseph 1877; Schoolcraft 1834; Scott 1826; Tanner 1974a, c, d, e, f; Tanner 1833; Tipton 1942; Tippecanoe 1878; Utter 1942; Weisenburger 1941; Whickar 1926; Whitney 1876; Winter 1917; Wolcott 1826, 1827; Writers Program 1940; White 1883; Warren 1883.

Illinois in 1830 was the homeland of about a third of the Potawatomi and less than 15 percent of the Winnebago, both groups living in the northern part of the state. Kickapoo still ranged through the central section, and affiliated Sauk and Mesquakie hunted west of the Illinois River. Remnants of the Kaskaskia and Piankeshaw resided on small reservations in the southern end of the state. This brief overview gives a static picture of the situation existing in 1830, after removal had been under way in Illinois and Indiana for a decade. Transient groups of several tribes would continue to move through the countryside during the decade to follow. Meanwhile, northward-advancing white settlers would engulf ever larger regions of the Indian hunting grounds in Illinois.

The map locates a total of 114 Indian villages, 64 within the state of Illinois, and an additional 50 villages in adjacent states and territories. The total represents an Indian population of approximately 16,300 for the area mapped, of 'whom about 7,300 should be attributed to the state of Illinois'. Discussion for this map covers all Illinois, as well as the western edge of Indiana now shown on map 25, and the Mississippi border region of Iowa and Missouri. Villages lying north of the Illinois state line are treated in connection with map 27.

The pattern of the four major tribal areas in Illinois in 1830 can be discerned with reasonable clarity by identifying the conspicuously mixed Indian villages situated along the borders between homogeneous territories of the Winnebago, Sauk, Potawatomi, and Kickapoo. Examples of boundary-line villages are: the Winnebago-Sauk villages on the lower Rock River, the Potawatomi-Kickapoo villages of Shikshak and Captain Hill on the Illinois River, and the Kickapoo-Potawatomi villages of Kannekuk's band south of the Iroquois River. Use of these indicators creates the tribal distribution pattern for Illinois in 1830 shown on map 22. Saukenuk, at the mouth of the Rock River, was exceptionally diverse as a consequence of the collection there of pro-British contingents from many tribes during the War of 1812 (map 21).

Potawatomi and Winnebago

Potawatomi villages and hunting grounds encompassed lands from the Kankakee and upper Illinois river valleys to the Rock River, the dividing line between Potawatomi and Winnebago country. Potawatomi lands in Illinois were only part of a total tribal estate extending from southwestern Michigan around the southern shore of Lake Michigan to southeastern Wisconsin. Of the 50 Potawatomi villages on the map, 40 within Illinois account for a population of about 3,600, a third of the total tribal population in 1830

and half the Indian population of Illinois.

The number of villages and total population of the Illinois Potawatomi rose sharply between 1815 and 1830, reflecting some Indian migration from southwestern Michigan motivated chiefly by the search for richer hunting grounds. The continued influx of Michigan Potawatomi, along with Ottawa and Ojibwa, increased the regional Potawatomi division identified by the federal government as the "United Band of Chippewa, Ottawa and Potawatomi." From this group emerged a coalition of influential leaders, several of mixed heritage, who supplanted traditional Potawatomi village leaders as tribal representatives in treaty negotiations during the critical years 1829-1833. A prominent trio in this group included an Ottawa, Shabbonee; Alexander Robinson or "Cheecheebinquay," Ottawa-British; and Billy Caldwell of Mohawk-Irish ancestry.

The Winnebago country, stretching north and west of the Rock River into central Wisconsin, is only partially shown on this map. The six Winnebago villages in Illinois represent about 600 or 700 out of a total population of 5,000, the majority living north of the Illinois state border. Winnebago remained generally responsive to traditional tribal leadership. Exceptional were the dissident Winnebago-Sauk villages on the lower Rock River who cast their political sympathies with Black Hawk's band (see map 29).

White miners spreading through the lead mining district had largely displaced the Winnebago in the northwestern corner of Illinois, pressing them northward into Wisconsin. Resentment against the 2,000 white inhabitants of the lead mining district had provoked a protest in 1827, followed by a land cession in 1829 (map 27).

Kickapoo

The Kickapoo, estimated at 2,200 in 1819, ceded their tribal estate that year and were under pressure to complete the process of removing west of the Mississippi. By 1830, white settlement advancing from southern Indiana and Illinois had forced them to abandon villages on the lower Wabash, Embarras, and Kaskaskia rivers. An estimated 600 had migrated to their assigned reservation on the Osage River, and another 600 to the White River of Missouri, but some straggled as far south as Texas.

Of the 1,000 or more not otherwise accounted for, perhaps all or at least 600 were still within the region covered by this map. A village of 15 to 20 lodges was located on the Mississippi River south of Saukenuk and Fort Armstrong. In Indiana, Little Duck's village on the Wabash River was the most easterly location noted for the Kickapoo. About

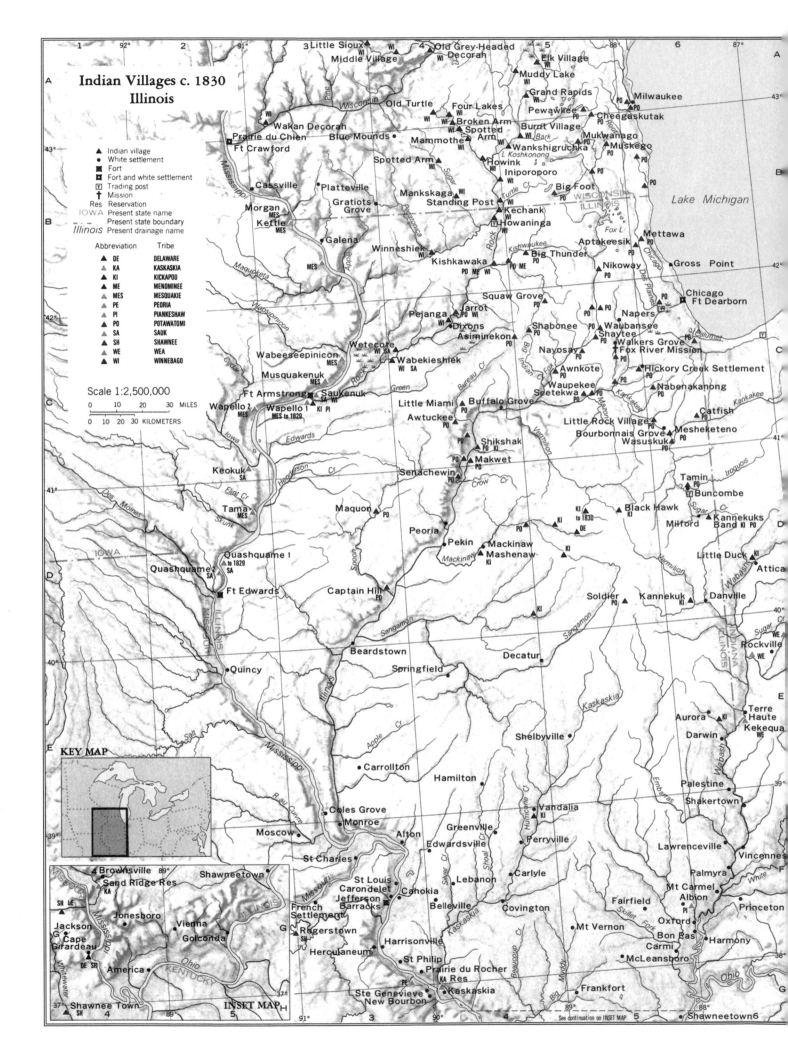

MAP
26

Wabonsee, Potawatomi who was influential in northern Illinois. From Viola, *The Legacy of Charles Bird King*. The Newberry Library.

Sauk and Mesquakie, and Remnant Groups

The ten Sauk and Mesquakie communities on the map, situated along the course of the Mississippi River, represent almost the total tribal membership estimated at 6,500. Probably 200 or so were farther west near the Missouri River. The Sauk and Mesquakie lived in large towns averaging more than 500 population, five times the size of the average Potawatomi or Winnebago towns. The significant variations in village size are best explained by their contrasting dependence upon agriculture and commercial hunting. The Sauk and Mesquakie cultivated extensive fields of corn and other crops and sold the surplus at forts and trading posts. In former times, their villages housed 2,000 inhabitants. On the other hand, the economy of the Potawatomi and most Upper Great Lakes Indians by 1850 was geared firmly to hunting, forcing a breakup into small hunting units, each group intensively exploiting a separate area.

Saukenuk, the last Sauk and Mesquakie village in Illinois, moved to the west bank of the Mississippi in late 1830. In that year, Black Hawk's people harvested their final crop of corn at their long-occupied village site. Wapello and Quashquame had abandoned their Illinois villages in 1829. For these two villages, consecutive locations on opposite sides of the Mississippi are shown on this map. Despite these moves, Sauk and Mesquakie continued to hunt in previously ceded lands in Illinois, viewing their eastern tribal boundary as the watershed between the Illinois and Mississippi rivers.

A population figure of 2,000 Sauk and Mesquakie ascribed to three towns, Saukenuk, Wapello, and Quashquame, is included in the estimate of total Indian population for Illinois in 1830. Sauk and Mesquakie were already involved with the Iowa and Dakota farther west, and relinquished claims to parts of Iowa by treaty in 1830.

The balance of the Indian villages mapped are found on the western edge of Indiana, the southern tip of Illinois, and the bordering area of Missouri. Coverage is extended to the southern boundaries of Illinois on the inset map. The main map and inset can be correlated by noting the location of Shawneetown on the right side of both maps.

In Indiana, three Wea villages with an estimated 350 inhabitants could be found near Terre Haute, but their fellow tribesmen had all removed west of the Mississippi. Downriver on the Illinois side of the Wabash River, a single Piankeshaw village lingered near Albion. The Kaskaskia reservation on the main map and Sand Ridge reserve on the inset probably had no more than 40 residents. Below St. Louis, Missouri, on lands originally granted by the Spanish government in 1784, population of the four remaining Delaware and Shawnee villages was reduced to about 600. A small Peoria enclave likewise persisted near Ste. Genevieve.

The Non-Indian Population

The predominantly rural, white population in Illinois had trebled since statehood in 1818, increasing to 157,000 in 1830. White settlement was concentrated in two areas, the lead-mining district of the northwest, and the southern part

200 were reported on the Mackinaw River in central Illinois.

The remaining Illinois Kickapoo had split into small, itinerant bands, moving frequently to evade state officials and harassment by white settlers. The largest aggregation of Kickapoo clustered near the headwaters of the Sangamon and the two Vermilion rivers. Some had been forced upstream from the site of Danville, where white operators took over their valuable saltworks. Probably as a result of stress and dislocation, they were experiencing a revitalization movement led by Kannekuk, the Kickapoo Prophet. Kannekuk's new religion attracted large numbers of converts, including neighboring Potawatomi.

The twelve Kickapoo village sites on this map were derived primarily from fragments of information in county histories, often less reliable sources than official reports prepared by resident Indian agents familiar with their Indian clients. Although a Kickapoo agricultural village in the midst of white settlement as late as 1830 seems unusual, the summer village near Vandalia was described by early Fayette county residents. It is impossible to verify simultaneous residence of all sites in central Illinois, but the distribution delineates the region occupied by Kickapoo in 1830.

The single Delaware site in the midst of the Kickapoo marks a transient group apparently including descendants of George Girty. He was the least conspicuous of the three "Girty Brothers," former Indian captives who moved permanently to the British-controlled Ohio frontier in 1778 (see map 15).

Potawatomi Traveling, c. 1837. Sketch by George Winter. Tippecanoe County Historical Association.

of the state. By 1830, most of Illinois had been ceded in a series of seven Indian treaties negotiated between 1815 and 1829, the year the valuable lead-mining district was relinquished by the Winnebago (map 30). The lead district was bounded on the east and north by the Pecatonica and Wisconsin rivers, and on the west by the Mississippi, extending south of Galena and the Apple River.

Advancing settlement had actually lagged behind the land cessions, extending only as far north as a line from Danville in the east to Quincy in the west. A few farms had been established between the Illinois and Mississippi rivers within the "military tract" set aside for soldiers of the War of 1812. Small numbers of squatters were lodged in Potawatomi territory along the Kankakee and Des Plaines rivers by 1830, but generally the non-Indian sites above Peoria were small trading communities with populations of mixed heritage (Metis) rather than commercial centers serving an agricultural hinterland.

Only the Potawatomi retained tribal land located in the northeastern section of the state. The Potawatomi reluctantly gave up this region, adjoining lands in Wisconsin and Indiana, and reservations in Michigan, in treaties signed in 1832 and 1833. By 1832, the remaining Kaskaskia, Piankeshaw, Wea, Peoria, Delaware, and Shawnee had all migrated to western reservations. During the late 1830s, the majority of the Potawatomi as well as Kickapoo, Sauk and Mesquakie, and Winnebago were relocated on reservations in Iowa and eastern Kansas. Land vacated by Indian residents was rapidly filled by the stream of American immigrants traveling west on the new road from Detroit to Chicago, or sailing across Lake Michigan from the new port at the mouth of the St. Joseph River.

Principal Sources: Beckwith 1879, 1880a, b; Brown 1922-1932; Center 1832; Chandler 1829; Clifton 1977; DeWard 1835; Farmer 1830; Gussow 1974; Hagan 1958; Harland 1961; Hubbard 1911; Indian Claims Commission 1974; Jablow 1974; Jones 1974; Kinzie 1829; Kuhm 1952; Menard 1830; National Archives 1829; Peck 1834; Pooley 1908; Scott 1954; Spector 1974; Tanner 1825, 1833; United States Census 1821; Voegelin 1974b, e; Vogel 1963; Whitney 1970-75; Wolcott, 1827.

INDIAN VILLAGES c. 1830: WISCONSIN REGION OF MICHIGAN TERRITORY, Map 27

The Wisconsin region, a part of Michigan Territory in 1830, retained its characteristic population of four major Indian tribes, Winnebago, Menominee, Ojibwa, and Potawatomi, as well as a small number of French and Metis trading families. American penetration into an area dominated by the British throughout the War of 1812 was indicated by three military forts along the Fox-Wisconsin waterway and a concentration of miners in the lead district south of Prairie du Chien (see also map 26). Two groups of New York Indians, the closely affiliated Stockbridge and Brotherton and the Oneida, were recent immigrants.

The subject area for this map is the present state of Wisconsin and the Upper Peninsula of Michigan west of the Carp River, present Marquette, plus the small Canadian border area on the northern shore of Lake Superior west of 81 degrees longitude, not shown on the map of the Minnesota region (map 28). Of the 134 Indian sites on the entire map, the subject area includes 123 villages with a population estimated at 13,500. The non-Indian population of Wisconsin, including garrison personnel, was about 3,600.

By far the largest tribal population in Wisconsin were the Winnebagos living in 40 villages in the southwestern part of the state, with six more villages on the lower Rock River in northern Illinois (map 26). By 1830, their communities stretched from Lake Winnebago to the mouth of the Wisconsin River and north along the east bank of the Mississippi River to the mouth of the Black River. A horticultural people with a dual chieftainship, the Winnebago still retained a far more settled village organization than had ever been attained by their Potawatomi, Ojibwa, or Menominee neighbors.

At one time the Winnebago had resided in a single large village at Red Banks, near present Benderville on the Door County peninsula, where they were surrounded by extensive fields of corn, squash, and beans. A later major settlement was located at Doty's Island in Lake Winnebago. By 1830, however, they had dispersed under new village leaders, many of them part-French descendants of the Old Queen and her husband, Decori (Dekaury or Decorah), in an apparent effort to maximize the profits of the fur trade. The shift in subsistence pursuits could be seen in the changed appearance of the Winnebago villages by the early decades of the nineteenth century. Less permanent oval wigwams, still multifamily dwellings, replaced the rectangular gabled multifire houses typical of the eighteenth century.

The Winnebago in 1830 were experiencing the aftermath of hostile incidents that occurred in 1827, but had yet to face problems created by the Black Hawk War of 1832 (map 29). During the summer of 1827, Winnebago attacked a boat descending the Mississippi River from Fort Snelling (present Minneapolis, Minnesota), killing two of the crew and committing other acts of violence. At the same time, evidence of Indian hostility practically brought lead-mining activities to a halt. Rumors circulated of war belts going to neighboring and southern Indian tribes.

In reprisal, an American expeditionary force of 700 assembled at Prairie du Chien, advanced up the Wisconsin River, and obtained a peace agreement and the surrender of principal offenders. The next summer, Fort Winnebago was established at the portage point of the Fox-Wisconsin waterway connecting Green Bay and the Mississippi River, The final settlement was a treaty in 1829 in which the Winnebagos gave up the lead district, the first surrender of their tribal lands. In two subsequent treaties, 1832 and 1837, the Winnebago lost the rest of their tribal lands in Wisconsin. By that time, a full-fledged split had developed between the "traditionals" who retained their old lifeway along the Wisconsin River and its tributaries, and "progressives" who came under the influence of missionaries and teachers after moving to Iowa following the 1829 and 1832 land cessions.

The Menominee in 1830 had a population of 3,000 or 4,000 people inhabiting their ancestral lands, but by 1830 had ceded all but the territory lying between the Wolf and upper Wisconsin rivers. Like the Winnebago, the Menominee had proliferated outward from their ancient seat at the mouth of the Menominee River and later from Green Bay. In 1830 they occupied 19 villages located between Lake Winnebago at the south, the Menominee River in the north, and the upper Wisconsin River to the west. The Menominee had long been linked to the fur trade, and their people showed considerable evidence of intermarriage with fur trade personnel. Because of game depletion in northeastern Wisconsin, the Menominee rotated their hunting reserves in western Wisconsin in a conservation effort. They also supplemented their rice harvesting and fishing activities by long winter hunts for beaver and deer in the largely uninhabited oak savanna between the northern coniferous forests and the prairie environment to the south (see maps 2 and 3).

Still regarded as friends by the antagonistic Dakota and Ojibwa, the Menominee continued to exploit the rich game reserves of the war zone extending across the present state of Minnesota (map 28). Dependence upon eastern Minnesota hunting lands resulted in the settlement of Menominee hunters among the Sioux on the west bank of the Mississippi and in permanent summer village sites near the mouths of the Bad Axe and Black rivers. Moreover, by 1830 the Menominee had established at least one village, L'Espanol, in what had formerly been regarded as Winnebago hunting territory. Pressure to obtain game during this period apparently led to cooperation between neighboring tribes as often as it did to competition and warfare.

The Stockbridge, Brotherton, and Oneida were occupy-

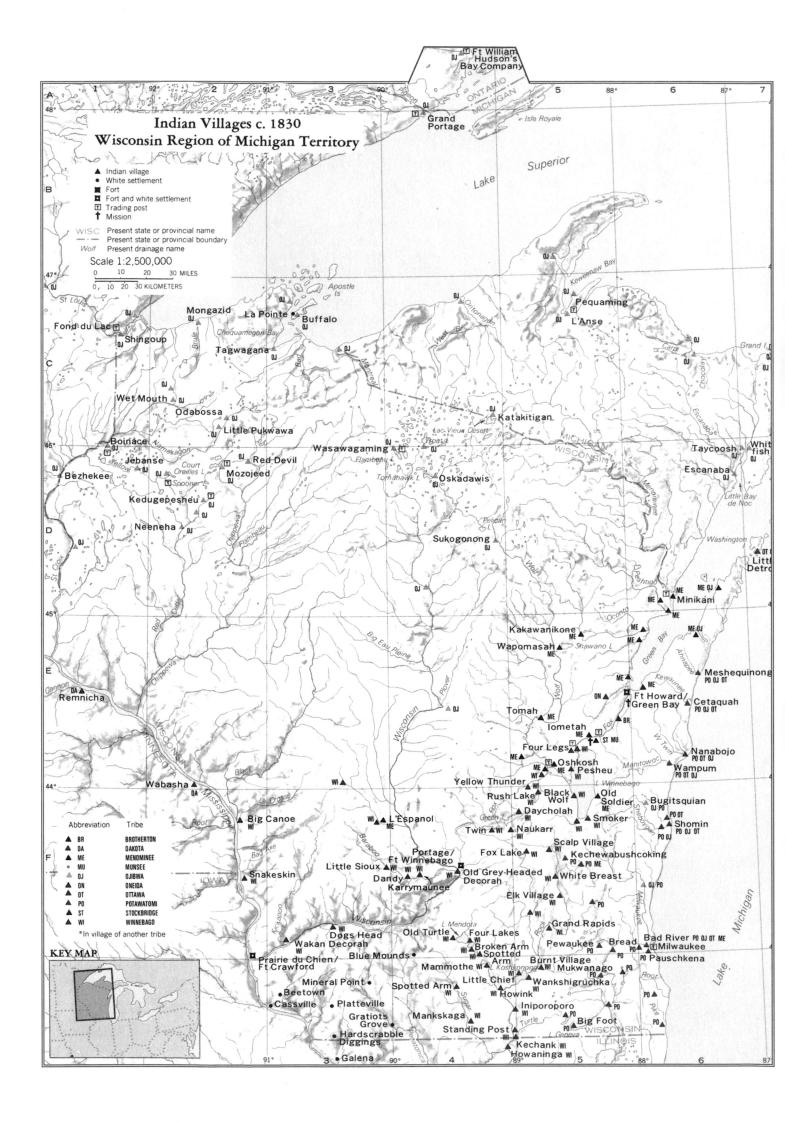

MAP
27

Indian Villages c. 1830
Wisconsin Region of Michigan Territory

▲ Indian village
● White settlement
■ Fort
🏠 Fort and white settlement
Ⓣ Trading post
✝ Mission

WISC — Present state or provincial name
— · — Present state or provincial boundary
Wolf — Present drainage name

Scale 1:2,500,000

0   10   20   30 MILES
0   10   20   30 KILOMETERS

Abbreviation	Tribe
▲ BR	BROTHERTON
▲ DA	DAKOTA
▲ ME	MENOMINEE
● MU	MUNSEE
▲ OJ	OJIBWA
▲ ON	ONEIDA
▲ OT	OTTAWA
▲ PO	POTAWATOMI
▲ ST	STOCKBRIDGE
▲ WI	WINNEBAGO

*In village of another tribe

KEY MAP

Lake Superior

🏠 Ft William
Hudson's
Bay Company

ONTARIO
MICHIGAN

Ⓣ Grand
Portage

Isle Royale

Pequaming
L'Anse

Fond du Lac
Shingoup
Mongazid
La Pointe
Buffalo
Tagwagana

Wet Mouth
Odabossa
Little Pukwawa
Katakitigan
Wasawagaming
Boinace
Jebanse
Red Devil
Mozojeed
Bezhekee
Kedugepesheu
Oskadawis
Neeneha
Sukogonong

Taycoosh
Whitefish
Escanaba
Little Bay
de Noc
Washington

Little
Detroit

ME Minikani

Remnicha

Kakawanikone
Wapomasah

Meshequinong

Tomah
Iometah
Ft Howard/
Green Bay
Cetaquah

Nanabojo
Wampum

Four Legs
Oshkosh
Pesheu

Yellow Thunder
Rush Lake
Black
Wolf
Old
Soldier
Bugitsquian
Shomin

Wabasha

Daycholah
Smoker

L'Espanol
Twin
Naukarr

Big Canoe

Scalp Village
Kechewabushcoking

Portage/
Ft Winnebago
Fox Lake
White Breast

Little Sioux
Dandy
Old Grey-Headed
Decorah
Karrymaunee
Elk Village

Snakeskin

Grand Rapids
Bad River
Bread
Milwaukee
Pauschkena

Dogs Head
Old Turtle
Four Lakes
Pewaukee
Wakan Decorah
Broken Arm
Blue Mounds
Spotted
Arm
Burnt Village
Mukwanago
Wankshigruchka

Prairie du Chien/
Ft Crawford
Mammothe
Little Chief
Howink

Mineral Point
Spotted Arm
Iniporoporo
Big Foot

Beetown
Cassville
Platteville
Mankskaga
Gratiots
Grove
Standing Post
Hardscrabble
Diggings
Kechank
Howaninga

Galena

WISCONSIN
ILLINOIS

Fort Howard on Green Bay, 1838. From Castlenau, *Vues et Souvenirs du L'Amerique du Nord*, pl. 16. The Newberry Library.

Party of Winnebago descending the upper Mississippi River using blanket sails on their log canoes, c. 1830. From Catlin, *Souvenirs of the North American Indians*, vol. 3, pi. 149. (London, 1850.)

Sheboygan, Wisconsin, in 1838. From Castlenau, *Vues et Souvenirs du L'Amerique du Nord* pl. 18, fig. 2. The Newberry Library.

ing three sites within the Menominee and old Winnebago country in 1830. These groups, jointly called "New York Indians," commenced land negotiations with the Menominee in 1821 and began moving to the lower Fox River valley about two years later (see map 23). The Stockbridge, shown across the Fox River from present Kaukauna, together with the Brotherton near present De Pere numbered about 300. Close to 400 Oneida had gathered on Duck Creek, which flowed into Green Bay. The Stockbridge and Brotherton were transferred in 1832 to a reservation on the east side of Lake Winnebago. This move was mandated by a federally supervised treaty made in 1831 that modified previous intertribal arrangements and included a large land cession (map 31).

In northern Wisconsin and western Upper Peninsula Michigan, Ojibwa numbering about 3,800 were distributed among the 35 principal locations in the subject area of this map. Although game was depleted farther south, the fur trade remained profitable in the Lake Superior region until the late nineteenth century. Continuing a pattern in existence for almost 200 years, traders intermarried with village women, contributing to a growing Metis population much in evidence by 1830 at such village-trading post clusters as La Pointe, L'Anse, Fond du Lac, and Lac du Flambeau (Flambeau Lake).

The map extension into the top margin of the plate shows Fort William, the Hudson's Bay Company post at the mouth of the Kaministikwia River in Canada. This new post was established in 1804, after British authorities determined that the Grand Portage site at the mouth of the Pigeon River lay within American territory and Americans had taken over Mackinac Island.

Near Lake Michigan, mixed Potawatomi-Ojibwa-Ottawa villagers lived by fishing as well as hunting, and maintained close contact with related people living around the northern shoreline and islands in Lake Michigan. The 11 villages on the map with these mixed tribal populations and the 14 Potawatomi villages in the southeastern section of Wisconsin represented about 1,800 people. Their existence was not particularly disturbed until their lands, ceded in 1833, were opened for settlement in 1835.

The non-Indian population of the Wisconsin region was not a prominent element in 1830, except for the military posts. Fort Howard at Green Bay and Fort Crawford at Prairie du Chien had been established in 1816 at the terminal points of the important Fox-Wisconsin waterway (map 21). Along with Fort Winnebago, the three forts had a total military population of about 600, principally young men. About 1,500 people, half the total Wisconsin civilian population, lived in the lead mining area in the southwest corner of the present state. Green Bay and Prairie du Chien, aside from the military personnel, were villages of around 500 people. A few hundred traders and employees in outlying areas accounted for the balance of the population.

In 1830, the vanguard of American settlers were driving herds of cattle into southern Wisconsin at a time when Potawatomi were still interring their deceased relatives in ancient mounds that continued to be objects of veneration. Winnebago villages bordered Lake Mendota, site of the future state capital, Madison. Milwaukee was only a post managed by French traders. Land speculators and Yankee immigrants coming by the Erie Canal route began to take over Milwaukee in 1835, and a separate Wisconsin Territory was formed in 1836. Although Potawatomi were given hospitality in kitchens of Milwaukee settlers up to 1838, wagons came that year with supplies for their removal from land ceded in the 1833 treaty at Chicago. Many Potawatomi fled north to Ojibwa country or took off in canoes for Manitoulin Island, recently established Canadian reserve (see also map 23).

Principal Sources: Allen 1860; Anon, map 1830; Arndt 1913; Atwater 1831; Barge 1918; Berrien 1835; Buck 1876; Chandler 1829; Clifton 1977; Doty 1876; Ellis 1856; Farmer 1830; Hall 1962; Hexom 1913; Jipson 1923; Jones 1974; Kinzie 1829-31; Kuhm 1952; Lawson 1907; Long 1860; Lurie 1952, 1980; Mack 1907; McKenney 1827; Martin 1888; Neuenschwander n.d.; Powell 1913; Radin 1923; Smith, 1973; Snelling 1868; Spector 1974; Storrow 1872; Tanner 1968; United States 1827; United States Land office, n.d.; Vieau 1888; Wisconsin n.d.

INDIAN VILLAGES c. 1830: MINNESOTA REGION, Map 28

The Minnesota region, the western borderland of Great Lakes territory, was occupied in 1830 by two large tribal groups, the long resident Dakota and the Ojibwa whose major advance into the area had taken place since the 1750s. Commentary for this map is limited to the estimated 10,500 Indians for which 62 population centers can be identified in present Minnesota and along the borders of Canada and South Dakota. An additional 16 Ojibwa and two Winnebago sites in Wisconsin are covered by map 27.

Before describing the Ojibwa and Dakota situation in 1830, it is important to point out that the Minnesota section of the present United States was only moderately under American influence at that time. The upper Mississippi Valley had figured in European treaties and American legislation since 1763 (map 12).Land east of the Mississippi was included in the Northwest Territory created by Congress in 1787, while land west of the river was considered by western nations as part of Louisiana, a province under the rule of France or Spain until the American purchase in 1803. Claims, to "sovereignty" in the vicinity of the St. Peter's (Minnesota) River continued to be largely theoretical, for Minnesota and northern Iowa effectively remained British Indian country until long after the War of 1812.

The joint commission surveying the American-Canadian border, carrying out terms of the Treaty of Ghent in 1815, did not reach the western section between Lake Superior and the problem area of Lake of the Woods until 1825. Final border settlement was delayed until a further British-American treaty was signed in 1842.

American presence in Minnesota was permanently established in 1819 with the construction of Fort Snelling, briefly called Fort St. Anthony, at modern Minneapolis. The fort was located on a tract of land rather dubiously ceded to the United States in 1805 as a consequence of a treaty made by Lieutenant Zebulon M. Pike during his explorations of the Mississippi River. No annuity payment in recognition of the treaty was made until 1819. The following year, 1820, the Dakota greeted their first American agent, Lawrence Taliaferro, who handled a difficult post in government-Indian relations with energy and integrity until 1840. As late as 1827, he predicted that if war should again break out with Great Britain, the Dakota would support the British. Among the first settlers around Fort Snelling were a few refugee families from the Selkirk Colony established on the Red River in Canada.

Taliaferro worked hard to acquire the allegiance of the Dakota, at the same time striving to quell Dakota warfare with the Ojibwa with no more success than the French and British before him. Lands north of the Minnesota River were still unoccupied and dangerous hunting ground; as a result they were extremely rich in furbearing animals and a prize worth contending for.

Wanaton, the Charger, Dakota leader of Sisseton and Yanktonnai heritage, with his son at the Lake Traverse Village. From Keating, *Expedition to the Source of the St. Peter's River.* The Newberry Library.

In Taliaferro's era a second war zone developed involving the Dakota and the Sauk and Mesquakie on the south. Having ceded former lands in southwestern Wisconsin and northwestern Illinois, the Sauk and Mesquakie were forced to concentrate their hunting activities west of the Mississippi in the Iowa and Minnesota border region long controlled by the Dakota. In defending their hunting territory, the Dakota came into frequent and bloody contact with the Sauk and Mesquakie, especially around the headwaters of the Des Moines River, an area that the Wapekute and Yankton divisions had long exploited.

It was Taliaferro's unrealistic idea that geographic boundaries might be set to resolve conflicting claims of the warring tribes. At his suggestion, a grand intertribal council was held at Prairie du Chien in the summer of 1825 to promote peace and establish boundaries for Indians living

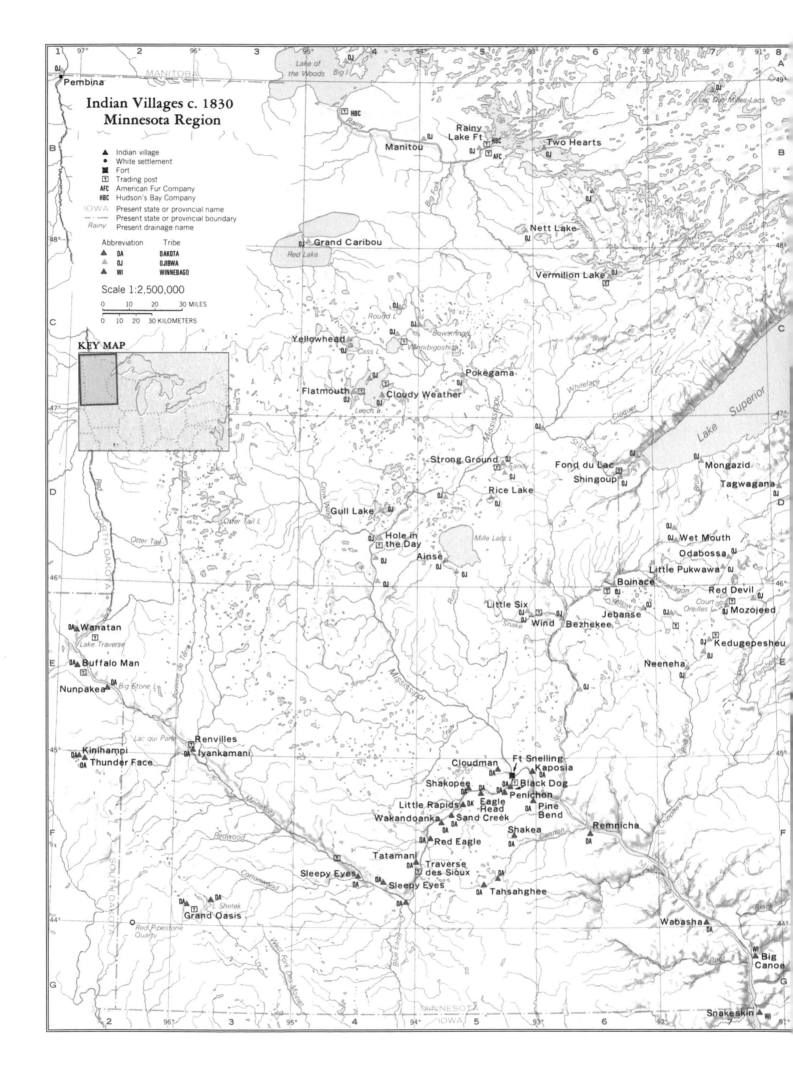

Indian Villages c. 1830
Minnesota Region

Indian village
White settlement
Fort
Trading post
AFC   American Fur Company
HBC   Hudson's Bay Company
IOWA   Present state or provincial name
Present state or provincial boundary
Rainy   Present drainage name

Abbreviation   Tribe
DA   DAKOTA
OJ   OJIBWA
WI   WINNEBAGO

Scale 1:2,500,000

0   10   20   30 MILES
0   10   20   30 KILOMETERS

KEY MAP

MAP
28

Pembina

MANITOBA

Lake of
the Woods   Big I

HBC

Manitou

Rainy
Lake Ft   HBC
AFC

Two Hearts

Lac Dux Milles-Lacs

Nett Lake

Grand Caribou

Red Lake

Vermilion Lake

Round L

Yellowhead

Cass L

Bowstring

L Winnibigoshish

Pokegama

Flatmouth

Cloudy Weather

Leech L

Whiteface

Cloquet

Lake Superior

Strong Ground

Sandy L

Fond du Lac

Shingoup

Mongazid

Tagwagana

Rice Lake

Mississippi

Gull Lake

Otter Tail L

Otter Tail

Hole in
the Day

Ainse

Mille Lacs L

Wet Mouth

Odabossa

Little Pukwawa

Boinace

Red Devil

Mozojeed

Court
Oreilles L

Little Six

Jebanse

Wind   Bezhekee

Kedugepesheu

Neeneha

Wanatan

Lake Traverse

Buffalo Man

Nunpakea

Big Stone L

Snake

Mississippi

Kinihampi

Lac qui Parle

Renvilles

Thunder Face   Iyankamani

Cloudman

Ft Snelling   Kaposia

Shakopee   Black Dog

Little Rapids   Eagle
Head   Penichon

Wakandoanka   Sand Creek   Pine
Bend

Red Eagle   Shakea

Remnicha

Tatamani

Sleepy Eyes

Traverse
des Sioux

Sleepy Eyes   Tahsahghee

Kinihampi

L Shetek

Grand Oasis

Red Pipestone
Quarry

Wabasha

Big
Canoe

Snakeskin

NORTH DAKOTA

SOUTH DAKOTA

Minnesota

Redwood

Cottonwood

West Fork Des Moines

Blue Earth

Cannon

MINNESOTA
IOWA

Root

Lake Traverse on the present Minnesota-South Dakota border, with scaffold burial in the foreground. From Keating, *Expedition to the Source of the St. Peter's River.* The Newberry Library.

west of Lake Michigan. Attending the council were representatives of the Dakota, Ojibwa, Sauk and Mesquakie, Iowa, Winnebago, Menominee, and a portion of the "United Band" Potawatomi, Ojibwa and Ottawa living on the Illinois River.

The Dakota-Ojibwa line set by the Treaty of Prairie du Chien in 1825 followed precise geographic markers from the Chippewa River in Wisconsin to the juncture of the Red River of the North and Goose Creek in present North Dakota (see map 22). Despite the treaty, during the summer of 1826 a party of Dakota attacked Ojibwa visiting Taliaferro almost under the walls of Fort Snelling. The line was not surveyed until 1835, and then both tribal groups pulled up the stakes. The 1825 treaty line drawn between the Dakota and the Sauk and Mesquakie fared little better. In an effort to create a neutral zone on the southern side of Dakota lands, American commissioners in 1830 secured the cession of twenty-mile strips north and south of the treaty line from Dakota bands and from the Sauk and Mesquakie. Both groups tried to gain control of the "neutral" zone. As a consequence of pressure on the Dakotas from the north and the south, an atmosphere of strife pervaded the Minnesota Region in the 1830s, with desperate struggles over dwindling hunting resources in an area where life had always been precarious, even in times of peace.

In Minnesota proper, Ojibwa expansion into former Dakota territory was virtually complete by 1830. Villages were safely entrenched in the headwaters of the Mississippi, as well as on Mille Lacs Lake, principal Dakota center during the seventeenth century (see map 9). South of the Crow Wing River, in the region claimed by both tribes, new Ojibwa villages had been established as far down as the mouth of the Elk River. These villages, like those at Mille Lacs and the upper St. Croix, were still subject to periodic Dakota attack. Similarly, while the Pillager band of Ojibwas from Leech Lake hunted with fierce determination in

the Otter Tail Lake, trying to secure a village location there, another decade and a half would pass before they achieved their objective.

The Ojibwa population of Minnesota and the border regions included in the map was approximately 3,800 in 1830. Prominent leaders of this era whose villages are shown were Flat Mouth on Leech Lake and Hole-in-a-Day on the upper Mississippi River. Some information was reported concerning the size of individual bands and groups within particular geographic districts. More than 1,800 Ojibwa were living in loosely organized bands in the upper Mississippi River area, and near 340 were on the St. Croix and Snake rivers closer to Wisconsin. A second large body of Ojibwa, estimated at about 1,200, was distributed at unspecified locations through northern Minnesota from the vicinity of Red Lake to Pembina, a settlement located on the Red River of the North at the Canadian border. Individual bands of Ojibwa ranging in size from 130 to 160 were based at Vermilion Lake, Rainy Lake, and Lake of the Woods.

The 28 Dakota villages on the map, chiefly in the Minnesota River valley, represent divisions having a combined population of about 6,700 in 1830. The Mdewakanton, leading eastern division of the Dakota with a population around 1,500, retained villages on the Mississippi and the lower Minnesota River. Fairly recently they had established new villages near Little Rapids in order to raise corn. The Mdewakanton, under the guidance of a succession of leaders named Wabasha, Little Crow, Shakopee, and Red Wing, were the most geographically stable division of Dakota. They had dealt with Europeans appearing on the Mississippi River since the seventeenth century.

During the winter of 1828-29, reports circulated that 175 Dakota, mainly from the more nomadic bands, had starved to death out on the prairies. Following this tragedy, Taliaferro's frustrated attempts to "civilize" the Dakota and turn

Falls of St. Anthony, on the Mississippi River at present St. Paul. From Schoolcraft, *History of the Indian Tribes of the United States*, pt. 6, p. 385. The Newberry Library.

them into white-style farmers took tentative root. In 1829 he convinced one near-victim, the Mdewakanton leader Cloud Man, to try farming. The experimental village near Lake Calhoun, called "Eatonville," attracted the services of missionaries, teachers, and farming instructors. Although a modest success, it had to be abandoned in 1839 because of vulnerability to Ojibwa attack.

A second division of the Dakota, the Wapekuta, numbering about 800, ranged uneasily about the headwaters of the Des Moines River near the Grand Oasis and on the upper Cannon River. The Wapekuta, whose living habits had always been less reliable than other divisions, were sometimes termed "renegade" or "vagabond."

Two other Dakota divisions, approximately 900 Wahpeton and 2,500 Sisseton, had gathering points upstream where the Minnesota River broadened at intervals to form lakes. The members of the Wahpeton division were established near Traverse des Sioux, an important river crossing, as well as on Lac Qui Parle and Big Stone Lake. Probably the best known civilization experiment among the Dakota in the 1830s was carried on at Lac Qui Parle, where missionaries received the support of the influential leader Joseph Renville. The shores and islands of Big Stone Lake at the headwaters of the Minnesota River were used as well by upper bands of Sisseton and North Yankton bands also called Yanktonnai. Sleepy Eye's people, the Lower Sisseton, still made the area near the mouth of the Blue Earth River (present Mankato) their rendezvous. The majority of the Upper Sisseton tended to congregate near Lake Traverse, located on the drainage of the Red River of the North.

Wanaton, leader of the Upper Sisseton and about 5,000 Yanktonnai and other Dakota, had gained his posi-

tion through bravery during the War of 1812 at the siege of Fort Stephenson (present Fremont, Ohio). Taliaferro had refused a permit to Wanaton's brother-in-law, British agent and trader Robert Dickson, to return to his trading post on Lake Traverse. After Dickson's death at Michilimackinac in 1823, Wanaton and his large following spent an increasing percentage of time in the upper Missouri River region. Although Wanaton occasionally returned to his eastern base at Lake Traverse until about 1836, his principal headquarters became the vicinity of present Bismarck, North Dakota, about 200 miles northwest of Lake Traverse. By 1830, approximately 4,000 Yanktonnai had moved westward permanently, while about 1,000 remained behind with the Upper Sisseton. These Dakota, like their Teton predecessors living on Big Stone Lake and Lake Traverse, faced the rolling country of the western plains outside the Great Lakes Region.

One final comment about the map concerns the small circle identifying the location of the Red Pipestone Quarry, source of the beautiful rock used especially for making ceremonial pipes. Although a particular responsibility of the Yankton, the site held spiritual significance for all Dakota people.

Principal Sources: Babcock 1945a, b; Blegen 1940; Boutwell 1830; Bray 1976; Bray 1970; Brower 1900; Forsyth 1880; Hickerson 1974; Hughes 1929; Kane 1978; Keating 1825; Meyer 1967; Minnesota Archaeological Survey n.d.; Morris n.d.; Nute 1942; Parker 1966; Pond 1908; Schoolcraft 1821, 1854, 1855; Tanner 1970; Upham 1920; Voegelin 1974g; Winchell 1911.

On April 5, 1832, under the leadership of an aging Sauk war leader, Black Hawk, some one thousand Sauk and Mesquakie warriors and their women and children crossed the Mississippi River at the Yellow Banks about halfway between Fort Madison and Fort Armstrong. Ostensibly, the band's intentions were peaceable. Sauk women carried bags of seedcorn to sow the fields at their ancestral village, Saukenuk, near present Rock Island, Illinois, which had served for nearly a hundred years as the principal residence of the Sauk tribe.

In 1832, Saukenuk no longer belonged to the Sauk. The village lay in territory ceded rather questionably by a few affiliated Sauk and Mesquakie in 1804, part of a vast tract bounded by the Illinois, Mississippi, Wisconsin, and upper Rock rivers. Signatories later disclaimed knowledge of the cession, charging that the treaty had been fraudulently obtained. Following the Peace of Ghent, ending the War of 1812, the Sauk and Mesquakie again touched the quill in 1816 to reaffirm the sale of their traditional lands, although many tribesmen persisted in the belief that Saukenuk had been excluded from the original cession. Most adamant were members of the so-called British Band, Sauk and Mesquakie who had held off American advances during the War of 1812 and continued to seek British support and advice after the war.

When, in 1829, the fields at Saukenuk were thrown open to American settlement, the majority of the Sauk followed the lead of the American accommodationist, Keokuk, and established new villages on the west bank of the Mississippi. The British Band, in contrast, spurned American calls for removal until the summer of 1831, when a force under General Edmund Gaines and 1,400 scalp-hungry militiamen sent Black Hawk and his followers fleeing to the Iowa shore under cover of darkness. By an extra-legal agreement of capitulation, the British Band agreed not to reenter the state of Illinois without presidential approval.

Black Hawk's return in 1832 was interpreted as an invasion. In response, Governor John Reynolds called out the Illinois militia, and General Henry Atkinson, at Jefferson Barracks south of St. Louis, ordered ten companies to Fort Armstrong at Rock Island. But the British Band did not attempt to reoccupy Saukenuk. Instead, they continued up the south bank of the Rock River, skirting territory ceded by the Potawatomi and Winnebago in 1829, to the multi-tribal village of sympathizers under Wabekieshiek, the Winnebago Prophet, at present Prophetstown, Illinois. There, American calls for retreat were ignored. By May 14, the growing band was encamped near the mouth of the Sycamore River, the site of a composite village and the gateway to remaining Potawatomi lands in northeastern Illinois.

The movements of the British Band before mid-May,

1832, confused white observers. Despite the amassing of troops and militia along the Rock and Illinois rivers, no Indian hostilities or armed clashes had occurred during the nearly five-week-long Sauk excursion into forbidden territory. Moreover, the continued presence of women and children argued against militaristic aims. Events of May 14 suggest that Black Hawk had decided to negotiate with, if not to surrender to, American authorities. Unfortunately, General Atkinson was still at Dixon, Illinois, with the main contingent when Sauk bearing a white flag approached an advance scouting party of Illinois militia under Captain Isaiah Stillman south of the Sycamore River. The untrained recruits attacked the Sauk envoys, pursuing them back to Black Hawk's camp, where the Americans panicked and were thoroughly routed by the Indian force.

The American disgrace at Stillman's Run signaled the onset of a war which called into service nearly 7,000 Americans against an Indian force of no more than 500 warriors. The ill-managed campaign dragged more than 3,000 militia and several hundred regulars through the mosquito-infested

Black Hawk (Makataimeshekaikiak), Sauk leader, sketched at Louisville, Kentucky, probably in 1833 when prisoners were en route from Jefferson Barracks, Missouri, to Washington, D.C. By James R. Lambdin. Original watercolor at The Newberry Library, gift of Robert O'Neill.

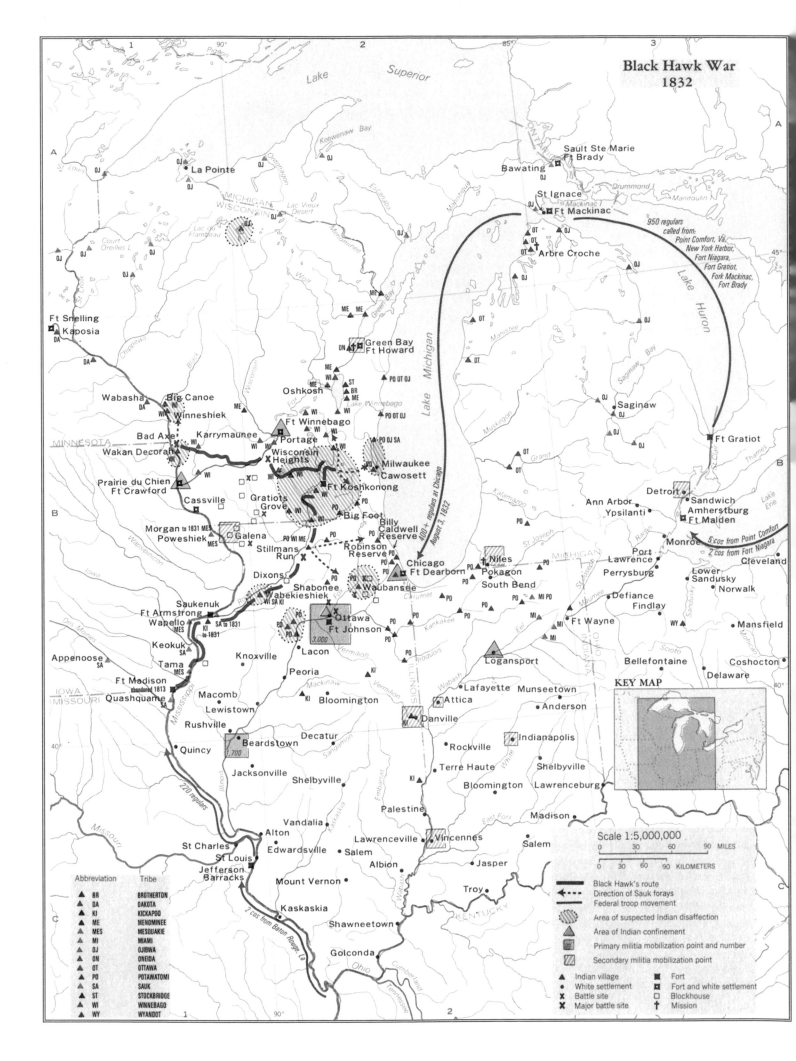

Black Hawk War
1832

950 regulars
called from:
Point Comfort, Va,
New York Harbor,
Fort Niagara,
Fort Gratiot,
Fork Mackinac,
Fort Brady

MAP
29

KEY MAP

Scale 1:5,000,000

| | 0 | 30 | 60 | 90 | MILES |
| | 0 | 30 | 60 | 90 | KILOMETERS |

Black Hawk's route
Direction of Sauk forays
Federal troop movement

Area of suspected Indian disaffection

Area of Indian confinement

Primary militia mobilization point and number

Secondary militia mobilization point

▲ Indian village   ■ Fort
● White settlement   ⊡ Fort and white settlement
✕ Battle site   □ Blockhouse
✕ Major battle site   † Mission

Abbreviation	Tribe
▲ BR	BROTHERTON
▲ DA	DAKOTA
▲ KI	KICKAPOO
▲ ME	MENOMINEE
▲ MES	MESQUAKIE
▲ MI	MIAMI
▲ OJ	OJIBWA
▲ ON	ONEIDA
▲ OT	OTTAWA
▲ PO	POTAWATOMI
▲ SA	SAUK
▲ ST	STOCKBRIDGE
▲ WI	WINNEBAGO
▲ WY	WYANDOT

swamps and timbered river valleys of south central and southwestern Wisconsin in pursuit of an elusive fugitive. About one thousand additional regulars were called or absorbed by General Winfield Scott, commander of the Northwest Army, from points as distant as Baton Rouge, Louisiana; Fort Monroe (Point Comfort), Virginia; New York Harbor; Fort Niagara, New York; and Fort Gratiot, Michigan. The majority of them either turned back, arrived too late for battle, or died in the first epidemic of Asiatic cholera to strike North America (see map 32).

For nearly two months, the British Band hid in the marshes of the upper Rock River, north of Lake Koshkonong. From this base, warriors launched attacks on the hastily thrown-up forts of Illinois and southwestern Wisconsin, burning homesteads, pillaging stores, stealing livestock, and killing some thirty settlers and militiamen. Some of the depredations were the responsibility of Indians living in areas of suspected disaffection shown on the map; Winnebago of the Rock and Wisconsin rivers, Kickapoo from Central Illinois, and Potawatomi of the Fox and Illinois rivers. Even in southwestern Michigan, pioneers erected defenses and the stream of immigration into the area temporarily halted.

Finally, in mid-July, 1832, scouts for Colonel Henry Dodge, noted frontier fighter and future governor of Wisconsin Territory, discovered the southward-leading trail of the British Band just south of the Rock River rapids at present Hustisford. Had Dodge not been informed by Winnebago spies of Black Hawk's general whereabouts, and had the British Band not been reduced to peeling bark from the trees for subsistence, the Sauk might have slipped undiscovered between Atkinson's forces to the south and Fort Winnebago to the north in their attempted escape across the Mississippi.

Dodge's forces dogged the retreating Sauk across the site of present-day Madison, Wisconsin, and on July 21 caught the rear of the British Band at Wisconsin Heights. Although outnumbered, the British Band turned to attack the Americans as women and children fled across the Wisconsin River in Winnebago canoes. Nightfall terminated the battle, and by morning the Sauk warriors had likewise disappeared.

Falling back for supplies, Dodge rendezvoused with Atkinson's troops a week later and again led the pursuit of the starving Sauk and Mesquakie up the Pine River valley, over the Kickapoo River to the mouth of the Bad Axe River. When they arrived in late July, the villages of sympathetic Winnebago were vacant. The Indian agent at Prairie du Chien had coerced reluctant Winnebago into eyeshot of his agency only a few days earlier. Raked by guns of an armed steamboat and attacked by land troops, the British Band on August 2 was squeezed onto the mud-flats and islands of the Mississippi, where they fell like "grass before the scythe."

Many of those who reached the opposite shore were cut down by Wabasha's Dakota band a few days later. Others who had escaped after the Wisconsin Heights battle were captured by Menominee from Green Bay and by Winnebago fearful of American reprisal. Only 150 to 200 Sauks and Mesquakies of the original 1,000 rejoined their kinsmen on the Iowa side of the Mississippi River. A few others found refuge among the mixed Ottawa, Ojibwa, and

Potawatomi villages dotting the western shore of Lake Michigan, eventually seeking asylum in Canada.

Black Hawk did not witness the final destruction and dispersion of his people. With the Winnebago Prophet and about fifty followers, he pushed toward Winnebago allies on the Black River. If they hoped for sanctuary or transport northward to friendly Ojibwa at Lac du Flambeau or to British territory, they were disappointed. The Winnebago leader One-Eyed Decorah provided the fugitives safe passage to officials at Fort Crawford at Prairie du Chien, once the ferocity of the American military campaign was revealed.

Black Hawk, his son, his principal lieutenant, Neapope, and the Winnebago Prophet were taken to confinement at Jefferson Barracks. In the spring of 1833 they went by steamboat from St. Louis up the Ohio River, then overland to one month more of incarceration at Fortress Monroe, Virginia. After his release, Black Hawk had a formal meeting with President Andrew Jackson and other high government officials in Washington. During his return trip to Iowa, the Indian delegation received considerable public attention when they stopped at Baltimore, Philadelphia, New York, and Albany.

The foregoing account covers the principal military action in the three-months-long Black Hawk War of 1832 and the end of punitive measures against Black Hawk personally. In the background of this brief frontier conflagration was a long sequence of inter-tribal alignments and re-alignments that had concerned Americans at intervals during the previous half century.

The westernmost Sauk, Mesquakie, and Winnebago had been active confederates since the American campaign for control of Ohio in the 1790s. Although the Sauk were pressured into aiding the British in 1812, once committed, under the leadership of Black Hawk and Ioway they staged a brilliant attack on Americans on the Mississippi River. Peace brought no hiatus in confederate activity. Throughout the winter of 1815-16 the Winnebago hereditary chief Karrymaunee traveled to different tribes making agreements to resist further land cessions. The allies, then consisting of the Sauk, Mesquakie, Iowa, Kickapoo, Menominee, Ojibwa, and Winnebago, were reluctant to accept the British withdrawal from the Great Lakes fur-trading zone. At the same time, British Indian Agent Robert Dickson was urging them to move to British protection in the Pembina region, on the lower Red River.

The "Winnebago War" of 1827 seemed to be a localized protest against the lead miners (map 27), but actually it was a sign of broader discontent. With the Winnebago subdued, the Sauk emerged by 1828 as the militant core of resistance to advancing American settlement in the western Great Lakes Region. A Sauk emissary passed the winter of 1828-29 near the falls of the Niagara River, rallying eastern sympathy. British contacts continued without any overt support. Chances of joint confederate action against Americans were dashed in 1830-31 by the involvement of the Menominee and the Wisconsin River Winnebago in the Dakota-Sauk feud. Retaliatory murders brought death to an important party of Menominee and nine Mesquakie chiefs, splintering the Wisconsin branch of the confederacy and leaving the Mesquakie virtually without leadership. Many Mesquakie, including the

The Winnebago Prophet (Wabekieshiek), sketched at Louisville, Kentucky, probably in 1833. He was known to Indian people as White Cloud. By James R. Lambdin. Original watercolor at The Newberry Library, gift of Robert O'Neill.

Menominee murderers, joined the British Band. Continuing hostility of the Menominee toward the British Band was a factor preventing Black Hawk from securing refuge in the Green Bay region in 1832.

The British Band suffered other set-backs before the outbreak of hostilities in 1832. In the search for additional allies, Black Hawk's chiefs and warriors traveled southwest into eastern Texas, at that time still Mexican territory. The party circulated black wampum among twelve tribes, inviting them to a grand council in 1831. The Sauk were warmly received by their former allies the Shawnee and Delaware, but only the Iowa and Osage promised warriors. During the journey, two Sauk leaders died of unknown causes, and a third died at home the following summer, weakening the Sauk at a time when the Mesquakie had lost nine principal men.

Although the drive for southern and western allies failed to yield militant supporters, the council at Saukenuk in May, 1831, did attract several hundred dissident Kickapoo, Potawatomi, Winnebago, and Osage, as well as the Sauk and Mesquakie. These allies later supported Black Hawk at the outset of warfare in May, 1832. When General Gaines and 1,400 troops arrived at Saukenuk in June, 1831, however, the concentration of warriors and leaders dispersed to the Iowa side of the Mississippi River. At this point, the Sauk themselves were divided, Keokuk and a majority of the tribe breaking with the anti-American militants.

These are the principal developments leading up to the events of the Black Hawk War already recounted. The war decimated the British Band, demoralized the non-belligerent members of the Sauk and Mesquakie tribes, and intimidated neighboring tribes. Black Hawk's rival, Keokuk, and other pro-American chiefs were forced to cede a portion of their tribal domain in eastern Iowa. Moreover, the shadowy involvement of the Winnebago and Potawatomi in Black Hawk's behalf rendered them vulnerable to government demands for removal. By 1836, all Indian lands in northern Illinois and southern Wisconsin had been ceded, clearing them for American occupancy. The Black Hawk War broke surviving Indian resistance to American domination of the Great Lakes Region.

Principal Sources: Black Hawk 1955; Brunson 1856; Decorah 1895; Dickson papers n.d.; Eby 1973; Hagan 1949, 1958; Jackson 1962; Lambert 1939; Lockwood 1856; Matson 1880; Stevens 1903; Wakefield 1834; Wallace 1970-1978; Whitney 1970-75.

The progressive loss of land by Indian tribes to the American and Canadian governments is illustrated in this map. The treaty-making procedure for acquiring Indian land is commonly called a land "cession" in the United States and a land "surrender" in Canada. By 1873, most land in the Great Lakes Region had been ceded in approximately 130American and 27 Canadian treaties. Only portions of Ontario east of Georgian Bay and around Lake Simcoe, along with the Red Lake region in northern Minnesota, were still under Indian jurisdiction in the view of Canadian and American governments. As the map shows, earliest cessions occurred in the eastern part of the Great Lakes Region. In New York and Pennsylvania, lands were ceded to states, but throughout the rest of the region national governments treated with Indians.

Dates of land cessions are grouped into three historical periods for Canadian territory and four periods for the United States, where additional warfare and greater white population growth caused a larger number of treaties. Periods are differentiated on the map by color. The printed dates indicate the specific time of land cessions in particular areas. Boundaries of individual land cessions, sometimes obscure or overlapping, have been omitted from this compilation. Within ceded lands, tracts reserved for Indians by treaty provisions are shown on "Reservations 1783-1889" (map 31).

Red Areas

Inclusive dates for the initial period of Indian land cessions were virtually identical on both sides of the international border created by the Treaty of Paris in 1783 (map 12). These years, indicated by red-tinted areas on the map, were 1783-1806 in British Canada, and 1784-1809 in the United States. The time period was concurrent with the first advancing wave of settlement after the American Revolution and the post-Revolutionary wars (see also map 20).

When war ended, British officials in Canada quickly secured surrenders of land from Iroquois and Missisauga Indians along the north shores of the upper St. Lawrence River and Lake Ontario. These treaties cleared the way for entry into Canada of British Loyalists leaving the former American colonies. Among the emigrés were loyal Indians of the Six Nations Confederacy, principally Mohawk from New York. Dotted lines mark the two tracts of land surrendered by Missisauga and designated for the Six Nations in 1784, a transaction confirmed in 1792. These tracts lay along the Grand River north of Lake Erie and the Bay of Quinte on the northeastern shore of Lake Ontario. Subsequently, lands between Lake Erie and the Thames River and inland from Lake St. Clair were secured for Loyalists entering Canada by way of the Detroit frontier. Land sur-

renders omitted Walpole Island at the delta of the St. Clair River (maps 22, 33, 9).

In American territory, the first major land cession at the Treaty of Greenville in 1795 opened up land for settlement northwest of the Ohio River and along the southern coast of Lake Erie as far west as present Cleveland at the mouth of the Cuyahoga River. The extension of ceded land westward to Sandusky Bay in 1805 encompassed the area that had been claimed by Connecticut as its "western reserve."

Treaties following the American Revolution also secured for the British and American governments parcels of land strategically located for controlling the water transportation routes throughout most of the Great Lakes Region. In these cases the purpose was military. In 1785 the British acquired control of the Severn River route from Lake Simcoe to Matchedash Bay, a southeastern arm of Georgian Bay (map 13). This river channel was the western extension of the Trent River waterway between Lake Simcoe and the Bay of Quinte on Lake Ontario. In 1798, land was purchased at the tip of the peninsula between Matchedash Bay and broader Nottawasaga Bay, later the location of the Penetanguishene naval base (map 21).

At that time, the British government was making adjustments in the defense of territory on the upper Great Lakes as a consequence of the need for vacating posts to Americans in 1796, fulfilling terms of the Jay Treaty of 1794 (map 12). In 1798, Ojibwas gave up St. Joseph's Island at the outlet of the St. Marys River into Lake Huron, new site for the British base moved from Mackinac Island. Further surrenders south of Lake Simcoe in 1805 and 1806 secured for the British an alternate route, via Toronto and Lake Simcoe, between Lake Ontario and Nottawasaga Bay.

In addition to ceding two-thirds of the present state of Ohio, the Greenville Treaty of 1795 specified parcels of land at a dozen locations of strategic importance in present Michigan, Indiana, Ohio, and Illinois for use of the American government. These tracts were located at critical portage points, heads of navigation on well-traveled streams, and sites for forts and major trading posts. The red area on this map includes a number of these parcels. None of them were situated along the Fox-Wisconsin waterway linking Green Bay and the Mississippi River. This channel was under British control.

Outside the main Greenville Treaty land cession, parcels were ceded in 1795 at: Loramie's trading post on the head-waters of the Miami River (maps 16 and 17), the heads of navigation on the Auglaize and St. Marys rivers, the confluence of the Auglaize and Maumee rivers where Fort Defiance was established (map 18), the foot of the rapids and mouth of the Maumee River (map 21 inset), the confluence

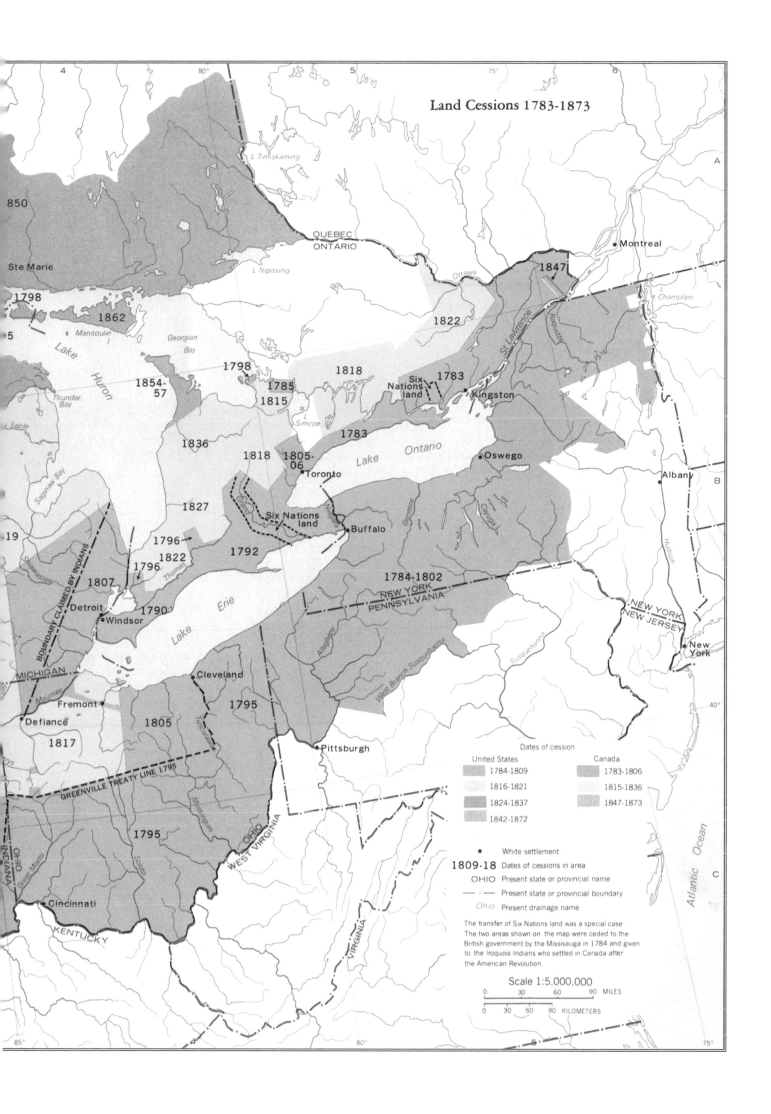

Land Cessions 1783-1873

MAP
30

Dates of cession

United States
- 1784-1809
- 1816-1821
- 1824-1837
- 1842-1872

Canada
- 1783-1806
- 1815-1836
- 1847-1873

● White settlement

1809-18 Dates of cessions in area

OHIO Present state or provincial name

— · — Present state or provincial boundary

Ohio Present drainage name

The transfer of Six Nations land was a special case.
The two areas shown on the map were ceded to the
British government by the Missisauga in 1784 and given
to the Iroquois Indians who settled in Canada after
the American Revolution.

Scale 1:5,000,000

0   30   60   90 MILES

0   30   60   90 KILOMETERS

Grand council of Ojibwa and American officials, held at Fond du Lac, at the head of Lake Superior. Indian councils usually took place under a large tree or an arbor of branches. From McKenney, *Tour to the Lakes,* p. 311. The Newberry

of the St. Marys and St. Joseph rivers where Fort Wayne was established (map 181, the portage point to the Wabash River eight miles west of Fort Wayne, Sandusky Bay and the lower Rapids of the Sandusky River at present Fremont, the mouths of the Chicago and Illinois rivers as well as a Peoria Lake site, Ouiatenon and Vincennes on the Wabash River, and the Fort Massac site on the lower Ohio River (map 9).

In the 1795 treaty, the United States also received Indian acquiescence to the takeover of large blocks of land at the Straits of Mackinac and Detroit River as well as approval of the 150,000-acre congressional land grant in southern Indiana for George Rogers Clark's veteran Revolutionary War contingent. Within Michigan territory not ceded until 1807, the United States in 1795 secured control of a strip of land six miles wide, too narrow for mapping, from the Raisin River to Lake St. Clair, taking in all the woods and cropland that French and British settlers had purchased from Indian people. At the Straits of Mackinac, the United States acquired title to similar land on both sides of the straits and to Mackinac Island, and further received larger Bois Blanc Island as a voluntary gift from the Ojibwa.

American troops moved by stages into most of these 10cations in the Indian hinterland. For example! the post at Chicago was established in 1803, and that at Peoria during the War of 1812. Land at the Straits of Mackinac was not surveyed until 1834, when Henry Schoolcraft broached the matter with local Ottawa and Ojibwa leaders who recalled terms of the 1795 treaty.

The red area highlights the westward penetration of American settlers down the Ohio River and up the Wabash

into both Indiana and Illinois. On the other hand, the 1808 land cession in Missouri represents a different population current stemming from the American purchase of Louisiana from the French in 1803. This land cession is barely within the initial time period, and only land close to the course of the Mississippi River lies within the defined Great Lakes Region (map 2).

By 1807, the looming spector of Indian hostilities in the United States and the general expectation of war between Great Britain and the United States curtailed pressure for further Indian land cessions until after the Peace of Ghent in 1815. The roadway across northwestern Ohio, although secured by treaty in 1808, was not developed until the region ceased being a theatre of war. Governor Harrison's 1809 cession in central Indiana evoked Tecumseh's organized protest against American land cession procedures.

Green and Brown Areas

After the War of 1812, substantial immigration into Upper Canada created the need and desire for more land (see also map 23). Concurrent with the expansion of white population, Indians in the southern regions of the province began to confine themselves to more stationary locations, partly through necessity and partly as a result of the new civilization program that came into effect officially in 1830 (map 31). These two considerations tended toward further surrenders of land. Accordingly, from 1815 to 1836, a series of treaties provided new lands for settlement in the second line, or back regions, of the province. The green section of Canadian territory covers the areas of present Ontario ceded by various groups of Ojibwa and Missisauga people during a time interval of twenty-two years.

The green areas within the boundaries of the United States also denote land cessions following the War of 1812, but only for the six-year period from 1816 to 1821. Treaties covering the Illinois Territory, some referring to previous treaties, were negotiated by Governor Ninian Edwards, whose major objectives were to secure the adherence of Sauk, Mesquakie, and Kickapooto treaty terms and to remove the Kickapoo from Illinois. Governor Lewis Cass of Michigan Territory carried out an intensive land cession policy, securing eleven land cession treaties from upper Great Lakes Indians between 1817 and 1821.

Most important of these treaties was the 1817 cession linking the northern Ohio land ceded in 1805 and the southeast Michigan tract ceded in 1807. An estimated 7,000 Indians gathered at the Foot of the Rapids of the Maumee River in September, 1817, to discuss terms. Because the treaty provided for private land ownership for Wyandot, Seneca, and Shawnee on the reservations to be established in Ohio, the treaty was not approved by the Senate. In conjunction with re-negotiating the treaty in 1818 at a different location, the St. Marys River of Ohio, five additional treaties were concluded.

Cass followed up these activities with an Ojibwa treaty at Saginaw in 1819. The following year, he ventured north of Lake Huron and ascended the St. Marys River. With some difficulty, he persuaded Ojibwa living on the south bank of the river to give up their British flag and grant land for an American fort at Sault Ste. Marie.

During his return trip, he secured cession of the St. Martin's Islands, valued for plaster deposits, situated east of present St. Ignace in Lake Huron. These islands are too small for the scale of this map, but the locations can be found on map 24. He went on to Chicago for the 1821 treaty that secured southwestern Michigan lands.

The brown-tinted area in the United States covers land cessions during the overall period 1824 through 1837, but the principal treaties were made after the American government established military supremacy in the western Great Lakes Region during the Black Hawk War. In the wake of Black Hawk's defeat, the Potawatomi were forced to cede their remaining lands in Illinois and Wisconsin, and cessions were also obtained from the Winnebago, Menominee, Sauk, and Mesquakie (map 29). Land acquisition was also promoted by the influx of settlers after the opening of the Erie Canal in 1825 and Michigan's advance to statehood between 1834 and 1837 (map 25). The pine forests of Michigan and Wisconsin (map 3) attracted lumbermen to northern areas avoided by farmers.

Blue Areas of the Map

The blue area covers land cessions during similar time periods on both sides of the international border, 1842-72

In the United States and Canada, Indian delegations often visited government headquarters for treaty negotiations and other discussions. This view shows an Indian deputation from the upper Mississippi River headed for Washington, D.C., in the 1850s. From Lewis, *Das Illustrierte Mississipithal*, p. 20. The Newberry Library.

in the United States and 1847-73 in Canada. Mining, lumbering, and railroad interests were primarily served by the government acquisition of these lands in the northwestern sector of the Great Lakes Region. In present Minnesota and central Iowa, however, treaties of cession from the Dakota, Sauk, and Mesquakie satisfied demands of settlers advancing across the prairies west of the Mississippi River.

Mining began in the Upper Peninsula of Michigan in the late 1840s. Although the existence of copper in the Lake Superior district had been known to Europeans since the seventeenth century, the first mining boom followed a Michigan geological survey report in 1841. Iron ore deposits were found in 1844. Mineral resources brought this remote area to public attention in the 1840s through newspaper accounts of the removal of a 6,000-pound copper boulder from the Ontonagon River (map 24).

In Canada, by 1850, new British companies pushed exploitation of recently discovered mineral deposits along the Canadian shield (map 3.). The completion of the Sault Ste. Marie ship canal by American engineers in 1855 further encouraged the growth of mining in the area west of Lake Superior in northern Minnesota and western Ontario. The timing of Indian land cession treaties was connected with mining and transportation developments. Most of these treaties were with bands of Ojibwa people.

The last of the major cessions in American territory during this period involved Ojibwa of northern Minnesota in 1863. Ojibwa at that time retained the region surrounding Red Lake extending north to Lake of the Woods. This area, ' uncolored on the map, was ceded in 1889 in one of a series of separate agreements between the American government and ten bands of Minnesota Ojibwa, signed between July and November that year.

The 1872 date refers to a portion of the land given up in an agreement involving Sisseton and Wahpeton bands of Dakota who by that time had been removed from their reservation on the Minnesota River in the aftermath of the "Sioux Uprising" of 1862 (map 33).

During the third quarter of the nineteenth century, five major treaties were concluded with Indians of Ontario. The first two, known as the Robinson treaties of 1850, involved Ojibwa on the northern shores of Lake Huron and Lake Superior between the lakes and the height of land to the north. Both treaties were negotiated in September at Sault Ste. Marie, Ontario, on the north shore of the St. Marys River. These were undertaken partly to open some lands for settlement, but principally for mining development.

Two smaller tracts of land were involved in surrenders near Georgian Bay of Lake Huron. In 1836, Lieutenant Governor Bond Head had designated the region north of the Saugeen River (map 23) on the Bruce Peninsula as a refuge for the Saugeen band of Ojibwa. This large area remained open to Indians until treaties securing this land for the government were concluded between 1854 and 1857.

Also in 1836, Bond Head had set aside the Manitoulin Island for the general use of all Indians of Upper Canada who would relocate there. Despite urgings from Indian Department officials, Indians did not migrate in large numbers, but white settlers began to covet the island, particularly notable for its fishing resources. Ojibwa and Ottawa surrendered the major portion of Manitoulin Island in 1862, but the eastern end of the island remained an unceded reserve occupied by the Indians of Wikwemikong (see map 33).

In 1873, Treaty No. 3 secured lands from the 14,000 Ojibwa Indians who occupied territory in Ontario to the west of the Robinson-Superior surrender. A small piece of Manitoba land ceded by Treaty No. 1 in 1871 also appears on the map. Total land area surrendered in 1871 and 1873 extended beyond this map. These treaties, among the first concluded after Canadian Confederation in 1867, secured the route from Thunder Bay to Manitoba, permitting the passage of immigrants into the newly acquired territories of the Canadian West. The 1873 treaty is also known as the North-West Angle Treaty, a name denoting the site for negotiations at the Lake of the Woods. The "Northwest Angle" is the rounded peninsula on the western shore, which became a northern projection of Minnesota as a consequence of Canadian-American boundary surveys completed for that swampy terrain in 1873. The survey linked the northwest point of the Lake of the Woods, specified as an international boundary marker by the 1783 Treaty of Paris, and the 49th parallel of latitude west of the Lake of the Woods, the boundary accepted by the Convention of 1818.

Commentary

Land concepts of Indian people differed markedly from the views motivating the British and American officials with whom they were dealing. In the belief system of Indian people, land, like air and water, was available to all on the basis of need. Personal ownership was limited to things individually crafted, crops raised, or proceeds of hunting and fishing activities. Tribal groups exercised stewardship over particular areas under their control. Only gradually did Indian people realize that the cession or surrender of land to a non-Indian government meant more than sharing use of the land, and actually threatened eventual dispossession.

The treaty-making procedure for acquiring Indian land in the Great Lakes Region grew out of eighteenth-century British legal theory. By the Royal Proclamation of 1763, the British government admitted the principle of Indian ownership of lands occupied by Indian people. The principle did not apply to settled portions of the former colony of New France east of the Ottawa River and along the St. Lawrence River. As a consequence, no land cession treaties have been concluded between Indian people and the present province of Quebec.

After the thirteen American colonies became independent in 1783, American officials at first approached treaty-making with the view that Indians, as allies of the defeated British army, had also been conquered. In 1786, American officials disavowed this theory and acknowledged Indian ownership rights to land, asserting nevertheless that Indians could sell land only to the federal government. This land cession map excludes treaties in 1785 at Fort McIntosh (map 15) and in 1786 at Fort Finney (map 17), made while the invalid "conquest theory prevailed, as well as the 1789 treaty at Fort Harmar (map 181, where Indians were inade-

Indians Traveling. From Schoolcraft, *History of the Indian Tribes of the United States*, pt. 2, p. 77. The Newberry Library.

quately represented. Land under discussion in those negotiations was definitively ceded in 1795 at Greenville.

Following adoption of the American constitution in 1787, the federal government made treaties with Indian people as it did with foreign nations. By federal law passed in 1871, however, treaty-making with Indians ended, and subsequent dealings between the American government and tribal people were in the form of agreements approved by acts of Congress. The map emphasizes the land dealings until 1871, the end of the treaty-making period in the United States and a time close to the 1867 end-date for British-Indian treaty making and the advent of Canadian Confederation.

Treaties in theory could have been simple transactions in which lands were ceded in return for payment in the form of trade goods or money. But the practice of Indian treaty-making developed a number of complications. In Canada, the original copies of a number of early post-Revolutionary War treaties with Great Lakes Indians were lost or destroyed. Efforts to correct improprieties of these early treaties even involved securing marks of approval on a blank deed. Lands east of Toronto between the Etobicoke River (map 23) and the Trent River remained a matter of dispute until 1923. At that time the matter was settled for the most part by a special government commission and a new treaty. This new treaty agreement, in addition to ending the longstanding dispute, also acquired for the Canadian government the territory lying northward between Georgian Bay and the Ottawa River, an area uncolored on this map.

The process of land acquisition by Indian treaty differed between Canada and the United States. British authorities generally obtained land surrenders before survey and opening the land to white settlement. American settlers frequently occupied Indian land as squatters before a treaty was signed turning the land over to the federal government for sale through land offices. Canadian treaties

were principally land transactions for which some immediate compensation or perpetual annuities were granted. American treaties usually limited annuity payments to 10 or 20 years, under the assumption that Indians as a distinctive people would no longer exist at the end of the period. Beginning in the 1820~~ American treaties with Great Lakes Indians specified that highly valued blacksmith services, as well as farmers, missionaries, and teachers, would be provided for Indian settlements.

As a matter of strategy, American commissioners at times secured the release of land from Indians with little claim to a specific area in order to force a cession from the tribe with the major claim. Traders, land speculators, and missionaries exercised significant influence in negotiating cessions of Indian lands. Great Lakes treaties usually provided substantial payments to traders to cover the claimed indebtedness of their Indian clients? although authorities tried to prevent the practice.

Treaty councils were major events usually lasting from one to four weeks. The proceedings brought together large numbers of Indian people, several hundred in Canada and up to a few thousand in American territory. These were times for ceremonies, feasting, and dancing as well as diplomacy and declamation. The subsequent distributions of annuity payments in money and goods were important social occasions on the Indian calendar and profitable commercial events for traders.

Principal Sources: Alvord 1908; Canada 1957, 1967, 1971; Clifton 1975; Ellwood 1977; Gates 1968; Guellet 1957; Hamil 1939, 1951; Higgins 1931; Horsman 1964; Hough 1866; Ireland-Smith 1980; Johnson 1973; Johnston 1964; Lajeunesse 1960; Lass 1980; Leighton 1977; Morris 1880; Morris 1943; Murray 1963; New York 1889; Ontario 1906; Paterson 1921; Paulin 1932; Quaife 1913; Rayback 1965; Robinson 1937, 1965; Royce 1899; Schmalz 1977; Smith 1982; Stagg 1981;Surtees 1982; Tanner 1973; Torok 1956.

This map locates and dates all the reservations set aside in the Great Lakes Region and fringe areas during the eighteenth and nineteenth centuries, mainly through land cession treaties (see map 30). Included are six mission stations on the St. Lawrence River founded earlier by the French. The area of each reservation is shown as it was first formed, either by symbol if the reserve was smaller than a township of 36 square miles, or in outline if it was larger. The map includes the maximum amount of land reserved, and does not indicate successive reductions in size.

Roughly estimated, about 25,000 square miles were reserved for the Indians in the Great Lakes Region of the United States and Canada. In addition close to 700 square miles in the United States were granted to individuals of Indian heritage named in the treaties, many of them Metis. With few exceptions, individual grants have not been mapped. The grant by Pennsylvania to the Seneca leader Cornplanter in 1790 is shown since that land was occupied by residents of his village. The 1966 end-date records the time the government took over the reserve for flooding as part of the Kinzua dam project. Because some tracts reserved in the United States were never located and others not surveyed, it is difficult to figure precisely the amount of land actually designated for Indian people when they ceded most of their territory.

Introduction of Reservations

Before the British and American treaty-making era, the French government established the earliest reservations along the lower St. Lawrence River in the present province of Quebec. These tracts were beneficies of the French monarch, setting aside land for Indian communities under the direction of missionary orders. Shown on the map without dates, these reservation villages were already in existence when the British acquired Canada in 1763 and have continued into the twentieth century. Of the reserves founded in the French era, farthest upstream on the St. Lawrence is St. Regis, straddling the borders of New York, Quebec, and Ontario.

Following the American Revolution, British and American officials established reservations in the eastern Great Lakes region in 1784. In Canada, the first post-war treaties settled pro-British Iroquois on reserves along the Grand River north of Lake Erie and on the Bay of Quinte west of Kingston, near the foot of Lake Ontario. Reservations in American territory began in the Iroquois country of western New York state.

Although most of the reservations on this map were established by treaties, some came into existence through executive or legislative measures. An Act of Congress in 1788 granted land on the Tuscarawas River in southeastern Ohio to Moravians as compensation for the "Gnadenhütten Massacre" of 1781 (see maps 17 and 20). Occupied in 1798, the Goshen reserve attracted few Christian Indians from Moraviantown on the Thames River, Canada, and added only a small number of wavering converts. The land was given up by Moravians in 1823 because of heavy financial obligations.

The 1790 British treaty with Wyandot living along the Detroit River established the first reserves in the heartland of the Great Lakes. Missisauga on Lake Ontario were assigned reservations in 1806. On the American side of the Detroit River, Hull's Treaty in 1807 set aside land for the first reservations in the "Old Northwest," aside from the Piankeshaw reserve near the lower Wabash River, dating from an 1805 treaty. The reservations in Michigan Territory in 1807 were made for Ojibwa of Swan Creek and Black River north of Lake St. Clair, for Potawatomi, mainly along the Huron River west of Detroit, and for Ottawa on the lower Maumee River. These reservations were surveyed in 1810, along with private property claimed under previous French and British title in the Detroit area.

The reservation principle in the United States was further extended in Michigan, Ohio, Indiana and the southern tip of Illinois through provisions of treaties made between 1817 and 1821. Congressional legislation in 1819 set up a "civilization fund" expended through Protestant missionary programs, notably on reservations for Upper Sandusky Wyandot and among Potawatomi at Carey mission near Niles, Michigan. Whenever possible, provisions were written into treaties to promote Christianity, English language education, and farming, objectives shared by American and British reservation programs.

The Reserve System in Canada

In Canada a vigorous new reserve policy came into existence in 1830. One element came from the humanitarian movement in England, evidenced by the formation of the Aboriginal Society, demanding empire-wide improvement of methods for dealing with native peoples. Another influence was the expanding missionary movement from the United States. The Methodist activities, led by half-Ojibwa Peter Jones, were particularly successful following the founding of the first Methodist Indian mission in Canada in 1827, at Grape Island in the Bay of Quinte. Since British officials feared that these missionaries were attempting to inculcate republican principles into the Indians, they advocated that civilization and religious programs be undertaken by the royal government.

The British reserve program of the 1830s called for

St. Regis, on the south shore, and Islands of the St. Lawrence River, 1838. Reserve is located at conjunction of boundaries for Quebec, Ontario, and New York. By W. H. Bartlett. From Willis, *Canadian Scenery*, vol. 1, p. 107. The Newberry Library

collecting substantial numbers of Indians in specific locations where they would be provided with housing, schools, and resident missionaries—preferably Church of England. In this setting artisans and farmers would instruct Indians in the skills associated with agricultural life requiring smaller tracts of land than the traditional hunting economy. With this system, British officials expected to reduce the expense of Indian administration as Indian people learned to handle their own affairs and to become self-sufficient citizens, generally indistinguishable from their non-Indian neighbors.

Although the special experiment at the Coldwater reserve on Lake Simcoe had only limited success and was abandoned in 1837, the policy continued (see also map 23). New experiments were begun, such as the grand scheme for gathering Indians at the Manitoulin Island in 1838. More than 9,000 Indians, two-thirds of them from the United States, came to Manitoulin during a single summer to receive gifts from the British, but the resident population never grew beyond about 1,200.

As new areas of land were surrendered and new missionaries became available, the reserve system was extended throughout the Great Lakes Region of Canada. Those in northwestern Ontario were all established by three Ojibwa treaties: the two Robinson treaties of 1850, one with Lake Huron bands and the other with Lake Superior bands; and by Treaty No. 3, signed in 1873. Lags occurred in the organization of some of the western Ontario reserves. The reserve at the juncture of the Roseau and Red rivers on the southern Manitoba border is the only reserve established by Treaty No. 1 that is included in the mapped area.

Reservations and Removal: Michigan, Indiana, Ohio

Reservations created in southern Michigan, northern Indiana and northwestern Ohio after the War of 1812 were but a prelude to removal in the late 1830s. Reservations in existence in 1830 are outlined at a larger scale on map 25. Here the removal program of the American government cleared reservations from the area where population was rapidly increasing. On the other hand, Ojibwa and Ottawa living in the Saginaw Bay drainage and in western lower Michigan, regions of scanty white population, were allowed to remain in the state, but with uncertain land bases.

Between 1837 and 1840, the removal program vacated reservations of the Ojibwa of Swan Creek and Black River in extreme southeastern Michigan, the Potawatomi of Michigan and Indiana, and the Ottawa, Seneca, Shawnee, and the Big Spring Wyandot in Ohio. Most reluctant to surrender final reservations were the Wyandot in Ohio and the Miami of Indiana. In 1838 the fifty gallons of alcoholic beverages supplied by the treaty commissioner failed to weaken Wyandot determination to retain their Grand Reserve at Upper Sandusky. It took trusted friend John Johnston, called from retirement, to persuade them to give it up in 1842. In Indiana, 1872 marks the date when the last Miami re-

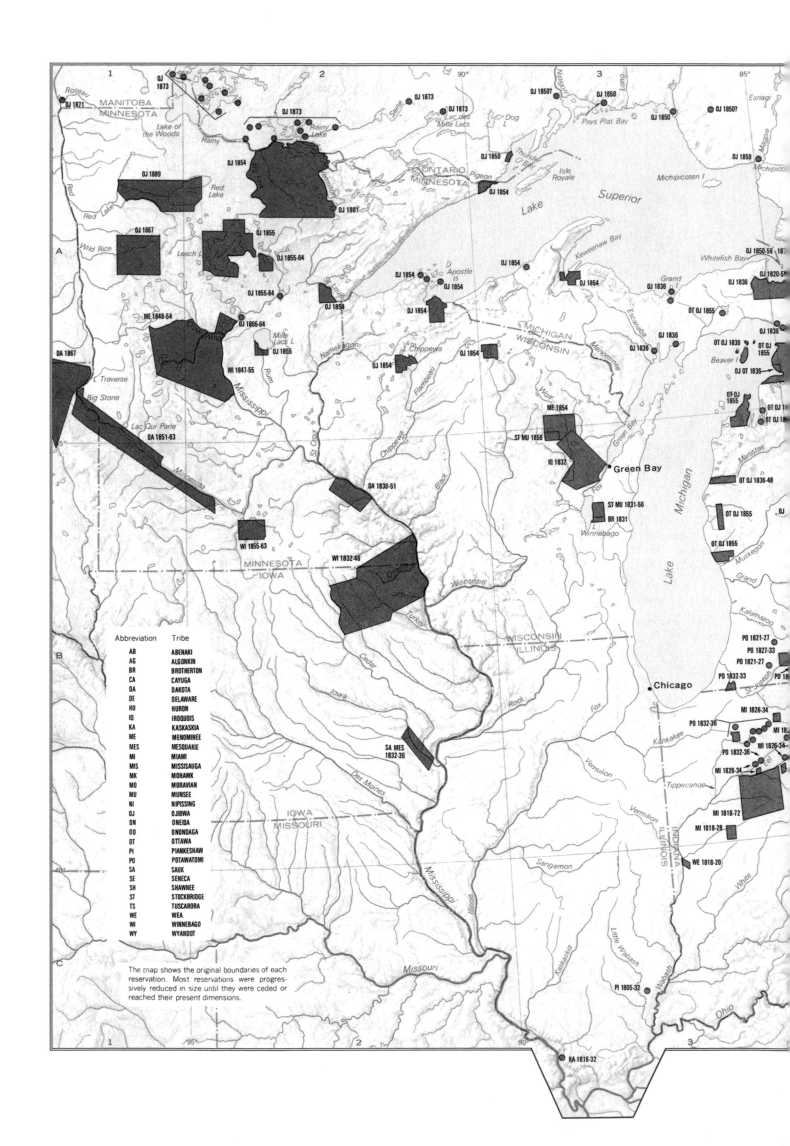

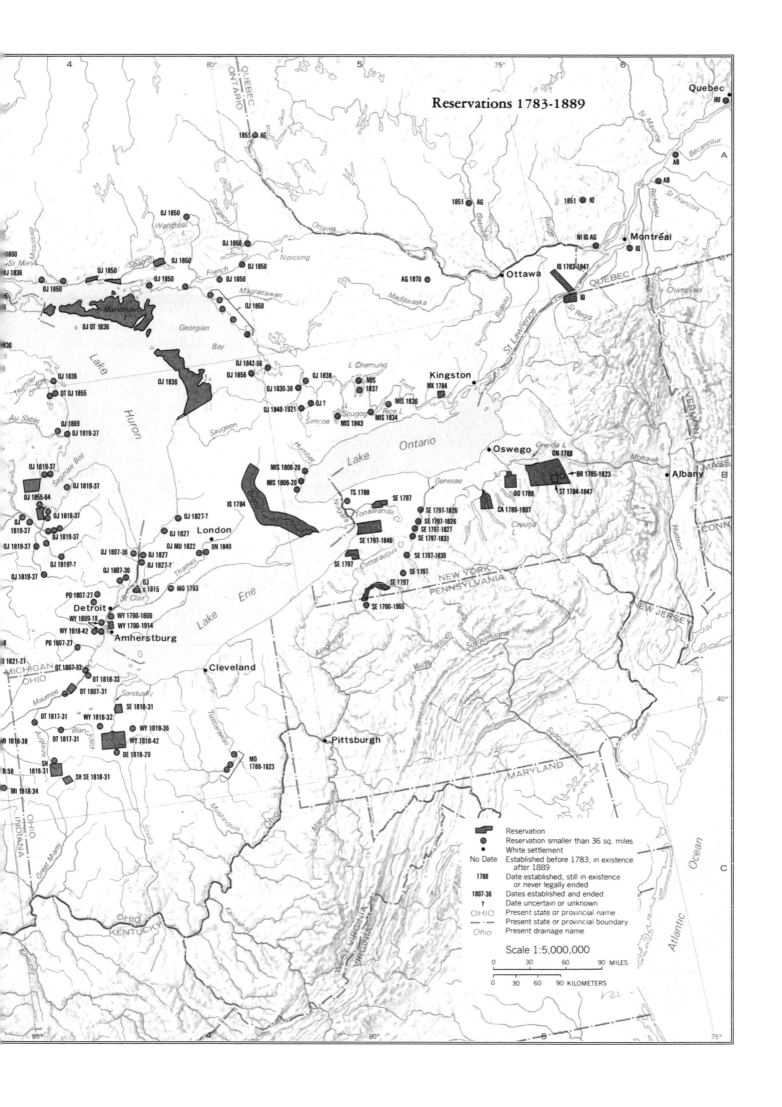

Reservations 1783-1889

MAP
31

	Reservation
	Reservation smaller than 36 sq. miles
•	White settlement
No Date	Established before 1783, in existence after 1889
1788	Date established, still in existence or never legally ended
1807-36	Dates established and ended
?	Date uncertain or unknown
OHIO	Present state or provincial name
— · —	Present state or provincial boundary
Ohio	Present drainage name

Scale 1:5,000,000

0 30 60 90 MILES

0 30 60 90 KILOMETERS

Between-the-Logs, Wyandot leader and licensed Methodist minister on The Grand Reserve at Upper Sandusky, Ohio. Accompanied by a fellow minister, Monocue, he spoke to large gatherings in Buffalo, New York, Philadelphia, Baltimore, and Washington during the summer of 1826. From *History of Wyandot County*, Ohio, p. 60. The Newberry Library.

served land was divided into allotments. At least half of the Miamis had ceded reservations in 1840 and had left the state in 1846.

Reservations in western and Upper Peninsula Michigan, described in the 1836 land cession treaty (map 30), were only partially carried into effect. Missionary pressure led to the survey of the reserve on the east arm of Grand Traverse Bay. Yet the large block of land around Whitefish Bay of Lake Superior, reserved for the Sault Ste. Marie bands, has never appeared on printed maps, probably because the river boundary called "Pississawinning" in the treaty is not found on any other map or document. Henry Schoolcraft's manuscript map drawn in 1837 shows that the stream is the present Waiska River (map 24). The reservation status of land on the Manistee River ended in 1840 because Ottawa did not move there from the Grand and Kalamazoo river valleys. In eastern Michigan, the Saginaw Valley reservations created in 1819 were ceded in 1837 by Ojibwa who suffered severe population loss and dispersion from a smallpox epidemic that year (map 32).

The federal government by 1841 abandoned plans to remove Ojibwa and Ottawa from Michigan, but delayed creating permanent reservations until the treaties of 1855. In the meantime, Potawatomis were returning to secluded parts of

southern Michigan. The reservation dated 1848 refers to land south of Battle Creek at present Athens, purchased by sympathetic white neighbors for Potawatomi who had been forcibly removed but returned to their homeland. This land, placed in trust with the governor of Michigan, is the only "state" reservation in the Great Lakes Region.

Wisconsin, Iowa, and Minnesota: Reservation Shifts

The first reservations in Wisconsin were introduced in 1831 for New York Indians who had begun negotiations with the Menominee ten years earlier and had already established farms along the Fox River and Duck Creek flowing into Green Bay. Arriving in the next several years were accumulating numbers of Stockbridge, Munsee, and Brotherton, who located along the eastern shore of Lake Winnebago. The Brotherton sold their reserve in 1833, and were unofficially dropped from federal jurisdiction. After 1832, additional Iroquois people, chiefly Oneida, transferred from New York to the new reservation between the Fox and Wolf rivers west of Green Bay. The Stockbridge, along with Munsee from Moraviantown in southern Ontario who joined them in 1837, were shifted northwest to a corner of the Menominee Reservation in 1856. This move followed a series of new reservation arrangements made in 1854 and 1855 for tribes in northern Michigan, Wisconsin, and Minnesota (see map).

The Sauk and Mesquakie reservation established in Iowa in 1832 was a short-term concession to followers of Keokuk, the Sauk leader who had remained pacific toward Americans during the Black Hawk War (map 29). In the same year, Fox River Winnebago were removed to a reservation on the present Minnesota-Iowa border, a part of the "neutral ground" between the Dakota and Sauk, after ceding the eastern portion of their territory. This initial Winnebago reserve was situated on the Mississippi River about fifty miles below the "half-breed" reservation near present Red Wing, Minnesota (map 33), set aside by treaty in 1830 but not occupied.

When Wisconsin became a state in 1848, pressure was exerted to remove the Menominee, but they never settled on the large reservation set aside on the Crow Wing River in Minnesota. In 1854 the Menominee were conceded a reservation in their traditional territory on the Wolf and Oconto rivers. Long resident in western Wisconsin, the Winnebago repeatedly returned to the state while their official reservation was shifted farther up the Mississippi to the Crow Wing River in 1846, then to Blue Earth River near the elbow of the Minnesota River in 1855.

In Minnesota, by the treaties of Traverse des Sioux and Mendota in 1851, the Dakota ceded their remaining lands in Minnesota in exchange for a reservation 20 miles wide straddling the Minnesota River between Lake Traverse and the mouth of the Yellow Medicine River. However, following the 1862 uprising of Dakotas in Minnesota (termed "Santees"), Dakota and Winnebago were exiled to starvation conditions on the Crow Creek reservation in present South Dakota. This location on the Missouri River is west of the mapped area. The further removal of these Dakotas in 1866 to the Santee reservation on the Niobrara River in Nebraska

Looking across the Wabash River to the Miami Reserve. Soft maple trees in the foreground, and maples and elms on Biddle's Island, in the middle of the river course. Watercolor by George Winter, c. 1845. From "Judge Horace Biddle's Journal," MS in Cass County Historical Society, Logansport, Indiana. Cass County Historical Society.

promised a better future. Winnebago at Crow Creek ultimately sought sanctuary among the Omaha in northeastern Nebraska (map 33). In an 1867 treaty Dakota identified as "friendlies" during the 1862 uprising were given a triangular reserve in Dakota Territory, a portion of which appears on the western margin of the map.

In the Ojibwa country of northern Wisconsin and Minnesota, most reservations date from treaties in 1854 and 1855. Before the creation of the first reserves in this district, a presidential order in 1850 attempted to remove Wisconsin bands to the headwaters of the Mississippi River. The La Pointe agency was closed, and Wisconsin bands were directed to receive annuities at Sandy Lake, in Minnesota (map 33). The agent planned to withhold the 1850 annuity distribution until weather conditions forced the Indians to remain for the winter. Reports indicated that as many as 400 died, near Sandy Lake or trying to walk home. The removal order was rescinded in late 1851. Treaties in 1863 and 1867 aimed to consolidate the Minnesota Ojibwa upon two large reserves at Leech Lake and at White Earth, directly west of Leech Lake. The latest reservation to be established in Minnesota was at Red Lake in 1889.

The Allotment Phase

A second stage in the reservation program for Great Lakes Indians began in 1854 when American treaties first allotted individual family plots within reserved areas. Government officials designed the allotment procedure ostensibly to transform Indians into horse and plow farmers, replacing the communal land usage among Indian people with private land ownership concepts considered superior in Anglo-American society. To white citizens, an equally important objective was the release of unallotted reservation land for sale through government land offices. Most reservation land in the Great Lakes Region was unsuitable for agriculture, but valuable for timber resources.

Between 1854 and 1864, American treaties with Ojibwa and Ottawa, Menominee, and Winnebago allotted reservation land in present Michigan, Wisconsin, and Minnesota. In Canada the earliest individual allotments were made to Ojibwa and Ottawa in the Manitoulin Island treaty of 1862. The size of family allotments in the United States was officially computed on the basis of 80 acres for heads of families and 40 acres for individuals in other categories. Canadian allotments generally provided 100 acres for heads of families and 50 acres for others.

On the American side of the border, the more northern reservations with allotted lands were set up in four geographic groups, with some omissions and overlaps of constituent bands. From west to east, the four groups and treaty dates were: (1) 1855 for Ojibwa on the headwaters of the Mississippi River in Minnesota; (2) 1854 for a group called the Ojibwa of Lake Superior, extending from the St. Louis River eastward across Wisconsin to Keweenaw Bay in the Upper Peninsula of Michigan; (3) 1855 for northwestern Lower Michigan Ojibwa. and Ottawa, including Upper Peninsula bands east of Keweenaw Bay and Escanaba; and (4) 1855 for the combined Saginaw, Swan Creek, and Black River Ojibwa of southeastern Lower Michigan, including the band on the Au Sable River.

Two of the treaties in 1855 finally reserved blocks of land for "permanent homes," with individual allotments for Ojibwa and Ottawa remaining in Michigan with tacit presidential approval after ceding their lands. Permanent reserves for the combined Saginaw, Swan Creek, and Black River bands were located in the central Lower Peninsula and on Saginaw Bay, the latter site given up in 1864. In northwestern Lower Michigan, lands reserved in 1855 were more extensive than the reservations listed in the 1836 treaty. On the other hand, although all the Beaver Islands had been reserved in 1836, only High and Garden islands were set aside for allotment in 1855. Big Beaver Island was occupied by Mormons from 1849 until 1856, when the leader, "King" James Strang, was killed by mainland opponents of his religious colony. In the Upper Peninsula, the area reserved in 1855 for permanent homes for the Sault Ste. Marie bands lay within the Whitefish Bay and Sugar Island areas reserved by the 1836 treaty and does not carry additional dating on this map.

The lengthy procedure for allotting reservation land to Ojibwa and Ottawa in the Upper Great Lakes Region was not carried out according to plan. The treaties specified three main steps: listing individual selections of acreage, issuing certificates for selected land, and, finally, awarding presidential land patents. At every stage, interference came from , land speculators, loan sharks, lumbering interests, and aggressive settlers, at times working in collusion with Indian agents and the federal land offices. Lists of selections for the earliest allotment treaties, signed in 1854 and 1855, were still being changed in 1870. Delivery of land patents for these treaties generally did not take place until the 1880s, and in some cases was delayed until the twentieth century.

Government officials and the Ojibwa and Ottawa of the Upper Great Lakes Region experienced the problems of land allotment for over thirty years before passage of the Dawes Act in 1887, calling for general allotment of all reservation land. Close to 90 percent of allotted reservation land passed rapidly into non-Indian possession, usually before patents were received. Punitive taxation further reduced Indian land ownership. A number of Michigan Indians tried unsuccessfully to protect their lands by conveying them in trust to the state governor. Some reservation areas shown with no terminal date on the map were never actually ceded but are no longer in existence, largely because of the intricate and imperfect allotment procedures, or later loss through tax sales.

Special Cases, Conclusion

Because of delays and irregularities in executing terms of Indian treaties regarding reserved land, the location and exact boundaries of reserved tracts at times was difficult to determine. Manuscript maps of surveyed land recorded a number of reservations with ambiguous status. Question marks identify a controversial tract at modern Flint, Michigan, outlined on nineteenth-century maps. The land was reserved in the 1819 treaty in the names of Indian children of the resident trader. In litigation lasting into the 1860s, non-Indian descendants living in Detroit were declared the legitimate heirs to the land. An 1869 map shows a reservation on the AuSable River at modern Oscoda, Michigan, designated for trader Louis Chevalier, though no personal reservation is mentioned in treaty records. Parcels of land along the Chicago River in Illinois, granted to Potawatomi tribal representatives prominent in treaty-making during the 1829-33 era, have become incorporated into the county forest reserves.

Although Great Lakes Indians lost almost all the land originally reserved for their use, American and Canadian governments have retained or acquired tracts held in trust status as modern reservations. Canadian reserves along the St. Lawrence River and in Ontario have persisted to the present. In the American section of the Great Lakes Region, federal reservations continue in New York, Michigan, Wisconsin, and Minnesota.

Principal Sources: Canada 1845, 1847, 1858, 1971; Gray 1956; Herrington 1921; Irish University Press 1969; Johnson 1973; Leighton 1975, 1977; Milloy 1978; Monroe 1823; Morris 1880; Quealey 1968; Schmalz 1977; Smith 1975,1982; Surtees 1969; Torok 1956.

Descriptions of epidemics among Indians are found in reports by European settlers, travelers, military men who were in an area at the time of an outbreak, and native year-counts. The reports vary in accuracy, sometimes naming a specific disease such as measles or smallpox, and at other times describing a vague "distemper," "rash," or "fever" that proved fatal to Indians. The report may give information about disease in specific locations, or describe a particular illness over a wide geographic area.

From many details on epidemic episodes, it is possible to show the location of outbreaks throughout the Great Lakes area with some precision. Smallpox was the disease reported most frequently, although not all episodes reported actually were that disease, with measles second and cholera third. Other diseases are shown on the map as a collective fourth category including malaria, scarlet fever, diphtheria, yellow fever, typhoid fever, meningitis, whooping cough, influenza, dysentery, and ailments not identifiable from the available descriptions.

These diseases spread among Indians from initial contact with European carriers. Indians had little resistance to European diseases; smallpox and measles proved especially devastating to the Indian population. Epidemic outbreaks caused losses of one-third to one-half, or more, of the population afflicted. The diseases were spread by contact among Indians as they moved out of affected villages to other locations, and also by war parties.

The dates on the map show the chronological spread of specific epidemics, sometimes over wide geographic areas. For example, a series of contagious diseases decimated the Huron tribes beginning in 1634 and weakened them before their final attack by the Iroquois in 1649. These diseases spread throughout the eastern sector of the Great Lakes Region, and perhaps farther west. Nipissing living near the Huron villages carried smallpox back to their people. An unidentified epidemic or epidemics caused the Winnebago in Wisconsin to suffer a population drop from about 20,000 possibly to a low figure of 600 between 1634 and 1670. Yet these ailments afflicting Indians have seldom been differentiated by historians, who usually have labeled them all smallpox. On the other hand, as the map shows, smallpox epidemics appeared in the Great Lakes area in every decade, some outbreaks more widespread than others. In present New York, the term "Iroquois" is used to denote generalized epidemics among all five major divisions of the Iroquois, the intermediate Oneida, Onondaga, and Cayuga as well as the Seneca and Mohawk at the western and eastern ends of the territory.

The following chronology lists the sequence of major epidemics reported among Indians of the Great Lakes region, and indicates which episodes were part of wider contagions.

1633-34. The first episode was described by a French missionary as "a sort of measles" with stomach pains, although other survivors called it smallpox. It seems to have been transmitted by English colonists to New England Indians in the autumn of 1633, reaching the Seneca country by the winter of 1633-34. This outbreak began a decade of destructive epidemics among eastern and Great Lakes Indians. Huron and Montagnais traders returning from Trois Rivieres at the confluence of the St. Maurice and St. Lawrence rivers in 1634 spread it among their relatives. By early 1636, the epidemic had infected eastern natives south to Maryland, including the Delaware.

1636-37. A disease that caused a "purple" rash and high fever, probably scarlet fever or perhaps typhus, affected adult Europeans as well as causing significant Indian mortality. It was transmitted from the Susquehannock to the Mohawk; and spread among the Huron, Tionontati, Neutral, and Erie tribes, and probably marked the demise of the Wenroo All communities affected are not located. A count of villages north of Lakes Ontario and Erie indicates Neutral 40, Huron 25, and Tionontati 8. In 1637-38, the first smallpox epidemic struck the New York Iroquois. In reports of this period, it is difficult to distinguish between scarlet fever and smallpox.

1639-40. A major smallpox epidemic spread from coastal Abenaki to inland Allumette on their island in the Ottawa River, to other Northern Algonquin, and to Huron. This epidemic probably affected Ottawa on Manitoulin Island or the Georgian Bay region, though the specific places cannot be identified.

1641. Indian canoe traders at Trois Rivieres contracted another contagious disease and transmitted it to the Onondaga, Seneca, Cayuga, and other tribes.

1645. A red rash-producing disease broke out among the Iroquois, perhaps the same one that swept through tribes in New Spain that same year.

1649. Iroquois attacks caused less mortality than the "loathsome fever" that laid low 5,000 malnourished Huron refugees during the 1649-50 winter.

1669-70. Epidemic disease spread widely among the tribes of Eastern Canada, New England, and upper New York, and west up the St. Lawrence River.

1676-79. In late June of 1676, a respiratory malady spread among the Indians of Massachusetts and Connecticut who were allied in King Phillip's War, forcing them to disband. The following year, the current epidemic illness, probably influenza, spread to Great Lakes tribes and also destroyed most of the natives around Delaware Bay. In 1679, the Iroquois were too desolated by smallpox to think of war, only

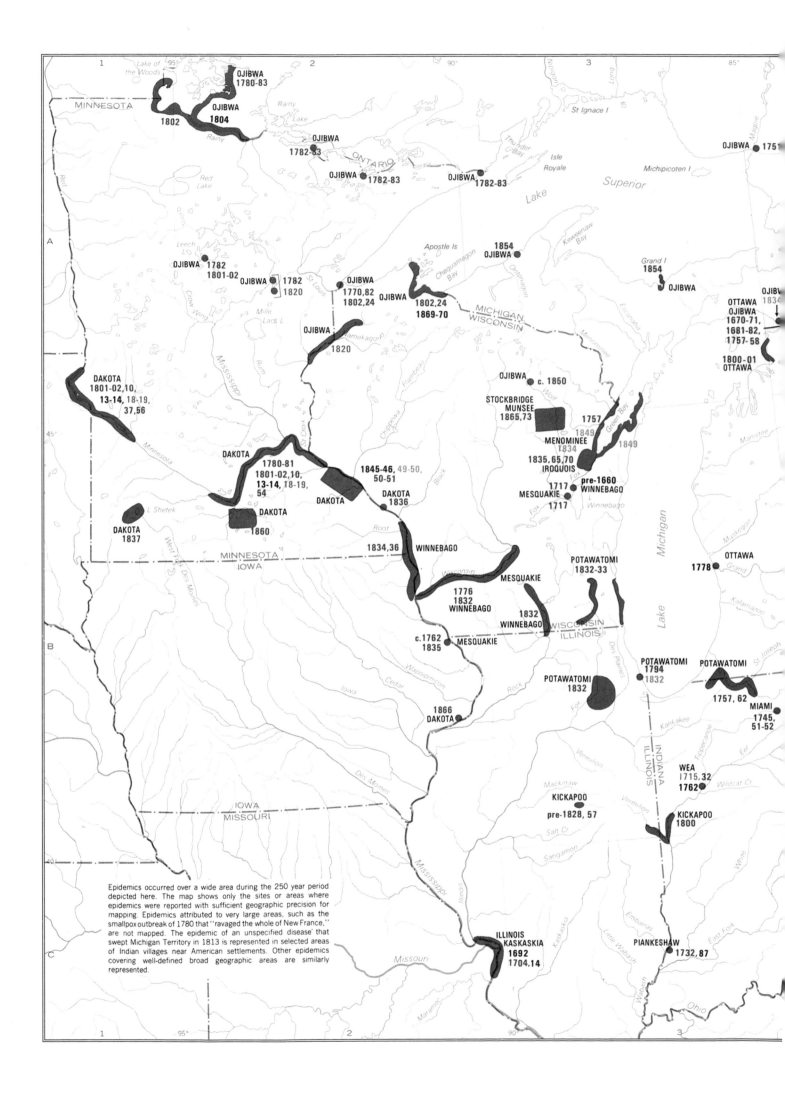

OJIBWA 1780-83

OJIBWA 1802 OJIBWA 1804

MINNESOTA

OJIBWA 1782-83

OJIBWA 1782-83

OJIBWA 1782-83

OJIBWA 175

OJIBWA 1782 1801-02

OJIBWA 1782 1820

OJIBWA 1770,82 1802,24

OJIBWA 1802,24 1869-70

1854 OJIBWA

OJIBWA 183

1854

OJIBWA

OTTAWA OJIBWA 1670-71, 1681-82, 1757-58

1800-01 OTTAWA

OJIBWA 1820

OJIBWA c. 1850

STOCKBRIDGE MUNSEE 1865,73

1757 1849

1849

DAKOTA 1801-02,10, 13-14, 18-19, 37,56

MENOMINEE 1834 1835,65,70 IROQUOIS

pre-1660 WINNEBAGO

DAKOTA 1780-81 1801-02,10, 13-14, 18-19, 54

1845-46, 49-50, 50-51

DAKOTA

DAKOTA 1836

1717 MESQUAKIE 1717

DAKOTA 1860

DAKOTA 1837

1834,36 WINNEBAGO

POTAWATOMI 1832-33

OTTAWA 1778

MINNESOTA IOWA

1776 1832 WINNEBAGO

MESQUAKIE

1832 WINNEBAGO WISCONSIN ILLINOIS

c.1762 1835 MESQUAKIE

POTAWATOMI 1832

POTAWATOMI 1794 1832

POTAWATOMI

1757, 62

MIAMI 1745, 51-52

POTAWATOMI 1832

1866 DAKOTA

WEA 1715,32 1762

IOWA MISSOURI

KICKAPOO pre-1828, 57

KICKAPOO 1800

INDIANA ILLINOIS

Epidemics occurred over a wide area during the 250 year period depicted here. The map shows only the sites or areas where epidemics were reported with sufficient geographic precision for mapping. Epidemics attributed to very large areas, such as the smallpox outbreak of 1780 that "ravaged the whole of New France," are not mapped. The epidemic of an unspecified disease' that swept Michigan Territory in 1813 is represented in selected areas of Indian villages near American settlements. Other epidemics covering well-defined broad geographic areas are similarly represented.

ILLINOIS KASKASKIA 1692 1704,14

PIANKESHAW 1732,87

Epidemics among Indians c. 1630-1880

MAP 32

ALGONQUIN HURON
1634,50
72-73,90
1760,78

QUEBEC
ONTARIO

ALGONQUIN IROQUOIS
1669
1716, 33, 48

ALGONQUIN IROQUOIS
1649, 69
1716, 33, 55-57

1835

ALGONQUIN
1639

1637-38
NIPISSING

Manitoulin I

Lake Huron

Georgian Bay

Muskoka Lakes

Simcoe

HURON
1633, **37**, 39-40

TIONONTATI
1637, 39-40

Lake Ontario

SENECA
1633-34, 37-38, 40
1755, 81-82

MOHAWK
1637, 69
1759

MOHAWK
1776

VT

B

MASS
CONN

NEUTRAL
1637, 39-40

1757,
81-82
IROQUOIS

WENRO
1637

SENECA
1865-66

IROQUOIS
1642,45, 49, 57, 61-63, **76,** 79, 90
1716-17, 31-33, 46-47, 51,
76-77, **94,** 95

1834, 37
OJIBWA

OJIBWA
1813

ERIE
1637

SENECA
1862

Lake Erie

NEW YORK
PENNSYLVANIA

NEW YORK
NEW JERSEY

POTAWATOMI
1752

1813
POTAWATOMI

1787-88
1813
WYANDOT

MICHIGAN

636-37   1748,57
DELAWARE

1833
OTTAWA

MUNSEE
1787-88

1787-88
WYANDOT

DELAWARE
1763-64

SUSQUEHANNOCK
1636-37, 61

AMI
32, 52

WYANDOT
1752

1764
MINGO

MARYLAND

DEL

SHAWNEE
1764

DELAWARE
1763

SHAWNEE
1762, 64

OHIO
WEST VIRGINIA

OHIO
INDIANA

KENTUCKY

VIRGINIA

Atlantic Ocean

MAP 32

MIAMI	Indian tribe
●	Indian village
⬤	Generalized region
1748	Date of smallpox epidemic
1820	Date of measles epidemic
1835	Date of cholera epidemic
1672	Date of epidemic of other or unknown disease
OHIO	Present state of provincial name
–·–·–	Present state or provincial boundary
Ohio	Present drainage name

Scale 1:5,000,000

0   30   60   90 MILES

0   30   60   90 KILOMETERS

Dakota Burial Ground, on plateau near the mouth of the Minnesota River. By Seth Eastman. From Schoolcraft, *History of the Indian Tribes of the United States*, pt. 2, p. 96. The Newberry Library.

bewailing their dead. The widespread epidemic frightened Dakota and Assiniboine away from Montreal, where they had promised to send delegations.

1690-91. Smallpox originating among the English and Mahican in the Hudson River Valley before a battle with the French at Quebec was carried by Iroquois returning to their villages. Losses were also severe among the Mahican the following winter.

1692-93. During the winter all of the Illinois tribes suffered high child mortality.

1704. Smallpox was reported causing local high mortality among Illinois Indians.

1714-17. Epidemic disease killed hundreds of Illinois Indians at Kaskaskia in 1714. This may have been the measles that caused many deaths among the Wea near modern Lafayette, Indiana, in 1715. Smallpox struck the Iroquois in 1716-17.

1731-33. For the Great Lakes tribes, the deadly century of pestilence that had begun in 1633 closed with yet another smallpox epidemic that began among the Iroquois tribes in 1732. It affected Montreal that same year. By 1733, it had ravaged Indians as far west as the Miami village at the head of the Maumee River and the Wea and Piankeshaw along the Wabash, as well as the Indian communities at Sault St. Louis and Lac des Deux Montagnes near Montreal. Miami warriors mobilized by the French against the Chickasaw may have transmitted the infection

to the Southern Indians. The neighboring Chickasaw, Choctaw, and Creek suffered from smallpox in 1733-34.

1752. Appearing first among the Miami, this widespread smallpox epidemic passed to Detroit, inflicting heavy losses among the Potawatomi and the Ottawa and Wyandot across the Detroit River. Wyandot living temporarily on the Muskingum River in Ohio were also struck by this epidemic.

1755. At times disease was carried over long distances after Indian contact with outbreaks among Europeans. During the French and Indian War, two waves of contagion swept from Euroamerican colonists through tribal peoples. In 1755, French Canadian settlements suffered what was reported as smallpox. The disease spread to the Seneca, and by the spring of 1756 to most tribes in eastern Canada and New England. Disease at Fort Frontenac and Fort Niagara disrupted not only warfare but also Indian trade because Upper Great Lakes tribes did not want to risk infection by visiting such posts. The illness also spread south through the Delaware.

1757. A French expeditionary force captured English Fort William Henry in 1757. Many of the nearly 2,000 Indian warriors belonging to over 40 tribes or bands mobilized in the French army contracted smallpox from the surrendered garrison. They spread the contagion as they returned to homes from southern Labrador to Lake Superior. Menominee suffered heavily, losing 300 warriors. This epidemic reached Potawatomi on the St. Joseph River, who had missed the 1752 epidemic affecting the Detroit Potawatomi.

1762-64. Beginning in 1762, a serious communicable disease, possibly smallpox, spread among the Mingo, Delaware, and Shawnee of the upper Muskingum and Scioto river valleys of Ohio. British officers at Fort Pitt, where smallpox broke out in 1763, deliberately gave Indians blankets and a handkerchief "out of the smallpox hospital." Their goal was to spread the disease among tribes involved in Pontiac's uprising against British authority in 1763, and thus to diminish their military power. Sir Jeffrey Amherst, the British commander-in-chief in North America, ordered this biological warfare. This epidemic became broad in geographic extent, affecting Creek, Choctaw, and Chickasaw in the southeast, and southwestern tribes living in the present Mexican-American border region.

1770. The epidemic among the Ojibwa of Fond du Lac at the western end of Lake Superior appears to have been an isolated outbreak.

1781-83. Epidemics caused great loss of life and sudden reductions in population. Reports of the 1781-83 smallpox episode among the Ojibwa variously tell of the deaths of many families, of 1,500 to 3,000 dying and of 3 to 4 children expiring daily. The epidemic struck both the eastern and western sectors of the Great Lakes area. The Iroquois on the Genesee River, some of them survivors of the 1776 epidemic, succumbed to the disease which spread to those at Niagara~. To the west, smallpox hit the Ojibwa in their villages in present Wisconsin and Minnesota. As Indians left their own villages and moved to other settlements, the disease spread to Grand Portage on the north shore of Lake Superior, then through the boundary waters region to Rainy River and Lake of the Woods. At the same time, it was carried to Sandy Lake and Leech Lake at the head of the Mississippi River. This pandemic began in the area of present Mexico in 1779 and advanced northward to Alaska, paralyzing the fur trade for two years throughout all of western North America, including the upper Missouri River drainage and Saskatchewan.

1787-88. A more localized epidemic of smallpox affected Wyandot at Detroit and Upper Sandusky, along with neighboring Munsee in Ohio, and Piankeshaw on the Wabash.

1793-94. Miami Indians who visited Kaskaskia in midsummer of 1793 suffered from scarlatina, probably the disease that killed 50 Potawatomi at Chicago in mid-1794 and alarmed the Indians at Michilimackinac.

1801. The nineteenth century opened with a smallpox pandemic that swept through the Indian population from Canada to the Gulf of Mexico. In the Great Lakes Region, the disease was reported among the Kickapoo on the Wabash and Ottawa-Ojibwa villages on Little Traverse Bay of Lake Michigan. The largest area of contagion encompassed the Ojibwa of Chequamegon Bay of Lake Superior, northern Minnesota, Rainy River on the Canadian border, and Dakota along the Minnesota River. The Dakota winter count indicated smallpox again in 1810.

1813-14. An epidemic of whooping cough or possibly typhoid swept Michigan Territory. At the same time an epidemic struck the Dakota on the Minnesota River.

Indian Burial, on raised scaffold. Seth Eastman, artist. From Schoolcraft, *History of the Indian Tribes of the United States,* pt. 2, p. 70. The Newberry Library.

1820. Measles took a heavy toll among the Ojibwa on the St. Croix River in Wisconsin.

1825. Dakota representatives contracted dysentery at the council held by federal Indian officials at Prairie du Chien. Many died there or on the way home after the conclusion of inter-tribal peace negotiations.

1832. As Americans settled in tribal areas, Indians fell victim to diseases they brought. Smallpox epidemics in Wisconsin between 1832 and 1834 spread from Americans to the Potawatomi in Illinois and Wisconsin, and afflicted one-third to one-fourth of the Menominee and Winnebago in Wisconsin in 1834-35. The mortality rate among Indians was at least twice as high as that for settlers. Smallpox might kill about 16 percent of the settlers, while Indians lost one-third of their people.

1832-34. Asian cholera reached North America in 1832, breaking out among European immigrants in Quebec on June 8 and Montreal on June 10. United States troops sent to the Black Hawk War theatre by Great Lakes steamers from Buffalo carried cholera to Detroit, reached Fort Dearborn at Chicago on July 10 and continued to Fort Crawford at Prairie du Chien. Chicago's small civilian population fled, and possibly spread the disease among friendly Indians. Although this initial epidemic did not affect large Indian populations, some Potawatomi attending a council at Milwaukee contracted cholera, and a councilwoman died. An influential Winnebago chief died from cholera he contracted while meeting with General Winfield Scott, and at least one Menominee representative at the same council came down with the disease but recovered.

Cholera reappeared in 1834 and spread to many Great Lakes Indian settlements. The contagion was specifically located at the Indian village of Cheboygan on the Lower Peninsula of Michigan. It also proved fatal to some Indians near Mackinac on the upper Peninsula and struck the Menominee on Green Bay.

1837-38. Although Wabasha's band of Dakota on the upper Mississippi River suffered from smallpox in 1836, an extremely virulent pandemic took place during the two following years. Among the Ojibwa of the Saginaw Valley in Michigan, estimates of fatalities in 1837 ran as high as two-thirds, although the official count was 354 deaths, leaving a population of 993. Reportedly introduced by new European settlers, the malady circulated through the Grand River valley between 1835 and 1840 with varying severity. During the winter of 1837-38, many Dakota on Lake Traverse in Minnesota succumbed to smallpox. The greatest loss of life in these years came as a result of infection carried up the Missouri River by active cases on board a steamer from St. Louis. This smallpox epidemic killed an estimated 17,000 Indians between the Missouri Valley and the Rocky Mountains.

1849. Cholera returned in 1849. Deaths occurred among Ojibwa at Sault Ste. Marie and on Drummond Island, but more critically affected were Menominee who lived near Green Bay. Mortality among Great Lakes Indians was lower than on the Central Plains. Especially hard-hit were tribes adjacent to the emigrant trail leading to the California gold fields.

1869-70. Vaccination by traders, missionaries, and federal Indian agents curbed smallpox epidemics in the later nineteenth century, but epidemic disease continued to occur in reservation and non-reservation communities. The malady afflicting the Ojibwa of western Lake Superior in the winter of 1869-70 was described as "something like lung fever," and several hundred died from the effects.

Principal Sources: Blasingham 1956; Duffy 1951; Edmunds 1979; Glover ed. 1962; Hubbard 1887; Jameson 1909; Kellogg 1925; Kip 1846; Lawson 1908; Le Baron 1978; Lurie 1960; Mallery 1877; Mooney 1928; Newcomb 1956; Nouvelle c. 1630?; Schleiser 1956; Schoolcraft 1860; Stearn and Stearn 1945.

In 1870, Indian people occupied customary areas but restricted space in the northern Great Lakes Region, though they had become a negligible part of the population in the southern section. Outstanding examples of continuity of residence are the Iroquois in present western New York State and along the St. Lawrence River, Ojibwa spread from Lake Huron to Lake Superior, Ottawa near the Straits of Mackinac, and Menominee along the Menominee River west of Green Bay, Wisconsin. The map shows that fragments of dispersed tribes still lived in familiar surroundings: Potawatomi in southwestern Michigan, Miami near the Wabash River in Indiana, Winnebago in Wisconsin, and Dakota near the headwaters of the Minnesota River. The distribution of most Indian sites on this map corresponds closely to the locations of reserved areas shown on map 31.

Scattered through the southern Great Lakes Region, Indian people in 1870 were also living in predominantly white towns and rural communities. They had purchased land and lived inconspicuously, usually adopting English family names. ThE; Shawnee villages in Ohio and Indiana were examples of the type of settlement not reported in official records. One group of Ohio Shawnee avoided removal by taking refuge in the wooded hills of West Virginia until lumbering began, then moved back to rugged terrain in southern Ohio, far from traveled roads. The Shawnee settlement in existence in 1870 near Indianapolis included a dozen families, followers of Tecumseh and the Prophet, who returned from Canada about 1821, purchased land, and maintained a council form of community government until the 1880s. Probably there was also a small Kaskaskia community, not mapped, in a remote section of southern Illinois at this time.

The Civil War era in the United States, 1861-65, had left its mark on Indian people along with other parts of the American population. Indians from the northern states served with distinction, even forming special sharpshooter brigades. In Kansas and the Indian Territory of present Oklahoma, reservation lands were devastated by opposing armies, and Great Lakes Indians were among those who had to flee for safety. Annuity payments in devalued script during the war years were still a subject of discussion in 1870. Anxiety about the security of the Canadian border had brought troops to Fort Wilkins at Copper Harbor on the Keweenaw Peninsula of Lake Superior and led to the reoccupation of Fort Brady at Sault Ste. Marie in 1866. The impact of land cessions was delayed until the post-Civil War years in the northern Great Lakes Region, where lumbering hit boom years in the 1870s.

New York and Southern Canada

The Iroquois people occupying seven reservations in Western New York numbered over 4,800 in 1870. More than half lived on the two Seneca reservations, Cattaraugus and Allegany-including the Cornplanter reserve on the Pennsylvania border. These two reservations had adopted a written constitution in 1849 with executive, legislative, and judicial divisions and written ballots. The new form of government operated satisfactorily, although it specifically excluded women, who had traditionally exerted considerable influence in tribal affairs. The Iroquois were good farmers. Well attended agricultural fairs featuring displays of choice fruits and vegetables and skilled needlework took place at the Cattaraugus, Tonawanda, and Onondaga reservations.

Farther from the farm country was the Awkwesasne community on the St. Regis reservation, with about 700

War dance of Ojibwa from Lake Huron before Queen Victoria and royal party in London, 1845. Many Indian parties performed in Europe in the nineteenth century. Catlin, *Catlin's Notes on Eight Years Travel in Europe*, vol. 1, no. 6, p. 138.

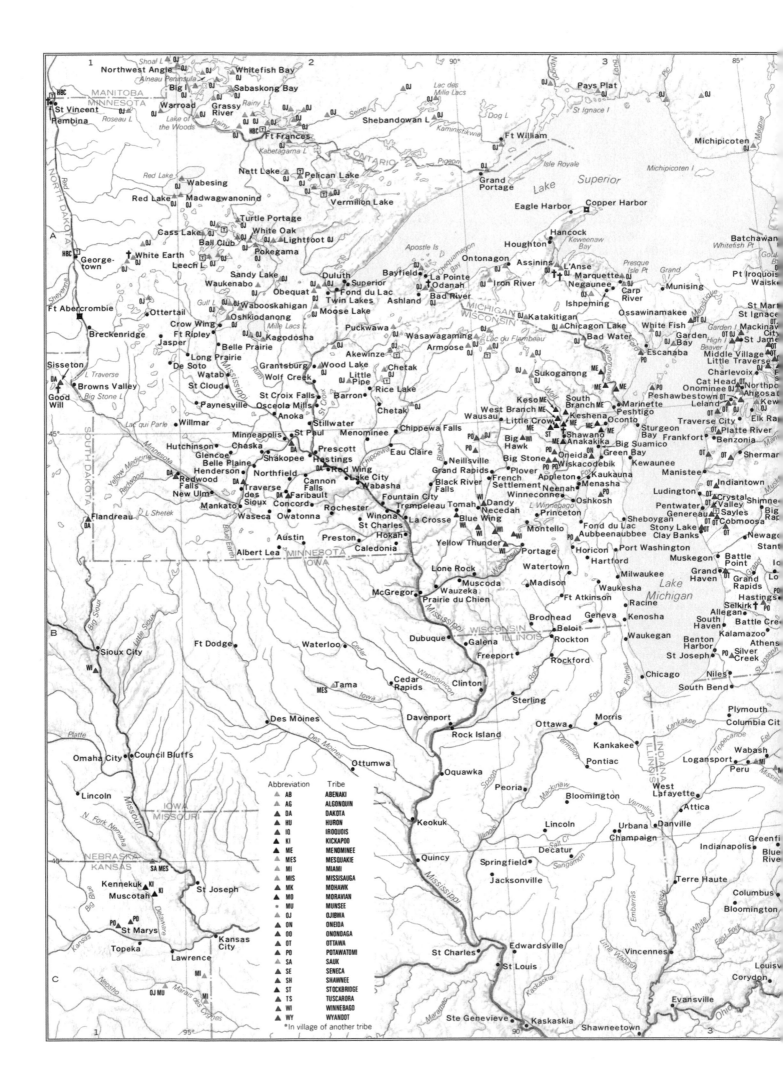

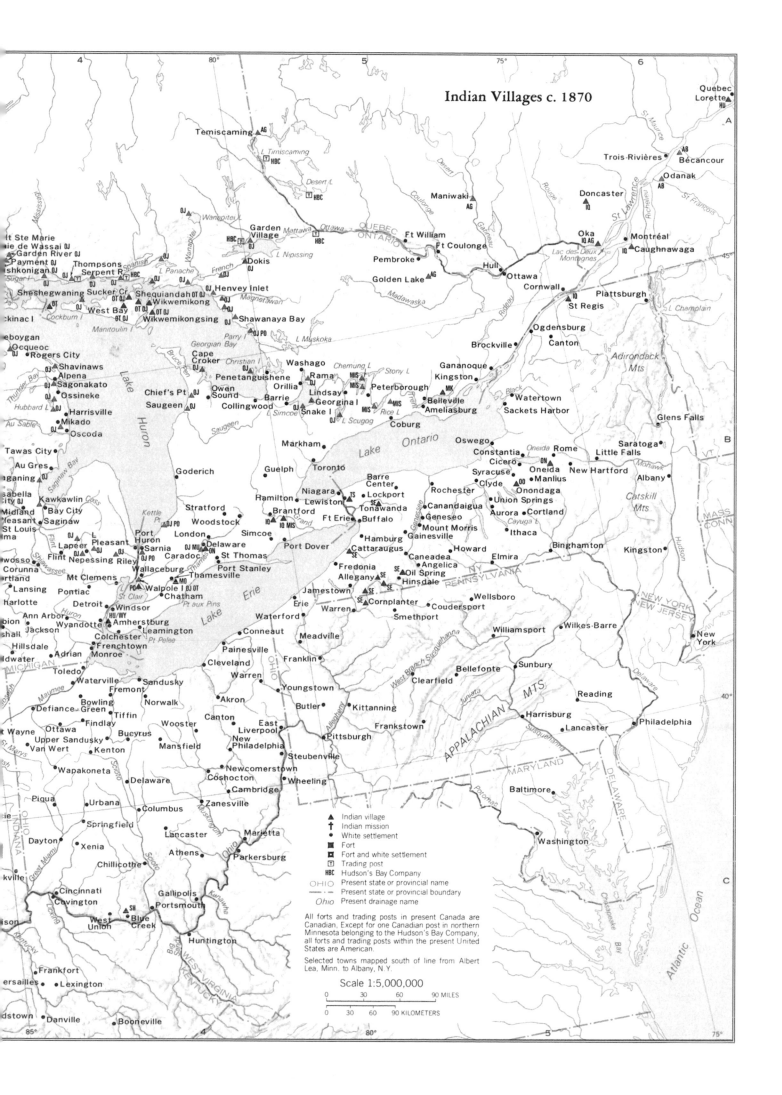

Indian Villages c. 1870

MAP
33

Legend:
▲ Indian village
† Indian mission
• White settlement
◼ Fort
◪ Fort and white settlement
⊤ Trading post
HBC Hudson's Bay Company
OHIO Present state or provincial name
— — Present state or provincial boundary
Ohio Present drainage name

All forts and trading posts in present Canada are
Canadian. Except for one Canadian post in northern
Minnesota belonging to the Hudson's Bay Company,
all forts and trading posts within the present United
States are American.

Selected towns mapped south of line from Albert
Lea, Minn. to Albany, N.Y.

Scale 1:5,000,000

0   30   60   90 MILES

0   30   60   90 KILOMETERS

Recruiters swearing in two Stockbridge Indians of Wisconsin during Civil War. Special Indian brigades were formed for some of the approximately four thousand Indians who served with the Union army. An estimated ten to twelve thousand Indians joined the Confederate forces. State Historical Society of Wisconsin.

Quinte, or between the villages at Sault Ste. Marie and the Manitoulin Island. Internationally, back and forth, the movement continued between Little Traverse Bay of Lake Michigan and Manitoulin Island, as well as across the St. Marys and St. Clair rivers.

The seasonal migrations were also more restricted for Indian people, at least in southern Ontario. For this district, the total Indian population remained fairly constant at about 9,000, while the white population had risen from 250,000 in 1830 to 1,620,000 in 1870. This pressure precluded, to a large extent, the lifestyle of previous generations. Furthermore, the surrender of reserves or portions of reserved lands restricted movement, and the program of civilization begun in 1830, while hardly as successful as its creators would have hoped, also promoted a more sedentary existence. By 1870 virtually every Indian settlement in southern Ontario was located on an institutionalized reserve. Smallest tribal population was the 75 Wyandot, at Anderdon, south of Windsor. More mobility was possible among the northern Ojibwa in the areas of the Robinson-Huron and Robinson-Superior treaties signed in 1850. There, some 3,400 Indians continued their traditional pursuits, although each band had received a reserve location.

On Manitoulin Island, tension lingered in the aftermath of the Indian protest in 1862 against efforts of white companies to take over the local fishing industry. The commissioner of fisheries, who had come from Ottawa to make an investigation, was drowned in Georgian Bay under circumstances giving rise to reports that his death was not accidental. The Manitoulin Island incident was contemporary with the Dakota uprising in Minnesota, described in a later section of the text for this map.

population on the American side of the border and 800 in Canada. South of Montreal the Caughnawaga reservation (now officially spelled "Kahnawake") at Sault St. Louis continued to be one of the largest Indian communities, with a population of 1,650. By 1870 these principally Mohawk people were already recognized for their skill in high steel construction, through their work on major railroad bridges. In southern Ontario the 2,900 residents of the Six Nations Reserve near Brantford and 700 Mohawk at Tyendinaga, located west of Kingston on the Bay of Quinte, were largely dependent upon farming operations.

Throughout the balance of southern Ontario, the migrations of an additional 5,700 Indian people were virtually ended. The years since 1830 had, nonetheless, witnessed changes. A group of Oneida had moved from New York into the Thames valley in the 1840s; Potawatomi had joined Ojibwa on the Saugeen Peninsula and Walpole Island; a portion of the Moravians had departed from the Thames River and were living in Kansas; and a band of Missisauga had moved from the Credit River to the Six Nations Reserve on the Grand River.

There was also some individual change of residence among bands; for example, between the Six Nations Reserve near Brantford and the Tyendinaga settlement on the Bay of

Michigan, Indiana, Wisconsin

In 1870, southwestern Michigan was the home of two recognized Potawatomi groups. About 300 Indians designated by the government as Ojibwa, Ottawa and Potawatomi lived near Silver Creek in the vicinity of present Hartford. These were principally families from Pokagon's village who had been exempted from Potawatomi removal by special provisions of the Treaty of Chicago in 1833. As Catholics, they were allowed to remain in Michigan, with the expectation that they would join Ottawa and Ojibwa of that faith living around the mission at La Croix on Little Traverse Bay. These remnants of the old St. Joseph River Potawatomi instead lived temporarily at several locations, then purchased land. The government made a final financial settlement with this group in 1866. A smaller community numbering under 100 identified as Potawatomi of the Huron, indicating earlier residence near the Huron River of eastern Michigan, cultivated small garden patches at Athens, south of Battle Creek. Contemporary reports indicate that other Potawatomis were scattered all across southern Michigan, but were outside the purview of the Indian agency headquarters at Detroit.

In Indiana, the government officially counted only 345 Miami. The reservation communally held by the Meshingomesia band was ordered divided into individual allotments in 1872. The two other Miami bands remaining in the state after the removal in 1846 had lost most of their property and financial resources, partially through litigation. Although their leaders of the Godfroy and Richardville families had been men of considerable wealth in 1840, the generation of the 1870s lived in reduced circumstances.

Along the eastern side of Michigan's Lower Peninsula, small white-populated towns bordered the shore of Lake Huron north of Saginaw Bay. With the occupation of Oscoda at the mouth of the AuSable River and Alpena on Thunder Bay, the Indians of the vicinity moved inland to Mikado and Hubbard's Lake. Ossineke retained only the middle syllables of the original long Ojibwa name (map 25).

The majority of the 9,000 Indians in Michigan lived north of Saginaw and Grand Rapids in tracts reserved for their permanent homes by the treaties of 1855. Sites mapped in the interior of the state were focal points of population identified by schools, missions, or trading posts.

At Isabella reservation in the central part of the state, the 1,650 Saginaw Ojibwa by this time included bands from the Black River and Swan Creek, streams flowing into the St. Clair River and Lake St. Clair (map 25). Isabella City, headquarters for the main reservation, was already losing its importance and declined rapidly after the Indian mill burned in 1871. A mile and a half away at Mt. Pleasant, a business block constructed in 1869 promoted growth of a new center for sawmill enterprises. Although the Saganing reservation on the shore of Saginaw Bay had been ceded in 1864, Ojibwa still remained in the vicinity.

On the western side of Michigan's Lower Peninsula, a concentration of Ottawa and Ojibwa on the Leelanau Peninsula, northwest of Traverse City, was under way before the area was reserved by the 1855 treaty. The movement to the Leelanau Peninsula began in 1849, when the Old Wing mission colony moved from the vicinity of Holland to a point near the western entrance to Grand Traverse Bay. Named Wakazooville for their leader, the townsite shortly was taken over by a lumbering firm and named Northport. New Indian villages were formed at Cat Head Bay and Onominee on the Lake Michigan shore. In 1852 the mission established on Grand Traverse Bay in 1841 moved from Old Mission point in the middle of Grand Traverse Bay to the Western arm. The new site, present Omena, became identified with the Indian leader Ahgosa. Peshawbestown, originally called Eagletown, was founded in 1856 as an offshoot of the mission at La Croix, north of Little Traverse Bay.

The removal of the Ottawa from the lower Grand River Valley took place in 1857. The non-Indian population had grown rapidly as a result of completion in 1855 of a road between Grand Rapids and Kalamazoo, a major railroad terminal fifty miles to the south. In the summer of 1857, over 900 Indians embarked at Grand Haven for the first leg of their trip to inland reservations near Ludington and Pentwater in present Ocean a and Mason counties. New communities developed, forming a line south from Indiantown (see map).

In the northwestern tip of the Lower Peninsula, new towns crowd the map area, leaving insufficient room for complete identifications. Mackinaw City had only a single house in 1870, but lumbering and dock building were under way. Cheboygan as a white town, formerly called "Duncan," was only a year old. Of the Indian villages, the names of four have been omitted. Two are longstanding sites: Cheboygan, the mixed Ottawa-Ojibwa band at present Burt Lake, east of Middle Village on the map; and La Croix, at present Cross Village, north of Middle Village on the map. On the south shore of Little Traverse Bay, the Ojibwa village west of Petoskey was called Kawgachewing. The Ottawa site west and a little north of Traverse City was located at Hidden Lake near Pyramid Point. In 1870, Little Traverse, present Harbor Springs, was the principal trading settlement in the region. Change came suddenly in 1874, when the railroad line from Chicago reached Petoskey, and land sales began.

At the eastern end of the Upper Peninsula, Ojibwa settlements were located on reserved land along Waiska Bay and at Point Iroquois, where a Methodist mission had been particularly active in the 1850s. Sugar Island, with four or five Indian communities, was densely settled. In the L'Anse district on Keweenaw Bay, a Methodist mission on the east side and Father Frederick Baraga's Catholic mission on the west shore were focal points. Baraga purchased land subsequently divided among families of his mission. Assinins was the local leader of the band to whom land was conveyed in 1863.

In Wisconsin, admitted to the Union in 1848, settlers did not penetrate the north woods in large numbers. Ojibwa had relatively little contact with whites in 1870, retaining a portion of their own domain and traditional lifeways. The Menominee on the upper Wolf and Oconto rivers fought lumbering depredations and agency attempts to convert them to farming. Their lands were too poor to attract the attention of white farmers or dairymen. The Oneida, Stockbridge and Munsee, however, engaged in farming operations similar to their non-Indian neighbors.

The leading Ojibwa band included the Red Cliff and Bad River communities of the La Pointe district. Unfortunately, there was a considerable landless Ojibwa population, such as the St. Croix River and Mole Lake bands, who were left out of, or neglected by, the treaties of 1854 and 1855 that provided reservations for other bands.

Also without land assignments were many former residents of the composite Potawatomi communities on the western shores of Lake Michigan. Dispossessed as a result of the Menominee cession of 1831 and the Treaty of Chicago in 1833, some of these people eventually joined their Potawatomi brethren on reserves in western Iowa and, later, Kansas. Others eluded federal roundup agents by moving into the marshy areas of the upper Rock River, or north to the Door Peninsula, or into the densely forested north central portion of Wisconsin and the Michigan-Wisconsin border region.

In 1870 there were still more than a thousand "strolling" Potawatomi and Ojibwa camping and hunting along the Eau Claire and upper Wisconsin river drainage system. These migratory bands had to await the twentieth century for federally recognized land bases. In the early twentieth century, Potawatomi were granted a reservation at Hannahville, near present Bark River, west of Escanaba, Michigan. In 1913 the federal government purchased discontinuous parcels of land for other homeless Potawatomi in present Forest County, Wisconsin. These refugee communities included Potawatomi from the entire tribal estate.

Little Crow's Village, about 1848. Little Crow fled to Canada following the outbreak of hostilities in 1862, but was later captured. From Lewis, *Valley of the Mississippi,* ed. by Bertha Heilbrun, 1967, p. 29. The Newberry Library.

Winnebago of western Wisconsin had similar experiences. Although the Fox River Winnebago had ceded land and migrated in 1832 (map 31), several hundred Wisconsin River Winnebago never reconciled themselves to the 1837 cession of the remaining Winnebago lands in Wisconsin. Unwilling to follow their brethren to the Crow Wing and Blue Earth reserves in Minnesota, the "disaffected" Winnebago repeatedly resisted capture, or stole back to campsites along the Lemonweir, Black, and Wisconsin rivers. Finally these refugees were granted the right to avail themselves of the Indian Homestead Act of 1875. Winnebago group identity remained strong after they took up 40- to 80-acre homesites among white settlers. In 1881 the federal government created a separate tribal roll for the Wisconsin Winnebago.

In northern Wisconsin and Michigan, Indian people were an integral part of the regional economy in the 1870s. They worked at mining and lumber camps, on survey crews, as stevedores on vessels plying the Great Lakes, and carried the mail. One factor enabling the Winnebago to remain in Wisconsin was their usefulness as farm laborers. Fishing remained an important occupation, and some hunting and trapping continued in this region as in Minnesota and Canada. Great Lakes tribes in the late nineteenth century profited from the sale of hundreds of pounds of maple sugar and bushels of strawberries, raspberries and blueberries. They made baskets, birch bark containers, bark and carved-pine canoes. The Peshawbestown (Eagletown) community constructed their own sailboat. On Sugar Island, using local maple sugar and berries, Indians produced the twelve tons of jam sold to passengers at the steamboat landing during a single summer excursion season in 1862.

In addition to an economic role, Michigan Indians had a significant political role for about a quarter of a century after revisions in the state constitution in 1850 gave them the right to vote, with certain requirements. Men of Indian heritage were elected to office in counties that remained predominantly Indian until the increase in white population in the 1870s. During the 1860s the Indian agency in Michigan, largest in the United States at that time, was a showcase for experiments in day-school education. Though there had been 32 schools in 1865, the number was cut in half by 1871 and dwindled to only six by 1885, as treaty payments came to an end and denominational support decreased. By terms of treaties, payments of annuities to most Michigan and Wisconsin Indians were scheduled to end in 1871.

Minnesota, Canadian Border, Outlying Reservations

Minnesota achieved statehood in 1858 and numbered 440,000 whites by 1870. Yet the northern section could still be classified as Indian country, inhabited almost exclusively by over 7,000 Ojibwa and their Metis relatives plus a scattering of traders, missionaries, agency personnel, and hangers-on. The move to consolidate Minnesota Ojibwa on Leech Lake and White Earth reservations was only partially completed in 1870. New settlements existed at White Oak Point and White Earth, but a few Ojibwa villages remained south of Leech Lake.

Among the new leaders at White Earth was Enmegahboth (John Johnston), an Ottawa minister adopted by the Ojibwa. His Episcopal mission had been broken up in 1862, but he removed with Ojibwa from Gull Lake and resumed mission activities at White Earth in 1869. Catholic missionaries continued to work among the Ojibwa from their station at Grand Portage.

In 1870 the Dakota population formerly inhabiting Minnesota was recovering from the disruption of the 1862 "Sioux Uprising." Dissension between the miss ionized and traditional elements, as well as dissatisfaction with government observance of treaty terms, led to the killing of white settlers around New Ulm in late summer of 1862. At that time, most Dakota fled in terror, some crossing into Canadian territory. Several hundred were imprisoned in Davenport, Iowa, before being sent to join kinsmen transported to the Santee Reservation in Nebraska. A few "friendly" Dakota were allowed to remain, for whom an 1863 act authorized the secretary of state to assign 80-acre plots on the old reservation on the Minnesota River. The press of white settlement and anti-Indian resentments foiled this plan, and in 1866 the 374 Dakota still in Minnesota lived as landless outcasts, clustering in small groups at Faribault, on Sibley lands at Mendota, near Redwood Falls, on the Yellow Medicine River, at Wabasha, and at the head of Big Stone Lake. Good Will marks the mission at the Sisseton Agency, government headquarters for the triangular reservation established in eastern South Dakota in 1867.

Some of the Dakotas transferred in 1866 from the Crow Creek Reservation to the Santee Reservation refused to remain. In 1869 they moved back to establish a farming community near Flandreau, South Dakota, on Big Sioux River. This group was granted lands by the Homestead Act of 1875, and two years later numbered 227 persons living in 51 log houses.

The Canadian border region adjoining the northwest corner of Minnesota was in a state of turmoil in the opening months of 1870 because of the Red River insurrection that had commenced in October, 1869. Led by Louis Riel, the rebellion protested arrangements made by the new Canadian Confederation government, formed in 1867, to take over territory administered for two hundred years by the Hudson's Bay Company. The transfer was virtually complete in 1869, when the government sent surveyors to mark tracts in anticipation of land sales.

For Métis, the key issue was recognition of their rights to ribbon farms lining the Red River from the international border north to Winnepeg, a town north of the mapped area. Regional Ojibwa leaders also wanted assurance that their band territory would be recognized by treaty. Considerable sympathy for the insurrection prevailed on the American side of the border. Ojibwa of the Red Lake area of Minnesota still had unceded lands and shared the concerns of their near neighbors under Canadian jurisdiction. Frequent interchange occurred among members of bands based near Pembina and along the Roseau River in Minnesota and Manitoba.

In aggressive action, Riel seized control of the fort, established a provisional government, and blocked the incoming lieutenant governor's advance north of Pembina. This town, founded as a center for Red River Ojibwa and Metis trade, had been determined by surveys to be in American territory. Unable to proceed farther, the incoming Canadian official finally had to retreat to St. Paul, Minnesota, to spend the winter of 1869-1870. A series of conferences in the summer of 1870 reassured the Metis and Ojibwa groups, permitting establishment of Manitoba and preparing the way for Indian treaties in 1871 and 1873 (map 30). About 7,000 Ojibwa belonged to bands living in the portion of the treaty areas included in the 1870 map.

When the Hudson's Bay regime came to an end in 1870, the firm still had a trading post near present Georgetown, Minnesota. The following year, the Great Northern railroad stretched to Breckenridge, Minnesota, connecting the fertile Red River Valley with St. Paul and eastern commodity markets. Transportation advances heralded the beginnings of large scale agriculture on the northern plains and the end of the fur trade as the principal economic activity.

South of Minnesota, the western margin of the map includes some of the late nineteenth-century reservation communities of Indian people formerly living in the Great Lakes Regions, but does not extend to the Indian Territory of present Oklahoma. While the federal government was endeavoring to concentrate tribal people in the Indian Territory, segments that had migrated or been removed still lived on reserved lands in Nebraska and Kansas.

The government also maintained supervision over the Mesquakie settlement at present Tama, Iowa. This group, numbering about 250, purchased 80 acres of land in 1857 and increased their holdings to 400 acres by 1870, using money from the sale of ponies. The Tama community followed a traditional lifestyle, dispersing for winter hunting and returning to plant crops after making sugar in the spring. Some of the men augmented their income by working as farmhands.

The population of the Winnebago reservation in Nebraska, numbering 450 in 1870, increased with 60 new arrivals from Wisconsin in 1873, but movement continued between the reservation and the Winnebago settlements in ten Wisconsin counties. The Sauk and Mesquakie at Nohart, Richardson County, Nebraska, were expecting to join other tribal members in the Indian Territory.

Kansas still retained a diverse population of former Great Lakes Indians. The tiny group of 56 Ojibwa and Munsee included a few from the Swan Creek and Black River bands of southeastern Michigan, as well as former residents of the Moravian settlement on the Thames River in Canada. The 400 members of the Prairie Band of Potawatomi, who had forged a separate identity during their years in Iowa, clung to their Kansas home. Potawatomi living near the St. Mary's Mission planned to move but did not actually leave until several years later.

The two Kickapoo communities in Kansas, one named for their earlier religious leader Kennekuk, expected to join their Mexican branch in selecting a new reservation site in Indian Territory. But in 1871 the Mexican Kickapoo refused the offer of American officials for a home in the United States. Affairs of the Miami in Kansas, where lands had been allotted, were in a state of transition in 1870.

Final Population Summary

At the close of the period covered by the Atlas, Great Lakes Indian settlements continued in a band of territory extending from Kingston, Ontario, and western New York across southern Ontario and the northern sections of Michigan, Wisconsin, and Minnesota. Indian communities in the vicinity of Montreal and along the St. Lawrence River had few regular contacts with the Indian population concentration on the upper Great Lakes. Similarly isolated were the Algonquin on the Ottawa River and its tributaries-the river itself no longer the main artery of communication it had been in the seventeenth and eighteenth centuries. Montreal, supplanted by Ottawa as the Canadian capital, had also ceased being the focal point of Indian trade and politics. Also outside the arena of Great Lakes Indian affairs were former residents living on reservations southwest of the Missouri River.

Spearing Muskrat in Winter. In the 1870s, hunting remained a primary occupation for Ojibwa living in the northwestern section of the Great Lakes region. By Seth Eastman. From Schoolcraft, *History of the Indian Tribes of the United States,* pt. 2, p. 51. The Newberry Library.

Indian population in the Great Lakes Region from Kingston westward to Lake of the Woods totaled roughly 48,000 in 1870, with approximately 20,000 in Canada and 28,000 in the United States. These figures, which may represent local undercounting, are subdivided as follows:

Geographical District	Approximate Indian Population
Southern Ontario	9,300
North of Lakes Huron and Superior	3,400
Fort William to Lake of the Woods	7,000
Western New York State	4,800
Michigan	9,000
Wisconsin	7,200
Minnesota	7,800
Total	48,500

White population in 1870 surpassed the million mark in Ontario, Michigan, Indiana, and Wisconsin, but dropped off sharply to 440,000 in Minnesota and only 15,000 in Dakota Territory west of the Red River. The population of Illinois had passed 2,500,000, and New York State had grown to 4,300,000.

Probably the most fragmented tribal people were the

Potawatomi, who in 1870 could be found in southern Michigan, northern Wisconsin, on Canadian reserves at Walpole Island and Parry Sound, as well as on reservations in Kansas and Oklahoma. Despite dispersion, all Indians maintained contacts throughout the states and provinces and across international borders. Indian people continued living in the sections of the Great Lakes Region where their communities are mapped for 1870.

Principal Sources: Aguar 1971; Aguar Jyring Whiteman and Moser 1967, 1968; Allen 1976; Andrea 1874, 1883; Arthur 1978; Belknap 1927; Blackbird 1897; Blanchard 1980a, b; Brower 1900; Brown Papers n.d.; Canada 1871, 1913, 1978; Chapman 1884; Cheboygan 1887-95; Church 1862; Coleman 1967, 1968; Cooperative 1962; Cowperthwait 1850; Craker 1937; Cumming 1972; Danziger 1979; Dickinson 1951; Dobson 1978; Ensign 1855; Fancher 1911; Farmer 1867; Folwell 1921; Hatch 1880; Inglis 1898; Isabella 1884; Keesing 1930; Kemble 1850; Kohl 1860; Leach 1883; Levi 1956; Littell 1937; McClung 1870; Maguire 1980; Manistique 1960; Maps 1968; Meacham 1878; Meyer 1967; Mitchell 1870; Mittleholtz 1957; Morris 1880; Oliver 1903; Oppen 1978; Ourada 1978; Page 1882; Rezek 1907; Strang 1894; Tiedke 1951; Traverse 1884; Tucker 1913; United States 1870, 1872; Upham 1969; Verwyst 1900; Vizenor 1968; Walkerville 1976; Walling 1873.

BIBLIOGRAPHIC ESSAY

Information for mapping Great Lakes Indian history comes from a broad range of sources, printed, manuscript, oral, and visual. Included are personal letters, diaries, histories, biographies, literary works, travelers' descriptions, military dispatches, treaty journals, missionary observations, ships' logs, Indian agency documents, trade and commercial records, reports of legislative bodies, traditional accounts of Indians and early settlers, captivity narratives, anthropological studies, geological and archaeological researches papers, judicial proceedings, surveyors' notes, maps, sketches, paintings, and photographs.

Most of the pertinent original documents on Great Lakes history are held in the Public Archives of Canada, in Ottawa, and in the National Archives, in Washington, D.C., but many are preserved in smaller provincial, state, and local collections in North America as well as in repositories in Great Britain, France, and Spain. The basic sources in the Public Archives of Canada are Record Group 10, Indian Affairs, and Record Group 8, Military Affairs. In the United States, comparable sources in the National Archives are Record Group 75, Indian Bureau, and Record Group 77, War Department. Significant sequences from the large bodies of official and personal correspondence have been published under the auspices of state historical societies, as well as by government authority.

The long series *Documents Relating to the Colonial History of New York*, edited for the most part by E. B. O'Callahan, throw light on the Upper Great Lakes frontier as well as the region adjacent to New York. A rare selection of primary accounts of western Pennsylvania and Ohio Indian traders, with some discussion and a slender narrative thread, is found in Charles A. Hanna's two-volume work, *The Wilderness Trail* (1911).

Many crucial records concerning the Upper Great Lakes during both the French and the British colonial eras appeared under the editorship of Reuben Gold Thwaites. Louise Phelps Kellogg, in cooperation with Thwaites, edited four volumes of source material covering the Ohio Valley frontier from 1774 to 1781, using documents from the Draper Collection of manuscripts and personal interviews, important holdings of the State Historical Society of Wisconsin.

Under the heading "Cadillac Papers" correspondence of the early French period at Detroit was translated for volumes 33 and 34 of the *Collections and Researches of the Michigan Pioneer and Historical Society*. The printing of British documents from Canadian Archives dealing with the colonial period to the end of the War of 1812 progressed at intervals through volumes 9 to 25 of the Michigan *Collections*.

Among the other notable publications of state and provincial historical organizations in the Great Lakes Region are French documents with English translation in *Illinois on the Eve of the Seven Years' War*, volume 29 in the Illinois State Historical Library series, edited by Theodore Calvin Pease and Ernestine Jenison. In the same collections, the British era in the Illinois country, 1765-69, is chronicled in volumes 11 and 16, edited by Clarence W. Alvord and Clarence E. Carter. Of the many publications of the Indiana Historical Society, the most distinctive contribution for mapping purposes is probably the three volumes of papers of John Tipton, American Indian agent and trader at present Logansport, Indiana, whose records cover the period 1809-39.

In the vast field of federal government publications, the two volumes of the *American State Papers* dealing with Indian affairs are a principal source of detailed information on Indian-white relations for the period of post-Revolutionary War hostilities and treaty making in the early national period. These volumes are supplemented by selected documents in the series of *Territorial Papers of the United States* compiled by Clarence E. Carter.

As part of the *18th Annual Report of the Bureau of American Ethnology* (1899), Charles C. Royce produced a chronological list of American Indian treaties, including an abstract of the principal provisions regarding land cessions and reservations. In Royce's tabular information land cessions are consecutively numbered and keyed to an accompanying set of state and territorial maps. The maps are an indispensable reference work, although they are poor for all of Michigan except the southeastern section.

The complete texts of American treaties to the end of the Indian treaty-making period in 1871 can be found in volume 2 of Charles C. Kappler's *Indian Laws and Treaties*, reissued in 1965 with a useful map and a new introduction. Many researchers still prefer to consult the *United States Statutes at Large*, where the treaties are printed in the form signed by Indian representatives, with notations of the clauses modified, added, or struck out by the Senate before ratification. The early Canadian Indian treaties to 1890 were first brought together for official publication in two volumes appearing in 1891. These have been reissued through Coles Publishing Company in a three-volume paperback edition, including copies of manuscript maps for many of the land surrenders.

Canadian publications emphasizing primary source material for *Atlas* mapping include three of the Champlain Society series, each with a special geographic focus in southern Ontario: *The Windsor Border Region* edited by Ernest Lajeunesse, *The Valley of the Trent* by Edwin C. Guillet, and Charles M. Johnston's study of the Grand River Indian lands, *Valley of the Six Nations*. Richard Glover's edition of the David Thompson travels beyond the northwest sector of the Great Lakes Region and William Wood's maps and fine selection of documents on the War of 1812 are other valuable Champlain Society publications. The most thorough documentation of the military aspect of the War of 1812 along the Detroit-to-Niagara frontier is the work of Ernest Cruikshank, whose research has been published by the Canadian government and by historical societies in the Niagara area.

A few people in official capacities accumulated a preponderance of information gathered from Indian traders, military scouts, and other personal contacts. The voluminous papers of Sir William Johnson, British Indian superintendent based near present Rome, New York, span the period from the Seven Years' War to the American Revolution. For the period of post-Revolutionary warfare culminating in 1794, revealing correspondence comes from military opponents, British Lieutenant Governor John Graves Simcoe and American General Anthony Wayne.

A balance for the official dispatches of the latter half of the eighteenth century is found in the recollections of men captured by Indians in their youth. For the region covered by the *Atlas,* five captivity narratives of particular importance should be cited. Indian life in the Ohio country is illuminated by accounts of Charles Stuart (1755-57), James Smith (1756-57), and Oliver M. Spencer (1791-92). The interior of Indiana and Indian settlements around Fort Wayne in 1787 and 1788 were described by Thomas Rideout, who later became surveyor general of Canada. The most thorough account of a former captive is the story of John Tanner taken down by a physician at Mackinac Island in the 1830s after Tanner had been living more than forty years among , the Ottawa and Ojibwa in the area from Lake Huron to southern Manitoba.

For the early nineteenth century and the era of the War of 1812, the papers of Indiana territorial governor William Henry Harrison are major sources of information for Indian people in Indiana and Ohio. At that time the non-Indian with the greatest knowledge of the Indians in the territory north and west of Lake Michigan was Robert Dickson, British Indian superintendent for the Western District of Canada, whose trading interests stretched to the Red River country of present South and North Dakota and Manitoba. The papers of William Claus and other members of his family associated with the British Indian Department cover the region between Malden, opposite Detroit, Michigan, and the Niagara frontier and extend to the 1830s. During the 1820s and 1830s a number of American governors and Indian agents in the Old Northwest became well informed on Indian affairs. Lewis Cass, governor of Michigan Territory, negotiated sixteen treaties with Great Lakes Indians. Henry R. Schoolcraft, intellectually inquisitive Indian agent based at Sault Sainte Marie and later at Mackinac Island and Detroit, produced several small volumes of travels and local memoirs as well as the six comprehensive volumes of information respecting the Indian tribes ultimately entitled *Archives of Aboriginal Knowledge.* His introduction to Indian society came through his wife and relatives of Ojibwa heritage.

On the western border of the Great Lakes Region a principal information source by the 1830s was Lawrence Taliaferro, a plucky Indian agent assigned to Fort Snelling, present Minneapolis, Minnesota, when the post was established in 1819. Throughout the nineteenth century several descendants of the original French traders at

Green Bay, represented by the Grignon family, were the best informants concerning the interior of present Wisconsin. Along the Ontario shores of Lake Huron, including Manitoulin Island, a major information resource of the 1830s was Thomas G. Anderson, who had been stationed at British bases in Wisconsin during the War of 1812.

Although Indian interpretations of contemporary and past events have generally come into the historic record through non-Indian reporters, several authors of Indian heritage have contributed works based on their own experience and accumulated knowledge. For example, Black Hawk's recollections of his career as a Sauk leader, climaxing in his capture at the end of the short but intense war in 1832, have appeared in several editions. William W. Warren, educated and bilingual son of an Ojibwa woman and an Indian trader, wrote a carefully prepared history of the Ojibwa living south and west of Lake Superior, first published in volume 5 of the *Minnesota Historical Collections.* The Methodist missionary Peter Jones, son of a British surveyor in Ontario, eloquently pleaded for reserves needed by his mother's Missisauga people.

In addition to the variety of printed matter, the *Atlas* staff used an assortment of maps. The earliest maps with pertinent information were the seventeenth- and eighteenth-century French maps representing the work of Jean Baptiste Franquelin and Claude and Guillaume Delisle. A number of French manuscript maps are available in photostat form in the Karpinski Collection of Photographs of Maps from England, France, Spain and Portugal. The Newberry Library is one of several repositories of the complete collection reproduced by Louis Karpinski, mathematics professor and cartophile in the University of Michigan. Portions of maps covering sections of the Great Lakes Region appear in *Indian Villages of the Illinois Country* compiled by Sarah Jones Tucker with a later supplement by Wayne Temple.

Mapping the Great Lakes progressed by spurts. Lake Superior, at the far end of the canoe thoroughfare west from Montreal, was the first of the lakes to be well drawn. The remarkably accurate Jesuit map of 1671 was not generally known, however, and printed maps up to the 1830s were plagued by errors, the most conspicuous being nonexistent islands. The first reasonable map of the Ohio country was the Lewis Evans map of 1755, superior in this region to John Mitchell's more famous map of 1755 because Evans tapped the knowledge of better-informed Pennsylvania traders. Thomas Hutchins, who accompanied Colonel Henry Bouquet on his march west from Pittsburgh in 1764 and made an overland journey northward to Lake Michigan, was the pioneer map maker and surveyor of the Ohio country. On all printed maps the configuration of the five Great Lakes was long distorted by lack of geographic knowledge of the size of Michigan's Peninsula. The eastern shoreline of Lake Michigan was not correctly represented until 1840, when initial land surveys were completed for the Grand and Little Traverse Bay areas.

By the 1830s printed maps, including those in atlases and emigrant guides, could be used with care for identifying Indian communities in the Great Lakes region. Still more reliable were the often crude manuscript maps, such as those preserved in the State Historical Society of Wisconsin and other repositories. Henry S. Tanner's regional map and John Farmer's maps of Michigan and Wisconsin territory, regularly revised and updated, were of great utility. It is interesting to note that the only Farmer map carrying extensive Indian village data is the 1834 map of Michigan printed in German and produced in collaboration with Traugott Bromme for a book to promote German immigration. Among the important state guides with maps for new settlers are those published by John Kilbourn and Warren Jenkins for Ohio and by John Scott for Indiana. County historical atlases appearing in the late nineteenth century were sources of critical bits of information. The county and township maps preserve information about Indian occupancy in the names of lakes, creeks, and roadways.

The published results of several modern research projects were particularly helpful. Wilbur Hinsdale's large *Archaeological Atlas of Michigan* (1927) includes many eighteenth- and nineteenth-century Indian village sites, purposely mapped with slight errors to protect the actual sites from vandalism. Hinsdale's original field notes in the University of Michigan archaeological files record the accurate sites. E. Y. Guernsey's masterful compilation of Indiana's eighteenth- and early-nineteenth-century Indian villages and early Euro-American settlements was published by the Indiana Department of Conservation in 1933, but the research notes are unfortunately lost. An exceptionally fine product of modern mapping is the legacy of William Trygg, who used original. surveyor's notes to construct maps for appraising the value ~f Indian land in areas of Minnesota, Wisconsin, and Michigan. These maps, originally prepared for Indian Claims Commission litigation, show village sites, sugar camps, trails, saltworks, and garden plots as they were recorded by surveyors in the 1840s and 1850s.

A key to this broad range of sources, only sampled in the preceding paragraphs, has been a group of reports prepared for legal cases heard by the Indian Claims Commission, a federal court established in 1946 to consider claims of American Indian tribes against the government based on provisions of treaties. Litigation for the several hundred dockets covering the United States was organized on a geographical basis under the land cession numbering system devised by Charles C. Royce. Evidence presented to the court stressed mappable data such as the locations of villages and hunting grounds, areas of tribal conflict, and regions jointly used by tribal groups.

The initiation of land-claims research stimulated interest in Indian history throughout the United States, including the Great Lakes Region and the Ohio country's

little-known eighteenth-century Indian inhabitants. To investigate this particular area, a research project was instituted at Indiana University, Bloomington, in 1956 under the direction of Erminie Wheeler-Voegelin, with financial support from the U.S. Department of Justice. The results of the staff's systematic research, which continued until 1969 , are preserved in the Ohio Valley-Great Lakes Ethnohistory Archive, housed in the Glen Black Laboratory on the university campus. Most of the project reports appeared in 1974 as part of the Garland Publishing Company Ethnohistory Series. These research reports and supporting documentary evidence served as short cuts for finding primary source material for *Atlas* maps.

The onset of similar land-claims cases in Canada is producing concentrated research on Indian land use in Ontario, summarized in reports being published by the Research Division of the Rights and Treaties Division of the Indian Department, in Ottawa. Since all this litigation is in the form of adversary proceedings, varying interpretations of the historical record and traditional information have been brought forward. Yet without the work of joint research teams and expert witnesses, the complex multitribal history of the Great Lakes Region could not be mapped.

In the actual process of entering information on manuscript maps for the *Atlas*, modern maps and reference works were used constantly. Erwin Raisz's graphic *Landforms of the United States*, mounted on the office wall, kept in view the total geographic scene. For general information the staff consulted *The Columbia Lippincott Gazetteer of the World* (1970), *The National Atlas of the United States of America* (1970), and *The Times Atlas of the World* (1975) which has the same scale (1:2.5 million) used for the two groups of *Atlas* single-page maps, the "Frontier in Transition" series and the sequence of maps for the 1830s. For intensive examination of specific areas, the United States Geological Survey Quadrangles at a scale of 1:250,000 were used to prepare preliminary drafts. For basic geographic information on Canadian territory the staff used standard topographical maps at scales of 1:250,000 and 1:500,000 published in Ottawa by the National Resources Intelligence Branch of the Department of Interior (1919-37). The publication in 1978 of *The Northeast,* edited by Bruce Trigger, volume 15 in the new Smithsonian Handbook Series, provided a specialized reference work for cross-checking data, though *Atlas* maps and text differ in selection and presentation of source material.

A comprehensive bibliography with appropriate commentary on the subject of Great Lakes Indian history would require a separate volume. The selected bibliography for the *Atlas* includes significant items from all types of sources.

Aguar, Charles E.
1971   *Exploring St. Louis County Historical Sites.* Duluth: The St. Louis County Historical Society.

Aguar, Jyring, Whiteman, and Moser. Planning Associates.
1967   *Historical Resources Inventory: Supplement to the Outdoor Recreation Plan for Koochiching County, Minnesota.*

————
1968   *Outdoor Recreation Resources-Itasca County, Minnesota.*

Ainse, Joseph
1888   Statement at Michilimackinac 16 August 1787. *Michigan Pioneer and Historical Society Collections* 11: 50 1-506. Lansing.

Aldrich, Lewis Cass
1889   *History of Erie County, Ohio.* Syracuse, N.Y.: D. Mason & Co.

Allen, James
1860   Report of Lieutenant Allen, of the Army, of H. R. Schoolcraft's Exploration of the Country at and beyond the Sources of the Mississippi, and a Visit to the Northwestern Indians in 1832. *American State Papers, Military Affairs* 5:312-432.

Allen, Robert S.
1976   *The British Indian Department and the Frontier in North America 1755-1830.* Canadian Historic Sites no. 14. Ottawa: Queens Printer.

Alvord, Clarence Walworth
1908   The Genesis of the Proclamation of 1763. *Michigan Pioneer and Historical Society Collections* 36, 20-52. Lansing.

————
1922   *The Illinois Country, 1678-1818. The Centennial History of Illinois.* Vol. 1. Chicago: A. C. McClurgh & Company.

———— and Clarence Edward Carter
1916   *The New Regime: 1765-1767. Collections of the Illinois State Historical Society Library* 11. Springfield: Illinois State Historical Library.

————
1921   *Trade and Politics, 1767-1769. Collections of the Illinois State Historical Library,* 16. Springfield: Illinois State Historical Library.

Alway, S.
1838   Plats of government Surveys of rapids of the Grand River, Michigan. MS. National Archives. Res. Schools, A 473-1838. L-1899. Copy, Grand Rapids Public Museum.

American State Papers
1832-1861   *American State Papers.* Class II, *Indian Affairs 1789-1827,* 2 vols. Class V, *Military Affairs 1789-1838,* 7 vols. Washington: Gales and Seaton.

Andrea, Alfred T.
1874   *Illustrated Historical Atlas of the State of Minnesota.* Chicago: A. T. Andrea.

————
1883   *History of the Upper Peninsula of Michigan.* Chicago: The Western Historical Co.

————
1884-86   *History of Chicago from the Earliest Period to the Present.* 3 vols. Chicago: A. T. Andrea.

Anson, Bert
1970   *The Miami Indians.* Norman: University of Oklahoma Press.

Arndt, John Wallace
1913   Pioneers and Durham Boats on the Fox River. *Proceedings of the State Historical Society at its Sixteenth Annual Meeting* (1912), 180-220. Madison: Wisconsin Historical Society.

Askin, John
1928-1931   *The John Askin Papers.* Ed. by Milo M. Quaife. 2 vols. Detroit Mich.: Detroit Library Commission.

Arthur, Elizabeth, ed.
1973   *Thunder Bay District, 1821-1892, a collection of documents.* Toronto: Champlain Society.

Atwater, Caleb
1831   *Indians of the Northwest, Their Manners, Customs, etc., or Remarks Made in a Tour to Prairie du Chien and then to Washington City in 1829.* Columbus, Ohio: Jenkins and Grover.

————
1938   *A History of the State of Ohio, Natural and Civil.* 2nd ed. Cincinnati: Stereotyped by Glezen & Shepard.

Aupaumut, Hendrick
1827   A Narrative of an Embassy to the Western Indians. *Memoirs of the Historical Society of Pennsylvania.* 2 (Pt. 1):60-131.

Babcock, Willoughby M.
1945a   Sioux Villages in Minnesota Prior to 1837. *Minnesota Archaeologist* 11: 126-46.

————
1945b   The Taliaferro Map of the St. Peter's Indian Agency. *Minnesota Archaeologist* 11: 118-25.

Barreis, David Albert and Erminie W. Voegelin and Remedios Wycoco-Moore
1974   *Anthropological Report on the Chippewa, Ottawa, and Potawatomi Indians in Northeastern Illinois.* New York: Garland Publishing Co.

Baker, Ronald L. and Marvin Carmony
1975   *Indian Place Names.* Bloomington, Ind.: Indiana University Press.

Bardon, Richard and Grace Lee Nute, eds.
1943   A Winter in the St. Croix Valley, 1802-03; A Fur Trader's Reminiscences by George Nelson. *Minnesota History* 28(1); (2): 142-59; (3): 225-40.

Barge, William D.
1918   *Early Lee County, Being Some Chapters in the History of the Early Days in Lee County, Illinois.* Chicago: Barnard & Miller, printers.

Barnhart, John D.
1951   *Henry Hamilton and George Rogers Clark in the American Revolution with the Unpublished Journal of Lieut. Gov. Henry Hamilton.* Crawfordsville, Ind.: R. E. Banta.

_____
1953   *Valley of Democracy, The Frontier versus the Plantation in the Ohio Valley, 1755-1818.* Bloomington, Ind.: Indiana University Press.

Baughman, Abraham J.
1909   *History of Huron County, Ohio.* Chicago: S. J. Clarke Publishing Co.

_____
1913   *Past and Present of Wyandot County.* Vol. 1. Chicago: S. J. Clarke Publishing Co.

Bauman, Robert F.
1949   The Migration of the Ottawa Indians from the Maumee Valley to Walpole Island. *Northwest Ohio Quarterly* 21 (2):86-113.

Bauxar, J. Joseph
1959   The Historic Period. *Illinois Archaeology.* Illinois Archaeological Survey Bulletin 1:4058. Urbana: University of Illinois.

Beckwith, Hiram W.
1879   *History of Vermilion County, together with Historic Notes on the Northwest.* Chicago: H. H. Hill and Co.

_____
1880a   *History of Iroquois County.* Chicago: H. H. Hill and Co.

_____
1880b   *History of Park and Vigo Counties.* Chicago: H. H. Hill and Co.

_____
1884   *The Illinois and Indiana Indians.* Fergus Historical Series No. 27. Chicago: Fergus Printing Co.

Belknap, Charles E.
1927   *The Yesterdays of Grand Rapids.* Grand Rapids: The Dean-Hicks Company.

Berrien, J. M.
1835   Green Bay and Chicago Road, Surveyed and Located Under the Orders of Lieut. J. M. Berrien by Lieut. A. J. Center assisted by J. D. Doty-Esq. Drawn by Lt. Center, 1835. MS, State Historical Society of Wisconsin, Madison.

Berrien
1880   *History of Berrien and Van Buren Counties, Michigan.* Philadelphia: D. W. Ensign & Co.

Berthrong, Donald J.
1974   *Indians of Northern Indiana and Southwestern Michigan.* An Historical Report on Indians' Use and Occupancy of Northern Indiana and Southwestern Michigan. New York: Garland Publishing Co.

Bidlack, Russell E.
1965   *The Yankee Meets the Frenchman: River Raisin, 1817-1830.* Lansing: Historical Society of Michigan.

Biddle, Horace
c. 1845   Judge Horace Biddle's Journal. MS. Cass County Historical Society.

Bigsby, John J.
1850   *The Shoe and Canoe, or Pictures of Travel in the Canadas.* 2 vols. London: Chapman and Hall.

Billingston, Ray A.
1944   The Fort Stanwix Treaty of 1768. *New York History* 25:182-294.

Bird, Henry
1815   *Narrative of Henry Bird.* Bridgeport, Conn. (Reprinted by Clements Library, Ann Arbor, Mich., with introduction by Howard H. Peckham, 1971.)

Blackbird, Andrew J.
1897   *Complete Both Early and Late History of the Ottawa and Chippewa Indians.* Revised Edition. Harbor Springs, Mich.: Babcock & Darling.

Black Hawk (Ma-ka-tai-me-she-kia-kiak)
1955   Black Hawk: An Autobiography. Ed. by Donald D. Jackson. Urbana: University of Illinois Press.

Blair, Emma Helen, trans. and ed.
1911   *The Indian Tribes of the Upper Mississippi Valley and Region of the Great Lakes as Described by Nicolas Perrot, French Commandant in the Northwest; Bacqueville de la Pothene, French Royal Commissioner in Canada; Morrell Marston, American Army Officer; and Thomas Forsyth, United States Agent at Fort Armstrong.* 2 vols. Cleveland: Arthur H. Clark and Company.

Blanchard, David S.
1980a   *Kahnawake: A Historical Sketch.* Kahnawake, Quebec: Kanien'kehake Raotitiohkwa Press.

_____
1980b   *Seven Generations: A History of the Kanienkehaka.* Kahnawake, Quebec: Kahnawake Survival School.

Blasingham, Emily J.
1956   The Depopulation of the Illinois Indians. *Ethnohistory* 3: 193-224, 361-412.

Blegen, Theodore c., ed.
1940   Two Missionaries in the Sioux Country; The Narrative of Samuel W. Pond. *Minnesota History* 21:15-32,158-75,272-83.

Blois, John T.
1839   *Gazetter of Michigan.* Detroit: S. L. Rood & Co.

Bond, Beverly W., Jr., ed.
1927   The Captivity of Charles Stuart, 1755-57, *Mississippi Valley Historical Review* 13: 58-81.

Boutwell, Rev. W. T.
1850-1856   Schoolcraft's Exploring Tour of 1832. *Collection of the Minnesota Historical Society* 1:153-76. St. Paul.

Braider, Donald
1972   *The Niagara.* New York: Holt, Rinehart & Winston.

Bray, Edmund C. and Martha Coleman, trans. and eds.
1976   *Joseph N. Nicollet of the Plains and Prairies:* the Expeditions of 1838-39 with Journals, Letters, and Notes on the Dakota Indians. St. Paul: Minnesota Historical Society Press.

Bray, Martha, ed.
1970   *The Journals of Joseph N. Nicollet: A Sci, entist on the Mississippi Headwaters with Notes on Indian Life, 1836-37.* St. Paul: Minnesota Historical Society Press.

Brickell, John
1842   John Brickell's Narrative. *American Pioneer.* 2 vols. 1 :43-56. Cincinnati: J. S. Williams.

Brisbois, B. W.
1882   Traditions and Recollections of Prairie du Chien. *Collections of the State Historical Society of Wisconsin* 9:282-302. Madison.

British
1969   *British Parliamentary Papers,* vol. 12. *Correspondence, Returns and other Papers relating to Canada and to the Indian Problem Therein,* 1839. Shannon: Irish University Press.

Brower, Jacob Vraderberg and David I. Bushnell, Jr.
1900   *Memoirs of Explorations in the Basin of the Mississippi.* Vol. 3. *Mille Lacs.* St. Paul: H. L. Collins Company.

Brown, Charles E.
[1922-1932]   [Charles E. Brown Papers.] MSS., State Historical Society of Wisconsin, Madison.

————
       Chippewa Indians, Potawatomi Indians, Winnebago Indians. MSS., State Historical Society of Wisconsin, Madison.

Brown, Margaret Kimball
1979   *Cultural Transformations Among the Illinois: An Application of a Systems Model.* Publications of the Museum of Michigan State University, Anthropological Series 1 (3). East Lansing.

Brunson, Alfred
1856   Memoir of Hon. Thomas Pendleton Burnett, Appendix No. 8. *Collections of the State Historical Society of Wisconsin* 2:233-325. Madison.

Buck, James S.
1876   *Pioneer History of Milwaukee, From the First American Settlement in 1833, to 1841.* 2 vols. Milwaukee: Milwaukee News Company Printers.

Burnett, William
1967   *Letterbook of William Burnett, Early Fur Trader in the Land of Four Flags.* St. Joseph: Fort Miami Heritage Society of Michigan.

Bushnell, David I., Jr.
1919   The Virginia Frontier in History-I778. *The Virginia Magazine of History and Biography.* 23:4.

Butterfield, Consul W.
1848   *History of Seneca County.* Sandusky: D. Campbell & Sons.

————
1873   *An History of the Expedition Against Sandusky Under Col. William Crawford in 1782.* Cincinnati: R. Clarke.

————
1890   *History of the Girtys.* Cincinnati: R. Clarke.

Campbell, Isabelle
1966   *The Story of Seaforth.* Seaforth, Ont.: Huron Expositor.

Canada
1845   Report on the Affairs of the Indians in Canada, Section I and II, *Journals of the Legislative Assembly of Canada, 1844-1845.* Appendix E.E.E.

————
1847   Report on the Affairs of the Indians in Canada, Section III. *Journals of the Legislative Assembly of Canada, 1847.* Appendix T.

————
1858   *Report of the Special Commissioners appointed on the 8th of September, 1856 to Investigate Indian Affairs in Canada.* Toronto: Queen's Printer.

————
1871   Report of the Indian branch of the department to the Secretary of State. *Sessional Papers* (No. 23).

————
1876   *Censuses of Canada, 1665-1871. Statistics of Canada,* vol. 4. Ottawa: I. B. Taylor.

————
1913   *Handbook of Indians of Canada.* Appendix to the Tenth Report of the Geographic Board of Canada. Ottawa: C. H. Parmalee.

————
1957   *Copy of a treaty made November 15, 1923 between His Majesty the King and the Mississauga Indians of Rice Lake, Mud Lake, Scugog Lake and Aldersville.* Ottawa: Queens Printer.

1967   *Copy of a treaty made October 31, 1923 between His Majesty the King and the Chippewa Indians of Christian Island, Georgian Island and Rama.* Ottawa: Queens Printer.

1971   *Atlas of Indian Reserves and Settlements.* Ottawa: Indian and Inuit Affairs Program, Reserves and Trust Group.

1973   *Indian Treaties and Surrenders from 1690 to 1890.* Reprinted in 3 vols. Toronto: Coles Publishing Co.

Carey, H. C. and I. Lea
1822   *A complete Historical and Geographical American Atlas.* Philadelphia: Carey and Lea.

Cappon, Lester L., ed.
1976   *Atlas of Early American History: The Revolutionary Era 1760-1790.* Princeton, N.J.: Princeton University Press.

Carte du Fort
1731   Carte du fort ou les Renards ont Ete defaits dressee dur des Relations Envoyees et Sur Ie Rapport des Officiers qui Etoient a l'Action a la Nouvelle Orleans Ie vingt six mars 1731. MS. Archives Nationales, Section Outre-Mer Depot des Fortification des Colonies. Louisiane: 46C. Paris.

Carter, Clarence E., ed.
1934   *Territorial Papers of the United States.* Vols. 2 and 3, *The North West Territories 1787-1803.* Washington: Government Printing Office.

1939   *Territorial Papers of the United States.* Vol. 7, *Territory of Indiana, 1800-1810;* Vol. 8, *1810-1815.* Washington, D.C.: Government Printing Office.

1942   *Territorial Papers of the United States.* Vol. 10, *Territory of Michigan, 1805-1820.* Washington, D.C.: Government Printing Office.

1943a   *Territorial Papers of the United States.* Vol. 11, *Territory of Michigan, 1820-1829.* Washington, D.C.: Government Printing Office.

1943b   *Territorial Papers of the United States.* Vol. 12, *Territory of Michigan, 1820-1829.* Washington, D.C.: Government Printing Office.

1948   *Territorial Papers of the United States.* Vol. 16, *Territory of Illinois, 1806-1814.* Washington, D.C.: Government Printing Office.

Carver, Jonathan
1781   *Travels through the Interior Parts of North America in the Years 1766, 1767, and 1768.* 3rd ed. London: Printed for the author.

Castlenau, Francis de
1842   *Vues et Souvenirs du L 'Amerique du Nord.* Paris: Arthus Bertrand.

Cass, Lewis
1835   Letter to E. A. Brown, November 3, 1835. National Archives Record Group 75. Office of Indian Affairs, Letters Received. Vol. 17.

Catlin, George
1850   *Catlin's Notes on Eight Years Travel and Residence in Europe.* 2 vols. London: Published by the author.

Center, Lt. A. J.
1832   Map of the Route of the Military Road from Fort Crawford to Fort Howard via Fort Winnebago. MS. State Historical Society of Wisconsin, Madison.

Chalou, George
1971   The Red Pawns Go to War: British-American Indian Relations, 1810-1815. MS. Ph.D. dissertation, Indiana University.

Chandler, R. W.
1829   Map of the United States' Lead Mines on the Upper Mississippi River. Cincinnati: E. B. Martin, Engraver.

Cheboygan
1887-1895   Correspondence concerning lands of the Cheboygan band near Burt Lake. Records of the Executive Office, 1810-1910, R.G. 44, Box 177 folder 6, Box 139 folder 1, Box 188 folder 12. Michigan State Archives, Lansing. Xerox in *Atlas* files.

Church, Philetus Swift
1862   Manuscript Journal No.6, L. H. Morgan Papers, University of Rochester, Rochester, New York.

Claus, William
n.d.   The Claus Papers. Manuscript Group 19, Public Archives of Canada, Ottawa.

Cleland, Charles E.
1966   *The Prehistoric Animal Ecology and Ethnozoology of the Upper Great Lakes Region.* University of Michigan Museum of Anthropology, Anthropology Papers 29. Ann Arbor.

1982   The Inland Shore Fishery of the Northern Great Lakes: Its Development and Importance in Prehistory. *American Antiquity* 47(4): 761-84.

Clench, J. B.
1810   Observations Relating to Indians. MS. Public Archives of Canada Record Group 10, vol. #792.

Clifton, James A.
1975   *A Place of Refuge for All Time: Migration of the American Potawatomi into Upper Canada, 1830-1850. Mercury Series Paper 26.* Ottawa: National Museum of Man, Ethnology Division.

1977   *Huron of the West: Migrations and Adaptations of the Ontario Iroquoians.* Ottawa: Research Report, Canadian Ethnology Service. National Museum of Man.

——————

1977 *The Prairie People: Continuity and Change in Potawatomi Indian Culture 1665-1965.* Lawrence, Kans.: The Regents Press.

Coates, John
1888 Number of Indians Resorting to Michili-mackinac, September 10, 1782. *Michigan Pioneer and Historical Society Collections* 10: 635-63.

Coleman, Sister Bernard
1967 *Where the Water Stops (Fond du Lac Reservation).* Duluth, Minn.: College of St. Scholastica.

——————, Sister Verona LaBud, and John Humphrey
1968 *Old Crow Wing, History of a Village.* Duluth, Minn.

Coleman, Thelma
1978 *The Canada Company.* Stratford, ant.: County of Perth and Cumming Publishers.

Cooperative
1962 This is Schoolcraft County. [Mimeographed publication of the Cooperative Extension Service, Schoolcraft County, Mich.]

Corbett, Theodore G.
1977 The Soldier as Settler: The Case of St. Frederic on Lake Champlain. MS. Atlas files.

Coues, Elliott, ed.
1897 *New Light on the Early History of the Greater Northwest: The Manuscript Journals of Alexander Henry, Fur Trader of the Northwest Company and David Thompson, Official Geographer and Explorer of the Same Company 1799-1814.* 3 vols. New York: Francis P. Harper. Reprinted in two volumes by Ross & Haines, Inc., 1965.

——————

1965 *The Expeditions of Zebulon Montgomery Pike, To Headwaters of the Mississippi River, Through Louisiana Territory, and in New Spain, During the Years 1805-6-7.* Newed., 2 vols. Minneapolis: Ross & Haines.

Cowperthwaite, Thomas
1850 *Map of the Original Counties of Minnesota.* Philadelphia: Thomas Cowperthwait & Co.

Coyne, James H.
1895 *The Country of the Neutrals.* Saint Thomas, Ont.

Craig, Gerald M.
1963 *Upper Canada: The Formative Years, 1784-1841.* Toronto: McClelland and Stewart.

Craig, Oscar J.
1892 Ouiatenon, A Study in Indiana History. *Indiana Historical Society Publications,* 2 (8): 317-438.

Craker, Ruth
1937 In the Wake of Ja-Geh-Ask. *Leelanau Enterprise,* August 12.

Crevecoeur, St. John de
1787 Esquisse des Rivieres Muskinghum et Grand Castor, Esquisse du Sioto. *Lettres d'un Cultivateur Américain addressées a Wm. S. Ecuyer.* 3 vols. 3:413. Paris: Chez Cuchet.

Croghan, George
1939 *George Croghan's Journal of His Trip to Detroit in 1767.* Ed. by Howard H. Peckham. Ann Arbor: University of Michigan Press.

Cruickshank, Ernest Alexander
1892 *Robert Dickson, The Indian Trader.* Madison: Wisc. Historical Collections, Vol. 12: 133-53.

——————

1896 The Employment of Indians in the War of 1812. *American Historical Association Annual Report for 1895,* 321-35.

——————

1896-1908 *Documentary History of the Campaign on the Niagara Frontier in 1812, 1813, 1814.* 9 vols. Welland, Ont.: Lundys Lane Historical Society.

——————,ed.

1902 Campaigns of 1812-1814: Contemporary Narratives by Captain W. H. Merritt, Colonel William Claus, Lieutenant Colonel Matthew Elliott and Captain John Norton. *Niagara Historical Society Paper* 9:5-46. Niagara-on-the Lake, Ont.

——————

1913 *Documents Relating to the Invasion of Canada and the Surrender of Detroit.* Ottawa: Government Printing Bureau.

Cumming, P. A. and N. H. Mickenburg, eds.
1972 *Native Rights in Canada.* 2nd ed. Toronto: Indian-Eskimo Association of Canada.

Currie, J. G.
1898 The Battle of Queenston Heights. *Niagara Historical Society Paper* No. 4:15-23. Niagara, Ont.

Cutler, H. G., ed.
1916 *History of St. Joseph County, Michigan.* 2 vols. Chicago, New York: The Lewis Publishing Company.

Danziger, Edmund J.
1979 *The Chippewas of Lake Superior.* Norman: University of Oklahoma Press.

Dean, William G.
1969 *Economic Atlas of Ontario.* Toronto: University of Toronto Press.

Decorah, Spoon
1895 Narrative of Spoon Decorah. *Collections of the State Historical Society of Wisconsin* 13: 448-62. Madison.

DePeyster, Col. Arendt Schuyler
1888 *Miscellanies by an Officer.* Ed. by J. Wats DePeyster. New York: A. E. Chasmar & Co.

Desruisseau, Paul
1777 Memoire d'Observations. Public Archives of Canada. War Office 28, vol. 10:393-95.

DeVorsey, Louis, Jr.
1961 *The Indian Boundary in the Southern Colo-*

nies 1763-1775. Chapel Hill, N.C.: University of North Carolina Press.

DeWard, Charles
1835   Sac & Fox Lands South of the 40 mile Point on Cedar River. MS. William Clark Papers, U.S. Superintendency of Indian Affairs Papers, vol. 1, 168. Kansas State Historical Society. Topeka, Kans.

Dickens, Charles
1968   *American Notes,* with introduction by Christopher Lasch. Gloucester: P. Smith.

Dickinson, Julia Terry
1951   *The Story of Leelanau.* Omega, Mich.: Solle's Bookshop.

Dickson, Robert
            The Robert Dickson Papers. St. Paul: Minnesota Historical Society. (From Indian Affairs, Record Group 10. Public Archives of Canada, Ottawa.)

Dillon, John B.
1859   *A History of Indiana, from Its Earliest Exploration by Europeans to the Close of Territorial Government, in 1816.* Indianapolis: Bingham and Doughty.

————
1897   The National Decline of the Miami Indians. *Indiana Historical Society Publications* (4).

Dobbs, Arthur
1744   *An Account of the Countries Adjoining to Hudson's Bay, in the North-west Part of America.* London: J. Robinson.

Dobie, Richard, et al.
1888   Memorandum for Sir John Johnson Baronet submitted to his consideration by the Committee of Merchants, Montreal April 13, 1786. *Michigan Pioneer and Historical Society Collections* 11 :485-88. Lansing.

Dobson, Pamela, ed.
1978   *The Tree That Never Dies.* Grand Rapids: Grand Rapids Public Library.

Dodge, John R.
1859   *Redmen of the Ohio Valley.* Springfield, Ohio: Ruralest Publishing Co.

Donehoo, George P.
1928   *A History of the Indian Villages and Place Names in Pennsylvania with numerous historical notes and references.* Harrisburg, Pa.: The Telegraph Press.

Doty, James D.
1876   Northern Wisconsin in 1820. *Collections of the State Historical Society of Wisconsin* 7: 195-206, Madison.

Dougherty, Peter
n.d.   Peter Dougherty Papers. MSS. Michigan Historical Collections, Bentley Library. Ann Arbor.

Downes, Randolph C.
1940   *Council Fires on the Upper Ohio: A Narrative of Indian Affairs in the Upper Ohio Valley Until 1795.* Pittsburgh, Pa.: University of Pittsburgh Press.

Drake, Benjamin
1852   *Life of Tecumseh and his Brother the Prophet.* Cincinnati: H. S. and J. Applegate & Co.

Duffy, John
1951   Smallpox and the Indians in the American Colonies. *Bulletin of the History of Medicine* 25.

Dunbar, Willis F.
1969   *All Aboard, A History of Railroads in Michigan.* Grand Rapids: W. B. Eerdmans Pub. Co.

Durant, Samuel W.
1877   *History of Oakland County, Michigan.* Philadelphia: L. H. Everts and Co.

————
1880   *History of Kalamazoo County, Michigan.* Philadelphia: Everts and Abbott.

Eaton, John Henry
1829   Report from the Secretary of War, February 9, 1829. 20th Congress 2nd Session. #72.

Eby, Cecil
1973   *That Disgraceful Affair, the Black Hawk War.* New York: W. W. Norton & Co.

Edmunds, R. David
1978   *The Potawatomis, Keepers of the Fire.* Norman: University of Oklahoma Press.

Edwards, Ninian Wirt
1870   *History of Illinois, from 1778 to 1833; and Life and Times of Ninian Edwards.* Springfield: Illinois State Journal Company.

Eid, Leroy V.
1979   The Ojibwa-Iroquois War: The War the Five Nations Did Not Win. *Ethnohistory* 26 (4): 297-324.

Ellis, Franklin
1879   *History of Genessee County Michigan.* Philadelphia: Everts and Abbott.

Ellis, Albert G.
1856   Some Account of the Advent of the New York Indians into Wisconsin. *Collections of the State Historical Society of Wisconsin* 2: 415-49. Madison.

Ellwood, E. M.
1977   The Robinson Treaties of 1850. MS. B.A. Thesis, Wilfred Laurier University.

Ensign
1855   *Map of Minnesota and Part of Wisconsin.* New York: Ensign, Bridgman & Fanning.

Epping, Charlotte S. J., trans.
1911   *Journal of DuRoithe Elder, Lieutenant and Adjutant, in the Service of the Duke of Brunswick, 1776-1778.* New York: Publications of the University of Pennsylvania, Americana Germanica No. 15, D. Appleton & Co.

Esarey, Logan
1915-1918   *History of Indiana.* Indianapolis: B. F. Bowen & Co.

————,ed.
1922   *Messages and Letters of William Henry Harrison.* 2 vols. Indianapolis: Indiana Historical

Commission.

Espenshade, A. Howry

1925   *Pennsylvania Place Names.* State College, Pa.: The Pennsylvania State College.

Everett, Franklin

1878   *Memorials of the Grand River Valley.* Chicago: The Legal News Company.

Fancher, Isaac A.

1911   *Past and Present of Isabella County, Michigan.* Indianapolis: B. F. Bowen.

Farmer, John

1830   *Map of the Territories of Michigan and Ouisconsin.* Engraved by R. Clarke & Co., Albany, N.Y. Detroit: John Farmer.

———

1836   An Improved Edition of a map of the Surveyed part of the Territory of Michigan. New York: J. H. Colton.

———

1860   *Map of the States of Michigan and Wisconsin embracing a great part of Iowa, Illinois & Minnesota and the whole Mineral Region with Charts of The Lakes.* Inset maps: A Geological Map of Isle Royal, Lake Superior, Beaver Isles, Connection of Private Claims with Public Surveys at Pte. Ste. Ignace. Detroit. John Farmer.

———

1867   *Map of the State of Michigan and Surrounding Country.* Detroit: John Farmer.

——— and Traugott Bromme

1834   *Karte von Michigan.* Bound in Traugott Bromme, *Michigan.* Baltimore: C. Shield & Co.

Faulkner, Charles H.

1961   *An Archaeological Survey of Marshall County.* Indianapolis: Indiana Historical Bureau.

Feiler, Seymour, ed. and trans.

1962   *Jean-Bernard Bossu's Travels in the Interior of North America 1751-1752.* Norman: University of Oklahoma Press.

Fenton, William N.

1940   Problems Arising from the Historic Northeastern Position of the Iroquois, in *Essays in Historical Anthropology of North America.* Smithsonian Miscellaneous Collections, 100. Washington, D.C.

Ferguson, Roger James

1972   The White River Indiana Delawares: An Ethnohistorical Synthesis, 1795-1867. MS. Ph.D. dissertation, Ball State University. Muncie, Indiana.

Finley, James B.

1840   *History of the Wyandot Mission at Upper Sandusky, Ohio, under the Direction of the Methodist Episcopal Church.* Cincinnati: J. F. Wright and L. Swormstedt.

———

1853   *Pioneer in the West, the Autobiography of Rev. James B. Finley.* Cincinnati: Printed at the Methodist Book Concern, for the Author.

Fliegel, Carl J., comp.

1970   *Index to the Records of the Moravian Missions among the Indians of North America.* New Haven: Research Publications. Xerox copy, The Newberry Library.

Folwell, William Watts

1921   *A History of Minnesota.* 4 vols. St. Paul: Minnesota Historical Society.

Forsyth, Thomas

1812   Chart of the Country Southwest of Lake Huron. MS. State Historical Society of Wisconsin, Madison.

———

1880   Fort Snelling: Col. Leavenworth's Expedition to Establish it, in 1819. *Collections of the Minnesota Historical Society,* 3:139-67. St. Paul.

———

Thomas Forsyth Papers. Missouri Historical Society, St. Louis.

Fowler, Melvin L.

1969   Explorations into Cahokia archaeology. *Illinois Archaeological Survey Inc. Bulletin* 7. University of Illinois, Urbana.

Fox, Truman B.

1868   *History of Saginaw County, from the year 1819 down to the present time.* East Saginaw: Enterprise Print.

Franquelin, Jean Baptiste Louis

[1684]   Carte de la Louisiane ou des voyages du Sr. de la Salle & des pays qu'il a découverts depuis la Nouvelle France jusqu'au Golfe Mexique, les années 1679, 80, 81 & 82. Paris. Reproduced in *The Jesuit Relations and Allied Documents,* 63. Ed. by Reuben G. Thwaites. Cleveland, 1900.

———

[1686]   Amerique Septentrionelle. Composée corrigée et aumentée Sur les Journaux et Observations les plus justes que en on ete ftes en l'annee 1685-1686 parplusieurs Particuliers. Service Hydrographique Bibliothèque, Paris. MS. B 4040-6. Photostat in Karpinski Collection.

———

[1688]   Carte de I'Amerique Septentrionnelle depuis le 25 :jusqu'au 65: deg. de latt. & environ 140: & 235 deg. de longitude Contenant les pays de Canada ou Nouvelle France, la Louisiane, la Floride, Virginie, Nlle. Suede, Nlle. York, Nlle. Angleterre, Acadie, Isle de Terre-Nueve & C: . . . en l'Anne 1688. Reproduced in *Indian Villages of the Illinois Country,* Sara Jones Tucker, comp. Springfield: Illinois State Museum, 1942.

Fulkerson, Alva Otis, ed.

1915   *History of Davis County, Indiana.* Indianapolis: B. F. Bowen & Co.

Gagnieur, Fr. William, S. J.

1918   Indian Place Names in the Upper Peninsula and their Interpretation. *Michigan History Magazine* 2:526-55.

———

1919   Some Place Names in the Upper Peninsula of Michigan and Elsewhere. *Michigan History Magazine* 3:412-19.

Gates, Charles M.
1933   *Five Fur Traders of the Northwest, Being the Narrative of Peter Pond and the Diaries of John Macdonell, Archibald N. McLeod, Hugh Faries, and Thomas Connor.* Minneapolis: Minnesota Historical Society.

Gates, Lilliam F.
1968   *Land Policies of Upper Canada.* Toronto: University of Toronto Press.

Gibson, Arrell M.
1963   *The Kickapoos: Lords of the Middle Border.* Norman: University of Oklahoma Press.

Gilpin, Alex R.
1958   *The War of 1812 in the Old Northwest.* East Lansing: Michigan State University Press.

Gist, Christopher
1893   *Christopher Gist's Journals.* Ed. by William M. Darlington. Cincinnati: Arthur H. Clarke.

Glover, Richard, ed.
1962   *David Thompson's Narrative 1784-1812.* Toronto: The Champlain Society.

Gorrell, James
1903   Lieutenant James Gorrell's Journal of 1762. *Collections of the State Historical Society of Wisconsin* 1 :25-48, Madison.

Gratiot Co.
1884   *Portrait and Biographical Album of Gratiot County, Michigan.* Chicago: Chapman Brothers.

Gray, Elma E. and L. R. Gray
1956   *Wilderness Christians: The Moravian Mission to the Delaware Indians.* Toronto: Macmillan and Co.

Gray, Leslie R., ed.
1954   From Bethlehem to Fairfield. Part II, *Ontario History,* 46 (2):107-31.

Graymont, Barbara
1972   *The Iroquois in the American Revolution.* Syracuse, N.Y.: Syracuse University Press.

Greeley, Aaron
1847   Plan of private claims in Michigan Territory 1810, in U.S. 19th Congress. 2nd Session. 1846-47. Senate Doc. 221. Ser. 495.

Green, Evarts B. and Virginia D. Harrington
1932   *American Population before the Federal Census of 1790.* New York: Columbia University Press.

Griffin, James B.
1943   *The Fort Ancient Aspect, Its Cultural and Chronological Position in Mississippi Valley Archaeology.* Ann Arbor: University of Michigan Press.

———

1960   A Hypothesis for the Prehistory of the Winnebago. *In Culture in History: Essays in Honor of Paul Radin,* ed. by Stanley Diamond. New York: Columbia University Press.

Guernsey, E. Y., comp.
1933   *Indiana: The Influence of the Indian upon its History–with Indian and French Names for Natural and Cultural Locations.* State of Indiana Department of Conservation, Publication No. 122.

Guillet, Edwin C., ed.
1957   *The Valley of the Trent.* Toronto: Champlain Society.

Gussow, Zachary
1974   An Anthropological Report on Indian Use and Occupancy of Royce Areas 64 and 120, and An Ethnological Report on the Historic Habitat of the Sauk, Fox and Iowa Indians. *Sac, Fox and Iowa Indians* I: An Anthropological Report. New York: Garland Publishing Co.

Hagan, William T.
1949   Black Hawk's Route Through Wisconsin. (Mimeographed publication of the State Historical Society of Wisconsin, Madison.)

———

1958   *The Sac and Fox Indians.* Norman: University of Oklahoma Press.

———

1976   *Longhouse Diplomacy and Frontier Warfare: The Iroquois Confederacy in the American Revolution.* Albany, N.Y.: New York State American Revolution Bicentennial CommisSIon.

Haldimand Papers
n.d.   British Museum Additional Manuscripts 21, 760, 223. Public Archives of Canada, Ottawa.

———

1765?   A list of the Number of Men able to bear arms in the different Indian nations. British Museum, 21, 671, 312 (B11, 436).

———

1782   Denobrement des Indiens residents dans le district du Detroit pour l'anée 1782. British Museum 21, 783, 282 (B123, 352). Public Archives of Canada, Ottawa.

Hall, Robert L.
1962   *The Archaeology of Carcajou Point, with an Interpretation of the Development of Oneota Culture in Wisconsin.* 2 vols. Madison: University of Wisconsin Press.

Hamil, Frederick Coyne
1939   *Sally Ainse, Fur Trader.* Detroit: Algonquin Club.

———

1951   *The Valley of the Lower Thames 1640 to 1850.* Toronto: University of Toronto Press.

Hanna, Charles A.
1911   *The Wilderness Trail.* 2 vols. New York and

London: G. P. Putnam's Sons.

Harland, Elizabeth Taft, et aI., eds.
1961 *1830 Federal Census: Territory of Michigan.* Detroit, Mich.: Society for Genealogical Research.

Hast, Adele
1978 Mapping Iroquois History, presented at Iroquois Conference, Rensselaerville, N.Y., October 15. MS and maps in *Atlas* files.

Hatch, Judge
1880 Centennial Address. *Leelanau County, Historical and Descriptive.* Traverse Bay: A.]. Johnson, Compiler.

Heckewelder, John
1820 *Narrative of the Mission of the United Brethren among the Delaware and Mohegan Indians from its commencement, in the year 1740 to the Close of the year 1808.* Philadelphia: McCarty and Davis.

———
1884 *Map and Description of Northeastern Ohio by Rev. John Heckewelder, 1796.* Cleveland: W. W. Williams.

Heidenreich, Conrad
1971 *Huronia, A History and Geography of the Huron Indians, 1600-1650.* Toronto: McClelland & Stewart.

Herrington, M. Eleanor
1921 Captain John Deserontyou and the Mohawk Settlement at Deseronto. *Queens Quarterly* 29 (2):165-80.

Hexom, Charles Philip
1913 *Indian History of Winneshiek County.* Decorah, Iowa: A. K. Bailey & Son, Ine.

Hickerson, Harold
1956 The Genesis of a Trading Post Band: The Pembina Chippewa. *Ethnohistory* 3 (4):289-345.

———
1974a *Chippewa Indians II:* Ethnohistory of Mississippi Bands and Pillager and Winnibigoshish Bands of Chippewa. New York and London: Garland Publishing Co.

———
1974b *Chippewa Indians III:* Ethnohistory of Chippewa of Lake Superior. New York: Garland Publishing Co.

———
1974c *Chippewa Indians IV:* Ethnohistory of Chippewa in Central Minnesota. New York and London: Garland Publishing Co.

———
1974d *Sioux Indians I:* Mdewakanton Band of Sioux Indians. New York: Garland Publishing Co.

Hicks, Trudy
1978 Iroquois and the Fur Trade of Western Canada. MS. Revision of paper presented at Fur Trade Conference, May 4-6, Winnipeg.

Higgenbotham, Don
1971 *The War of American Independence, Military Attitudes, Policies, and Practices, 1763-1789.* New York: The Macmillan Company.

Higgins, Ruth L.
1931 *Expansion in New York.* Columbus: Ohio State University Press.

Hildreth, Samuel P.
1848 *Pioneer History: Being an account of the first examination of the Ohio Valley and the early settlement of the Northwest Territory.* Cincinnati: H. W. Derby & Co.; New York: A. S. Barnes.

Hill, Leonard U.
1957 *John Johnston and the Indians in the Land of the Three Miamis.* Piqua, Ohio: Printed for the author by the Stoneman Press, Columbus.

Hinman, Marjory Barnum
1975 *Onaquaga: Hub of the Border Wars of the American Revolution in New York State.* Windsor, N.Y.: Valley Ofsett.

Hinsdale, Wilbur B.
1931 *Archaeological Atlas of Michigan.* Ann Arbor: University of Michigan Press.

Historical Society of Michigan
1980 Historical Madison, *The Historical Society of Michigan Newsletter* 5, 5.

Hodge, Frederick Webb, ed.
1907-1911 *Handbook of North American Indians.* 2 vols. Bureau of American Ethnology Bulletin 30. Washington.

Horsman, Reginald
1964 *Matthew Elliott: British Indian Agent.* Detroit: Wayne State University Press.

Houck, Louis
1909 *The Spanish Regime in Missouri.* 2 vols. Chicago: R. R. Donnelley & Sons.

Hough, Franklin B.
1866 *Proceedings of the Commissioner of Indian Affairs.* 2 vols. Albany: J. Munsell.

Howard, James J.
1976 Yanktonnai Ethnohistory and the John K. Bear Winter Count. *Plains Anthropologist* 21 (2).

Howe, Henry
1898 *Historical Collections of Ohio.* 2 vols. Norwalk, Ohio: The Laning Printing Col.

Hubbard, Bela
1887 *Memorials of a Half Century.* New York: G. P. Putnam's Sons.

Hubbard, Gurdon Saltonstall
1911 *The Autobiography of Gurdon Saltonstall Hubbard.* Chicago: The Lakeside Press.

Hughes, Thomas
1929 *Old Traverse des Sioux.* St. Paul, Minnesota: Herald Publishing Company.

Hunt, George T.
1967 *The Wars of the Iroquois: A Study in Intertribal Trade Relations.* Madison, Wisc.

Hunt, John Elliott
1979 *The John Hunt Memoirs: Early Years of the Maumee Basin, 1812-1835.* Ed. by Richard J.

Wright. Maumee, Ohio: Maumee Valley Historical Society.

Hutchins, Thomas
1778   *A Topographical Description of Virginia, Pennsylvania, Maryland and North Carolina, comprehending the Rivers Ohio, Kenhawa, Sioto, Cherokee, Wabash, Illinois, Mississippi, etc. . . .* London: Printed for the author.

_____
1942   *The Course of the Ohio.* Ed. by Beverly W. Bond, Jr. Cincinnati, Ohio: Historical and Philosophical Society of Ohio.

Illinois
1960-1961   Illinois Archaeological Survey. Bulletins 1 and 2. Springfield.

Indian Claims Commission
1974   Commission Findings of the Sac, Fox and Iowa Indians. *Sac, Fox and Iowa Indians,* 3. New York: Garland Publishing Co.

Inglis, James Gale
1898   *Northern Michigan. Handbook for Travelers. Including the Northern Part of Lower Michigan, Mackinac Island and the Sault St. Marie River.* Petoskey, Mich.: G. E. Sprang

Ireland-Smith, A.
1980   *Research Report on the Issues Concerning the Interests of the St. Regis Akwesasne Indian Band in the St. Lawrence River and the Islands Therein.* Toronto: Ministry of Natural Resources, Office of Indian Research Policy.

Isabella
1884   *Portrait and Biographical Album of Isabella County.* Chicago: Chapman Bros.

Jablow, Joseph
1974   *Indians of Illinois and Indiana: Illinois, Kickapoo, and Potawatomi Indians.* New York: Garland Publishing Co.

Jackson, Donald D.
1962   The Black Hawk War, *The Palimpsest* 43:65-94.

James, James Alton, ed.
1912   *George Rogers Clark Papers 1771-1781. Collections of the Illinois State Historical Library,* 8. Springfield: Illinois State Historical Library.

Jameson, Anna Brownell
1838   *Winter Studies and Summer Rambles in Canada.* 3 vols. London: Saunders and Otley.

Jameson, J. F., ed.
1909   *Narratives of New Netherland 1609-1664.* New York: Scribner's.

Jenkins, Warren
1837   *The Ohio Gazeteer and Traveler's Guide.* Columbus: I. N. Whiting.

Jenks, Albert E.
1900   The Wild Rice Gatherers of the Upper Lakes: A Study in American Primitive Economics. *19th Annual Report of the Bureau of American Ethnology for the years 1897-1898,* 1013-113 7 . Washington.

Jenks, William Lee
1912   *St. Clair County, Michigan, Its History and Its People,* New York and Chicago: Lewis Publishing Co.

Jipson, N. W.
1923   Winnebago Villages and Chieftains of the Lower Rock River Region. *The Wisconsin Archaeologist* 2:125-39. New Series.

Johnson, Crissfield, ed.
1880   *Allegan and Barry Counties of Michigan.* Philadelphia: S. W. Ensign & Co.

Johnson, Guy
1781   General Abstract of the Ohio Dependents and Confederates of the Six Nations as returned by Mr. McKee, Niagara, 1 June 1781 in Haldimand Papers Britsih Museum 21, 769, 122.

Johnson, Ida A.
1919   *The Michigan Fur Trade.* Lansing: Michigan Historical Commission.

Johnson, Leo
1973   *History of the County of Ontario.* Whitby: Corporation of the County of Ontario.

Johnson, Thomas H.
1912   The Indian Village of Cush-og-wenk. *Ohio Archaeological and Historical Publications* 21 :432-35. Columbus.

Johnson, Sir William
1921-1951   *The Papers of Sir William Johnson.* Eds. James Sullivan, Alexander C. Flick, Almon W. Lauber, Milton W. Hamilton, and Albert B. Corey. 15 vols. Albany: The University of the State of New York.

_____
1942   Memorandum on the Six Nations and other Confederacies 1763. *Johnson Papers* 4:240-46.

_____
1951   Letter of July 29, 1761. *Johnson Papers* 10:324.

Johnston, Charles Murray, ed.
1963   Joseph Brant, the Grand River Lands and the Northwest Crisis. *Ontario History.* 15 (4): 267-82.

_____
1964   *The Valley of the Six Nations: A Collection of Documents on the Indian Lands of the Grand River.* Toronto: University of Toronto Press.

Johnston, John
1960   An Account of Lake Superior 1792-1807. *Les Bourgeois de la Compagnie du Nord-Ouest.* Ed. by L. R. Masson. 2 vols, 2:135-74. Quebec: A. Coté et Cie.

Johnston, William
1909   Letters on the Fur Trade 1833. *Michigan Pioneer and Historical Society Collections* 37: 132- 207. Lansing.

Jones, Dallas Lee
1952   The Survey and Sale of the Public Land in

Michigan, 1815-1862. MS. M.A. thesis, Cornell University, Ithaca, N.Y.

Jones, David
1865   *A Journal of Two visits made to some Natives of Indians on the West Side of the River Ohio in the Years 1772 and 1773.* New York: Reprinted for Joseph Sabin.

Jones, H. Bedford
1917   *L'Arbre Croche Mission.* Santa Barbara: [The Author].

Jones, J. A.
1974a   Anthropological Report on the Indian Occupancy of Royce Area 87. *Indians of Western Illinois and Southern Wisconsin.* New York: Garland Publishing Co.

——— 1974b   Winnebago Ethnology. Winnebago Indians. New York and London: Garland Publishing Co.

Jones, Peter
1860   *Life and Journals of Kay-Ke-Wa-Qua-Na-By* (Peter Jones) Toronto: Wesleyan Printing Establishment.

Kaatz, Martin
1955   The Settlement of the Black Swamp of Northwestern Ohio. Ph.D. Thesis, The University of Michigan, MS No. 3150.

Kane, Lucille M., June D. Holmquist, and Carolyn Gilman, eds.
1978   *The Northern Expeditions of Stephen H. Long: The Journals of 1817 and 1823 and Related Documents.* St. Paul: Minnesota Historical Society Press.

Kappler, Charles J., comp. and ed.
1972   *Indian Treaties 1778-1883.* New York: Interland Publishing Co. (Reprint of Vol. 2 of *Indian Affairs: Laws and Treaties* pub. by Government Printing Office, Washington, 1904.)

Kay, Jeanne
1977   The Land of La Baye: The Ecological Impact of the Green Bay Fur Trade, 1634-1836. MS. Ph.D. dissertation, University of Wisconsin.

——— 1979   Wisconsin Indian Hunting Patterns, 1634-1836. *Annals of the Association of American Geographers* 69 (3):402-18.

Keating, William H.
1826   *Narrative of an Expedition to the Source of St. Peter's River, Lake Winnepeek, Lake of the Woods, etc. Performed in the Year 1823.* 2 vols. Philadelphia: H. C. Carey and I. Lea.

Keesing, Felix M.
     Leaders of the Menomini Tribe: A Sketch from the Contemporary Records and from the Memories of Old Indians Today. Typescript circa 1930. MSS., State Historical Society of Wisconsin, Madison.

——— 1939   The Menomini Indians of Wisconsin: A

Study of Three Centuries of Culture, Contact and Change. *Memoirs of the American Philosophical Society* 10. Philadelphia.

Kellogg, Louise Phelps
1916   *Frontier Advance on the Upper Ohio, 1778-1779.* Madison: State Historical Society of Wisconsin.

——— 1917   *Frontier Rétreat on the Upper Ohio, 1779-1781.* Madison: State Historical Society of Wisconsin.

——— 1925   *The French Régime in Wisconsin and the Northwest.* Madison: State Historical Society of Wisconsin.

——— 1935   *The British Regime in Wisconsin and the Northwest.* Madison: State Historical Society of Wisconsin.

Kemble, W. Esq.
1850   *Map of Minnesota.* New York: Harper & Brothers.

Kent, Donald H.
1938   The Frontier Forts and Trails Survey of Northwestern Pennsylvania, *Pennsylvania Archaeologist,* 8:3-5.

——— 1974   History of Pennsylvania Purchases from the Indians. *Iroquois Indians* 1. New York: Garland Publishing Co.

Kentucky Gazette
1787   Speeches of Captain Johnny, Chief of the Shawnee Nation, and Colonel Benjamin Logan at Limestone, August 20, 1787, published August 25, 1787. (Photostat from Lexington Public Library by University of Michigan Library in 1918. Vol. 1 1787-1788.) Copy in The Newberry Library, Chicago.

Kilbourn, John
1831   *The Ohio Gazetteer: or Topographical Dictionary.* 10th ed. Columbus: J. Kilbourn.

Kingsbury, Robert C.
1970   *An Atlas of Indiana.* Bloomington: Dept. of Geography, Indiana University.

Kinietz, W. Vernon
1940   *The Indians of the Western Great Lakes, 1617-1760.* University of Michigan Museum of Anthropology, Occasional Contribution 10. Ann Arbor.

Kinnaird, Lawrence
1932   The Spanish Expedition Against Fort St. Joseph in 1781: A New Interpretation. *Mississippi Valley Historical Review* 19:173-91.

——— 1964-1949   *Spain in the Mississippi Valley, 1651-1794.* 3 parts. Annual Report of the American Historical Association for the Year 1945. Washington, D.C.

Kinzie, John Harris
1829   Winnebago Census enclosed in Cass to Mc-

Kenney 15 March, 1830. Record Group 77, Office of Indian Affairs "Letters Received."

——

1829-1831   Schedule of the Number and names of the different Winnebago villages–number of lodges and persons in each, with the names of the Head chiefs of each village. MS. U.S. Manuscripts, Transcripts from Indian Office Files, Box 63, 1829-1831, State Historical Society of Wisconsin, Madison.

Kinzie, Juliette A.
1932   *Wau-bun, The Early Days in the Northwest.* Intro. by Milo M. Quaife. Chicago: The Lakeside Press, R. R. Donnelley and Sons.

Klinck, Carl F. and James J. Talman, ed.
1970   *The Journal of Major John Norton, 1816.* Toronto: Champlain Society.

Kip, William I.
1846   *The Early Jesuit Missions in North America.* New York: Wiley & Putnam.

Klopfenstein, Carl G.
1976   The Removal of the Indians from Ohio. *The Historic Indian in Ohio.* Ed. by Randall L. Buchman. Columbus: Ohio Historical Society.

Knapp, Horace S.
1872   *History of the Maumee Valley.* Toledo, Ohio: Blade Publishing House.

Kohl, Johann G.
1860   *Kitchi-Gami: Wanderings Round Lake Superior.* London: Chapman and Hall.

Konrad, Victor A.
1977   Iroquois Villages on the North Shore of Lake Ontario: Change and Continuity in Late Seventeenth Century Illinois Settlement. Preliminary draft. MS copy in *Atlas* files, The Newberry Library, Chicago.

——

1981   An Iroquois Frontier: The North Shore of Lake Ontario during the late seventeenth century. *Journal of Historical Geography,* 7 (2):129-44.

Krauskopf, Frances, ed.
1955   Ouiatenon Documents. *Indiana Historical Society* 18 (2):[131]-234. Indianapolis.

Kuchler, A. W.
1964   *Potential Natural Vegetation of the Conterminous United States.* Special Publication No. 36. New York: American Geographical Society.

Kuhm, Herbert W.
1952   Indian Place-Names in Wisconsin. *The Wisconsin Archaeologist,* 33:1-157.

Lajeunesse, E. J., ed.
1960   *The Windsor Border Region, Canada's Southernmost Frontier: A Collection of Documents.* Toronto: The Champlain Society.

Lambert, Joseph L.
1939   The Black Hawk War: A Military Analysis. *Journal of the Illinois State Historical Society* 32:442-73.

Lang, William
1880   *History of Seneca County from the Close of the Revolutionary War to July,* 1880. Springfield, Ohio: Transcript Printing Co.

Lanman, James H.
1839   *History of Michigan, Civil and Topographical, in a Compendious Form; with a View of the Surrounding Lakes.* New York: E. French.

Lass, William E.
1980   *Minnesota's Boundary with Canada: Its Evolution Since 1783.* St. Paul: Minnesota Historical Society Press.

Lawson, Publius V.
1907   The Habitat of the Winnebago, 1632-1832. *Proceedings of the State Historical Society of Wisconsin,* 144-66.

——

1908   *History of Winnebago County, Wisconsin.* Chicago: C. F. Cooper & Co.

Leach, Morgan
1884   *A History of Grand Traverse Region.* Traverse City, Mich.: The Grand Traverse Herald.

Le Baron, William
1978   *History of Will County.* Chicago: W. Le Baron Jr. & Co.

Lees, John
1911   *Journal of John Lees, of Quebec, Merchant.* Ed. by C. M. Burton. Detroit: Speaker-Hines Press.

Leeson, Michael
1881   *History of Saginaw County, Michigan.* Chicago: C. C. Chapman & Co.

Leggett, Conway & Co.
1884   *History of Wyandot County, Ohio.* Chicago: Leggett, Conway & Co.

Leighton, Douglas
1975   The Development of Federal Indian Policy in Canada, 1840-1890. MS. Ph.D. thesis, University of Western Ontario.

——

1977   The Manitoulin Incident of 1863: An Indian-White Confrontation in the Province of Canada. *Ontario History* 69, (2):113-24.

Lemon, James T.
1972   *The Best Poor Man's Country, A Geographical Study of East Southeastern Pennsylvania.* Baltimore: Johns Hopkins Press.

Levi, Sister M. Clarissa
1956   *Chippewa Indians of Yesterday and Today.* New York: Pageant Press.

Lewis, Henry
1854   *Das Illustrierte Mississipithal.* Dusseldorf: Institute von Arnz & Co.

——

1967   *Valley of the Mississippi.* Ed. by Bertha L. Heilbron. St. Paul: Minnesota Historical Society.

Lewis, Rundall M.
1957   Diary of Mahlon Burwell. *Ontario History* 49 (4):199-219.

Libby, Dorothy
1974   *An Anthropological Report on the Piankashaw Indians.* New York: Garland Publishing Co.

Lindley, Jacob, Joseph Moore and Oliver Paxon
1892   Expedition to Detroit, 1793. *Michigan Historical Collections* 17: 565-671. Lansing.

List
1892   List, Location and Number of Indians, (Probably in 1789) *Michigan Pioneer and Historical Society Collections* 20: 305-307.

Littell, Edmund M.
1937   Leelanau County. *Leelanau Enterprise,* July 15.

Lizars, Robina and Kathleen Macfarlane Lizars
1896   *In the Days of the Canada Company:* The Story of the Settlement of the Huron Tract and a view of the social life of the Period. Toronto: W. Briggs; Montreal: C. W. Coates.

Lockwood, James H.
1856   Early Times and Events in Wisconsin. Appendix No.6. *Collections of the State Historical Society of Wisconsin* 2: 98-196. Madison.

Long, John
1791   *Voyages and Travels of an Indian Interpreter and Trader.* London: Printed for the author.

———
1904   (*Voyages and Travels*). Ed. by Reuben Gold Thwaites. *Early Western Travels* 2. Cleveland: Arthur H. Clarke.

Long, Major Stephen H.
1860   *Voyage in a Six-Oared Skiff to the Falls of Saint Anthony in 1817.* Philadelphia: Henry B. Ashmead, printer. Printed in *Collections of the Historical Society of Minnesota* 2:9-82.

Lossing, Benson J.
1868   *The Pictorial Field Book of the War of 1812.* New York: Harper & Brothers.

Lurie, Nancy Oestreich
1952   The Winnebago Indians: A Study in Cultural Change. MS. Ph.D. dissertation in anthropology, Northwestern University, Evanston, Ill.

———
1960   Winnebago Protohistory. *Culture in History: Essays in Honor of Paul Radin.* Ed. by Stanley Diamond, 790-808. New York: Columbia University Press.

———
1980   *Wisconsin Indians.* Madison: State Historical Society of Wisconsin.

Lyon, Lucius
1846   Transcript of a certified copy of one from the Office of Indian Affairs exhibiting the relative positions of the fishing and encamping ground, the stop selected for the use of the Indian Department, and the various claims to public lands; transmitted to the Secretary of War by Henry R. Schoolcraft, Esqr., August 9, 1823, and now on file in that office. MS.

Detroit: Surveyor General's Office. Feb. 9, 1846. Copy R.G. 59-4 Folder 01027, Michigan State Archives, Lansing.

MPHC
1877-   *Collections and Researches of the Michigan Pioneer and Historical Society.* 40 vols. Lansing: Michigan Historical Commission.

McAfee, Robert B.
1816   *History of the Late War in the Western Country.* Lexington, Ky.: Worlsey & Smith.

McAllister, J. Gilbert
1932   *The Archaeology of Porter County. Indiana History Bulletin,* 10 (1).

Macaulay, J. B.
1839   Report on Indian Affairs submitted to Lieutenant Governor Sir George Arthur. MS. Record Group 10, vol. 718. Public Archives of Canada, Ottawa.

McCarty, Richard
1779?   List of the Different Indian Nations up the Mississippi. . . Toward Michilimackinac. Draper MSS 2U68. State Historical Society of Wisconsin, Madison.

McClung, J. W.
1870   *Minnesota as it is in 1870.* St. Paul: By the Author.

McCord, Shirley, comp.
1970   *Travel Accounts of Indiana 1679-1961: A Collection of Observations by Wayfaring Foreigners, Itinerants, and Peripatetic Hoosiers.* Indiana Historical Collections, 47, Indianapolis: Indiana Historical Society.

McCoy, Isaac
1840   *History of the Baptist Indian Missions.* New York and Washington: William M. Morrison.

McDonald
n.d.   McDonald Collection. MSS. Hiram Walker Museum, Windsor, Ont.

McDowell, John E.
1972   Madame La Framboise. *Michigan History* 56 (4):271-86.

Mack, Edwin S.
1907   The Founding of Milwaukee. *Proceedings of the State Historical Society of Wisconsin:* 194-207. Madison.

McKenney, Thomas L.
1827   *Sketches of a Tour to the Lakes, of the Character and Customs of the Chippeway Indians and of incidents connected with the Treaty of Fond du Lac.* Baltimore: Fielding Lucas, Jr.

———
1830   Letter to John Bell. March, 1830. Microfilm Publication 21, Roll 6. Washington: National Archives.

———
1846   *Memoirs, Official and Personal with Sketches of Travels among the Northern and Southern Indians, etc.* New York: Paine and Burgess.

McKenney, Thomas L. and James Hall
1854   *History of the Indian Tribes of North America.* 2 vols. Philadelphia: D. Rice and A. N.

Hart.

MacLeod, Normand
1978   *Detroit to Fort Sackville, 1778-1779: The Journal of Normand McLeod.* Ed. by William A. Evans. Detroit: Wayne University Press.

McLoughlin, John
c. 1807   Dr. McLoughlin's Description of the Indians from Fort William to Lake of the Woods. MS. John McLoughlin Papers, Minnesota Historical Society. Original in Masson Papers, McGill University Library, Montreal.

MacNeish, Richard S.
1976   The *In Situ* Iroquois Revisited and Rethought. In *Culture Change and Continuity: Essays in Honor of James Bennett Griffin.* Ed. by Charles E. Cleland. New York: Academic Press, Inc.

McPherron, Alan
1967   The Juntunen Site and the Late Woodland Prehistory of the Upper Great Lakes Area. *University of Michigan Museum of Anthropology, Anthropological Paper No. 30.* Ann Arbor.

Maguire, Ronald C.
1980   *An Historical Reference Guide to The Stone Fort Treaty.* (Treaty One, 1871) Ottawa, Canada: Department of Indian and Northern Affairs.

Mahon, John K.
1972   *The War of 1812.* Gainesville: University of Florida Press.

Mallery, Garrick.
1877   A Calendar of the Dakota Nation. *Bulletin of the United States Geological and Geographical Survey of the Territories* 1877, 3.

Manistique
1960   *Manistique Centennial; Official Souvenir Book.* Manistique, Mich.

Maps
1968   *Maps of Indiana Counties in 1876.* Indianapolis: [Reprinted from *Illustrated Historical Atlas of the State of Indiana.* Chicago: Baskin, Forster and Co., 1876.]

Marin, Joseph
1975   *Journal of Joseph Marin, French Colonial Explorer and Military Commander in the Wisconsin Country, August 7,1753-June 20, 1754.* Ed. and trans. by Kenneth P. Bailey. Los Angeles: Printed for the Author.

Marshall, Peter
1967   Sir William Johnson and the Treaty of Fort Stanwix, 1768. *American Studies* 1: 149-79.

Martin, Morgan L.
1888   Narrative of Morgan L. Martin. *Collections of the State Historical Society of Wisconsin* 11 :385-415. Madison.

Martindale, Charles, ed.
1888   Loughery's defeat and Pigeon Roost Massacre. *Indiana Historical Society Publications* 2:128-34. Indianapolis: The Bobbs-Merrill Company.

Mason, Carol I.
1976   Historic Identification and Lake Winnebago Focus Oneonta. In *Culture Change and Continuity: Essays in Honor of James Bennett Griffin.* Ed. by Charles E. Cleland. New York: Academic Press, Inc.

Masson, Louis F., ed.
1889-1890   *Les Bourgeois de fa Compagnie du Nord-Ouest.* 2 vols. Quebec: A. Coté et Cie.

Matson, Nehemiah
1880   *Memories of Shaubena.* Second edition. Chicago: Donnelley, Gassette & Lloyd.

Meacham, J. L.
1878   *Illustrated Historical Atlas of Frontenac, Lennox and Addington Counties, Ontario.* Toronto: J. L. Meacham & Co.

Mealing, Stanley R., ed.
1967   *The Jesuit Relations and Allied Documents; a Selection.* Toronto: Macmillan of Canada.

Melish, John
1819   *Map of Indiana,* prepared by John Melish, the surveys furnished by Burr Bradley. Philadelphia: Melish & Harrison.

Melsheimer, F. V.
1861   Journal of the Voyages of the Brunswick Auxiliaries from Wolfenbuttel to Quebec . . . *Literary and Historical Society of Quebec, Transactions,* New Series, No. 20.

Menard, Peter
1830   Letter to William Clark, 12 November, 1830. MS. William Clark Papers. Kansas State Historical Society. Topeka, Kans.

Meyer, Alfred H.
1954   *Circulation and Settlement Patterns of the Calumet Region of Northwest Indiana and Northeast Illinois. The First Stage of Occupance, the Potawatomi and the Fur Trade-1830.* Albany, N.Y.: Reprint from *Annals of the American Geographers* 44: 245-74.

Meyer, Roy H.
1967   *History of the Santee Sioux.* Lincoln: University of Nebraska Press.

Michigan Archaeological Files
            MSS. Museum of Anthropology, The University of Michigan, Ann Arbor.

Milloy, J. S.
1978   The Era of Civilization: British Policy for the Indians of Canada, 1830-1860. MS. Ph.D. thesis, Oxford University.

Mills, James Cooke
1918   *History of Saginaw County.* Saginaw, Mich.: Seeman & Peters.

Minet
[1685]   Carte de la Louisianna—A. embouchure de la Riverre, comme monsieur de la Salle le marque dans sa cart B. costes, et lacs par la hauteur de sa Riverre, comme nous les avons trouvez. MS. C 4044-4, Service Hydrographique Bibliotheque. Paris. Photostat in Kar-

...pinski Collection.

Minnesota

n.d.   Minnesota Archeological Survey, James Jerome Hill House, St. Paul.

Mitchell, Waldo F.

1914   Indiana's Growth 1812-1820. *Indiana Magazine of History,* 10:369-95. Bloomington.

Mitchell, S. Augustus

1870   *Mitchell's New General Atlas.* Philadelphia: S. August Mitchell, Jr.

Mittleholtz, Erwin F., ed.

1957   *Historical Review of the Red Lake Indian Reservation.* Bemidji, Minnesota: General Council of the Red Lake Band of Chippewa Indians and the Beltrami County Historical Society.

Montgomery, Thomas L., ed.

1916   *Report of the Commission to Locate the Site of the Frontier Forts of Pennsylvania.* 2 vols. 2nd ed. Harrisburg, Pa.: W. S. Ray.

[Monroe, James]

1823   Message from the President of the United States Transmitting Information in relation to Certain Christian Indians. . . , 17th Congress, 2nd Session. *Senate Papers.* No.3. Washington: Gales & Seton.

Montour, Enos T.

1973   *The Feathered United Empire Loyalists: an account of the Life and Times of Certain Canadian Native Peoples.* Toronto: Division of Communication (CEMS), United Church of Canada.

Mooney, James

1928   The Aboriginal Population of America North of Mexico. Ed. by John R. Swanton. *Smithsonian Miscellaneous Collections* 80 (7). Washington: The Smithsonian Institution.

Morgan, George

1776-1778   George Morgan Letterbooks. MSS. Carnegie Library, Pittsburgh. Transcripts, Ohio Valley Great Lakes Archives, Indiana University, Bloomington, Ind.

Morris, Alexander

1880   *The Treaties of Canada with the Indians of Manitoba and the North-West Territories.* Toronto: Bellefords, Clarke & Co.

Morris, H. S.

n.d.   *Historical Stories, Legends and Traditions: Roberts County and Northeastern South Dakota.* Sisseton, S.D.: The Sisseton Courier.

Morris, James L.

1943   Indians of Ontario. Toronto: Ontario Department of Lands and Forests.

Morse, Jedediah

1822   *A Report to the Secretary of War on Indian Affairs.* New Haven, Conn.: S. Converse.

Mueller, Paul E.

1963   David Zeisberger's Official Diary. *Transactions of the Moravian Historical Society.* 19 (1).

Murray, Florence B., ed.

1963   *Muskoka and Haliburton 1615-1875: A Collection of Documents* (Ontario Series 6). Toronto: The Champlain Society.

Musick, James B.

1941   *St. Louis as a Fortified Town.* St. Louis: Press of R. R. Miller.

Nasatir, Abraham P.

1928   The Anglo-Spanish Frontier in the Illinois Country During the American Revolution. *Journal of the Illinois State Historical Society* 21 :291-358.

_____

1952   *Before Lewis and Clark: Documents Illustrating the History of the Missouri 1785-1804.* 2 vols. St. Louis: St. Louis Historical Documents Foundation.

_____

1976   *Borderland in Retreat, From Spanish Louisiana to the Far Southwest.* Albuquerque: University of New Mexico Press.

National Archives

1829   Map of Southwestern Wisconsin and Northern Illinois. MS. National Archives, Record Group 77, Map 043. Photostat, State Historical Society of Wisconsin, Madison.

_____

c. 1830   Map of eastern Wisconsin in about 1830. Records of the War Department, Record Group 77, Office of the Chief of Engineers Map 015. Photostat.

Neuenschwander, Herbert E.

1958   Indian Trails and Villages of Dodge County 1834 to 1837. *The Wisconsin Archaeologist,* new series 39 (2):127-29.

New York Legislature: Assembly

1889   *Report of the Special Committee to Investigate the Indian Problem of the State of New York, Appointed by the Assembly of 1888.* Doc. #51. Albany: The Troy Press Co.

Newcomb, William W., Jr.

1956   *The Culture and Acculturation of the Delaware Indians.* University of Michigan Museum of Anthropology, Anthropological Papers 10. Ann Arbor.

Norton, Thomas Elliot

1974   *The Fur Trade in Colonial New York 1686-1776.* Madison, Wisc.

Nouvelle

[c. 1630?]   Nouvelle France, original map on deerskin, undated, in Naval Institute, Taunton, Somerset, England. Copy. The Newberry Library.

Nute, Grace Lee, ed.

1942   *Documents Relating to Northwest Missions, 1815-1827.* St. Paul, Minn.: Minnesota Historical Society Press.

O'Callaghan, Edmund B., ed.

1853-1887   *Documents relative to the Colonial History of the State of New York.* 15 vols. Albany: Weed and Parsons and Co.

———

1857   *Documents Relative to the Colonial History of the State of New York* 8. Albany: Weed and Parsons.

Ojibwe

1973   *Land of the Ojibwe,* developed by the Ojibwe Curriculum Committee, American Indian Studies Department, and Educational Services Division, Minnesota Historical Society. St. Paul: Minnesota Historical Society.

Oliver, David

1903   *Centennial History of Alpena County, Michigan.* Alpena: Argus Printing House.

Ontario

1906   *Third Report of the Bureau of Archives for the Province of Ontario,* 1905. Toronto.

Oppen, William A.

1978   *The Riel Rebellions: A Cartographic History.* Cartographica Monograph No. 21-22. Supplement Nos. 1-2 to *Canadian Cartographer* 15.

Ourada, Patricia K.

1979   *The Menominee Indians: A History.* Norman: University of Oklahoma Press.

Page, H. R.

1882   *History of Manistee, Mason and Oceana Counties, Michigan.* Chicago: H. R. Page & Co.

Parker, Donald Dean, ed.

1966   *The Recollections of Philander Prescott, Frontiersman of the Old Northwest, 1819-1862.* Lincoln: University of Nebraska Press.

Parker, John, ed.

1976   *The Journals of Jonathan Carver and Related Documents.* St. Paul: Minnesota Historical Society Press.

Paterson, Gilbert C.

1921   *Land Settlement in Upper Canada, 1783-1840. Sixteenth Report of the Department of Archives for the Province of Ontario.* Toronto: C. W. James.

Paullin, Charles O. and John K. Wright

1932   Indian Cessions, 1750-1890. *Atlas of the Historical Geography of the United States.* Baltimore: Carnegie Institute of Washington.

Pease, Theodore and Ernestine Jenison, eds.

1940   *Illinois on the eve of the Seven Years War. Collections of the Illinois State Library* 29. Springfield: Illinois State Historical Library.

Peck, John Mason

1834   *A Gazetteer of Illinois in Three Parts.* Jacksonville, Ill.: R. Goudy.

Peckham, Howard H.

1961   *Pontiac and the Indian Uprising.* Chicago: University of Chicago Press.

Peeke, H. L.

1925   *The Centennial History of Erie County, Ohio.* Cleveland: Penton Press.

Perrault, Jean Baptiste

1910   Narrative of the Travels and Adventures of a Merchant Voyageur in the Savage Territories of Northern America Leaving Montreal the 28th of May 1786 to 1820. Edited by John Sharpless Fox, *Michigan Pioneer and Historical Society Collections* 37:508-619. East Lansing.

Peterson, Jacqueline

1978   Prelude to Red River: A Social Portrait of the Great Lakes Metis. *Ethnohistory* 25 (1): 41-67.

Peyser, Joseph

1980   New Cartographic Evidence on Two Disputed French-Regime Fort Locations: Niles' Fort St. Joseph (1691-1781) and the Illinois Fox Fort (1730). *Indiana Military History Journal* 5: (2). Indianapolis: Indiana Historical Society.

Phillips, Paul C.

1926   The Fur Trade in the Maumee-Wabash Country. *Studies in History.* Nos. 66-68. Bloomington: Indiana University.

Pond, Samuel

1908   The Dakota or Sioux in Minnesota as They Were in 1834. *Collections of the Minnesota Historical Society* 12:319-501. St. Paul.

Pooley, Thomas Vipond

1908   The Settlement of Illinois from 1830-1850. *Bulletin of the University of Wisconsin. History Series.* 1 (4):287-595. Madison.

Powell, William

1913   William Powell's Recollections in an Interview with Lyman C. Draper. *Proceedings of the State Historical Society of Wisconsin at its Sixtieth Annual Meeting* (1912),146-79. Madison.

Putnam, Rufus

1903   *The Memoirs of Rufus Putnam.* Rowena Buell, comp. Boston and New York: Houghton, Mifflin & Co.

Quaife, Milo M.

1913   *Chicago and the Old Northwest, 1673-1835.* Chicago: The University of Chicago Press.

———, ed.

1921   *Alexander Henry's Travels and Adventures in the Years 1760-1776.* Chicago: The Lakeside Press.

———

1940   *War on Detroit, The Chronicles of Thomas Vercheres de Boucherville and the Capitulation by an Ohio Volunteer,* Chicago: The Lakeside Press.

Quealey, Francis M.

1968   The Administration of Sir Peregrine Maitland, Lieutenant Governor of Upper Canada 1818-1828. MS. Ph.D. thesis, York University.

Radin, Paul

1923   The Winnebago Tribe. *37th Annual Report of the Bureau of American Ethnology for the Years 1915-1916:* 33-550. Washington.

Rafert, Stewart J.

1982   The Hidden Community: The Miami Indians of Indiana, 1846-1940. MS. Ph.D. dissertation, University of Delaware.

Raisz, Erwin
1957   *Landforms of the United States.* Sixth revised edition, Cambridge, Mass.: Erwin Raisz.

Rawlyck, George A.
1975   The Rising French Empire in the Ohio Valley and the Old Northwest. *Contest for Empire 1500-1775.* Ed. by John B. Elliott. Indianapolis: Indiana Historical Society.

Rayback, Robert J., et al. eds.
1965   Land Patents, Grants, Purchases in New York, 1624-1800. Map in *Richard's Atlas of New York State,* revised and supplemented by Edward L. Towle. Phoenix, N.Y.: F. E. Richards.

Rezek, Antoine Ivan
1906-1907   *History of the Diocese of Sault Ste. Marie and Marquette.* 2 vols. Houghton, Mich., 1906. Vol. 2. Chicago: M. A. Donohue & Co.

Richardson, John
1842   *War of 1812.* Brockville, Ontario.

Rideout, Thomas
1890   An Account of my Capture by the Shawanese Indians dwelling on the River Ohio in North America, and of my residence among them during the Spring and part of the Summer of the Year 1788, in Matilda Edgar, *Ten Years in Upper Canada in Peace and War: 1805-1815.* Appendix, 341-81. Toronto: William Briggs.

Risdon, Orange
1825   *Map of the Surveyed part of the Territory of Michigan.* Albany: Rawdon, Clarke & Co. Map Collection, The University of Michigan Library, Ann Arbor.

Roads
1888   Roads from Detroit to the Illinois by Way of the Forts Miamis, Ouiattenon and St. Vincent with some Remarks. (1774?) *Michigan Historical Collections* 10:247-48, Lansing.

Robinson, Percy
1937   The Chevalier De Rocheblave and the Toronto Purchase. *Royal Society of Canada Transactions,* 31, 3rd series, Section II: 131-52. Toronto.

1965   *Toronto During the French Regime.* 2nd ed. Toronto: University of Toronto Press.

Roland, Charles G.
1979   Medical Aspects of the War in the West, 1812-1813, MS. Paper delivered at the Western District Historical Conference, University of Windsor, October 13-14.

Rostlund, Erhard
1952   Freshwater Fish and Fishing in Native North America. *University of California Publications in Geography* 9. Berkeley.

Rowe, John S.
1972   *Forest Regions of Canada.* Department of the Environment, Publication No. 1300. Ottawa: Canadian Forestry Service.

Royce, Charles C.
1899   *Indian Land Cessions in the United States. 18th Annual Report of the Bureau of American Ethnology for the Years 1896-1897.* Pt. 2. Washington: Government Printing Office.

St. Joseph Co.
1877   *History of St. Joseph County,* Michigan. Philadelphia: L. H. Everts & Co.

Sarchet, Cyrus P. B.
1911   *History of Guernsey County,* Ohio. Indianapolis: B. F. Bowen & Co.

Sault
n.d.   Map of the Village at Sault Ste. Marie. Scale: 400 feet to the inch. MS. RG 59-4 Folder 01014. Michigan State Archives, Lansing.

Schleiser, Karl H.
1956   Epidemics and Indian Middlemen: Rethinking the Wars of the Iroquois, 1609-1653. *Ethnohistory* 3.

Schmalz, Peter S.
1977   *The History of the Saugeen Indians.* Ottawa: Ontario Historical Society.

Schoolcraft, Henry Rowe
1821   *Narrative Journal of Travels through the Northwestern Regions of the United States extending from Detroit Through the Great Chain of American Lakes, to the sources of the Mississippi River. . . in the Year 1820.* Albany: E. E. Hosford.

1834   Discourse Delivered before the Historical Society of Michigan. *Historical and Scientific Sketches of Michigan.* Detroit: Stephen Wells and George Whitney.

1851   *Personal Memoirs of a Residence of Thirty Years with the Indian Tribes on the American Frontier: With Brief Notices of Passing Events, Facts, and Opinions A.D. 1812 to A.D. 1842.* Philadelphia: Lippincott, Grambo & Co.

1851-1857   *Information Respecting the History Condition and Prospects of the Indian Tribes of the United States.* 6 vols. [Titles vary.]. Philadelphia: Lippincott, Grambo & Co.

1855   *Summary Narrative of an Exploratory Expedition to the Sources of the Mississippi River, in 1820.* Philadelphia: Lippincott, Grambo, and Co.

1860   *Archives of Aboriginal Knowledge.* 6 vols. Philadelphia: J. B. Lippincott & Co. (Reissue of 1851-1857 Publication.)

Schuyler, Philip
1764   List of Indians. MS. Schuyler Papers, Box 13. New York Public Library, New York.

Scott, James
1966   *The Settlement of Huron County.* Toronto: Ryerson Press.

Scott, John
1826   *The Indiana Gazeteer or Topographical Dictionary.* Centreville: J. Scott & W. M. Doughty.

———
1954   *Indiana Gazeteer or Topographical Dictionary.* Ed. by Gayle Thornbrough. Indiana Historical Society Publication 18 (1). Indianapolis.

Shea, John D. G.
1882   *History of the Catholic Missions Among the Indian Tribes of the United States.* New York: P. J. Kennedy.

Shelby
1887   *History of Shelby County.* Chicago: Brent & Fuller.

Simcoe, John G.
1923-1931   *The Correspondence of Lieut. Governor John Graves Simcoe.* Ed. by Ernest A. Cruikshank. 5 vols. Toronto: Ontario Historical Society.

Slocum, Charles E.
1905   *History of the Maumee River Basin.* 3 vols. Indianapolis: Bowen.

Smith, Alice E.
1973   *The History of Wisconsin: Volume I From Exploration to Statehood.* Madison: State Historical Society of Wisconsin.

Smith, Donald B.
1975   *The Mississaugas, Peter Jones and the White Man.* MS. Ph.D. thesis, University of Toronto.

Smith, James
1870   *An Account of the Remarkable Occurances in the Life and Travels of Col. James Smith.* Ed. by William M. Darlington. Cincinnati: R. Clarke & Co.

Smith, Thomas H.
1977   *The Mapping of Ohio.* Kent, Ohio: Kent State University Press.

Smith, William
1868   *Historical Account of Bouquet s Expedition against the Ohio Indians, in 1764.* Cincinnati: Robert Clark & Co.

Smith, William Henry
1882   *The St. Clair Papers.* 2 vols. Cincinnati.

Smyth, David William
1799   *A Short Topographical Description of His Majesty's Province of Upper Canada, in North America.* London: W. Faden.

Smyth, John F. D.
1784   *A Tour in the United States of America.* 2 vols. London: G. Robinson, J. Robson, and J. Sewell.

Snelling, William J.
1868   Early Days at Prairie Du Chien. *Collections of the State Historical Society of Wisconsin* 5:123-53. Madison.

Sosin, Jack M.
1971   *Whitehall and the Wilderness: The Middle West in British Colonial Policy, 1760-1775.* Lincoln: University of Nebraska Press.

———
1975   Britain and the Ohio Valley, 1760-1775. Ed. by John B. Elliott. *Contest for the Empire, 1500-1775.* Indianapolis: Indiana Historical Society.

Spector, Janet D.
1974   Winnebago Indians, 1634-1829: An Archaeological and Ethnohistorical Investigation. MS. Ph.D. dissertation, University of Wisconsin.

Spencer, Oliver M.
1968   *The Indian Captivity of O. M. Spencer.* Ed. by Milo M. Quaife. New York: Citadel Press.

Stagg, Jack
1981   *Anglo-Indian Relations in North America to 1763, and An Analysis of The Royal Proclamation of 7 October 1763.* Ottawa: Research Branch, Indian and Northern Affairs, Canada.

Stanley, George F. G.
1950   The Indians in the War of 1812. *Canadian Historical Review,* 31:145-65.

———
1963   The Significance of the Six Nations Participation in the War of 1812. *Ontario History,* 55:215-31.

Stearn, E. W. and A. E. Stearn
1945   *The Effects of Smallpox on the Destiny of the Amerindian.* Boston: Bruce Humphries.

Stevens, Frank E.
1903   *The Black Hawk War.* Chicago: F. E. Stevens.

———
1904   Illinois in the War of 1812-1814. *Transactions of the Illinois State Historical Society for the Year 1904,* 62-197. Publication No. 9 of the Illinois State Historical Library. Springfield: Phillips Brothers, State Printers.

Stevens, Sylvester K. and Donald H. Kent, eds.
1940   *Journal of Joseph Chaussegros de Lery.* Harrisburg, Pa.

Stone, Lyle M.
1974   *Fort Michilimackinac 1715-1781: An Archaeological Perspective on the Revolutionary Frontier.* East Lansing: Michigan State University.

Stone, William L.
1865   *The Life and Times of Sir William Johnson.* Albany: J. Munsell.

Storrow, Samuel A.
1872   The Northwest in 1817. *Collections of the State Historical Society of Wisconsin* 6:155-87. Madison.

Stout, David B.
1974a   Ethnohistorical Report on the Saginaw Chippewa. *Chippewa Indians.* New York: Garland Publishing Co.

———
1974b   Report on the Kickapoo, Illinois and Potawa-

tomi Indians. *Indians of Illinois and Northwestern Indiana,* Pt. 2. New York: Garland Publishing Co.

Strang, James J.
1894 *Ancients and Modern Michillimackinac,* with Supplement. (First Edition, 1854) Mackinac, Mich.

Strickland, Samuel
1853 *Twenty-Seven Years in Canada West; or, the experience of an early settler.* London: R. Bentley.

Summary
1908 Summary of the Indian Tribes of the Misuri River, San Luis de Ylinneses, 15 November 1777. From MS in Archivo General de Indias, Seville in papeles Procedentes de la Isla de Cuba. *British Regime in Wisconsin,* ed. by Reuben Gold Thwaites. Wisconsin Historical Collections, 18:358-68.

Surtees, Robert J.
1969 The Development of the Indian Reserve Policy in Canada. *Ontario History,* 61:87-98.

———
1971 *The Original People.* Toronto: Holt, Rinehart & Winston.

———
1982 Indian Land Cessions in Ontario, 1763-1862: The Evolution of a System. MS. Ph.D. dissertation, Carleton University, Ottawa.

Talbert, Charles Gano
1962 *Benjamin Logan—Kentucky Frontiersman.* Lexington: University of Kentucky Press.

Tanner, Helen Hornbeck
1968 Report on the Indians of Southeastern Wisconsin and Northern Illinois, with Special Reference to the Treaty of Chicago, 1833. MS. Indian Claims Commission Docket 29A. *Atlas* Files.

———
1970 The Sisseton and Wahpeton Treaty of 1867 and Agreement of 1872. MS. Report for Indian Claims Commission Docket 363. *Atlas* Files.

———
1973 Educational Provisions of Michigan Indian Treaties. MS. Michigan Historical Collections, Bentley Library, The University of Michigan, Ann Arbor.

———
1974a The Chippewa of Eastern Lower Michigan. *Chippewa Indians,* 5:347-74. New York: Garland Publishing Co.

———
1974b The Greenville Treaty, 1795. *Indians of Ohio and Indiana Prior to 1795.* 2 vols. 1:51-128. New York: Garland Publishing Co.

———
1974c The Location of Indian Tribes in Southeastern Michigan and Northern Ohio. *Indians of Northern Ohio and Southeastern Michigan.*

New York: Garland Publishing Co.

———
1974d Historical Report for Appraising Value of Wyandot Reservation in Ohio. MS. Indian Claims Commission Dockets 212 and 213. *Atlas* Files.

———
1974e Historical Report for Land Valuation of Royce 188, 189, 190 MS. Indian Claims Commission Docket 29A. *Atlas* Files.

———
1974f Land Valuation Report for Royce 98 Ceded by the Potawatomi October 2, 1818. MS. Indian Claims Commission Docket 29. *Atlas* Files.

———
1974g Historical Report on the Sault Ste. Marie Bands. MS. *United States vs. Michigan.* No. M 26-73. C.A., USDC Western District of Michigan, Northern Division.

———
1978 The Glaize in 1792: A Composite Indian Community. *Ethnohistory* 25 (1):15-39.

Tanner, Henry S.
1825 *New American Atlas.* Philadelphia: H. S. Tanner.

———
1833 *A New Universal Atlas.* Philadelphia: H. S. Tanner.

Tanner, John
1956 *A Narrative of the Captivity and Adventures of John Tanner.* Ed. by Edwin James. Introduction and notes by Milo M. Quaife. Minneapolis: Ross & Haines.

Temple, Wayne C.
1958 *Indian Villages of the Illinois Country: Historic Tribes.* Illinois State Museum Scientific Papers 2 (2). Springfield.

Thomas, David
1819 *Travels Through the Western Country in the Summer of 1816.* Auburn, N.Y.: David Ramsey.

Thompson, Charles N.
1937 *Sons of the Wilderness, John and William Connor.* Indiana Historical Society Publication 12. Indianapolis.

Thornbrough, Gayle, ed.
1961 *Letter Book of the Indian Agency at Fort Wayne 1809-1815.* Indiana Historical Society Publications 21. Indianapolis.

Thwaites, Reuben Gold, ed.
1869-1901 *The Jesuit Relations and Allied Documents: Travels and Explorations of the Jesuit Missionaries in New France, 1610-1791.* 73 vols. Cleveland: The Burrow Brothers.

———
1902 *The French Régime in Wisconsin 1634-1727.* Collections of the State Historical Society of Wisconsin 16. Madison: The Society.

———
1904   *Early Western Travels 1748-1846.* Vols. 1-3. Cleveland, Ohio: The Arthur H. Clark Co.

———
1906   *The French Régime in Wisconsin, 1727-1748.* Collections of the State Historical Society of Wisconsin 17. Madison: The Society.

———
1908   *The French Régime in Wisconsin, 1743-1760. The British Regime in Wisconsin 1760-1821.* Collections of the State Historical Society of Wisconsin 18. Madison: The Society.

——— and Louise Phelps Kellogg, eds.
1905   *Documentary History of Dunmore's War 1774.* Madison: Wisconsin State Historical Society.

———
1908   *The Revolution on the Upper Ohio 1775-1777.* Madison: Wisconsin State Historical Society.

———
1912   *Frontier Defense on the Upper Ohio 1777-1778.* Madison: Wisconsin State Historical Society.

Tiedke, Kenneth E.
1951   *A Study of the Hannahville Indian Community* (Menominee County Michigan). Michigan State College, Agricultural Experiment Station. Special Bulletin 369:5-43. East Lansing.

Tippecanoe Co.
1878   *Combined Atlas Map of Tippecanoe County, Indiana.* Chicago: Kingman Bros.

Tipton, John
1942   *The John Tipton Papers,* with an introduction by Paul Wallace Gates. 3 vols. *Indiana Historical Collections* 24-26. Indianapolis: Indiana Historical Bureau.

Tohill, Louis Arthur
1926   Robert Dickson, British Fur Trader on the Upper Mississippi: A Story of Trade, War, and Diplomacy. MS. Ph.D. dissertation, University of Minnesota.

Tooker, Elizabeth
1963   The Iroquois Defeat of the Huron: A Review of Causes, *Pennsylvania Archaeologist* 33:115-23.

Torok, Charles H.
1956   The Tyendinaga Mohawks: The Village as a Basic Factor in Mohawk Social Structure. *Ontario History,* 57 (2):69-77.

Traill, Catherine Parr (Strickland)
1838   *The Backwoods Country: Being letters from the wife of an emigrant officer, illustrative of the domestic economy of British America.* London: C. Knight.

Traverse
1884   *Traverse Region, Historical and Descriptive.* Chicago: H. R. Page & Co.

Trelease, Allen W.
1960   *Indian Affairs in Colonial New York: The Seventeenth Century.* Ithaca, N.Y.

Trent, William
1871   *Journal of Captain William Trent from Logstown to Pickawillany.* Ed. by Alfred T. Goodman. Cincinnati: Robert Clarke & Co.

Trigger, Bruce
1960   *The Destruction of Huronia: A Study in Economic and Cultural Change, 1609-1650.* Royal Canadian Institute Transcripts 33:14-45.

———
1976   *The Children of Aataentsic: A History of the Huron People to 1660.* 2 vols. Montreal: McGill-Queens University Press.

———,ed.
1978   *The Northeast, Handbook of North American Indians* 15, Gen. ed. William C. Sturtevant. Washington, D.C.: The Smithsonian Institution.

Trygg, J. William
1964-1969   *Composite Map of United States Land Surveyors' Original Plats and Field Notes.* 46 sheets. Ely, Minn.: Trygg Land Office.

Tuck, J. A.
1971   *Onondaga Iroquois Prehistory: A study in Settlement Archaeology.* Syracuse: Syracuse University Press.

Tucker, Sara Jones, comp.
1942   *Indian Villages of the Illinois Country. Illinois State Museum Scientific Papers* (2) 1. Pt. 1. Springfield.

Tucker, Willard D.
1913   *Gratiot County, Michigan.* Saginaw, Mich.: Press of Seemann & Peters.

Tyrell, J. B., ed.
1916   *David Thompson's Narrative of His Expeditions in Western America 1784-1812.* Toronto: Champlain Society.

United States
1827   *Report of the Commissioner of Indian Affairs for 1827.* Reports of the Commissioner of Indian Affairs, 1824-1837. Ayer Collection, The Newberry Library, Chicago.

———
1870   *Report of the Commissioner of Indian Affairs to the Secretary of the Interior for the Year 1870.* Washington: Government Printing Office.

———
1872   *Report of the Commissioner of Indian Affairs to the Secretary of the Interior for the Year 1871.* Washington: Government Printing Office.

United States Census Office
1821   *Fourth Census, Census for 1820.* Washington.

———
1832   *Fifth Census or Enumeration of the Inhabitants of the United States, 1830.* Washington, D.C.: Duff & Green.

1903   *Statistical Atlas of the United States 1900.* Washington.

United States Land Office

n.d.   *Land Office Plat Books.* Madison, Wisc.: State Historical Society of Wisconsin.

Upham, Warren

1969   *Minnesota Geographic Names: Their Origin and Historic Significance.* St. Paul: Minnesota Historical Society Press, [lst ed. 1920].

Utter, William T.

1942   *The Frontier State 1803-1825.* Vol. 2. Ed. by Wittke, Carl. *The History of the State of Ohio.* 6 vols. Columbus: Ohio State Archaeological and Historical Society.

Ver Wyst, P. Chrysostomus

1900   *Life and Labours of Rt. Rev. Frederic Baraga.* Milwaukee: M. H. Wiltzius & Co.

Vieau, Andrew J., Sr.

1888   Narrative of Andrew J. Vieau Sr. *Wisconsin Historical Collections* 11:218-37. Madison.

Viola Herman

1976   *The Legacy of Charles Bird King.* Washington and New York: Smithsonian Institution and Doubleday.

Vizenor, Gerald Robert, comp. and ed.

1968   *Escorts to White Earth* 1868 to 1968; *100 Year Reservation.* Minneapolis: The Four Winds.

Voegelin, Erminie Wheeler

1941   Indians of Indiana. *Indiana Academy of Science Proceedings.* 50:27-32.

1962   An Ethnohistorical Report on the Indian Use and Occupancy of Royce Area 66. MS. Ohio Valley Great Lakes Historical Archive, Glenn Black Laboratory, Indiana University, Bloomington. Copy, *Atlas files.*

1974a   An Anthropological Report on Indian Use and Occupancy of Northern Michigan. *Chippewa Indians* 5. New York: Garland Publishing Co.

1974b   Anthropological Report on the Ottawa, Chippewa and Potawatomi Indians. *Indians of Illinois and Northwestern Indiana.* Part 1. New York: Garland Publishing Co.

1947c   An Ethnohistorical Report on the Wyandot Potawatomi, Ottawa and Chippewa of Northwest Ohio. *Indians of Northwest Ohio.* New York: Garland Publishing Co.

1974d   Ethnohistory of Indian Use and Occupancy in Ohio and Indiana Prior to 1795. *Indians of Ohio and Indiana Prior to 1795.* 2 vols. New York: Garland Publishing Co.

1947e   Anthropological Report on the Indian Use and Occupancy of Royce Areas 77 and 78. *Indians of Western Illinois and Southern Wisconsin.* New York: Garland Publishing Co.

1974f   Ethnohistorical Report on the Wyandot, Ottawa, Chippewa, Munsee, Delaware, Shawnee, and Potawatomi of Royce Areas 53 and 54. *Indians of Northern Ohio and Southeastern Michigan.* New York: Garland Publishing Co.

——and Emily J. Blasingham, Dorothy R. Libby

1974   *An Anthropological Report on the Miami, Wea, and Eel-River Indians.* New York: Garland Publishing Co.

——and Harold Hickerson

1974   The Red Lake and Pembina Chippewa. *Chippewa Indians* 1. New York: Garland Publishing Co.

Vogel, Virgil J.

1963   *Indian Place Names in Illinois.* Springfield, 111.: Illinois State Historical Society, Pamphlet Series, no. 4.

Volwiller, Albert T.

1926   *George Crogban and the Westward Movement.* Cleveland: Arthur E. Clarke Co.

Voorhis, Ernest comp.

1930   Historic forts and trading posts of the French regime and of the English fur trading companies. Ottawa: Department of Interior, National resources and intelligence service. Mimeograph copy.

Vrooman, John J.

1943   *Forts and Firesides of the Mohawk Country.* Philadelphia: E. E. Brownwell.

Wakefield, John A.

1834   *History of the War Between the United States and the Sac and Fox Nations of Indians.* Jacksonville, Ill.: Printed by C. Goudy.

Walkerville

1976   *Bicentennial Collection of Walkerville Area, Colfax, Elbridge, Leavitt Townships.* Walkerville, Mich.: Bicentennial Committee.

Wallace, Anthony F. C.

1970-1978   Prelude to Disaster: The Course of Indian-White Relations Which Led to the Black Hawk War of 1832. Ed. by Ellen B. Whitney. *The Black Hawk War, 1831-32* 1:1-51.

1972   *The Death and Rebirth of the Seneca.* New York: Random House.

Walling, Henry F.

1873   *Atlas of the State of Michigan.* Detroit: R. M. & S. T. Tackabury.

Warner, Robert M.

1974   Economic and Historical Report on Northern Michigan. *Chippewa Indians* 5. New York: Garland Publishing Co.

Warren Co.

1883   *Counties of Warren, Benton, Jasper and New-*

ton, *Indiana. Historical and Biographical.* Chicago: F. A. Battey & Co.

Warren, William Whipple
1885   History of the Ojibways, Based Upon Traditions and Oral Statements. *Collections of the Minnesota Historical Society* 5:29-394. St. Paul: Minnesota Historical Society.

Wedel, Mildred Mott
1974   LeSueur and the Dakota Sioux. Ed. by Elden Johnson. *Aspects of Upper Great Lakes Anthropology.* St. Paul: Minnesota Historical Society.

Weisenburger, F. P.
1941   *The Passing of the Frontier.* Vol. 3. Ed. by Carl Wittke. *The History of the State of Ohio.* 6 vols. Columbus, Ohio.

Whickar, J. Wesley
1921   Shabonee's Account of Tippecanoe. *Indiana Magazine of History* 17:353-61.

————

1926   The Potawatomi Reservations in Benton, Fountain, Warren and Tippecanoe Counties, *Indiana Magazine of History,* 22:28-36.

White Co.
1883   *Counties of White and Pulaski, Indiana, Historical and Biographical.* Chicago: F. A. Battey & Co.

White, Marian E.
1961   *Iroquois Culture History in the Niagara Frontier Area of New York State,* Museum of Anthropology, University of Michigan, Anthropological Papers, No. 16, Ann Arbor.

Whitney, Ellen M., comp. and ed.
1970-1975   *The Black Hawk War, 1831-1832.* 3 vols. Springfield, 111.: Illinois State Historical Library.

Whitney, W. A. and R. I. Bonner
1876   *History and Biographical Record of Lenawee County, Michigan.* 2 vols. Adrian: W. Steams & Co.

Whittlesey, Charles
1867   *Early History of Cleveland, Ohio.* Cleveland: Fairbanks, Benedict and Co., Printer.

Williams, William W.
1879   *History of the Firelands Comprising Huron and Erie Counties.* Cleveland: Leader Printing Company.

Willis, N. P.
1840   *American Scenery,* with illustrations by W. H. Bartlett. 2 vols. London: George Virtue.

————

1842   *Canadian Scenery,* with illustrations by W. H. Bartlett. 2 vols. London: George Virtue.

Wilson, George Robert and Gayle Thornbrough
1946   *The Buffalo Trace.* Vol. 15, No. 2. Indianapolis: Indiana Historical Society Publications 15 (2):183-269.

Winchell, N. H.
1911   *The Aborigines of Minnesota,* A Report Based on the Collections of Jacob V. Brower and on the Field Surveys and Notes of Alfred J. Hill and Theodore H. Lewis. St. Paul, Minn.: The Minnesota Historical Society.

Winter, George
1948   *The Journals of George Winter 1809-1876 and Indian Paintings 1837-1839.* Ed. by Howard H. Peckham. Indianapolis: Indiana Historical Society. Chicago: Lakeside Press.

Winter, Nevin O.
1917   *A History of Northwest Ohio.* Chicago and New York: Lewis Publishing Co.

Wisconsin
n.d.   Archaeological Survey of the State of Wisconsin. Department of Anthropology, Museum of the State Historical Society of Wisconsin, Madison.

Wolcott, Alexander
1826-1827   A List of Chiefs of the Potawatomi Tribe of Indians to whom Annuities were paid by Alex Wolcott Jr. Indian Agent Chicago July 15, 1826, and July 18, 1827. MS. Indian Department Collection, Chicago Historical Society, Chicago.

Wood, William C. H., ed.
1920-1928   *Select British Documents of the Canadian War of 1812.* 3 vols. Toronto: Champlain Society.

Woodford, Frank B. and Albert Hyma
1958   *Gabriel Richard, Frontier Ambassador.* Detroit: Wayne State University Press.

Wright, Gordon K.
1963   *The Neutral Indians: A Source Book,* New York State Archaeological Association Occasional Papers, No. 4, Rochester, New York.

Wright, James V.
1966   *The Ontario Iroquois Tradition. National Museum of Canada Bulletin* 210. Ottawa.

Writers Program
1940   *The Ohio Guide,* compiled by Workers of the Writers Program of the Works Progress Administration in the State of Ohio, sponsored by the Ohio State Archaeological and Historical Society. New York: Works Progress Administration.

Yarnell, Richard A.
1964   *Aboriginal Relationships Between Culture and Plant Life in the Upper Great Lakes Region.* University of Michigan Museum of Anthropology, Anthropology Papers 23, Ann Arbor.

Zeisberger, David
1885   *Diary of David Zeisberger, a Moravian Missionary Among the Indians of Ohio, 1781-1798.* Ed. and trans. by Eugene F. Bliss. 2 vols. Cincinnati: Robert Clarke.

Zoltvany, Yves
1974   *Philippe de Rigaud de Vaudrueil, Governor of New France, 1703-1725.* Toronto: McClelland & Stewart.

INDEX

The index combines references to the maps and accompanying text. Citations to text pages appear in regular type, while map pages are in italics. The letter and number coordinates, following the map page number, identify the section on the map in which a site can be found. For example, the location of Michipicoten, an Ojibwa village on the northeast shore of Lake Superior, is noted as 98:A3.

Since many of the lakes and rivers are on several maps, the index generally cites the location on selected maps at different scales. The index reference notes the place that the river or lake name is printed on the map, not the entire course of the stream, nor all of the sections of the map covered by parts of one of the Great Lakes.

Unnamed Indian villages, identified on maps only by tribal abbreviations, are included under the main tribal heading. Following the map page number and letter-number coordinates, the numbers in parentheses indicate the number of unnamed tribal villages in that single section.

Atlas of Great Lakes Indian History

was designed by Emmy Ezzell, Bill Cason, and Ed Shaw. The cartography and map negatives were done by Rand McNally under the supervision of Miklos Pinther and the author. The text was set in various sizes of Alphatype Garamond by the University of Oklahoma Press. The jacket and text were printed by the University of Oklahoma Printing Services, the latter on 80-pound Mohawk Superfine, in five colors. The binding is by John H. Dekker & Sons.